MERCENARIES

The Changing Character of War Programme is an inter-disciplinary research group located at the University of Oxford, and funded by the Leverhulme Trust.

Mercenaries

The History of a Norm in International Relations

SARAH PERCY

Great Clarendon Street, Oxford OX2 6DP

Oxford University Press is a department of the University of Oxford.
It furthers the University's objective of excellence in research, scholarship,
and education by publishing worldwide in

Oxford New York

Auckland Cape Town Dar es Salaam Hong Kong Karachi
Kuala Lumpur Madrid Melbourne Mexico City Nairobi
New Delhi Shanghai Taipei Toronto

With offices in

Argentina Austria Brazil Chile Czech Republic France Greece
Guatemala Hungary Italy Japan Poland Portugal Singapore
South Korea Switzerland Thailand Turkey Ukraine Vietnam

Oxford is a registered trade mark of Oxford University Press
in the UK and in certain other countries

Published in the United States
by Oxford University Press Inc., New York

© Sarah Percy 2007

The moral rights of the author have been asserted
Database right Oxford University Press (maker)

First published 2007

All rights reserved. No part of this publication may be reproduced,
stored in a retrieval system, or transmitted, in any form or by any means,
without the prior permission in writing of Oxford University Press,
or as expressly permitted by law, or under terms agreed with the appropriate
reprographics rights organization. Enquiries concerning reproduction
outside the scope of the above should be sent to the Rights Department,
Oxford University Press, at the address above

You must not circulate this book in any other binding or cover
and you must impose the same condition on any acquirer

British Library Cataloguing in Publication Data

Data available

Library of Congress Cataloging in Publication Data

Data available

Typeset by SPI Publisher Services, Pondicherry, India
Printed in Great Britain
on acid-free paper by
Biddles Ltd., King's Lynn, Norfolk

ISBN 978–0–19–921433–4

1 3 5 7 9 10 8 6 4 2

Foreword

Sir John Hawkwood, the most infamous mercenary in the late 14th century between the Middle Ages and the Renaissance, was buried with majestic and solemn panache in the Duomo in Florence after a career of murder and extortion. Uccello painted his equine portrait on the gospel side of the church. All this was a remarkable but doomed attempt to give a veneer of civic respectability to a bloody-handed merchant of death. Machiavelli's dismissal of mercenaries and the danger they posed to leaders was infinitely more wise and to the point.

In her excellent account of the role of mercenaries from King John's hired hands (denounced by his barons at Runnymede) to the usually incompetent guns for rent of modern times in Africa, Sarah Percy points to the moral opprobrium that has usually attached to their activities. The rise of the nation state in the wake of the war of American Independence and the French Revolution saw a growing preference for citizens' armies and the abandonment of the military trade in flesh.

Sarah Percy is particularly skilful in showing how the Private Military and Security Companies of recent times, whose use has grown by leaps and bounds from the Gulf War to Iraq, fit into this debate. We plainly need greater transparency about their role and a clearer sense of how their actions are subject to domestic and international law.

Ms Percy's book is an admirable historical and theoretical foundation to what is likely to be a growing debate.

The Rt Hon the Lord Patten of Barnes

Oxford
July 2007

Acknowledgements

Books based on doctoral theses have a long gestation period, and consequently long lists of people and institutions to acknowledge. This book is no exception.

The book began life as a doctoral thesis completed under the supervision of Neil MacFarlane at the University of Oxford. I am grateful to Neil for his provocative and insightful assistance, and working to meet his exacting standards has undoubtedly resulted in a better book. I was surrounded by friends doing doctorates, all of whom provided notable assistance: Vivien Collingwood, Nicole Evans, Terry Macdonald and Dominik Zaum were a wonderful intellectual support group. My thesis examiners, Henry Shue and James Mayall, provided helpful comments. Henry has gone beyond the call of duty as a colleague in the past two years as a sounding board about the role of norms in international relations.

The doctoral thesis developed into a book while I was a research associate in the Oxford Leverhulme Programme on the Changing Character of War. The programme's generosity has allowed me to focus full time on my research for the past two years and provided me with stimulating and helpful colleagues. Adam Roberts, Audrey Kurth Cronin, and Alexandra Gheciu have all read or commented on parts of this book and I am grateful for their assistance. I have been lucky to participate in the many spirited discussions we have had in the programme about war, private force, and ethics. Keith Stanski provided able, intelligent and remarkably efficient research assistance.

The Commonwealth Scholarship funded my doctoral studies, and provided me with a boost of confidence as well as financial support. Queen's University in Canada offers scholarships to its alumnae for graduate study, and I have been fortunate in receiving financial aid from the Royce and Lynnett Fellowships. The University of Western Australia provided a congenial environment in which to work during my time away from Oxford. The staff at the United Nations Archive in New York were helpful and the Archive was of great assistance.

I have also been able to draw on the specific expertise of colleagues, all of whom have been generous with their assistance. Ernie Jones, John Tonkin, and Maurice Keen helped me to understand medieval warfare better and Joanna Harrington and Guy Goodwin-Gill helped me sharpen my arguments about international law. It goes without saying that any deficiencies in these areas are my responsibility alone.

Some parts of this book develop work that has appeared elsewhere. Portions of Chapters 4 and 7 are included in 'Morality and Regulation', in *From Mercenaries to Market: The Rise and Regulation of Private Security Companies*, eds. Simon Chesterman and Chia Lehnhardt, (Oxford University Press, 2007). Parts of Chapter 5 appear in 'Mercenaries: Strong Norm, Weak Law', *International Organization*, vol. 61(2), pp. 367–97 (2007). Permission to reprint the relevant passages is gratefully acknowledged.

As anyone who has ever had the misfortune of spending a lot of time around a doctoral student or someone finishing their first book knows, support and encouragement are necessary elements of the process. My friends and family have done this beautifully, while suffering through more dinner party conversations about dangerous men with guns in dangerous places than they probably would have liked. Leslie Preston, Vanessa Gruben, Christine Whelan, Helen Scott and Carman Yung have been pillars of support; Mark Siford deserves special mention for reading and commenting on the whole book. My family, David and Tikker, and Matthew and Jennifer, have given me all the things that matter, most notably words of wisdom measured with love and considerable doses of laughter. My husband, James Edelman, provided unstintingly all the things I needed while I was writing. He was a source of inspiration, love, humour, and extensive encouragement, as well as some original ideas about international relations, and it is to him that I dedicate this book.

Contents

Introduction   1
I.1. Existing Literature on Mercenaries   2
I.2. Outline of the Argument   11

1. Norms, Their Influence, and How They Can be Studied   14
   1.1. What Is a Norm?   14
   1.2. The Relationship between Norms and the Related Concepts of Law, Morality, and Interests   18
   1.3. The Influence of Norms on Politics   23
   1.4. Narrative Methodology   32
   1.5. The Challenges of Dealing with Norms   42
   1.6. Conclusion   48

2. The Definition of a Mercenary and the Definition of the Proscriptive Norm   49
   2.1. Definitions and Revelations: What Makes Mercenaries Different?   50
   2.2. A Different Definition   54
   2.3. The Spectrum of Private Violence   58
   2.4. How the Definition Indicates the Proscriptive Norm   64

3. The Origins of the Norm against Mercenary Use, 1100–1600   68
   3.1. Attachment to a Cause   69
   3.2. The Need to Control Mercenary Forces   78
   3.3. Conclusion: Revelations   90

4. Competing Explanations for the Nineteenth-Century Shift Away from Mercenary Use   94
   4.1. Materialist or Realist Explanations of the Shift Away from Mercenary Use   96
   4.2. Avant: Domestic Politics, Path Dependency, and the Transition From a Mercenary to a Civilian Army   105
   4.3. Thomson: Ideas Can Explain the Shift Away from Mercenary Use   111
   4.4. A Common Problem: Why Did States Prefer Citizen Armies, and Why Were They Willing to Take a Leap of Faith to Adopt Them?   119

5. How Citizens Became the Standard: A Normative Explanation
   of the Shift Away from Mercenary Use 121
   5.1. America 123
   5.2. France 128
   5.3. Prussia 136
   5.4. Britain 148
   5.5. Conclusion 165

6. The Norm against Mercenary Use and International Law 167
   6.1. Strong Norms Do Not Lead to the Creation of Strong Law:
        How the Law's Weaknesses Are Explained by the
        Anti-Mercenary Norm 169
   6.2. The Heightened African Interest in Law Demonstrates that the
        Norm Was Not Universal 179
   6.3. The Proscriptive Norm against Mercenary Use Is Most
        Challenged by Other Norms 192
   6.4. Conclusion: The Significance of the Norm against Mercenary
        Use in International Law 203

7. New Model Mercenaries: PMCs, PSCs, and the Anti-Mercenary
   Norm 206
   7.1. The Anti-Mercenary Norm in the 1990s: PMCs 207
   7.2. Private Force and the Shift Away from Combat Operations 225
   7.3. The Anti-Mercenary Norm and its Influence on the Provision
        of Private Force Today 232
   7.4. The Future of the Anti-Mercenary Norm 238
   7.5. Conclusion 243

Conclusion 244

Appendix 1: Definition of a Mercenary from the International
Convention against the Recruitment, Use, Financing and
Training of Mercenaries 248

References 249
Index 265

Introduction

Mercenaries are part of the fabric of the history of war. Battles have been fought by soldiers of fortune since classical Greece and Rome, and their use has continued until the present day, albeit with occasional absences and with new types of mercenary appearing on the international stage. Today, we see both old-fashioned and modern mercenaries operating around the world, with mercenaries who would not have been out of place in 1960s Africa staging a bungled coup in Equatorial Guinea at the same time as highly organized corporations have provided combat assistance to troubled governments, and similar companies provide security on a contract basis in Iraq.

While mercenaries have always been with us, moral disapprobation has accompanied them from battle to battle, from century to century. Simply because they have been common does not mean that mercenaries have had or have today an accepted place among the armies of the world. For as long as there have been mercenaries, there has been a norm against mercenary use.

The norm against mercenary use has two components. First, mercenaries are considered to be immoral because they use force outside legitimate, authoritative control. That control has been imposed by popes, princes, rulers of sovereign states, states in the contemporary international system, and international organizations like the United Nations (UN). Second, mercenaries are considered to be morally problematic because they fight wars for selfish, financial reasons as opposed to fighting for some kind of larger conception of the common good. Mercenaries fight for themselves rather than for any cause; they do not fight for the pope, the prince, the sovereign state, or even for an ethnic or national group. This ethical objection lies at the centre of the norm against mercenary use, and has been present in essentially the same form from the Middle Ages until today.

But given that this norm against mercenary use has not resulted in the disappearance of mercenaries from the world stage, or even, at any point in history, an effective formal international agreement limiting their use, why should we care that there has been an anti-mercenary norm from the earliest days of mercenary use?

The norm against mercenary use is crucial for our understanding of how states have chosen the type of soldier they would use to compose their armies. Without it, we cannot understand why states used mercenaries less and less, even when they were still militarily useful. Without it, we cannot understand why mercenaries were used ultimately only under tight control and even tighter agreements between states. Without it, we cannot understand why states eventually insisted upon using only their own citizens to make up their armies. Without it, we cannot understand why states struggled to create effective international law regulating mercenaries in the second half of the twentieth century. Without it, we cannot understand how today's private military industry developed and the obstacles it faces. I argue that the norm against mercenary use has influenced states in their decisions about which type of force to employ, and has thus shaped the opportunities available for mercenaries.

An analysis of the norm against mercenary use is also beneficial because it fills a gap in existing work on mercenaries. Despite the fact that mercenaries have been a common part of warfare, there are very few works focusing on the subject, and even fewer on the history of mercenaries. Before I turn to an outline of my argument, I first situate this discussion of mercenaries among others, and explain more clearly why a normative account of mercenaries is necessary.

1.1. EXISTING LITERATURE ON MERCENARIES

Existing work on mercenaries focuses primarily on the twentieth and twenty-first centuries. There are only six examinations which make a serious and in-depth attempt to deal with pre-nineteenth-century mercenaries. Two of these are very specific in focus: McCormack's discussion of Swiss mercenaries[1] and Fowler's discussion of the free companies of the twelfth and thirteenth centuries.[2] The remaining three deal exclusively with the nineteenth-century shift away from mercenary use.[3] Mockler is the only author to discuss mercenaries in more than one period, working from the medieval era to the 1980s, and in more than one place.[4]

The bulk of current writing on mercenaries deals with 1960s mercenaries in Africa and the private military and private security companies of the 1990s.

---

[1] McCormack (1993) and Kinsey (2005, 2006).   [2] Fowler (2001).
[3] Posen (1993), Thomson (1994), and Avant (2000). These authors are discussed extensively in Chapter 4.
[4] Mockler (1969, 1985).

This work takes two major forms, some of which overlap. First, there are accounts of mercenaries from an operational perspective. These range from discussions of the precise details of mercenary operations, often providing chronological and detailed discussion of conflicts in which mercenaries have been involved,[5] to discussions of how private military companies (PMCs) have influenced the course of battle,[6] to analyses of the corporate and practical organization of PMCs.[7] Many discussions of the latter type are also case-study analyses of mercenary involvement which make some sort of assessment of PMC conduct and its impact on state politics and the conflict itself.[8]

Second, some authors explicitly attempt to probe the concept of privatization of force and how it affects state politics. These analyses look at military privatization in both weak and strong states. Reno argues that PMCs are particularly attractive to weak state rulers, but that the privatization of force in a weak state context can undermine the state.[9] PMCs, he argues, can link 'their interest in private profit to collaboration with officials in weak states in ways that *diminish* the tendency of these officials to promote the Weberian ideal of an internally capable state'.[10] Clapham argues that privatization of force is more problematic in weak than in strong states.[11] Brauer analyses some of the economic theory underlying military privatization,[12] while Fredland and Kennedy examine the potential for privatization of force in strong states.[13] Avant differentiates the impact of privatizing security in both weak and strong states.[14]

There are four significant gaps in existing literature on mercenaries: first, most accounts focus more on empirical details and less on questions of what the presence or absence of mercenary use means for the state and relations between states; second, most writers do not situate their accounts in a theoretical framework, which while not necessarily problematic leaves space for important analysis; third, a case could be made that many accounts suffer from historical inaccuracies; and fourth, the combination of theoretical and historical difficulties has led to an absence of the analysis of norms, perhaps because those making empirical analyses do not consider norms to be important.

---

[5] Mockler (1969), Burchett and Roebuck (1977), Tickler (1987*a*), Arnold (1999), and Rogers (2000).
[6] See Ventner (1995), Howe (1996, 1998).
[7] Shearer (1998*a*, 1999), Pech (1999), Vines (1999), Singer (2003*a*), Avant (2005*a*), and Kinsey (2006).
[8] Harding (1997), Shearer (1997*a*, 1997*b*, 1998*b*, 1999), Howe (1998), O'Brien (1998, 2000), Dinnen (1999), and Douglas (1999).
[9] Reno (1997).   [10] Reno (2000: 59).   [11] Clapham (1999).
[12] Brauer (1999).   [13] Fredland and Kennedy Ibid.   [14] Avant (2005*a*).

A striking feature of the present literature on mercenaries is its lack of theoretical analysis, particularly with respect to international relations.[15] The accounts outlined above tend to look at *how* mercenaries behaved in a particular state, or the nature of their organization and operation, rather than what the behaviour or type of organization *means* for international relations. While not every account of mercenaries needs to be theoretical, mercenaries cut to the heart of some of the central issues of international relations. The use of mercenaries raises questions about the nature of the state and to what extent the state needs to monopolize force or the control of force, and questions about the type of force states choose to employ. Krasner has asserted that there are very few strategic arguments against state use of mercenaries, and it is hard to explain in strategic terms why states do not use mercenaries more frequently.[16] If strategy cannot explain why states use the troops they do, what can? Mercenaries can also provide evidence for theoretical claims about the nature of force, one of which underlies the main argument of this book: that norms can and do influence state decisions even in the realm of national security.

Very little, if any, of this type of theoretical analysis exists in current work on the subject. Peter Singer's *Corporate Warriors*[17] is a good example of the absence of theoretical grounding common in accounts of mercenaries and the private military industry.[18] Singer does provide an admirable analysis of the development of private military and security companies, and considers the political implications and morality of mercenary use, but he does so outside a theoretical framework. Singer argues that his book 'organizes and integrates what we know about [the private military industry] in a systematic manner, allowing for the development of underlying theories that can guide us in the future'.[19] While there is undoubtedly a place for this kind of account, Singer not only has left theoretical analysis for others, but asks questions that a greater attention to theory would help him to answer more thoroughly.

One of Singer's main preoccupations is the idea that the private military industry undermines the state monopoly on the control of force. When 'the government delegates out part of its role in national security through the recruitment and maintenance of armed forces, it is abdicating an essential responsibility. When the forms of public protection are hired through private means, the citizens of society do not enjoy security by right of their membership in a state'.[20] It is true that part of the objection to the use of private

---

[15] On the latter point, see Nossal (1998: 18).   [16] Krasner (1989: 91–2).
[17] Singer (2003*a*).
[18] Kinsey (2006) provides a similar account of private security companies (PSCs), focusing on the United Kingdom and dealing very briefly with theoretical questions.
[19] Singer (2003*a*: ix).   [20] Ibid. 226.

militaries and mercenaries has been that they not only do a job which the state itself should do, but they do not provide security as a public good; indeed, part of the norm against mercenary use that this book examines includes precisely this concern. However, fears about the undermining of the state's control over the monopoly on force are only part of a larger norm against mercenary use, and perhaps the less influential part. Chapter 7 argues, for example, that within the UN and in the international media the main objections to PMCs are not that they undermine the monopoly on force but that there is something morally problematic about fighting for money rather than for the public good.

Deborah Avant provides a more theoretical account of the private security industry and its relationship to the state's control over force.[21] She argues that control over force is actually best understood as three different types of control: functional (or the effectiveness of the military), political (or which actors, organizations, or individuals control force), and social (the degree to which the use of force is congruent with broader social values, including democracy, international law, human rights, and the protection of civilians in warfare). To assess whether or not privatization has changed a state's control over force, Avant seeks to discover whether or not change has occurred in a functional sense (is the use of force more or less effective?); in a political sense (has there been a shift in the relative power of actors who control force?); and in a social sense (has there been a change in the way security reflects societal values?). In addition, Avant looks at how well these three facets of control 'fit' together. She argues that examining 'fit' is vital, as most scholars tend to assume one feature of control is more important than the others. All the facets of control and 'how they fit together...hold the key to stable, legitimate, and effective civil-military relations—the situation we recognize as effective control'.[22] Accordingly, Avant aims to discover whether or not privatization enhances or detracts from the integration of these three elements, as an 'indicator of the longer term prospect of either the stability often associated with effective control or the instability and change associated with its absence'.[23] Avant's book does not seek to analyse the normative structures that are associated with the control over force, and she does not consider in depth how questions of legitimacy and morality play into the privatization of force. Moreover, its main focus is on the private security industry rather than earlier types of private force.

Janice Thomson[24] is also explicitly interested in the relationship between mercenaries and state sovereignty. Unlike Singer, Thomson explicitly asks theoretical questions about state sovereignty and the nature of the monopoly on force. She is particularly interested in mercenaries because they reveal truths about the nature of state sovereignty. She argues that 'the

[21] Avant (2005a).   [22] Ibid. 45.   [23] Ibid.   [24] Thomson (1990, 1994).

contemporary organization of global violence is neither timeless nor natural. It is distinctively modern. In the six centuries leading up to 1900, global violence was democratized, marketized, and internationalized. Non-state violence dominated the international system'.[25] Thomson asserts that the development of state sovereignty meant that the global market for violence needed to be controlled. Sovereignty was the mechanism used to achieve this control. Accordingly, sovereignty should 'be treated not as an attribute, nor as a set of normative constraints, but as an institution that empowers states vis-à-vis people'.[26] According to Thomson, states stopped using mercenaries because the developing institution of sovereignty required them to gain control over the actions of their citizens.

Although Thomson does seek to probe the interesting questions mercenaries pose about the relationship between sovereignty and the monopoly on force, her approach obscures the reality of when and how states stopped using mercenaries. As Chapters 5 and 6 argue, neither the timing of the state decision to first control and then abandon mercenaries nor the reasons states stopped using mercenaries can be explained by the development of state sovereignty and the increasing power of the state over its citizens. In fact, the decision to stop using mercenaries was not made until very late in states that were emphatically sovereign actors on the international stage, like Britain. An approach focusing on sovereignty also cannot account for the fact that rulers made attempts to rein in mercenaries long before the nineteenth century, and indeed before the development of the sovereign state.

Examinations of mercenaries in the light of the threat they pose to the state's monopoly on force, like those of Singer, Thomson, and Avant, obscure the fact that, while mercenaries were indeed disliked because they challenged the state's ability to control force, dislike of mercenaries on ethical grounds is a deeper, older, and harder to shake objection. Concerns that mercenaries might challenge a state's control can be addressed through regulation and legislation; mercenaries can become less objectionable if they are more tightly controlled. The objection that mercenaries, because they fight for financial gain rather than a cause, are inherently objectionable is more problematic because it is significantly harder to overcome. Concern about mercenaries on the basis of their motivation runs through from medieval Europe to Machiavelli to the British government's Green and White Papers responding to PMC use. Regardless of whether or not it is right or fair to object to mercenaries on the grounds that they are inherently immoral actors, this objection has influenced states and rulers for centuries.

---

[25] Thomson (1994: 3). [26] Ibid. 5, 11.

Introduction

The existing literature on mercenaries is also problematic for empirical reasons. Mercenaries prior to the twentieth century are generally understudied. Those few accounts which do examine mercenaries in earlier periods argue that rulers, commentators on politics, and the general public only began to find mercenaries morally problematic sometime after the nineteenth century. Some take the position that the French Revolution was the earliest date mercenaries were considered to be a moral problem,[27] and others argue that mercenaries were only considered to be immoral in the twentieth century.[28] Most of the literature takes the position that mercenaries fell out of use in the nineteenth century.[29] However, an argument can be made that mercenaries have been considered morally problematic at least since the twelfth century.

Another analytical problem stems from the absence of attention to pre-nineteenth-century mercenaries and the norm against mercenary use. There are, in fact, two shifts away from mercenary use. The first shift took place between the fifteenth and seventeenth centuries, when an early history of mercenary dislike and the moral and practical problems raised by independent mercenaries led states to control tightly the exchange of mercenaries and limit their use. By the end of the seventeenth century, the independent mercenary, or a mercenary contractor free to choose his own clients or indeed wage war in his own right, had almost completely disappeared.[30] The second shift took place in the nineteenth century and ended even the state-regulated practice of selling military units to other states or legally allowing recruitment by foreigners within state boundaries. During the nineteenth century, states almost entirely ended the practice of buying and selling soldiers from and to other states.[31] Existing accounts of mercenaries fail to account for either shift. As we have seen, Thomson cannot really explain why states stopped using mercenaries in the nineteenth century, and Chapter 4 argues that other explanations of the nineteenth-century shift are also inadequate. There has been no systematic attempt to explain when and why rulers controlled independent mercenaries.[32]

Some of these gaps in the existing accounts occur because most writers working on the mercenary question rely heavily on Mockler's history of mercenaries.[33] Relying on Mockler as a significant or in some cases the main

---

[27] Lynch and Walsh (2000: 133).   [28] Zarate (1998: 4) and Spicer (1999a: 37).
[29] Posen (1993), Thomson (1994: ch.4), Shearer (1998b: 70), Avant (2000: 41), and Singer (2003a: 31).
[30] See Chapter 3.   [31] See Chapter 5.
[32] The only two accounts that come close are Fowler (2001) and Tilly (1990). Fowler explains why mercenaries needed to be controlled, and sets out how rulers started to do so. Tilly examines how states monopolized force internally and considers incidentally the part mercenaries played in this process.
[33] Mockler (1969) and also Mockler (1985).

historical authority on mercenaries[34] has led to his arguments simply being taken for granted. While informative, Mockler's book has neither footnotes nor a bibliography, and it is difficult to verify his claims. Without reading other military histories and accounts of mercenaries focusing on the pre-nineteenth-century period, those relying on Mockler run the risk of merely repeating his arguments rather than trying to get to grips with whether or not they are correct. In his introduction, Mockler states that mercenaries prior to the nineteenth century were considered to be normal and unobjectionable actors in the international system. He argues that 'it was only with the growth of the nation-state in Europe that mercenary soldiering has become disreputable and that it is only with the introduction of universal conscription that it has fallen out of use'.[35] However, careful reading of his later chapters provides numerous examples of cases in earlier periods where mercenaries were out of control and behaved reprehensibly, including the reviled Free Companies of the fourteenth century,[36] Swiss mercenaries in the fourteenth century,[37] and the problems in France leading to the establishment of the *compagnies d'ordonnance* in the sixteenth century, a prototype standing army.[38] There are instances of profound moral dislike and fear of mercenaries in all these cases, as we will see later. It is important to examine pre-nineteenth-century mercenaries using other sources to get a more nuanced picture of mercenaries during this period, and doing so challenges the impression that fear of mercenaries is a post-nineteenth-century phobia.

The final gap in the literature comes from a combination of the historical and theoretical lacunae outlined above. One of the main consequences of inattention to the historical record and international relations theory is an insufficient discussion of normative positions on mercenaries. While discussions which argue for or against mercenary use on normative grounds are common,[39] they do not tend to analyse the assumptions behind a particular normative position. These accounts argue either for the use of mercenaries because they are considered to be either morally neutral or potentially positive, or against their use because of a belief that mercenaries are morally wrong. This type of analysis does not question *why* we might consider mercenaries to be morally problematic.

---

[34] Thomson (1994), Zarate (1998), and Singer (2003a).   [35] Mockler (1969: 14).
[36] Ibid. 31–41.   [37] Ibid. 82–8.   [38] Ibid. 69.
[39] Examples of those supporting mercenary use include O'Brien (1998) and Shearer (1999) while Howe (1998) is less explicitly supportive. Those opposing the use of mercenaries include Burchett and Roebuck (1977), Arnold (1999), Mills and Stremlau (1999a), and Musah and Fayemi (2000a). Enrique Ballesteros, the former UN Special Rapporteur on mercenaries, falls strongly in this category.

Singer's work provides an excellent example of some of the problems with failing to probe normative concerns about mercenaries. While Singer's book does usefully analyse the development of private military and security companies, and considers the political implications of mercenary use, it examines the question of morality only briefly. Indeed, many of the supposedly normative objections to mercenaries Singer outlines are not really normative at all. For example, Singer argues that a 'moral area of concern' is the idea of adverse selection, which means that 'the privatized military industry provides an employment opportunity for those previously drawn toward mercenary work or who have been forced out of public military activities for past misdeeds'.[40] The concern that the private military industry may attract bad people might be a valid objection, but it is hard to see how it violates a particular norm or moral code.

Singer's arguments on the normative implications of the private military industry focus on what the industry *does* rather than what it *is*. For Singer, objections to the industry can only come from its actions, and cannot be levelled at what underlies the industry: the use of force for private gain. However, as Singer himself acknowledges, the private military industry has suffered from the accusation that private military firms are merely a new type of mercenary, and 'as such, the firms often provoke quite a hostile reaction and have been viciously attacked in the public arena'.[41] It is hard to understand why the private military industry has been seen as so objectionable, given its relative successes, without understanding that PMCs, like mercenaries, are believed to be *inherently* objectionable, no matter what they do. One of the arguments made in the UN, outlined in Chapters 6 and 7, is that there is no such thing as a good mercenary; the fact of being a mercenary cannot be obscured by good works or good behaviour. It is not enough, as Singer does, to argue that 'to simply paint all PMFs as purely good or purely evil is plain wrong'.[42] Without considering why some people paint the private military industry as evil, it is impossible to understand the prospects for the industry and state reactions to it.

Moral objections to mercenary use are deeper and have greater influence than Singer recognizes. As we will see, objections to mercenaries have centred around the fact that there is something morally problematic with being a mercenary and killing for money rather than for an appropriate cause. In turn, because mercenaries are perceived as inherently immoral actors, they have been considered more likely to behave in immoral ways. Singer fails to

---

[40] Singer (2003a: 221).   [41] Ibid. 217.

[42] Ibid. Singer uses the term PMF, or private military firm, to refer to both private security and private military companies. See Chapter 2 for an explanation of the difference between these two terms.

describe this link. The idea, for example, that a private military firm might be less accountable than a national army makes more sense if we recognize that mercenaries themselves are perceived as morally problematic. Singer argues that public military forces are more tightly controlled by a series of domestic political and legal institutions, public opinion, and international law than are private militaries.[43] But surely there is an underlying question here: why does lack of control make an actor inherently untrustworthy? Why do we assume that accountability is going to be a problem for the private military industry? Singer states that mercenaries might be dangerous and that the private military industry is 'not altruistic by any measure'[44] without realizing what this statement means. We need to understand why PMCs are not altruistic and what the implications of lack of altruism are. Part of the reason PMCs, like their mercenary predecessors, are unaccountable is that they are associated with the group which hires them only by a financial commitment; there is no deeper attachment to a cause which would bind them to the community for which they fight. Public opinion cannot be a constraint on mercenary activity in the same way it can be on a national army's activities, because mercenaries are detached from the public for whom they fight. Without understanding the depth and range of moral reactions to mercenaries, we cannot really understand why states, the media, and public opinion respond to the privatization of force in the way they do.

Taking a normative position without probing its origins and the nature of its influence ignores an obvious and important avenue for research. Those critics who support the private military industry, or regard it is as neutral, must be able to explain why, if PMCs might be good and useful for states, there has been such a strong reaction to them and why some types of company, like Executive Outcomes (EO)and Sandline, have disappeared. Normative objections to mercenary use, even if they are unfair, have had a powerful influence on the prospects and shape of the private military industry. Those who oppose the private military industry might find it worthwhile to examine where the position that mercenaries are dangerous comes from, and see whether or not there is a historical basis for these concerns.

A more detailed analysis of the influence of the proscriptive norm against mercenary use will add to the growing literature about the influence of norms on international politics generally.[45] It will also contribute to the more specialized debate over how, even in decisions regarding the use of force and the nature of force, norms influence state behaviour.[46] If norms play a role in situations where realists have argued that a state ought to be purely interested in

---

[43] Ibid. 220. [44] Ibid. 228.
[45] Finnemore (1993, 1996a), Katzenstein (1996a), and Risse, Ropp, and Sikkink (1999).
[46] On this debate, see Legro (1995), Price (1997a), Price and Tannenwald (1996), and Thomas (2001).

calculating its relative power position, such as the decision about which type of soldier, mercenary, or citizen, should be used to fight wars, then it suggests that norms can play a very profound role in influencing state decision-making.[47]

Filling these gaps will allow this book to make a contribution to the existing international relations literature. A historically thorough, theoretically grounded account of mercenaries which questions the influence of norms does not exist. Moreover, this book could provide a practical guide for policymakers. The accounts that take a particular position for or against the use of mercenaries make their judgements on PMCs based on an implicit comparison with 1960s mercenaries. PMCs are either good or bad because they are different from or the same as mercenaries in the 1960s. However, none of these accounts actually provides a comparative analysis of mercenaries between the two periods. Given that this is a specific policy issue for governments today,[48] as well as part of a larger debate about the crisis in military capacity among Western democracies, it is important that the content of this implicit comparison be made explicit. This book begins to do so by looking at types of mercenaries across the years, and by examining whether or not mercenaries deserve their reputation for immorality.

This book also contributes to policy debates because it points out a crucial obstacle to the widespread use of private force. The impact of such a long-standing and powerful norm against mercenaries has undoubtedly influenced the prospects for private military and private security companies.[49] These companies, or states which wish to hire them, might be well advised to understand the norm against mercenary use and consider how to counter it. Alternatively, states and international organizations might reconsider whether there are good grounds for such a norm, and if there are not, how they might go about creating an effective regime for the use of private force. If, however, there are good grounds for the normative dislike of mercenaries, then states ought to think carefully about the continued use of private force. Establishing whether or not there is a reasonable basis for the norm against mercenary use requires an examination of its origins and development, and by doing so this book provides useful practical analysis for policymakers.

1.2. OUTLINE OF THE ARGUMENT

I argue that the anti-mercenary norm has restricted state use of mercenaries at the same time it has influenced, and often constrained, the opportunities

---

[47] See Chapter 2 for a detailed explanation of the realist position.
[48] House of Commons Foreign Affairs Committee 2001–2002. [49] See Chapter 5.

12   *Mercenaries*

available for mercenaries themselves. In particular, four puzzles about mercenary use are best explained by the norm against mercenary use. These puzzles correspond to the main empirical sections of the book.

I begin in Chapter 1 by setting out the theoretical framework of the book. I adopt a constructivist approach, which explains how norms influence behaviour and how their impact can be studied. Chapter 2 defines the term 'mercenary', and identifies the problematic qualities which differentiate mercenaries from other types of fighters: that mercenaries do not fight for an appropriate cause and that they are not controlled by the state or another legitimate actor.[50] I argue that these problematic qualities form the core of the proscriptive norm against mercenary use.

Before outlining the argument which is made in the four empirical chapters, it is important to note that because of the limited historical investigations into the mercenary phenomenon, there are very few accounts with which a normative approach can be contrasted. Rather than construct an artificial account of how different scholars might have approached the four puzzles I argue the anti-mercenary norm best explains, I have chosen to discuss in some depth the two areas where there is a significant body of work taking an alternative approach. Some of these approaches argue that norms are not important in explaining the puzzle, while others argue that another norm, rather than the norm against mercenary use, explains the puzzle. Chapters 4–6 examine alternate explanations for state behaviour.

The empirical analysis of the norm against mercenary use begins in Chapter 3, where I pinpoint the origins of the anti-mercenary norm and argue that examining it can help us answer the question of why states stopped hiring independent mercenary contractors who supplied their own forces and instead incorporated mercenaries into standing armies or began to hire foreign troops only from other states and only under a formal agreement. I argue that this decision represents the first shift away from mercenary use.

Chapter 4 sets the stage for a normative explanation of why states stopped using mercenaries in the nineteenth century. Chapter 4 analyses three explanations[51] of the nineteenth-century shift in some depth, because if any of these arguments can account for such a major transformation in the way states used private force, it would diminish the argument that norms have been centrally important to state policy on the question. To make the case in Chapter 5 that the norm against mercenary use explains why states stopped hiring mercenaries from other states in the nineteenth century, even though it

---

[50] Of course, the state might not always be a legitimate actor. That said, it is generally assumed in the modern world that states are the bearers of the legitimate right to control and wield force.
[51] See Posen (1993), Thomson (1994), and Avant (2000).

was a relatively effective and well-regulated process, I set out in Chapter 4 the three competing explanations and identify some of the areas they struggle to explain.

In Chapter 5, I examine the decision in the late eighteenth and early nineteenth centuries to adopt a citizen army and stop the long-standing practice of hiring mercenaries from abroad, using four case studies. Analysing the decision to adopt a citizen army in America during its Revolution, France, Prussia, and Great Britain demonstrate that it is not possible to understand why states stopped using mercenaries when they did without examining the role of norms.

In Chapter 6, I examine the absence of an effective international regulatory regime for mercenaries. At first glance, this absence might seem to suggest that there is no real international consensus, and therefore no norm, against mercenary use, and indeed there is a body of work that makes this argument. These arguments seek to account for some of the flaws in the international law dealing with mercenaries from the perspective that states were fundamentally disinterested in creating a legal regime to deal with private force. These arguments must be addressed because if international law, where we would expect an underlying norm to be especially influential, does not reflect that norm, it poses serious problems for the assertion that the norm against mercenary use has been a significant influence on state behaviour. I argue that the anti-mercenary norm is in fact so strong that it has prevented the development of effective international law, and that the significant problems with existing law can only be explained by normative factors.

In Chapter 7, I assert that the explosion of PMCs and military contractors beginning in the 1990s, and the subsequent boom in PSCs after the 2003 war in Iraq do not indicate that private force has become an acceptable part of international affairs. I argue that the opportunities for these companies, and the shape they take, have been directly influenced by the norm against mercenary use. A belief that the use of private force is wrong, whether or not it is grounded in the facts of how these companies have really behaved, provides a significant obstacle to the further development of the private military industry.

1

Norms, Their Influence, and How They Can Be Studied

Tracing the history of the norm against mercenary use and examining the ways in which it has influenced state behaviour first requires defining the word 'norm', and demonstrating not only the ways that norms influence politics but how we can capture and describe that influence. The first section of this chapter begins with explaining what a norm is, and defines proscriptive norms in particular. It moves on to explain the three main theoretical approaches to defining norms, and argues that a constructivist approach is the most appropriate for capturing the influence of the norm against mercenary use. Third, the chapter outlines the relationships between norms and the related concepts of law, morality, and interests. In the fourth section, the chapter examines the ways in which norms influence politics and state behaviour. If norms influence state interests, what is the relationship between the two? The fifth section argues that a narrative methodology is most appropriate to describe and explain the influence of norms on state behaviour. The chapter concludes by addressing some of the challenges inherent in a study of norms.

1.1. WHAT IS A NORM?

While there is agreement on the broad outlines of a definition of a norm, there is variation on the precise details of such a definition. Philpott argues that norms can be defined as 'rules viewed as obligatory by the broad majority of people living under them' which are usually or customarily practised.[1] Mearsheimer defines institutions essentially as norms, 'a set of rules that stipulate the ways states should cooperate and compete with each other. They prescribe acceptable terms of state behaviour, and proscribe unacceptable kinds of behaviour'.[2] Katzenstein defines norms as 'collective expectations

[1] Philpott (2001: 21).   [2] Mearsheimer (1994–95: 8).

for the proper behaviour of actors within a given identity'.³ Kratochwil and Keohane concur that a norm is a standard of behaviour defined in terms of rights and obligations.⁴

A norm that constrains behaviour or prohibits a course of action might be described as a taboo or a prohibitionary norm.⁵ Price uses these terms interchangeably,⁶ but both are difficult. The former is awkward because it carries with it a particular normative slant.⁷ The latter is a neologism, and perhaps an unnecessary departure from the term 'proscriptive'. The specific components of the proscriptive norm against mercenary use will be discussed in Chapter 2.

The basic agreement about the definition of a norm must be qualified by the fact that, while most scholars agree about what a norm is, they disagree fundamentally about what norms do, which has profound implications for this study. Not all theorists agree that norms can influence state behaviour, and so not all theorists agree that a normative explanation of state action is possible.

Structural realists⁸ argue that norms are not intrinsically influential, and maintain that they are 'basically a reflection of the distribution of power in the world. They are based on the self-interested calculation of great powers and they have no independent effect on state behaviour'.⁹ Norms are created to serve the interests of states, and will not be influential when they lie outside state interests. Because norms are at best epiphenomenal, and indirect causes of state action, they will only be useful as an adjunct to realist explanations.¹⁰

Both structural realist and neoliberal approaches are rationalist, in that they assume that a state's interests are exogenously given¹¹ and so do not seek to understand the origins of those interests.¹² Rationalists argue that actors make 'cost/benefit calculations and choose strategies designed to maximize certain interests'.¹³ Assuming interests are exogenously given is crucial because it closes off the possibility of one of the major forms of normative influence—that norms shape state identity, and therefore state interests.

The structural realist approach struggles to explain why mercenaries are very rarely openly used in combat by modern states. The 'virtual absence of mercenaries in the present world system is not so easily explained by a utilitarian calculus' because 'there are countries with material and financial

---

³ Katzenstein (1996b: 5).   ⁴ Keohane (1984: 57), Kratochwil (1989: 59).
⁵ Price 1995, 1997a, 1997b and Price and Tannenwald (1996).   ⁶ Price (1995: 85).
⁷ See Tannenwald (1999: 436).
⁸ The discussion of realism in this book focuses on structural, rather than classical realists, and the term 'realist' indicates the former throughout.
⁹ Mearsheimer (1994–5: 7).   ¹⁰ Desch (1998: 170).
¹¹ For an approach that treats interests as given, see Keohane (1984: 6).
¹² Goldstein and Keohane (1993: 4).   ¹³ Checkel (1998: 329).

resources whose citizens are reluctant to fight, for instance the United States; mercenaries would seem to be an optimal solution for such states'.[14] Without understanding the role of norms, it is difficult to understand why states do not find it in their interest to contract out their militaries and use private force.

Neoliberals give more weight to the idea that norms influence state behaviour, but because they begin from a rationalist standpoint, still see the role of norms as limited or instrumental. Neoliberals argue that norms are influential in that they 'not only reflect, but also affect, the facts of world politics'.[15] Norms can be viewed as 'intermediate factors, or "intervening variables" between fundamental characteristics of world politics such as the international distribution of power on the one hand and the behaviour of states and nonstate actors... on the other'.[16] Norms influence policy by providing 'road maps that increase actors' clarity about goals or ends-means relationships, when they affect outcomes of strategic situations in which there is no unique equilibrium, and when they become embedded in political institutions'.[17]

Adhering to a norm might create a 'cost' that states consider in making a decision.[18] However, norms can also provide benefits for states in that they make it easier to cooperate by reducing transaction costs and uncertainty.[19] As a result, states will calculate whether or not abiding by a norm makes sense in a cost-benefit fashion. If a norm is beneficial, states will be reluctant to stop following it, even if continued adherence affects the national interest.[20] Norms are important in understanding politics because they are instruments used by states which shape the pattern of state interaction.

The neoliberal approach would be more useful in a study of the norm against mercenary use, but still not sufficient, because it assumes interests are exogenously given and does not discuss where interests come from. Neoliberals might argue that the anti-mercenary norm has provided benefits for states, in that it has assisted them in gaining control over an occasionally problematic type of force.[21] Alternatively, violating the norm against mercenary use might impose a cost, in that other states might disapprove and apply sanctions or otherwise make life uncomfortable for the violating state. But the norm against mercenary use has arguably shaped state interests to begin with; the idea that a state is able to provide for its own security using its own citizens has become such a crucial part of state identity that it is simply no longer in state interests to use mercenaries, because to do so would undermine state identity. The way norms shape state identity will be discussed in some depth below.

[14] Krasner (1989: 92).　　[15] Keohane (1984: 57).　　[16] Ibid. 64.
[17] Goldstein and Keohane (1993: 3).　　[18] Tannenwald (forthcoming).
[19] Keohane (1988: 386).　　[20] Müller (1993: 388).　　[21] See Chapter 3.

As soon as we begin to discuss how state identity is shaped by norms, we move into a constructivist argument. Constructivism departs significantly from both neoliberalism and realism. Constructivists argue that not only are norms important for understanding behaviour in the neoliberal sense, but that they are crucial to explaining politics because they constitute state identity, and therefore interests.[22] We cannot understand why states pursue a particular interest without understanding how they have been shaped by norms. A basic constructivist definition of a norm might be a rule or standard of appropriate behaviour that an actor accepts as part of his identity and follows most of the time.

Constructivists further argue that norms of all kinds are characterized by the fact that they are not individually held. The idea that a particular course of behaviour is the correct one presupposes a community which is judging the correctness of that behaviour.[23] As Thomas points out, a norm would not be a norm at all if only one person held it.[24] In other words, for norms to guide behaviour, there must be agreement among actors that the norm does, or should, in fact do so; that agreement means that the norm is held by a group. In turn, that group judges adherence to the norm. On the international level, the community that sets the standard for behaviour and assesses the extent to which behaviour meets the standard is composed of states.

Norms can be held internationally as well as within societies. Thomas defines an international norm as a norm that commands a broad range of international support and makes implicit demands on state foreign policy, even if the foundations of the norm are not shared among all states.[25] International support might come in the form of actions and words. States might make statements supporting the norm, or join an organization that relies upon the norm. States might act in a way that supports the norm, and explain that their action does so. Even states that do not ascribe to a norm are frequently affected by it; for example, states that violate or do not abide by human rights norms can face censure, sometimes in a serious form, from those states adhering to these norms.

A loosely constructivist approach is best suited to explaining the norm against mercenary use. This book demonstrates that this norm is neither epiphenomenal nor merely an intervening variable, but that it has shaped state interests in such a way that the use of private force has been restricted and the opportunities for mercenaries themselves have been constrained. Given that state interests on the desirability of deploying private force have changed enormously, in ways that cannot always be accounted for by material

---

[22] Finnemore (1996a), Checkel (1998: 326), and Wendt (1999: 21).
[23] Risse and Sikkink (1999: 7).   [24] Thomas (2001: 28).   [25] Ibid.

factors,[26] attention to the norm against mercenary use can help explain how state interests on the question of private force have changed and if they are likely to remain the same. While norms cannot explain all aspects of state behaviour, they are necessary to understand the decisions states have made about the use of private force. As Finnemore points out, attention to international norms and the way they structure interests illuminates how interests change.[27]

Moving from a basic definition that tells us what a norm or a proscriptive norm is, and having explained why a constructivist approach is necessary to capture the influence of the anti-mercenary norm, it is essential to differentiate norms from other similar concepts and explain the often knotty relationship between norms and interests.

1.2. THE RELATIONSHIP BETWEEN NORMS AND THE RELATED CONCEPTS OF LAW, MORALITY, AND INTERESTS

Norms are related to other concepts that may constrain behaviour. To understand how norms influence politics, it is necessary to understand the extent to which they differ from the associated concepts of law, morality, and interests.

Laws and norms are similar. Both provide standards of behaviour to which people generally adhere. There are two key differences between laws and norms. First, a law is codified, whereas a norm need not be. Second, written international law actually *reflects* norms. International law is a body of rules that reflect the norms according to which states behave most of the time.[28] One crucial point for discussion is the relationship between customary international law and the kind of norm discussed in this book. Customary international law may also be unwritten, and otherwise closely fits the definition of a norm outlined above. The concepts can be differentiated in the following way.

A norm is usually regarded as reaching the status of customary international law only when it is reflected by state practice and *opinio juris*, or the belief that a norm is accepted as law. *Opinio juris* is found in the decisions of international judicial bodies, the writings of jurists, and the comments of states. As a result, it could be argued that customary international law is created through a far more formal process than an international norm. According to this argument, not all norms reach the status of customary international law, even though they may be internationally influential. There is, however, a large and complex debate on the relationship between customary international law, *opinio*

---

[26] See Chapters 4 and 5. [27] Finnemore (1996a: 157). [28] Thomas (2001: 41).

juris, and state practice.²⁹ Some international lawyers argue, from a natural law perspective, that customary international law is in fact 'systematically independent of the will of current society members',³⁰ meaning that there are fundamental rules of international society and even if state practice and *opinio juris* do not follow these rules, they retain the status of law. This perspective is but one contribution to an extremely complex debate about whether or not customary international law really needs to be reflected in state practice and *opinio juris* to be considered law.³¹ The complexities of this debate lie far outside the bounds of this book, but it is nonetheless important to highlight that disagreement on this question exists.

If we accept the position that a norm differs from customary international law because the latter is created through a formal process and the former need not be, then it is simple enough to see that not all internationally influential norms become customary international law. Even if we accept the natural law position outlined above, it could be argued that some international norms are influential without being part of the core group of norms which remain unaffected by violation.

Another key difference between formal international law and norms is that the former derives from the latter. Sometimes the norms guiding state practice change, because of repeated violations of an old norm or the birth of a new norm, and it takes some time for the law to 'catch up' and change accordingly. This lag time demonstrates that the law and norms are different but still related.³² The discussions around the creation or revision of international law can, as we see in a later section and throughout the book, provide a very useful window onto the evolution of a particular norm.

Morals and ethics, like norms, prescribe a particular course of action and implicitly indicate that other courses are incorrect. Goertz and Diehl point out that critics have 'often failed to deal with the reality that norm means *normative*, that there are issues of justice and rights of a moral and ethical character'.³³ Unlike norms, morals are individual rather than collective, and each individual may take a different moral position from every other individual. Norms, as described above, must be held collectively to make any sense.³⁴ A principled idea which separates right from wrong (a moral judgement) can become a norm, or a 'collective expectation' about behaviour.³⁵ Because norms are used to separate right from wrong and guide behaviour,

---

[29] Higgins (1994: 18). [30] Allott (2000: 76).
[31] See the contributions of the New Haven School: McDougal and Lasswell ([1959] 1996). For an outline of the natural law perspective, see Beck, Arend, and Van der Lugt (1996: 34–8). For a discussion of *opinio juris* and custom see Price (2004: 113).
[32] Thomas (2001: 42). [33] Goertz and Diehl (1992: 639). [34] Thomas (2001: 28).
[35] Risse and Sikkink (1999: 7).

they often, but not always, have an ethical component. The norm against torture, for example, is built on an ethical position of respect for humanity and basic human rights, while the series of norms governing the international movement and exchange of diplomats does not have an ethical grounding. As we see below, the norm against mercenary use has a strong ethical component.

Thomas characterizes the difference in the following way. Moral principles are abstract propositions expressing judgement. By contrast, norms provide a concrete guide to action that may be based on an abstract moral rule. Mercenaries can be used to illustrate the distinction between norms and morals. The moral prohibition against killing in the abstract, as we see, has become part of a concrete political norm suggesting that states ought only to use their own citizens as soldiers.

Just as it is important to discuss how norms are related to similar concepts, it is necessary to ascertain how norms are related to concepts which may at first glance seem different. Carefully delineating the relationship between norms and interests is crucially important to the argument of this book. If norms guide state behaviour, then what role do interests play? We must assess how norms and interests are related to understand the role of each in determining state behaviour. This assessment takes three steps. First, it is necessary to define 'interest'. Second, the influence of material interests on norms and vice versa must be examined. Third, a discussion of how the interrelated nature of norms and interests prevents a study using one to the exclusion of the other is necessary. The section concludes by arguing that although the close relationship between norms and interests means that they both influence state behaviour, understanding the influence of norms on questions like the decision to employ private force remains of central importance.

Definition of 'Interest'

According to structural realist theory, states behave not according to norms but according to self-interest, defined in material terms or as power. Interests are exogenously given, exist prior to beliefs or norms, and might include status and power in addition to strictly material factors.[36] A state determines its interests by examining the distribution of power in the system; in other words, by assessing its material capacity in relation to the material capacity of other states. Waltz writes that 'interest provides the spring of action; the necessities of policy arise from the unregulated competition of states; calculation based on these necessities can discover the policies that will best serve a state's interests'.[37] For structural realists, as we have seen, norms play at best a

[36] Goldstein and Keohane (1993: 4).   [37] Waltz (1979: 117).

secondary role; 'rules reflect state calculations of self-interest based primarily on the international distribution of power'.[38] The decision to use a weapon in war, then, is governed by the extent to which it will help the state gain power vis-à-vis other states, not whether or not there are rules about the deployment of that type of weapon. The difficulty with this argument is that norms and interests are often interwoven. Interests are strongly affected by normative factors, just as normative factors are affected by interests.

How Norms and Interests Influence Each Other

Norms and interests are closely intertwined, in the deep sense that norms can shape state interests and in the more obvious sense that norms and interests are related simply because they might coincide.

State behaviour can be interpreted as following one of two basic logics. States might think of the costs and benefits of their actions, conscious that other states are doing the same, and thus behave following a logic of consequences.[39] Structural realists would assume that states calculate their interests in this fashion. Alternatively, a state might assess a situation, think about the kind of state it is, and the sorts of rules it follows, and then decide on the appropriate action. This is the logic of appropriateness.[40] Constructivists argue that states act according to this logic.

Juxtaposing a logic of consequence against a logic of appropriateness ignores the intertwining of interest-driven and norm-driven behaviour.[41] An actor might have an interest in avoiding negative consequences *and* a belief that the action was inappropriate. For example, a cyclist may wear a helmet because it is against the law not to do so, and she senses an obligation to obey the law. She might also have a strong self-interest in wearing the helmet for her own safety and protection.[42] A norm may draw strength because it is built on interest in this way.[43] Whether an action is 'costly' or 'beneficial' may rest on normative factors. A state choosing to profit from the international slave trade might find such a decision economically beneficial, but the action would be extremely costly in normative terms, as other states might choose to sanction the slave-trading state on purely moral grounds.

Norms and interests affect each other in ways more profound than the fact of their simultaneous presence. Norms are extremely influential because

---

[38] Mearsheimer (1994–5: 13).   [39] March and Olsen (1998: 950).   [40] Ibid. 951.
[41] Thomas (2001: 37).
[42] Goertz and Diehl (1992: 637). See also Nadelmann (1990: 480).
[43] Goertz and Diehl (1992: 637).

they shape what states define as their interests to begin with,[44] and because they set the rules of the game. The 'social nature of international politics creates normative understandings among actors that, in turn, coordinate values, expectations, and behaviour'.[45] Even if highly realist calculations based on material factors like economic and military power do drive state behaviour, norms have defined 'in the first place which material factors are perceived as relevant and how they influence understandings of interests, preferences and political decisions'.[46] When Canada calculates its policy towards the United States, the significant material factor of American military might play less of a role than economic factors, because shared norms between the two nations and the participation of both in a number of institutions simply means that the material differences in military capability are far less relevant to policy calculations. Even on military issues, Canada does not always support the United States, as evidenced by the recent Canadian refusal to support the American military effort in Iraq.

Norms can also shape how states perceive their interests. Because norms shape state identity,[47] they can affect the sorts of issues states see as falling into their national interest. Sikkink argues that the adoption of human rights policies by states does not reflect a neglect of the national interest but rather a 'fundamental shift' in the perception of what the national interest *is*.[48] The increased importance of human rights norms has caused states to calculate their national interests in a way that takes human rights into consideration. For example, military action to protect human rights abroad might now be considered a part of a state's national interest, even if such an action is strategically unimportant.

In nineteenth-century Britain, the decision to abandon mercenaries came about because of a change in norms that led to the reconfiguration of state interests. Britain's identity as the most civilized state in a system of civilized states was increasingly threatened by the trade in able-bodied soldiers. Many critics equated the trade in soldiers with the trade in slaves, which Britain was a leader in banning.[49] Trading in mercenaries was doubly immoral because the soldiers were bought to kill and be killed. At the same time, the idea that civilized states fought wars with armies of their own citizens was growing. As these norms gained influence, Britain reconfigured her interests and abandoned the use of mercenaries.[50]

---

[44] Thomas (2001: 3).   [45] Finnemore (1996*a*: 157).
[46] Risse and Sikkink (1999: 6–7).
[47] See next section for a discussion of the mechanics of this process.
[48] Sikkink (1993: 140). Price also argues that norms shape the national interest (Price 1997*b*: 48).
[49] See Ray (1989).   [50] See Chapter 5.

To sum up, norms and interests are not easily separated. Norms, interests, and calculations based on the distribution of power can all cause behaviour in the international system,[51] and it is difficult to argue that any one is the sole determinant of state behaviour. However, the fact that norms may play a role in shaping state interests suggests that norms cannot be neglected. Some strategies to deal with these difficulties are outlined in the fourth section.

1.3. THE INFLUENCE OF NORMS ON POLITICS

With a clear picture of what constitutes a norm in hand, we can now turn to a discussion of the ways in which norms influence politics. This section will set out four ways that norms affect state behaviour. First, as already indicated, norms shape state identity. Second, norms are powerful because they are embedded in institutions and set basic rules. Third, norms do not necessarily influence states to pursue courses of action that provide benefits to the state or are otherwise 'functional'. Fourth, norms can be supported or undermined by other norms. A norm that might not otherwise be strong enough to have an influence on a state can nonetheless shape state behaviour if it is supported by a stronger norm. Alternatively, a strong norm we might expect to influence states might be prevented from doing so because of a conflict with another strong norm.

Norms Shape Identity

Norms are an important influence upon state action because they shape state identity. States can hold a particular view of themselves, and act accordingly. States can follow an identity set out by the role they occupy within the system—as strong or weak or civilized or uncivilized states—which will also have a profound effect on state behaviour. State identity has two components: how a state views itself, and how it is viewed by other states. Norms can shape both types of identities. A state might change its behaviour because of the fear of being perceived negatively by other states, or the desire to be seen positively. Alternatively, a state's self-image might be undermined by a particular course of action.

The first way identity influences behaviour is straightforward. Sikkink and Risse point out that 'What I want depends to a large degree on who I am.'

---

[51] Thomas (2001: 20).

Identity sets out which interests are possible or appropriate for a state.[52] A state with a view of itself as extremely moral will find some actions impossible. A state with a powerful normative agenda might pursue that agenda even if it is damaging for the state. For example, South Africa persisted with its system of apartheid despite facing international sanctions. States conform to norms because norms define them, their goals, and their views of international politics.[53] This is not to say that interests do not play into the equation; as we have seen, they remain important. It is to say that norms shape and limit the possibilities for state action because they are central to how a state views itself, and how it is viewed by other states.

States with a certain identity will see themselves as like some states and different from others, which in turn will influence how they treat (and are treated by) other states. Identity comes from states differentiating or associating themselves with other states and existing in relation to each other within a particular systemic context.[54]

One of the strongest examples of how identity influences state behaviour comes from Gong's explanation of the influence of the standard of civilization. During colonization, colonies that aspired to statehood had to meet a certain 'standard of civilization', a measure to test the extent to which they shared Western values and characteristics.[55] Meeting the standard of civilization required, in effect, a change in identity that came from accepting a series of norms and behaviours. Aspiring states had to guarantee a certain level of rights for their citizens, with rights defined according to European norms, and had to share or adopt other European norms, like a European mode of jurisprudence.[56]

Another example comes from the relations of liberal democracies. States which identify themselves as liberal democracies do so by recognizing that they are the same as other such states, and different from non-liberal democracies.[57] As a result of this identification, liberal democracies are in a mutually trustworthy relationship.[58] States which see themselves as 'civilized' will worry about becoming 'uncivilized' if they pursue a certain course of action.[59] It follows that states wishing to be treated as civilized nations might begin following certain rules or going down certain paths which are considered critical to an identity as a civilized state.

---

[52] Risse and Sikkink (1999: 9). See also Tannenwald (1999: 440).
[53] Thomas (2001: 17).   [54] Wendt (1992: 397–8).   [55] Gong (1984: viii).
[56] Ibid. 15.   [57] Risse and Sikkink (1999: 8).
[58] For a specific discussion of why liberal democracies may be less prone to wars with each other see: Doyle (1983), Russett (1993), Owen (1994), Brown, Lynn-Jones, and Miller (1996).
[59] Price (1995) and Price and Tannenwald (1996: 129).

Abiding by or violating certain norms indicates ' "who we are"—to be a certain kind of people we just do not do certain things'.[60] In this way, norms provide a way for states to adjudicate between right and wrong. By, for example, deciding not to torture, a state becomes part of a group of states who do not torture. The decision becomes part of a state's identity and signals that it is a certain type of nation: perhaps Western, or just, or democratic. A modern state that uses mercenaries signals its fundamental weakness as a state—the fact that it uses mercenaries suggests that it *needs* to use them, and thus the state's own armed forces must not be particularly strong. A ruler relying on mercenaries will find it difficult to convince others of his legitimacy. In a world in 'which national armies and the attendant patriotic fervour are ubiquitous, the need for mercenaries becomes a litmus test for the illegitimacy of those rulers who require them'.[61] States that do not use mercenaries are thus strong or real, and states that do use private force are weak, illegitimate, and not 'proper' states. Rulers who rely on mercenaries threaten their legitimacy. In the twentieth century, the association of mercenary use with weak states and an effective national army with strong states, as we see, has a profound impact on state identity.

Normative influence on state identity also dictates the parameters of the possible. States that identify in a particular manner will find it difficult, if not impossible, to behave in a way which threatens that identification. During the American Revolution, for example, the newly declared state identified itself as a republic made virtuous by the use of a citizen army, and doubly virtuous because it fought against mercenaries. To use private force in this context, or to fail to condemn it, would have been difficult because it would have been deeply at odds with American identity.

Norms Can Influence States through Institutionalization

The term 'institution' may refer to a '*general pattern or categorization* of activity or to a *particular* human-constructed arrangement, formally or informally organized'.[62] Norms can be institutionalized in specific institutions like political institutions or international law, and also in general institutions which shape state behaviour, like the institution of war. This section examines how both types of institutions can assist norms in influencing politics.

Norms embedded in specific political institutions[63] provide an extremely visible form of influence upon the state. The UN, for example, is built on several norms, including the norm that all sovereign states are equal and the

---

[60] Price (1997a: 10). [61] Lynch and Walsh (2000: 104). [62] Keohane (1988: 383).
[63] Goldstein and Keohane (1993: 3).

norm of non-intervention. Norms may also become institutions in the form of international law.

Once embedded in institutions, norms can exert a greater influence on state behaviour because the institution provides organizational support for the norm and the means for it to be expressed.[64] In other words, the mechanisms of the institution can mobilize state support, or indeed dictate that state support for the norm is a condition of membership in the institution. The institution can be used to propagate the idea that the norm is a good thing.

Swift institutionalization can strengthen a norm. Price argues that the very early decision to make chemical weapons illegal at the Hague Conference of 1907 had a strong influence on the long persistence of the norm against the use of chemical weapons. The Hague Conference and the norms institutionalized within it became a part of the 'standard of civilization'.[65] This early institutionalization, and its ties to the concept of 'civilization', made further deviations from the law difficult.

Similarly, the formal institutionalization of the norm against mercenary use in international law in the 1960s had a profound impact on the continued influence of the norm. Almost immediately after mercenaries had reappeared during the African wars of decolonization in the 1960s, various attempts were made to make them illegal. These attempts are examined in detail in Chapter 6, but it is important here to highlight that very swift action by individual states and the UN led to a lingering sense later on that mercenaries were illegal, even when they appeared in forms that might not contravene the law. In addition, as in the case of chemical weapons at the Hague, the institutionalization of the norm against mercenary use was tied to developing norms about the nature of statehood in the international system. Part of the reason mercenaries were considered so heinous during the decolonization period was that they were largely used to undermine the project of national self-determination. The institution of law against mercenaries was strengthened by the norms and institutions promoting national self-determination.

Once part of an institution, norms can have an impact on states even when they are no longer considered to be a useful moral guide to action.[66] The institution can promote, protect, and prolong the existence of a norm. The development of legal institutions against mercenaries is a good example of how this type of prolonging can occur. The early creation of an international legal regime against mercenaries promoted the idea that mercenaries were immoral actors requiring legal control, and protected that idea throughout the 1970s. Even when types of mercenaries have appeared that arguably did not violate the letter of international law, the law has had lingering effects. As

[64] Yee (1996: 88).   [65] Price (1997a: 35).   [66] Goldstein and Keohane (1993: 21).

we see in Chapters 6 and 7, private military companies and PSCs often have to explain their legal position, because of a prevailing belief that there must be something illegal about the use of private force.[67] Norms can be institutionalized across a number of issue areas, further enhancing their effects.[68]

Another example of the power of institutionalization comes from the UN. The UN acted very early on the mercenary problem, through both the Security Council and the General Assembly. These actions set the stage for further institutionalization, as the development of the UN International Convention against the Recruitment, Use, Financing and Training of Mercenaries in the 1980s demonstrates. As an institution, the UN has been geared towards disapproval of mercenaries, despite changes in the nature of mercenary action. The reports of the former UN Special Rapporteur on mercenaries, Enrique Bernales Ballesteros, reflect the moral disapproval of mercenaries by the UN High Commission for Human Rights (now the Human Rights Council) in language which closely reflects the 1960s and 1970s fears, and arguably ignores the differences between mercenary action then and now.[69]

General patterns of activity, like war, can also be institutions. In the sense that war is 'a settled pattern of behaviour, shaped towards the promotion of common goals, there cannot be any doubt that it has been in the past such an institution, and remains one'.[70] War fits the definition of an institution in that it is 'a set of persistent and connected rules prescribing behavioural roles, constraining activity and shaping expectations'[71] which might include both formal and informal rules.[72] The norm against mercenary use has been embedded in the institution of war, which has vastly increased its strength and its longevity.

The anti-mercenary norm has been strengthened because part of the task of the institution of war is to dictate who, and under what circumstances, has the right to kill.[73] A series of international laws created between 1859 and 1907 codified existing ideas on this question into law; 'to distinguish war from mere crime it was defined as something waged by sovereign states and by them alone. Soldiers were defined as personnel licensed to engage in armed violence on behalf of the state' and so private fighters were banned. To 'obtain and maintain their licence, soldiers had to be carefully registered, marked, and controlled, to the exclusion of privateering'.[74] One 'of the qualifications

---

[67] As is argued below, most PMCs and PSCs actually fall outside international legal definitions of a mercenary and are so not acting illegally.
[68] Klotz (1995: 23).
[69] The Ballesteros reports are discussed in more detail in Chapter 7, and the development of international law and statements about mercenaries in Chapter 6.
[70] Bull (1977: 178). [71] Keohane (1995: 167). [72] Keohane (1988: 383).
[73] Gong (1984: 74). [74] van Creveld (1991: 40).

for gaining the status of a civilized nation was to partake in the regulation of warfare that began among the European society of states in the mid-nineteenth century'.[75] The institution of war, as created through the latter half of the nineteenth century, explicitly excluded private force, and accepting this exclusion was one of the criteria states had to meet to be considered civilized. As Chapter 5 argues, the preference for citizen soldiers combined with this ban on private force made the use of mercenaries in the international system unthinkable from the 1850s to the 1960s.

Just as specific, purposely created institutions can prolong the effects of a norm, so too can the association of a norm with a general institution. Indeed, the institution of war has been remarkably resilient, and so it has lengthened the anti-mercenary norm's life as well as strengthened its effects. Van Creveld points out that Western governments have been loath to let go of the institution of war, which he defines as trinitarian, or composed of three strictly demarcated elements with their own roles to play: the people, the military, and the government, and deriving from the nineteenth century.[76] Despite evidence that the nineteenth century institution of war is no longer in touch with reality, 'the military establishments of developed countries clung to trinitarian war because it was a game with which they had been long familiar and that they liked to play'.[77] The association of the anti-mercenary norm with the institution of war suggests that change in the norm may require change in the institution of war. Even so, change in war might not lead to the death of the norm against mercenary use, because it is also made stronger and more resilient with the support of other norms.

The Effect of Norms on States Will Be Enhanced or Undermined by the Presence of Related Norms

The influence norms have on politics can be strengthened or weakened by the presence of other norms. Norms can draw strength from association in two different ways. First, the effect of a norm might be multiplied by support from another norm, enhancing the proscription or prescription of the norm, or by making it more influential than it otherwise would be. Second, the life of a norm, and so the influence it has on policymaking, can be prolonged if it becomes associated with a long-lived norm.

Price argues that the proscriptive norm against chemical weapons was tied to various other norms and ideas, like the norm against the use of poison or the idea that technology in general was dangerously stepping

[75] Price (1995: 95). [76] van Creveld (1991). [77] Ibid. 59.

outside human control.⁷⁸ These norms and ideas strengthened each other by association. Chemical weapons were tainted by the negative connotations of poison; if poison needed to be controlled, and chemical weapons were a form of poison, the need to control the latter was more clear. The proscriptive effects of the chemical weapon norm were reinforced by the norm against poison.

Norms can also gain influence in areas we might not expect them to as a result of the support of a different norm. Logical coherence between norms increases their legitimacy and power; European beliefs about inequality enhanced the decolonization norm because of their kinship.⁷⁹ Any 'new norm must fit coherently with other existing norms' to ensure its legitimacy.⁸⁰ The rapid spread of the anti-mercenary norm across Europe in the nineteenth century came about because of the close association between the anti-mercenary norm and the norm that citizens owe a military duty to the state. As Chapter 5 argues, states that had very little reason to give up mercenaries, or indeed relied on mercenaries as a substantial part of their economies, were forced to do so because the use of private force is wholly incompatible with the idea that citizens are the only appropriate soldiers.

The association between norms can also have an effect on state behaviour by prolonging the effect of a norm when we might otherwise expect to see its influence erode. It might appear, for example, as though the appearance of PMCs in the 1990s would have struck a serious blow at the norm against mercenary use. But because the anti-mercenary norm had been associated with the norm of national self-determination, which is a strong norm that has been repeatedly enshrined in law, various UN decisions, and even in the structure of UN committees, there was an unexpected direction from which to attack PMCs—that mercenaries in any form challenged national self-determination. The association between the norm against mercenary use and the norms of self-determination was sufficiently strong to influence the UN, even though there was little empirical evidence that self-determination was undermined by the 1990s variant of private force.⁸¹

The proscriptive norm against mercenaries is tied to other norms and a series of ideas, some of which have changed over the years. The ban against mercenaries is associated with norms as varied as the belief that the state ought to have control over the use of force⁸² and the norm against prostitution.⁸³ It has also been associated with the norms of self-determination and of

---

[78] Price (1997a: 12, 25).   [79] Finnemore (1996a: 173).   [80] Florini (1996: 376).
[81] See Chapter 7.   [82] Thomson (1990: 24).
[83] Finer (1976: 129) and Lynch and Walsh (2000: 134).

democracy, as some argue that PMCs undermine the state's ability to be responsible to its citizens.[84]

Clearly, the norms with which the proscriptive norm against mercenary use has been associated have evolved over time. Examining which norms and ideas are associated with the anti-mercenary norm at different junctures can reveal what particular states find dangerous about mercenaries at particular times. Price points out that examining the components of the chemical weapons taboo can reveal aspects of the 'practice of violence in international politics'.[85] Similarly, examining the associations of the anti-mercenary against mercenaries with other norms will reveal which types of force are considered valid in the international system at a given time. In addition, multiple associations explain why a prohibition remains strong; mercenaries might have been wrong because they threatened sovereignty, and later they might have been wrong because they challenge self-determination or democracy.

The effect of norms on state behaviour can also be increased or decreased as a result of a conflicting norm. The acceptance of a new norm can cancel out the effects of an old norm and so push states to change their behaviour. The institutionalization of the norm of self-determination made it impossible for states to pursue actions on the basis of the norm of colonization[86] because states cannot simultaneously hold two conflicting norms.[87] Likewise, states, once they had accepted the norm that citizens owed a duty to the state, foreclosed the option of using private force.

The presence of a conflicting norm can mean that a very strong norm, which we might otherwise anticipate would have a correspondingly strong influence on state policy, will be less influential. Alternatively, the presence of two strong conflicting norms might lead to unclear policy which does not accurately reflect the strength of either norm. During the creation of international law on mercenaries between the 1960s and the late 1980s, the norm of state responsibility was in direct conflict with the anti-mercenary norm. While the latter was extremely strongly held, once legal discussions turned to the question of state responsibility, states found themselves caught between two norms. States that adhered to the norm of state responsibility, which suggested that states ought not to be held internationally responsible for the actions of their citizens, found themselves unable to support a strong legal regime regulating mercenary use, because the two were incompatible. The anti-mercenary norm did not have the strong effect it might have done

---

[84] See the reports of the UN Special Rapporteur, including UN Doc E/CN.4/1998/31, p. 10. The Special Rapporteur's final report states that mercenaries still violate self-determination: UN Doc E/CN.4/2004/15, p. 20.
[85] Price (1997a: 9). [86] Jackson (1993: 113). [87] Florini (1996: 373).

on the resulting law, the incoherence of which can be explained partially by the conflict between the two norms.

It is worth noting that both institutionalization and the support of similar norms seem to have a noticeable effect on resilience. One explanation for the fact that some norms seem to be particularly long-lived might be that that norm has been fortunate in that it has coincided with other norms or been institutionalized in long-lived institutions. The norm against mercenary use, which has been extremely long-lived, has benefited from both types of support.

Norms Can Have a 'Negative' as well as a 'Positive' Effect on State Behaviour

Norms are not always 'logical' in that they do not necessarily lead to a beneficial outcome in utilitarian terms, or simply because we cannot easily use reason to understand why a particular norm exists. Norms do not always lead to 'functional' policy decisions for states.[88] Even though we can logically assess that there is no reason why a particular behaviour or course of action is proscribed by a norm, the norm may still remain a powerful guide to human action. For example, swear words alluding to bodily functions are considered taboo in most English-speaking cultures. It is hard to understand how these words became 'swears', or proscribed by society, in the first place, or why there is often a socially acceptable word that refers to the same bodily function.

The difference between what is a socially acceptable or a socially unacceptable word relies on social norms that dictate what is considered rude and polite. Proscriptive norms can be based on a particular moral code, which in turn might be contingent on a given society at a given time. The types of words considered profane vary from society to society, and within particular societies over time.

Similarly, some critics have argued that there is no longer any sensible reason to assume that PMCs or mercenaries are inherently bad.[89] As we see, the historical evidence suggests that mercenaries were not 'bad' for states in practice after the sixteenth century, and that any problems created by mercenaries in the nineteenth century were equally likely among native troops, meaning that there was not necessarily a reason to prefer the latter.[90] Arguments can be made that lack of accountability, potential for cruelty, and other commonly

---

[88] McElroy (1992: 54) and Tannenwald (forthcoming).
[89] Lynch and Walsh (2000: 134). For a discussion of how norms may not always be rational, see Tannenwald (forthcoming).
[90] See Chapter 3 for an extensive discussion of the early history of the anti-mercenary norm.

asserted mercenary dangers have no basis in fact.[91] A cost-benefit analysis of private military force (PMF) using a utilitarian calculus might suggest that private force is a good idea for states. Developed states, whose citizens are not keen to enlist and for whom casualties are extremely costly, might well prefer to hire mercenaries. Even though the reality of the situation suggests that mercenaries might not be dangerous, and indeed might be useful, moral qualms about their use persist.

Very strong norms might become internalized to the point that their influence on policy is automatic.[92] In this type of situation, a state or other actor will no longer necessarily consider whether or not it makes sense to abide by a norm. Alternatively, states and their citizens might automatically consider a norm to be correct and so be horrified by the prospect of its violation. This type of norm has become 'puritanical' in that it leads to relatively unreflective behaviour that persists regardless of reality.[93] To a large degree, the norm against mercenary use has become puritanical, in that its influence appears to be automatic and no longer tied to the facts.

The continued influence of norms, even when the action they constrain may no longer require control, demonstrates that norms have a profound and lingering influence that need not be positive for states. Explaining why it is not in American interests to hire mercenaries, even when evidence suggests that they might be useful and that their use would solve a problem of recruitment, requires attention to how the anti-mercenary norm creates a huge cost for states, both in terms of persuading domestic and international opinion about the decision, and also for American identity, which has relied on status as a military superpower. The influence of 'bad' or 'illogical' norms shows how strong a factor in political decisions norms can be.

1.4. NARRATIVE METHODOLOGY

If norms are important influences on behaviour in international politics, then how is it possible to trace their influence? Tracing the evolution of a norm through a changing historical context requires a particular kind of methodology. First, this section argues that a narrative method is a useful approach for understanding the role of norms in political behaviour. A narrative method is quite similar to a genealogical method, and so the genealogical method will be discussed, with its most useful features highlighted. Second, this section

---

[91] O'Brien (1998: 89), Lynch and Walsh (2000: 147). Chapter 7 assesses some of these claims.
[92] Thomas (2001: 38).
[93] I am indebted to Henry Shue for suggesting the term 'puritanical norm'.

outlines some of the specific tools of a narrative method. Finally, it discusses the sources necessary for a narrative approach.

A Narrative Approach

Answering the question of why states persistently view mercenaries as normatively problematic is really telling a story of how states and other actors came to believe the use of private force is wrong, and how that belief has influenced their behaviour. A narrative method traces the evolution of a norm through changing historical contexts, seeking to examine how the norm influences states and vice versa at different points in time.

The narrative approach argues that to see the influence of a norm on behaviour, it must be placed in context and then analysed historically. If the influence of the norm against mercenary use is visible in state policy, it is necessary to look at the historical record and use empirical research to trace it.[94] Historical evidence helps tell the story of how a norm has evolved.

A narrative approach is loosely based on the genealogical method advocated by Price.[95] The goal of both approaches is to explain the present in terms of the past, considering the road a norm has taken to lead it to where it is now. Price argues that a genealogical approach, following Nietzsche, questions structures which are now considered to be natural and normal and traces them back, looking at the historical context at the time of their growth and development.[96] Nietzsche's genealogical method is 'an approach that seeks to uncover the conditions under which moral institutions are devised and interpret the value that these norms themselves possess' and is specifically concerned with interpreting the origins of moral positions. In particular, the genealogical method seeks to uncover *how* rather than *why* a moral position becomes influential.[97] A genealogy tries to explain how the present became logically possible.[98]

Similarly, a narrative approach examines an existing norm's history to understand how it has influenced politics, and how that influence may have changed as it evolved. A narrative approach that seeks to construct plausible explanations is especially useful for looking at how the norm against mercenary use has changed over time. Norms embedded in institutions or crucial organizational norms require historical contextulization to be made

---

[94] Wendt (1987: 365), Yee (1996: 85), and Finnemore and Sikkink (1998: 890).
[95] Price (1995, 1997a).   [96] Price (1995: 85).
[97] Ibid. 85–6. For more on the method's focus on how rather than why questions see Price (1995: 84).
[98] Bartelson (1995: 8).

clear because the reasons they were initially implemented may have changed. Understanding the influence of the norm against mercenaries requires understanding its historical antecedents, looking at how these ideas became powerful over time and how they were adopted into international institutions, becoming a normal (and expected) part of state interaction.

A narrative method, like the genealogical method, focuses on crucial historical moments in the history of the norm, seeking to provide a window into the 'bursts of rich debate' that 'represent discussions of the crucial elements of the taboo'.[99] These defining moments, because they are characterized by extensive debate, allow us to see which aspects of the proscriptive norm are contentious and which are accepted and how norms are advocated or disputed.

A focus on the history of a norm, which seeks to tell the story of how the norm arrived where it has arrived by focusing on pivotal moments in its history, demonstrates the role of contingency in the evolution of a norm. Chance plays a powerful role in the construction of norms.[100] Changing circumstances can undermine a norm; a fortuitous change might strengthen it. The development of institutions or new norms might further challenge or support a norm. Analysing the history of a norm and focusing on its pivotal moments is vital because 'as a result of the marriage of chance occurrences, fortuitous connections, and reinterpretations, the purposes and forms of moral structures often change in such a way that they come to embody values different from those that animated their origins'.[101] If we assume that the reasons states support the norm today are the reasons that states supported the norm at the time of its creation, we run the risk of misunderstanding the norm's history. Moreover, the tale of how a norm embodied one set of values at its beginning and now embodies a different set reveals the process by which the norm remains important. Alternatively, if the norm has remained relatively constant throughout its history it is worth considering how and why this has been possible.

Admitting that chance plays a large role in the development of a norm means that the conscious interests and designs of states might have little effect on state behaviour.[102] In the case of chemical weapons, the initial taboo was developed at the Hague because chemical weapons had not yet been developed and were accordingly considered to be unimportant.[103] Later on, building the norm up was easy because the precedent had been set at the Hague and so the

---

[99] Price (1997a: 10).
[100] Florini (1996: 373), Price and Tannenwald (1996: 124), and Price (1997a: 8).
[101] Price (1995: 86).   [102] Price and Tannenwald (1996: 126–7).
[103] Price (1997a: 12).

norm was not entirely new.[104] The lucky break of the inclusion of chemical weapons at the Hague made it possible for the norm to develop later.

One of the central advantages of this kind of historical approach is that it reveals the connections between norms. Norms should be viewed not 'as individual "things" floating atomistically in some international social space but rather as a part of a highly structured social context'.[105] Tracing one norm in this linked pattern will reveal its relationship to other guiding norms; for example, tracing the norm of humanitarian intervention reveals how it relates to sovereignty, decolonization, and self-determination.[106] As we have seen, the norm against mercenaries is linked to several other norms, including the norm that citizens owe a military duty to the state, the norm of national self-determination, and the norms associated with the institution of war. Tracing the norm against mercenary use reveals its connections to these other norms.

Tools of a Narrative Methodology

Practically speaking, how are norms traced through history? What are some of the tools which can be used to trace the influence of norms? First, violations of the norm and the justifications for that violation provide a powerful lens through which to see the influence of norms. Second, tools that allow an understanding of the evolution of a norm will be proposed and a series of questions that can be used to trace the norm through history will be suggested. Third, the sources and nature of evidence used to make the argument will be set out.

Justifications and Violations

Examining the ways that states violate norms can reveal areas in which norms appear to have lost out to state interests but in fact remain important. The violation of the norm can provide evidence for its influence in five ways.

First, if a norm is violated often, it might mean that it is not powerful, or that it is no longer relevant to states because of historical changes. If a norm is rarely violated, it might suggest that it is considered to be so normal that states do not question it; alternatively, it might mean that it is simply insignificant and so states neither violate it nor uphold it. However, violations of norms, either singly or severally, do not mean that the norm is no longer significant. Only in cases where non-compliance is extremely widespread can it be argued that the norm is no longer playing a role at all.[107] Questions about the nature

[104] Price and Tannenwald (1996: 127).   [105] Finnemore (1996a: 161).   [106] Ibid.
[107] Kratochwil and Ruggie (1986: 768) and Philpott (2001: 26).

of the violation (what specifically was being violated?) and whether or not justification was necessary (did the state need to justify at all?) indicate the robustness of the norm.[108] If a state feels the need to justify its violation of a norm, then it suggests that the norm must still carry some weight. Examining the frequency and nature of violations, and finding explanations for them, shows how important a norm is in international relations. This type of analysis judges whether a norm is widely violated or not widely violated and what non-compliance might mean on the basis of a plausible explanation backed up by evidence.

Second, the reaction of other states to the violation of a norm is extremely important. Justification

> speaks directly to normative context... when states justify their interventions, they are drawing on and articulating shared values and expectations held by other decision makers and other publics in other states. It is literally an attempt to connect one's action to standards of justice, or perhaps more generically, to standards of appropriate and acceptable behaviour. Thus through an examination of justifications we can begin to piece together what those internationally held standards are and how they may change over time.[109]

If a state is internationally condemned for its decision to violate a norm, it suggests that the other states take the norm seriously. No reaction to the violation might indicate that the norm is no longer important, or that the violation was not egregious. Support for the violation would suggest that the norm might be falling out of favour. What happens after the violation is crucial: are there any future violations, and does state behaviour further undermine the norm, or support it?[110]

Third, *how* a state chooses to rationalize its violation is both interesting and useful. States justify their non-compliance to themselves and to others through official statements, in press conferences, and in submissions to international organizations. Violations of norms can thus leave 'an extensive trail of communication' which provides empirical data for study.[111] The methods states choose to justify the decision to violate a norm can also tell us something about how serious they consider the violation to be, and the extent to which they believe other states will see the violation as serious. The United States' decision to invade Iraq can be interpreted as a violation of the norm against pre-emptive strikes. Even though the United States ultimately did invade Iraq, they attempted to justify their decision through multiple avenues and in multiple institutions, working through bilateral negotiations and multilateral

---

[108] Price and Tannenwald (1996: 126).   [109] Finnemore (1996a: 159).
[110] Price (1997a: 10).
[111] Finnemore and Sikkink (1998: 892). Jackson (2000: 91) concurs.

discussions in the UN and NATO. The lengths to which the United States went suggest that they might have believed that other states took the violation of the norm against pre-emptive strikes very seriously.

Fourth, the motive behind the justification can reveal the importance of the norm. Even if the justification appears to be no more than a lip-service pronouncement totally divorced from the facts of state action, if the state must pay lip-service to the norm it demonstrates that the state believes the norm to be important enough so that it must be acknowledged. If the norm were wholly without importance, surely the state would not use normative language to justify its action. Moreover, a state may justify a norm-violating action in normative terms simply because doing so reinforces state identity. A Western state choosing to hold suspected terrorists illegally may attempt to argue that such a decision is perfectly consistent with, and in fact enhances, civil liberties, because otherwise the decision to detain may undermine the state's identity as an upholder of freedoms.

Fifth, the specific aspects of a justification point to which elements of a norm are most significant. States today argue that a violation of the proscriptive norm against mercenary use can be justified on the basis that a state's decision to use a private military company is an aspect of its self-determination. A state has the right to use whatever type of assistance it needs in order to ensure its viability, and hiring a PMC could help ensure the state's survival and continued independence, and so assist the project of self-determination. In the 1960s, a decision to use mercenaries could not have been justified by self-determination, as the norm against mercenaries rested on the grounds that private force threatened the independence of newly decolonized states. This shift might indicate that the relationship between self-determination and the anti-mercenary norm has changed, or that the former norm has itself changed, allowing for a different kind of justification. If a state's justification does not refer to a particular aspect of a norm, or refers to that aspect exclusively, it points to which grounds of that norm are still significant.

Examining violations of a norm and the justifications that states offer for doing so provides a useful empirical pool of evidence for the influence of norms on state policy.

Tracing the Evolution of a Norm

In addition to the broad sort of historical contextualization outlined above, it is useful to examine the specific evolution of the norm against mercenary use in order to explain how the present norm against mercenary use came into being. The evolution of a norm can basically be pinned down to three phases:

initial appearance, broad acceptance, and internalization (when acceptance of the norm becomes automatic).[112] During the first stage, norm entrepreneurs actively call attention to and pursue the creation of a norm.[113] The adoption of the norm by a particularly prominent or successful state may induce other states to follow suit.[114] Broad acceptance, the second stage, occurs when there is a critical mass of states supporting the norm, reaching a 'tipping point' after which the norm spreads rapidly. As in the first stage, it can help if powerful states whose acceptance is critical to the norm's success support it.[115]

The rapid spread of the norm, which Finnemore and Sikkink call a 'norm cascade', functions through a process of socialization, which in turn functions because of the power of state identity. At the tipping point, 'enough states and enough critical states endorse the new norm to redefine appropriate behaviour for the identity called "state" or some relevant subset of states'.[116] Socialization relies on 'peer pressure', where states are persuaded to adopt the norm because it provides a seal of international legitimacy, which can enhance domestic legitimacy, and the pressure to conform 'in order to avoid disapproval aroused by norm violation and thus to enhance national esteem'.[117] The third stage is reached when the norm becomes internalized, or embedded in state identity and international and domestic institutions, and adherence to it essentially automatic.[118]

The mechanisms of how states are influenced by norms, outlined above, are clearly at work in each phase of Finnemore and Sikkink's description of the evolution of a norm. State identity plays a crucial role in the second stage, and by the third stage adherence to the norm has become part of state identity. Institutionalization is also important, because institutions can assist norm entrepreneurs in disseminating the norm and indeed can be entrepreneurs themselves. Institutions are powerful sources of 'peer pressure' and legitimacy, and can encourage conformity. Finally, the association between norms is an important part of how norms develop. If a new norm is related to existing norms, it has a higher chance of success.[119]

The norm against mercenary use can also be usefully analysed using Finnemore and Sikkink's model. Given that the origins of the norm are extremely distant, the role of norm entrepreneurs was less important at the beginning but has become more important during each of the norm's crucial phases. During the medieval period, the Christian Church, particularly the Lateran Councils, propagated the norm. Political theorists,

---

[112] Finnemore and Sikkink (1998: 895).
[113] Florini (1996: 374–5) and Finnemore and Sikkink (1998: 896–7).
[114] Florini (1996: 375).   [115] Finnemore and Sikkink (1998: 901–2).
[116] Ibid. 902.   [117] Ibid. 904. See also McElroy (1992: 46).
[118] Finnemore and Sikkink (1998: 905).   [119] See above.

philosophers, and religious figures have also been strong advocates of the anti-mercenary norm, especially during the medieval period and the nineteenth century.

The anti-mercenary norm has reached two and possibly three 'tipping points'. The first tipping point occurred when states shifted from contracting with independent mercenaries to using their own standing armies, and the international exchange of mercenaries became a state-to-state enterprise. This tipping point is the first shift away from mercenary use, and the focus of Chapter 3. The second tipping point came when states stopped the state-to-state trade in mercenaries and began exclusively to use citizens in their armed forces, and this second shift away from mercenary use is the focus of Chapters 4 and 5. After this time, it can be argued that the norm against mercenary use was essentially internalized. The third tipping point could have been reached in the 1970s, with the creation of international law dealing with mercenaries, but because the norm had been so strongly internalized it paradoxically could not be translated into coherent international law, as we see in Chapter 6.

It is also worthwhile to consider some specific questions at each phase in the norm's evolution. First, it is necessary to identify the essential issues of a particular proscriptive norm.[120] Which aspects of the norm were considered crucial in debates over acceptable behaviour and the definition of the term 'mercenary'? What was the standard by which actions were deemed to be mercenary or not mercenary? Second, it is worthwhile to identify strategies and mechanisms used in extending the power of a norm. How did state action and interaction ensure that the norm against mercenary use held fast? Which states and which actors were advocating the norm, and why? Which states did not support the norm, and why not? Third, what reasons do states give for supporting a norm, and what reasons are given for violating it? Finally, how are states actually behaving? Are they using mercenaries? If so, it is necessary to examine in what circumstances mercenaries are being used and how their use is justified (or whether it is justified at all).

Answering these questions provides a clear picture of how and why a norm evolves over time. The analysis of a norm's evolution requires a careful examination of history, analysing state policy documents and discussions in international organizations. A review of primary sources such as texts of international instruments, diplomatic archives, diaries of delegates and policymakers, and interviews should reveal not only the existence of a norm,[121] but also how it has evolved.

---

[120] Price (1995: 88).   [121] Thomas (2001: 44).

Sources and Evidence

To grasp the impact of norms on state behaviour, documents from the United Nations General Assembly, Security Council, and High Commission for Human Rights, and the Organization for African Unity (now the African Union)were examined alongside national archives. These institutions have been and continue to be the main fora for the debate on mercenaries. Sources from these institutions, however, can occasionally be biased, because institutions themselves have been some of the chief advocates for formal control of mercenaries. As a result, national submissions to debates in the Fifth and Sixth committees of the General Assembly and to the various UN committees dealing more specifically with mercenaries have been carefully examined to ascertain the degree of state support for UN initiatives. Of course, just as any other kind of national statement, these documents can betray a bias, or be aimed to please domestic or international constituencies.

Mercenary use in the twentieth and twenty-first centuries has been predominantly by 'weak' states, and as Jackson points out, weak states are especially reliant on international institutions.[122] These states are also less likely to have accessible national archives. Examining institutions will reveal both tacit and formal norms; tacit norms will be apparent through recurring patterns of behaviour and the sanctions for violations, while formal norms will be visible in treaties.[123]

Interviews with people involved in policy on mercenaries, both at the national and international level, provide a second source of information. Interviews with policymakers at the national level reveal the reasons behind their policy on mercenaries, while interviews with those affiliated with the UN and other international organizations demonstrate how these organizations work to promote or support state policy on mercenaries.

Relying on interviews and documentary sources is not without methodological challenges. Interviews can reflect the bias of the interviewee. Moreover, as decision-makers 'justify their policies in moral terms all the time, how do we know when they are being truthful and how can the analyst trust such evidence'?[124] An interviewee's recollections might vary from day to day. The documentary record may be incomplete: some documents may not have survived or different reports might be contradictory.[125] Documents might also be biased, by the writer's ideas or because they were written for a specific audience.

In order to tackle these challenges, Goldstein and Keohane suggest that 'the analyst needs to consider how inferences about what happened would

---

[122] Jackson (1993: 138).
[123] Dessler (1989: 457–8). For more on tacit rules, see Kratochwil (1989: 82–3).
[124] Price (1997b: 65).   [125] Goldstein and Keohane (1993: 28).

have been affected had the available documents been somewhat different, had interviews been conducted in a different context, or had policies been adopted under other circumstances. Under these conditions, how different would the reported beliefs or policies have been?'[126] Unreliability need not present an obstacle; sensible judgements and interpretations and engaging alternate explanations should reveal the accuracy of the argument.[127] Dealing with the methodological challenges posed by unreliable data can be compensated for by the sorts of methodological tools already outlined, like attention to a counterfactual. A simple solution is to look for confirmation of information in more than one document or by more than one interviewee.[128]

Another methodological difficulty comes from the availability of pre-nineteenth century sources on mercenaries. The accounts of contemporary observers, like the medieval chroniclers, are a rich source of details about how mercenaries were viewed by their medieval contemporaries. There is a deep vein of information to be tapped in the history of political thought, as many different theorists, religious thinkers, and philosophers have considered the problems posed by mercenaries. One of the difficulties with relying on the views of political theorists is that they have sometimes been heavily biased against mercenaries. Machiavelli, for example, undoubtedly exaggerated some of the more nefarious mercenary deeds to assist in making a more compelling argument against them, and for his conception of a republic defended by its citizens.[129]

Because this book traces the history of a concept, however, some of these problems of bias are less awkward then they might be. A history of the norm against mercenary use does not seek to explain the realities of mercenary action on the ground in the sixteenth century. Rather, it seeks to explain how certain views about mercenaries were adopted, and spread. If political theorists can be understood to be 'norm entrepreneurs' then it makes sense that they would have a bias, and makes that bias essentially irrelevant. I am seeking to explain the history of moral dislike of mercenaries, and it is perfectly valid to examine how those who advocated the norm against mercenary use made their cases.

A final source of pre-nineteenth century evidence comes from governmental records and records of debate. The difficulty with this source is that many of these debates have been lost (as in the case of some Prussian records) or are unavailable in English. As a result, I have endeavoured to examine thoroughly the secondary literature and the detailed work of historians to ascertain how mercenaries were perceived.

---

[126] Ibid.   [127] Price (1997b: 65).   [128] Malone (1998: 74).
[129] See Chapter 3.

1.5. THE CHALLENGES OF DEALING WITH NORMS

While empirical evidence and specific methods can be used to trace norms, norms do cause several methodological difficulties. First, the influence of norms cannot always be easily seen. Second, the tight relationship between norms and interests might make it difficult to isolate the influence of the norm. Third, I examine the norm against mercenaries over a very long period, leading to potential problems of comparing unlike units. Finally, if norms are hard to see and it is hard to isolate their influence, it follows that empirically measuring norms might be a difficult project; however, empirical analysis of norms can still provide plausible explanations.

How can norms 'cause' behaviour? It is difficult to argue, in a positivist sense, that norms 'cause' behaviour. Norms are not causes of action 'in the sense that a bullet through the heart causes death or an uncontrolled surge in the money supply causes inflation'.[130] A bullet through the heart always causes death, while a norm may not always cause the same type of behaviour. The idea that x always causes y, in the tradition of positivist social science, is simply not true of norms.[131] To make matters worse, causality is hard to determine[132] because norms are difficult to measure, and often difficult to see. A powerful norm can seem completely natural, and its influence on people is so profound that they neither notice it nor do they use it to explain or justify their actions.[133] As a result, the influence of norms on states might be extremely subtle, and the failure of norms to influence behaviour is much more easily seen than successful influence.[134]

Norms cause behaviour in an indirect fashion, creating the conditions for action[135] or by helping a state adjudicate between competing policy choices. If we abandon thinking that there can only be causes in the positivist sense, and understand that x does not always lead to y, we are better equipped to understand how norms can indeed cause behaviour. The nature of the connection between x and y need not be mechanical; it can instead provide a bridge that 'allows us to get from "here" to "there". This is what we do when we provide an account in terms of purposes or goals, or when we cite the relevant rule that provides the missing element, showing us the reasons which motivated us to act a certain way.'[136]

To take the example of the bullet, a mechanical explanation of cause would be that the bullet was fired from the gun and entered the heart causing it to stop. But this does not explain cause in the sense that it does not tell us

---

[130] Kratochwil and Ruggie (1986: 768). [131] Kratochwil (2001: 62).
[132] Yee (1996: 70). [133] Price (1997b: 64). [134] Thomas (2001: 44).
[135] Finnemore (1996a: 158). [136] Kratochwil (2001: 66).

anything about *why* the bullet was fired in the first place. If we understand cause as a process, or a bridge from one point to another, then we can begin to ask questions about what caused the bullet to be fired.

Kratochwil argues that to understand cause in this fashion 'we reconstruct a situation, view it from the perspective of the actor, and impute purposes and values based on evidence provided by the actor himself (although not necessarily limited to his own testimony). This, in turn, provides us with an intelligible reason for acting'.[137] Examining the cause of an action requires putting it into context, which is logical, considering that norms cause behaviour by shaping the context of an actor's decisions; by defining his identity; or shaping the interests which affect policy choices.[138] We can understand whether an explanation of the cause of an actor's behaviour makes sense by examining the context of the decision and deciding if our explanation is plausible.[139] While the evidence for the influence of norms may be indirect and come in the form of justifications states give for their decisions, it is similarly indirect for most motivations behind political action.[140]

Norms and Interests Are Intertwined

Norms and interests clearly shape each other. As such, it is very difficult to assess whether a norm, or an interest, or both, is influencing state policy.[141] Goertz and Diehl argue that to study norms requires controlling for power and interests, to see the true impact of norms on state behaviour.[142] But if norms influence what states understand their interests to be, and interests influence the degree to which states might follow a norm, it might simply be impossible to analyse norms and interests separately.

That said, it is not impossible to see how a norm influences states nor is it useless to attempt to capture that influence. Thomas argues that we should discern as much as possible about a state's material interests in particular circumstances, create a null hypothesis, and then analyse the situation.[143] In examining the nineteenth century decision to adopt a citizen army in France, we might assess the material pressures which suggested citizens would make better soldiers, such as changes in military tactics and population growth. We can then set a null hypothesis: France adopted a citizen army because of a norm against mercenary use which was supported by a developing norm arguing that citizens owed a military duty to the state. As we see in Chapter 5,

[137] Ibid. [138] Jepperson, Wendt, and Katzenstein (1996: 66).
[139] Price (1997b: 64). [140] Finnemore and Sikkink (1998: 892).
[141] Tannenwald (1999: 439). [142] Goertz and Diehl (1992: 661).
[143] Thomas (2001: 44).

analysis of this situation suggests that material interests alone cannot tell the whole story. Tracing specific decision-making processes[144] can provide further evidence to back up the conclusions of the null hypothesis.

If material interests were the most influential factor in state decisions regarding the use of force, we would expect that in situations where it is emphatically more efficient for a state to adopt one course of action over another, the state would adopt that course. In some cases, it has undoubtedly been more efficient for states to hire private forces rather than use national armies, and yet, they have either decided to abandon the use of private force, and use normative language in their explanations, or they have not hired private force at all.

In reference to chemical weapons, Price argues that it was in many cases *more* rational to use chemical weapons than any other type of weapon in terms of cheapness, efficiency, and general appropriateness for the job. Many soldiers after the First World War, who had fought with or against gas, argued that it was actually a humane weapon and therefore ought to be used.[145] During cave warfare in the Pacific in the Second World War, military scholars argued that chemical weapons were the most efficient course of action.[146] As noted above, a structural realist would argue that states choose a course of action on the basis of whether or not it is beneficial in material or strategic terms; if it is beneficial, then the action is rational.

If an action is otherwise rational, why would a state not take it? In the case of mercenaries, as previously mentioned, there are clearly cases where it would be perfectly rational for a state to use mercenaries; nonetheless, it has been uncommon for states to do so. Finer goes so far as to suggest that the 'high moral line' against mercenaries is founded 'on confusion and error'.[147] The norm against mercenary use rests on a high moral line which enhances prohibitions against mercenary use but ignores the situations in which their use might represent the pragmatic course.

The decision to utilize private force, however, comes with costs as well as benefits. It is difficult to understand why states do not follow a course of action that makes material and strategic sense without understanding that there are significant normative costs associated with the use of private force. The option to use private force can only be understood to be rational in material or strategic terms; in terms of domestic public opinion or state identity, as Chapter 7 argues, the use of private force is extremely costly, and not rational. The difficulty is that the normative reaction against mercenaries is not logical. It does not make sense to assume that many of the negative qualities associated

---

[144] Ibid.   [145] Price (1997a: 80).   [146] Price and Tannenwald (1996: 117).
[147] Finer (1976: 129).

with mercenaries are particular to private fighters, or that all mercenaries are inherently immoral. If the normative objections to mercenary use could be overcome, then the use of private force on a wider scale would be possible.

An approach which takes norms seriously can explain variation among states with similar interests and similarities of behaviour among those with different interests. A structural realist conception would suggest that states with a similar place in the distribution of power would have similar reactions, and that powerful and weak states should have different reactions. If states with different material attributes or degrees of power share the same position against mercenary use, this suggests that the proscriptive norm against mercenaries may be influencing states.[148] States with a strong material interest in banning mercenaries advocate a strengthened legal regime banning private force, but so too do states with no material interest in doing so.[149] Discrepancies like these are impossible to address (and difficult to see) without attention to normative factors.

We would likewise expect that states with the *most* 'interest' in a particular situation would be most involved in dealing with that situation. In other words, we might anticipate that states which have a particular problem with mercenaries are the most vocal in advocating the proscriptive norm. If we see that states without a particular interest in the issue are still interested in and advocate the norm, it would suggest that the norm is having an influence.

Finally, if a state's material interests change over time, and its position on a particular issue stays the same, it might suggest normative influence. Some states over the years might have had a variety of material interests, depending on their power or wealth or other factors, and yet we see that despite changing interests, state policy on mercenaries has remained the same: states generally no longer use private force.

Historical Difficulties

It is important to emphasize that this book does not attempt to draw precise comparisons from either end of its very long historical reach. It is of course entirely possible that mercenaries in the twelfth century are different from mercenaries in the twenty-first century, and it is absolutely true that the state in the twelfth century has an entirely different set of capacities from the state in the twenty-first, if the former could be considered a state at all. One difficulty is that the 'literal meanings of key terms sometimes changes over time, so that a given [historical] writer may say something with quite a different sense and

[148] Finnemore (1996a: 158). [149] See Chapter 6.

reference from one which may occur to the reader',[150] or similarly, a term may have had a different nuance of meaning at one stage in history than it does now. That said, the goal of this project is not to try and draw out explicit points of comparison between mercenaries and states of long ago and their counterparts of today; it is to see how a norm against mercenaries held by states long ago has *evolved into* the norm we see today. The response of states to mercenaries today is the newest layer in a sedimentary accretion of responses, building on the attitudes and feelings of the past. Even if the actors responding to mercenaries have changed, in that today's modern state is a far cry from the fiefdom of a regional lord in thirteenth century France, the response of the latter has set the groundwork which shapes the response of the former. And even if modern states and regional lords are wildly different, their responses may be the same, although their capacity to implement those responses differs. Tracing responses throughout history to see how they build upon each other reduces the problems of a study with a long historical reach.

Norms Can Be Difficult to Measure Empirically

A careful historical narrative that traces the genealogy of the norm against mercenaries is practically useful and can provide empirical evidence. While a narrative approach seeking to trace the importance and composition of ideas throughout history falls into a generally constructivist category, properly implemented, such an approach can provide practical evidence for the influence of ideas through historical examination. Finnemore argues that members of the English School use a historical method with 'carefully crafted narratives that interpret events' that 'allows them to engage and challenge those who would dismiss arguments about culture based on more interpretive research methods'.[151] Claims about the causal power of norms—in this case, the influence of the anti-mercenarism norm—can be evaluated through careful historical and empirical research.[152] Tannenwald points out that 'it is sometimes argued that norms are difficult to study. This may be so, but in reality they are no more difficult to study than any other ideational phenomenon...nor...is studying normative structure different in principle from studying any other kind of social structure: it is studied through its effects and meaning (structure itself is unobservable)'.[153] A narrative approach is an example of 'methodological conventionalism', seeking useful

[150] Skinner (1988: 50–1). [151] Finnemore (1996b: 334).
[152] Finnemore and Sikkink (1998: 890). [153] Tannenwald (forthcoming).

empirical answers to thought-provoking questions rather than proposing a separate interpretive methodology.[154] As we see, this type of tracing history can be enormously revealing.

A narrative approach provides *plausible* answers. According to the historical record, is it plausible that ideas and norms were influential factors in state policy on mercenaries? The question of how a norm against mercenary use and the changing definition of sovereignty have influenced state policy can, like other normative questions, have empirical answers.[155] A careful examination of the historical record will reveal to what extent a normative approach provides a plausible explanation to the four empirical puzzles outlined in the book, and if the normative explanation is more plausible than other explanations.

A narrative approach focusing on the influence of norms reveals thought-provoking questions which other approaches ignore. As we have seen, in cases of the use of force, the fact that the norm seems to influence behaviour *at all* is interesting. In cases where we would expect states to be *most* influenced by a utilitarian power calculations, such as military decision-making, demonstrating the influence of a norm challenges the idea that in realpolitik calculations states will always rely first on their interest, defined as power. If a norm causes restraint, this represents a serious challenge to realism.[156]

Even though norms may be only one of the influences at work upon states, it is still useful and interesting to study their effects, in part because approaches based on national interest have neglected normative factors in the past.[157] Tannenwald notes that an argument based on norms is powerful because it does not exclude material interests, 'whereas the materialist explanation does exclude norms. Normative explanations do not claim that material factors do not matter; rather, they hold that material factors are important but are often indeterminate and are socially interpreted'.[158] Rationalist explanations 'too often fail to take into account how moral considerations shape...the national interest'.[159] Having accepted that norms do matter, the most important question then becomes *how* they matter,[160] without attempting to argue that interests play no role or that interests are trumped by norms.

Attention to norms may reveal interesting questions for study that an approach excluding norms misses. On many issues, 'norms researchers have made inroads precisely because they have been able to provide explanations substantiated by evidence for puzzles in international politics that other approaches have been unable to explain satisfactorily'.[161] A structural realist

[154] Jepperson, Wendt, and Katzenstein (1996). [155] Thomas (2001: 44).
[156] Ibid. 9. [157] Finnemore and Sikkink (1998: 890).
[158] Tannenwald (forthcoming). [159] Price (1997*b*: 48).
[160] Goldstein and Keohane (1993: 6). [161] Finnemore and Sikkink (1998: 890).

would find nothing puzzling in the fact that international law on mercenaries, formally created from the late 1960s to the late 1980s, is deeply flawed. If the law is flawed, it merely indicates that too few states or too few powerful states were really interested in creating a legal regime to deal with private force. Attention to normative factors, however, reveals that the law is flawed because states agreed about the norm against mercenary use and so insisted on a definition of the term 'mercenary' that was legally unworkable. The norm was so strong that states felt unable to tinker with it in order to ensure more effective law.

1.6. CONCLUSION

Norms clearly influence state behaviour, despite their association with interests and despite the empirical difficulties of describing that influence. The narrative method is a useful tool to trace the influence that norms have upon states.

The fact that state policy on mercenaries has remained condemnatory despite changes in the nature of mercenary action poses a puzzle. Why do states continue to argue that mercenaries are bad for states when in fact they might be good for states? The answer lies in the very strong proscriptive norm against mercenary use. In Chapter 2, the origins of the proscriptive norm will be examined, and a definition of the word 'mercenary' proposed.

2

The Definition of a Mercenary and the Definition of the Proscriptive Norm

There is a close relationship between the definition of the term 'mercenary' and the nature of the proscriptive norm against mercenary use. Conventional definitions of the term seek to break it down into its component parts, and do not focus on some critical questions. What makes a mercenary different from a soldier? And what does it mean to place a fighter in the category 'mercenary' rather than the category 'soldier'? Categorizing a fighter as a mercenary has important consequences, as mercenaries are considered at least to be irregular fighters, if not morally reprehensible. The definition of a mercenary relies on differentiating mercenaries from soldiers, and highlighting the criteria used in the differentiation. The differences between soldiers and other fighters and mercenaries then form the groundwork for the norm against their use. It is because mercenaries are different from regular fighters that states have sought to control or limit their use, and these differences are the root source of the proscriptive norm against mercenary use.

The chapter will begin explaining the importance of clear definitions and the difficulty of establishing them in a historical study. It continues by setting out the conventional manner of defining the term 'mercenary' and identifying problems with the criteria it uses. The second section argues that two basic factors make mercenaries different from other fighters: mercenaries lie outside legitimate control and are not motivated to fight by an appropriate cause. These two elements combine to provide a different, and more historically accurate, definition of the term 'mercenary'. The third section compares the degree to which fighters can be considered mercenary by creating a spectrum of force that categorizes different types of fighters on the basis of attachment to cause and degree of legitimate control. The spectrum of force provides a useful tool for understanding which type of force is properly considered to be 'mercenary'. The fourth section explains how the definition of the term 'mercenary' indicates the component parts of the proscriptive norm against mercenary use.

2.1. DEFINITIONS AND REVELATIONS: WHAT MAKES MERCENARIES DIFFERENT?

A basic definition of mercenaries is important for two reasons. First, it clarifies the rules of engagement by revealing which types of force are considered mercenary and which are not. Second, as already discussed, it reveals the component parts of the proscriptive norm against mercenaries. The argument proceeds in three stages. First, I discuss the pitfalls of defining terms in a historical project and try to address them. Second, I explain the conventional definitions of the term 'mercenary', which rely on the financial motivation and the foreign character of the mercenary. Third, I argue that the notions of appropriate cause and the degree of authority and control are essential to defining what makes a mercenary 'mercenary' and differentiating mercenaries from other types of fighter. To define a mercenary, it is helpful to consider how mercenaries fit on a continuum of force from purely mercenary to purely non-mercenary. Finally, the attributes that separate mercenaries from other fighters fall into two basic categories which form the proscriptive norm: control and motivation by an appropriate cause.

The Pitfalls of Definitions

Providing definitions at the beginning of a narrative examination of history is a risky business. The composition of a norm prohibiting the use of mercenaries today may be different from what it once was, as proscriptive norms can and do evolve according to political contexts. Thus, it is not enough merely to *define* a norm, because its definition will necessarily shift and evolve as time goes on. As Price points out, the 'present form of a moral interpretation' cannot 'account for its origins'.[1] At each phase of the development of the proscriptive norm against mercenary use, its exact content may differ.

What one generation considers to be 'mercenary' the next may not. Bartelson argues that defining sovereignty at the beginning of a study on the topic limits the discussion to what sovereignty is now as opposed to what it originally meant.[2] A good example of this is provided by the recent conflict in Iraq, where Iraqi officials referred to American troops as mercenaries and American officials referred to Islamic volunteers fighting alongside Iraqis as mercenaries. According to most definitions of the term, neither of these groups would qualify as mercenaries. The word mercenary has evolved into a pejorative term

[1] Price (1995: 85).   [2] Bartelson (1995: 13).

Definition of a Mercenary

used to denote a disliked soldier. The proscription against mercenary use is so strong that the word mercenary itself has become a powerful political tool, which can be used to brand another group's soldiers and attempt to make them appear illegitimate.

Hampson's definition of mercenaries also illustrates the difficulties of operating with a modern definition in a historical study. Hampson asserts that mercenaries are best defined in relation to three aspects: that they are foreign; that they are motivated by financial gain; and that they use force *not* as members of the armed forces of the state which hires them.[3] The addition of the third criterion means that, according to Hampson's definition, some mercenaries before the nineteenth century were not mercenaries at all, because states routinely hired units from abroad and integrated them with their own forces.[4]

To set out a definition of the proscriptive norm against mercenary use at this stage runs into the same problem. We can isolate the attributes of the proscriptive norm that tend to remain the same over time, but to set out a concrete and universal definition from the beginning renders the project of tracing the proscriptive norm impossible. To do so would be to start with what ought to come at the end: a complete understanding of the component parts of the proscriptive norm can only occur through understanding its shifts. However, it is possible to reveal basic aspects of the proscriptive norm and pay attention to how these aspects evolve, disappearing and reappearing over time.

The solution to this problem is to define both mercenaries and the proscriptive norm broadly at the beginning without making any attempt to nail down a precise definition. However, defining mercenaries even loosely is tricky simply because it is much harder than it at first seems to figure out exactly what separates them from regular soldiers or other fighters.

To provide a loose definition of what makes a fighter a mercenary is a twofold process. First, what are the conventional definitions provided and what are some of the problems with the attributes they identify as making mercenaries different from other fighters? Second, there are difficulties with relying on financial motivation and foreign status as the defining characteristics of a mercenary. Is there a sensible way to categorize different groups of fighters without running into the same difficulties? Answering the second question will provide a loose definition of mercenaries which is broadly true across time and place. The discussion of definitions in turn reveals the core

---

[3] Hampson (1991: 5–6). As we see in the next sections, there are difficulties with all three of these criteria.

[4] See Chapters 3 and 5. Hampson's definition, as she recognizes, also causes problems for mercenaries in their twentieth-century incarnations (ibid. 31).

aspects of the proscriptive norm by pointing out what makes mercenaries different from regular soldiers.

Conventional Definitions

Most critics argue that the definition of a mercenary has two components. First, mercenaries are foreign, having no national association with any of the parties to the conflict in which they fight. Second, a mercenary's dominant motive is financial gain.[5] This section examines the foreign and financial components of the definition in turn, and discusses the problems that each poses.

Foreign Component

One problem with using foreign status to define a mercenary is that it is historically inaccurate. The foreign nature of mercenaries is only remarkable as a defining feature in a world where it is extremely unusual for a soldier to be foreign. Historically, foreign soldiers were common.[6] Further, the notion of nationality narrows the definition of mercenaries to a time period in which the idea of nationhood makes sense, and thereby excludes many fighters considered by their contemporaries to be mercenaries, especially before the nineteenth century.

It might be more correct to define mercenaries as being external to a conflict[7] rather than merely foreign. This is an improvement, but it still falls into another trap created by relying on foreign status in defining a mercenary. Clearly, there are many foreign or external fighters who are *not* mercenary. Volunteers fighting in the Spanish Civil War,[8] *mujahideen* fighters in Afghanistan, UN peacekeepers, and soldiers on official secondment to another state,[9] like British soldiers in Oman,[10] are all types of foreign fighter not normally considered to be mercenary. Externality on its own is not sufficient to define a mercenary, and must be taken in tandem with the idea of a financial motivation to make sense. However, the financial motivation component is also deeply problematic, and can hardly act as a firm anchor for the more flimsy category of externality.

---

[5] Beshir (1972: 4), Burmester (1978: 37), Yusuf (1979: 114), Thomson (1994: 26), Nossal (1998: 18), Shearer (1998b: 69), Zarate (1998: 18), Adams (1999: 1), Sandoz (1999: 208), Singer (2003a: 41).
[6] Hale (1985: 147), and Thomson (1994: 10). [7] Musah and Fayemi (2000b: 16).
[8] Yusuf (1979: 15) and Thomson (1994: 27). [9] Zarate (1998: 18).
[10] Thomson (1994: 27).

Financial Motivation

Financial motives alone are also insufficient to define a mercenary. Modern-day soldiers might very well be motivated by financial gain as well as (or perhaps even instead of) patriotism. The military promotes itself as a 'career option'[11] with attractive pay and benefits. As Tim Spicer, former head of the PMC Sandline, puts it: 'There is nothing wrong with soldiering for pay. During my life as a professional soldier I expected to be paid'.[12] The idea that soldiers might be fighting for patriotism rather than money only makes sense in a particular time and place. Many medieval fighters fought for pay,[13] and not all of them were considered mercenaries. Some modern national armies might be *more* motivated by financial gain than mercenaries.[14] In the recent Sierra Leonean civil war, the rebels and the national soldiers were both fighting (sometimes together) for financial gain in the form of diamonds and looting.[15] Developing countries often provide peacekeepers to the UN specifically to generate revenues for the state, and creating jobs for individuals.

Like soldiers, mercenaries can also have mixed motivations. Some mercenaries might begin by fighting for money, but later adopt the cause of those for whom they fight. Some might have an ideological motive alongside their financial one.[16] Mercenaries might also be loyal to those with whom they fight, even though they are not motivated in the same way. It is difficult to distinguish between mercenaries and other fighters solely on the basis of financial motivation.

Two points need to be made about conventional definitions before we turn to another way to define a mercenary. First, international law on mercenaries demonstrates, among other tensions, the practical problems associated with using financial motive as a key definitional aspect. The internationally accepted legal definition proffered by Additional Protocol I of the Geneva Conventions is so full of holes that 'any mercenary who cannot exclude himself from this definition deserves to be shot—and his lawyer with him!'[17]

Second, it is obvious that foreign status or externality and financial motivation are meant to be taken together rather than separately. However, two flawed halves do not make a coherent whole. If neither one of these components is sufficient on its own, surely it is worthwhile to seek a definition of mercenarism which escapes some of these problems.

---

[11] Lynch and Walsh (2000: 135). [12] Spicer (1999*a*: 29).
[13] Mallett (1974: 13), Corvisier (1979: 41), Hale (1985: 146), and France (1999: 71).
[14] Mills and Stremlau (1999*b*: 11). [15] Kandeh (1998: 355).
[16] Mockler (1969: 18), and Lynch and Walsh (2000: 137).
[17] Quoted in Best (1980: 375 n. 83). These legal tensions are addressed at length in Chapter 6.

2.2. A DIFFERENT DEFINITION

Attachment to, and Motivation as a Result of, a Cause

Mercenaries should be defined by the extent to which they are motivated to fight for a cause. The idea of 'cause' encapsulates both the idea that mercenaries are external to a conflict and that they fight for financial gain, and furthermore recognizes that foreigners can fight without being considered mercenaries as long as they have a cause for their actions.

'Cause' in this sense need not, but sometimes can, relate to the idea of 'just cause' in warfare.[18] A cause might be the ideological or political goals of a group which fights, be it a state, the Church, or a national liberation movement. The concept of attachment to a cause cuts to the heart of what we find morally problematic about mercenaries.

Mercenaries are morally problematic because they cannot provide a plausible justification for killing; they cannot point to a cause in the service of which they fight, aside from financial gain. The rules of the *jus ad bellum,* or the right to go to war, define who can kill in warfare and separate out justifiable killing from unjustified homicide. Throughout history, the moral justification for killing comes from the presence of a plausible cause. The notion of cause thus captures a far wider historical range of mercenary action than does foreign status and financial motivation.

The idea of active combat is thus implicit in the cause element of the anti-mercenary norm. Mercenaries must engage in combat and run the risk of killing in order to be criticized for doing so without an appropriate cause.

In the medieval period, the plausible cause was 'just cause', which was determined by the Church. Only certain members of society had a just cause for war, and so could morally justify causing the deaths of others. The idea that a just cause led to a just war was part of the medieval social fabric.[19] In nineteenth-century Europe, as the Church-oriented concept of just war faded away, it was replaced by a web of laws that reinforced the idea that only the sovereign state could justly engage in war.[20] Related to this idea was the growing conception that war ought to be fought for nationalist purposes and by patriotically motivated citizens.[21] Foreigners fighting for a state other than their own no longer had cause to participate in war. During the twentieth century, this rubric was extended to include the idea that those fighting for self-determination as part of a recognized national liberation movement had the right to use force.[22] Again, mercenaries, because they were external to these causes, had no such right.

---

[18] See Keen (1966) and Clark (1988).   [19] Clark (1988: 39).   [20] Ibid. 41.
[21] See Chapter 5.   [22] See Chapter 6.

Mercenaries struggle to provide a plausible cause for why they kill. Of course, fighters of all different types, including mercenaries, will vary in the degree to which they can be seen to support a cause. The idea that mercenaries are not motivated by a cause and soldiers are is a generalization. Of course, soldiers can be motivated by fear or financial gain or obedience rather than a cause, and mercenaries might come to believe in the cause for which they fight, or fight for a cause as well as for money. But in practice, when states have compared the two types of fighters, they work with these generalizations. As the empirical chapters of the book demonstrate, state practice clearly indicates that the notion of cause is a crucial aspect of the definition of a mercenary.

The argument that soldiers are morally superior to mercenaries because they fight for a cause is not without problems. Pacifists may argue that it is never moral to fight, and the presence or absence of a cause is irrelevant. Others may assert that arguing that there ought to be some kind of moral distinction between fighters according to whether or not they are motivated to fight by a cause is problematic, particularly in terms of behaviour. There is no reason to assume a financially motivated soldier will be more badly behaved than a patriotically motivated one, and in fact the reverse may be true.[23] Lynch and Walsh point out that 'it remains simply unargued that organized violence centred on strong group identification is in itself morally better'.[24]

Identification with a cause, however, can provide a sort of moral armour for a fighter. Spicer argues that soldiering 'is about fighting, and if need be, killing. That fact can be cloaked in a wide range of fancy garments...but when you get right down to it, soldiering is about hitting the enemy hard, before they can kill you'.[25] War is about killing, and mercenaries have an inferior explanation for *why* they kill than just about any other type of fighter. Part of what makes mercenaries different from regular soldiers is that they make the decision to fight *alone*. They have complete independence in choosing to go to war, and have no profound reason to do so, because they do not fight for a cause.

Regular soldiers are often compelled to fight, and have no interest in fighting on their own. Just war theorists are divided about whether or not a soldier individually needs to worry about the justness of the cause for which they fight,[26] but the division results from the assumption that the soldier is fighting for a cause larger than himself and that therefore *someone else* is making the decisions about whether or not the cause is worth fighting for and whether or not the soldier is required to kill.[27]

---

[23] Finer (1976: 129) and Sandoz (1999: 210).   [24] Lynch and Walsh (2000: 134).
[25] Spicer (1999a: 17).   [26] See Lynch and Walsh (2000: 137–9).
[27] The manner in which the fighting and killing occurs is still a matter of individual responsibility and falls under international humanitarian law or the *jus in bello*.

Mercenaries are problematic because they make the decision to fight independently, and also because they cannot claim a direct association with the cause for which they fight. Because a mercenary might be foreign, or external to a conflict, or does not possess the ideological impulses that drive some volunteers to fight abroad, his financial motives are unmitigated by any sense of higher cause. And, as we have seen, unlike a conscripted soldier he has taken the decision to fight independently.

However, a fighter's decision to go to war need not be problematic simply because it is taken independently. Association with a cause can ameliorate a situation where a fighter has independently decided (rather than been compelled) to fight or where a fighter is an outsider, not from the group for which he fights and so not directly associated with their cause. Soldiers who are not conscripted, but volunteer, and individuals who fight for a foreign group out of shared beliefs are explicitly fighting for a cause; they join up because they believe profoundly in the cause of the army which they join. National soldiers who volunteer are directly involved in (and affected by) the cause for which they sign up to fight. International volunteers, like those in the Spanish Civil War or the war in Afghanistan in the 1980s, might also believe that they are directly involved in the cause of the army they join, because the failure of that cause might lead to an international situation that will affect them, or even worse, the victory of a cause which is perceived as wrong or incorrect. While national volunteers can overcome the difficulty of independence of their decision to fight by pointing to a cause with which they are directly associated, and international volunteers can overcome both the independence problem and the problem of their externality by closely associating with a cause, mercenaries cannot overcome the fact that they lie outside and are not affected by the cause for which they fight. A financial motive is insufficient to overcome the fact that mercenaries are outsiders, who have no association with the cause for which they fight.

Mercenaries are military entrepreneurs, who can freely choose to go (or not to go) to war. Even when the mercenary is incorporated as part of a unit there is surely a choice about joining that unit. Once on the battlefield, of course, mercenaries may find it hard to leave as they could be disciplined by their commanders. They face no similar pressure about going to the battlefield in the first place. The mercenary is not conscripted, nor recruited by evoking a group cause. Thus, the responsibility for killing by mercenaries can only be purely individual. The mercenary's killings cannot be excused because they are in fact following *someone else's* intentions, or pursuing a cause in which they have a stake, whether right or wrong. Lynch and Walsh argue that a group identification might excuse a fighter his participation in violence, but that an excuse is not a justification, as the former merely excuses something that we still consider wrong.[28] Mercenaries lack even the ability to *excuse* themselves from violence because they choose to do it themselves, and not on the basis of any belief in the cause of their employers. The weight of the decision to kill lies entirely on the mercenary's shoulders. Attachment to a cause provides the possibility of a selfless motive, even if in practice this is not true.

Legitimate Control

The second aspect that differentiates mercenaries from other fighters is the degree to which they are under legitimate control, in other words under the control of the entity which is understood to have the legitimate right to wage war. In modern times this has been the sovereign state, while previously it might have been a lord, king, city state, or even the papacy. Legitimate control is broad, in that it includes the idea that these soldiers are now working for the state and not for themselves, and specific, in that these soldiers are no longer under an independent command structure. The idea of control encapsulates the idea that the true mercenary is an independent, private contractor selling his services or the services of a company he commands. As Burmester argues, it is the 'essentially private, non-governmental nature [of mercenary intervention] which seems to be the basic problem which is raised by the use of mercenaries'.[29]

The control aspect of the definition is useful for two reasons. First, it fills in blanks left by the conventional definition and enhances the notion of cause. Second, it is historically accurate. Mercenaries, when placed under legitimate control, are regarded as less threatening and more 'normal' actors in the international system. They no longer represent private interests, even though they may still find that they are accused of not having an association with a cause.

Generally, foreign soldiers in permanent positions in other states' armies are not considered to be mercenary, and nor are fighters sent with the approval of their home state. The degree of legitimate control can explain why mercenaries are not soldiers, and conventional definitions relying on foreign status cannot. Soldiers or units in permanent positions in foreign armies are under two types of control. First, they remain broadly under the control of their home state, in that if they misbehave, they can be sanctioned by their home states. Canadian troops who committed human rights abuses while fighting under the UN flag in Somalia were held to account in Canada. Second, soldiers or units permanently attached to foreign armies are under the immediate control

[28] Lynch and Walsh (2000: 139).   [29] Burmester (1978: 38).

of the hiring state, in terms of behaviour and command. Thus, the French Foreign Legion and the Gurkhas are not mercenaries, and neither are troops on secondment to other states.

Troops sent as part of an alliance agreement or to the UN as peacekeepers, despite being foreign, are not considered mercenary because they remain under legitimate control. This control might remain that of the home state, as is the case in UN missions, or under an allied commander of a different state, as was the case in the Second World War. Soldiers of this type may also be strongly motivated by a cause, whether it is that of their home state, or something which the alliance stands for, or UN goals.

Another advantage of defining mercenaries according to the extent to which they are under legitimate control is that the difference between fighters who are considered mercenary, and therefore problematic, and fighters who are considered to be 'normal' actors in the international system, is how much they are under control of the authority of the time. Historically, mercenaries were differentiated from other fighters according to the degree of control they were under; that differentiation is still sensible today, when legitimate control is provided by the sovereign state and some international organizations composed of sovereign states. The 'international community's fear of mercenaries lies in that they are wholly independent from any constraints built into the nation-state system. The element of accountability is the tacit standard that underlies the international antipathy for mercenary activity and truly determines mercenary status'.[30] The more independent the fighter, the weaker the control of states and, potentially, the greater the threat to the stability of the international system. Mercenaries are military entrepreneurs, and in their purest form are independent contractors outside state control.

The degree of legitimate control placed over fighters indicates to what extent they can be understood to be mercenaries. Combined with the idea of cause the notion of legitimate control can provide a useful tool to assess whether or not fighters can be considered to be mercenary. We can define a mercenary as a fighter who engages in combat without a cause, for financial gain, and without being under the control of a state or other legitimate authority. Placing mercenaries in a spectrum with other fighters can allow us to understand what makes a mercenary.

2.3. THE SPECTRUM OF PRIVATE VIOLENCE

Actors who use force in the international system can be grouped largely according to the degree to which they are attached to, and motivated by, a

[30] Zarate (1998: 18).

Figure 2.1. Spectrum of private violence

cause and whether they are under a high or a low degree of legitimate control. Figure 2.1 shows the degree of attachment to a cause on the *x*-axis and degree of legitimate control on the *y*-axis.

The left- and bottom-most point represents any fighter fighting solely for no cause other than individual gain and responsible only to themselves. It includes the *routiers* or *cotereaux* who ravaged French society and prompted the excommunication of mercenaries by the Lateran Council of 1179.[31] The Free Companies of mercenaries formed during the Hundred Years War who worked for themselves pillaging in between formal employment (and sometimes in place of it) would also fit into this category.[32] In the twentieth century, this category would include the 'vagabond' mercenary, who fought for financial gain during African decolonization.[33] The term vagabond mercenary is a useful categorization for individual mercenaries fighting for themselves or in loosely knit and temporary organizations. Vagabond mercenaries are essentially under their own control. While part of that control may be ceded to an employer for a brief period of time, the danger with vagabond mercenaries is that their allegiance is minimal and they might desert or mutiny.

The point second from left represents fighters with a slightly more mixed motivation. These fighters may be formally incorporated into the armed forces but are fighting for financial gain, and are temporarily under the control of the entity which hires them. In the medieval period, this included many fighters, as pay could be a dominant motivation for soldiers as well as mercenaries,[34] and soldiers would often become mercenaries and vice versa.[35] The common use of foreign troops suggests that there were few controls over whether or

---

[31] France (1999: 70). See Chapter 3 for details. [32] Mallett (1974: 27–9).
[33] On the financial motives of these mercenaries see Mockler (1969), Beshir (1972), and Tickler (1987a). The term 'vagabond' is Mockler's.
[34] France (1999: 71). [35] Hale (1985: 147).

not a member of one group could fight for another.³⁶ As a result, medieval soldiers were neither particularly attached to a cause nor tightly controlled. This point also includes the *condottieri*, companies of mercenaries hired by Italian city states in the fourteenth and fifteenth centuries. They were led by a *condottiere*, a sort of chief contractor and military leader, who would sign a contract with a particular city state and work for that state through the terms of the contract. While under contract, the *condottieri* were under the state's control. Their lack of attachment to the cause of their employers meant that they were still regarded with suspicion, as Machiavelli's fears attest.³⁷

PMCs, which appeared on the scene in the 1990s, would likewise fit into this second category. PMCs can be defined as 'corporate bodies specializing in the provision of military skills to governments: training, planning, intelligence, risk assessment, operation support and technical skills'.³⁸ Operation support refers to the fact that PMCs will actually engage in combat.³⁹ PMCs are similar to *condottieri* as they are an organized group that works for a particular state and so are under that state's control for the duration of the contract. Again, because PMCs and their employees are not attached to the cause of their employers they have provoked fears that they are really working for their own interests and that they might undermine the state's interests.⁴⁰ PMCs are only under the control of the state which hires them, as unlike PSCs they do not have a relationship with their home states. Indeed, some states hosting PMCs, like South Africa, worked to close them down. As PMCs are not hired on a permanent basis, the degree of control is low, but still higher than that of vagabond mercenaries, as it is governed by contract with a host state.

The third point represents the outright hiring of units from one state by another. Prior to the mid-nineteenth century, states would hire units from other states in their entirety and armies remained multinational.⁴¹ Swiss soldiers hired by the French king are one good example,⁴² as are Hessians recruited by the English to fight in the American Revolution,⁴³ and in the Crimea in the 1850s.⁴⁴ These troops, while foreign, were in effect under two types of state control: their own state decided whether or not to send them, and the hiring state controlled and directed their movements. The selling state had a vested interest in ensuring the loyalty of the troops they rented out in order to keep their product desirable. These sorts of troops, as we will see, did not pose the same kinds of questions about loyalty as they were assumed to be

---

³⁶ As is argued in Chapter 3, the idea that a fighter might be external or foreign still made sense in medieval Europe despite the fact that the state was very different from today's state.
³⁷ Machiavelli ([1513] 1992: 34). Machiavelli is discussed at length in Chapter 3.
³⁸ Spicer (1999*a*: 15). ³⁹ Spicer (1999*b*: 168, 1999*a*: 41).
⁴⁰ Mills and Stremlau (1999*b*: 14). ⁴¹ Thomson (1994: 10).
⁴² See McCormack (1993). ⁴³ Mockler (1969: 117–26).
⁴⁴ The war ended before the Hessians were sent. See Bayley (1977).

employees of the hiring state. They were criticized heavily, however, because they were not considered to be motivated by the cause of the state which hired them, as their home state did not necessarily care about the cause of the hiring state. It was a pure moneymaking arrangement.[45]

PSCs are represented by the next point in Figure 2.1. They are similar to PMCs in that they are organized companies offering military services, like military advice and training, and guarding of facilities and individuals, but insist that they do not engage in combat. PSCs are under a higher degree of state control than PMCs. In the United States, companies like Military Professional Resources Incorporated (MPRI) and DynCorp work under a significant degree of state control. They undertake tasks authorized by the government and so are almost a branch of the national armed services. PSCs based in the United Kingdom have a more separate relationship but the UK government has vetoed PSC operations of which it does not approve.[46] PSCs do not engage in combat.[47] Moreover, today's PSCs (both UK- and US-based) work alongside national military forces and under their direction. It is important to note that the heightened control under which PSCs operate is *state* control rather than *popular* control, and that PSCs are criticized for being poorly monitored and under-regulated. While these criticisms may be true, and will be addressed in Chapter 7, the fact remains that PSCs are more under the direction of the sovereign state than other variants of private force, and if there are weaknesses in that direction they are the decision and the responsibility of the state rather than problems inherent with PSCs.

The next point indicates fighters who are foreign to a conflict but are entirely under state control, either permanently or almost permanently. The permanence of their contracts means that these fighters essentially adopt their employers' goals as their own, in the same way regular soldiers with mixed motivations are assumed to be fighting for their national army. They are employees of the state regardless of whether or not the state is actually at war. This category includes units on long-term secondment to Middle Eastern states like Oman in the 1970s, the French Foreign Legion, and the Gurkhas. The permanence of these arrangements and the degree of integration with regular services lead to a very high coincidence of motive between the foreign fighters and the state. In fact, after a certain period of service in the French Foreign Legion, legionnaires are offered French citizenship.[48]

The next point, the highest point on the y-axis, represents the highest point of state control; its position on the x-axis indicates a very high degree of

---

[45] See Chapter 5.
[46] See Chapter 7 for details of the UK relationship and a discussion of the problems associated with dileneating what constitutes active combat.
[47] Shearer (1999: 82–3).
[48] Thomson (1994: 91).

motivation by a cause. Soldiers may be motivated by financial gain but also may be motivated by patriotism or the desire to serve their home nation. National soldiers fight only for their own state and on projects approved by that state, like UN peacekeeping missions or NATO operations. National soldiers are prohibited by law from enlisting in the armies of other states, although this law is rarely enforced, as evidenced by the fact that none of the foreign mercenaries active since the 1960s have been charged under the various neutrality acts of their states. Nonetheless, their first duty is to their own state and they are tightly controlled by the state.

The next point shows a high degree of motivation by cause but a lower point of state control. Pure volunteers fighting for a cause fall into this category; it includes the International Brigade which fought in the Spanish Civil War for ideological reasons,[49] volunteer fighters for particular causes like the *mujahideen* in Afghanistan and foreigners fighting for the Taliban and al-Qaida later in Afghanistan. These international volunteers are not under the control of their home state. They can fight for a party to a civil war or for a state, like the international volunteers in the most recent Gulf War. Volunteers are less controlled than state soldiers in the sense that it is easier for them to desert or change their minds about fighting. They are not under the same range of controls as a citizen soldier. Whether a citizen soldier has been conscripted or has volunteered, they remain more tightly subject to their state's rules and regulations surrounding military service.

The final point encompasses freedom fighters and guerrillas, who are not under state control but are profoundly motivated by a cause, which offers at least some sort of alternative idea of organization[50] or political or ideological goal. It also includes terrorists, who are motivated by a cause to a large degree but are outside state control. The distinction between a legitimate freedom fighter and a terrorist is so subjective (and significantly outside the bounds of this enquiry) that for practical purposes they have been grouped together. It is interesting that both sides of the spectrum, representing diminished control, also represent entities which are perceived to be especially threatening. Terrorist organizations and mercenaries are considered to be dangerous, and they can be differentiated on the basis of attachment to a cause. Even though terrorists can claim a strong attachment to a cause, such a motive does not mitigate the fear which stems from the fact they operate outside state control.

Understanding mercenaries in terms of degree of attachment to a cause and the idea of legitimate control adds nuances missing from conventional definitions. Using this type of spectrum clearly separates out different types of private violence, while still recognizing that they are related.[51] First, using

---

[49] Thomson (1990: 30).   [50] Clapham (1999: 36).

[51] This answers Singer's concern that much of the literature on PMCs fails to put the PMC in the context of other forms of private violence. (Singer 2003*a*: 8 n.19).

the spectrum of attachment to cause and degree of control allows us to assess whether or not we can consider PMCs to be mercenaries. The answer, examining the spectrum, is mixed. PMCs engage in actual combat, and are still privately motivated. While they are under a degree of legitimate control, they are not as tightly controlled as other fighters. The spectrum enables us to distinguish clearly between a PSC and a PMC. PSCs are under a much tighter degree of control, usually by their home state.

It is only by understanding the importance of control that we can understand the full range of types of mercenary and some of the ambiguities in their treatment. A different degree of state control explains, for example, why more controlled mercenaries in the form of units hired from other states or units on long-term contract became a more 'normal' and less feared part of sixteenth-, seventeenth-, and eighteenth-century warfare while the lone and uncontrolled mercenaries joined together in loose and temporary bands during the medieval period were more threatening. It also explains why many (but not all) people find the prospect of a PMC[52] far less fearsome than the stereotyped 1960s mercenary of the Congo.

Relying on the ideas of cause and control is also useful because the idea that mercenaries are not motivated by a cause and that they are not controlled by an entity that is considered to have the legitimate control of force has remained constant throughout history. The precise meaning of each term has varied in different periods. Once, fighting for a noble or the Church gave a fighter a just cause; later, fighting for the state or the nation was seen to be the appropriate cause; later still, fighting for national liberation was considered to be the correct cause for war. Similarly, legitimate control might come from a different entity in different periods: from the nobility, the Church, or the Pope; from the sovereign state; or from a recognized national liberation movement. Mercenaries have been feared and judged accordingly when the entity which has the legitimate control over force at the time has the least control over mercenaries. Chapter 3 demonstrates that mercenaries under tighter state control are more ambiguously treated, and that states, kings, lords, and popes sought to control mercenaries from a very early stage. As a result, this definition of a mercenary does not cast back into the past a definition true only for today, but allows its component aspects of cause and control to evolve.

This book concerns itself mainly with those types of fighters to the left of the continuum: those with a low degree of state control and a low degree of attachment to a cause. Lone mercenaries in their various historical incarnations (*routiers*, vagabonds, and the like) and companies of these mercenaries (PMCs and *condottieri*) form the focus of this book. All the other categories represent fighters who are either under tight state control or strongly motivated by a

---

[52] See Chapter 7 for the debate over PMCs.

group cause, or, like national soldiers, both; they are not mercenaries because the definition of what makes a mercenary clearly rests on the combination of a financial, rather than cause oriented, motivation and loose legitimate control by a state or other entity considered to have the legitimate control of force. Treating PSCs, Gurkhas, and the French Foreign Legion as mercenaries, as many commentators do,[53] muddies the waters by including fighters who are clearly *not* mercenary on the basis of their own motivations and the degree of state control to which they are subject. PSCs fight for the goals of their home state; Gurkhas fight for Nepalese goals and for the goals created by a long association between Britain and Nepal; and the French Foreign Legion assumes that a fighter will adopt the cause of the French to such an extent that he can become French after a limited period of service. PSCs are examined in Chapter 7, in order to demonstrate the continued influence of the anti-mercenary norm in a market for force that seems to be rapidly growing.

Underlying the spectrum and the definition of mercenaries based on cause and control is the assumption that for mercenaries to be mercenaries they must actually engage in combat or be hired on the understanding that, should a war occur, they will fight. Similarly, a soldier would not be a soldier if the job description did not include fighting; he would be something else.

2.4. HOW THE DEFINITION INDICATES THE PROSCRIPTIVE NORM

Defining mercenaries according to the extent to which they fight for a cause, which manifests itself in the extent to which they are external to a conflict and financially motivated, and also by the degree of control to which they are subject, indicates the criteria according to which mercenaries are proscribed. The basis of the proscriptive norm is thus twofold: first, there are a series of objections based around the selfish motivation and absence of attachment to a cause that mercenaries demonstrate. These objections can be grouped together and placed under the broad heading of 'motivational'. Motivational objections to mercenaries stem from the idea that attachment to a cause makes war and killing in war more morally justified; the absence of such a motivation not only means that mercenaries have been considered to be inherently immoral but also that they are more likely to pursue immoral

---

[53] Several commentators refer to both Gurkhas and the French Foreign Legion as mercenaries or as a type of mercenary (Mockler 1969: 15–16, Thomson 1994: 89, Nossal 1998: 20, and Spicer 1999*a*: 33–4). Several commentators do not differentiate between PSCs and PMCs (Nossal 1998: 30, Zarate 1998: 2, Singer 2003*a*: 8).

tactics in war.⁵⁴ In other words, the fact that mercenaries were not attached to a cause and so were improperly motivated was not just perceived to be a moral problem, has also had practical consequences. A strong attachment to the appropriate cause of the day, whether or not it was a just cause of a noble or national glory of the state, was considered to lead to good behaviour.⁵⁵ Regular soldiers, then, were not greedy because they were also attached to the cause of their lord or state; they were less likely to be disloyal because they were held to their generals by more than fear and the desire for financial gain; they were less likely to change allegiances, because a belief in the army's cause would make it difficult to form a new attachment to a different army with a different cause; they were less likely to desert or mutiny because a common cause would hold them fast in times of trouble. Without attachment to the cause for which he was fighting, a mercenary could only be greedy, and was much more likely to be disloyal, to change sides for better wages, and to desert or mutiny. Assuming that mercenaries are inherently dangerous, as do some of the modern commentators cited above, assumes that national soldiers are not inherently problematic and so are superior.

The evidence in the next chapters suggests that national soldiers have not always been superior to mercenaries. As Sandoz argues, 'recent events and recent history have amply demonstrated that combatants driven by ideological, ethnic or religious fanaticism are capable of far worse behaviour toward the general population than that of persons popularly depicted as mercenaries'.⁵⁶ Nonetheless, this argument has been made over a long time period and now many automatically assume that mercenaries are immoral and so more dangerous than other fighters.⁵⁷ The persistence of the proscriptive norm in face of contrary empirical evidence demonstrates its strength.

The 'cause' aspect of the norm began to take on an additional connotation during the Italian renaissance, when the argument that mercenaries undermined the community that hired them because they did not share that community's goals became common. This later evolved, in line with a tradition of republican thought, into the view that soldiers must share the cause of their employers for two reasons: first, to avoid undermining the community, and second, to prevent tyranny on the part of the state. The use of mercenaries, who do not share the cause of a community, could make it easier for their employers to suppress rebellion at home or embark on unpopular wars abroad. This aspect of the norm is important because it further demonstrates

---

⁵⁴ Ballesteros Report, UN Doc E/C.N/2004/15 at page 10.   ⁵⁵ See Chapter 3.
⁵⁶ Sandoz (1999: 210). See also Lynch and Walsh (2000: 147).
⁵⁷ Finer (1976: 129), Nossal (1998: 17), Lynch and Walsh (2000: 133) all cite how commonly held is the assumption that mercenaries are inherently immoral.

the degree to which it is not financial motivation alone that makes a mercenary problematic. Rather, the absence of a shared cause can cause moral difficulty for a state. This variation on the norm can be seen after the fifteenth century and is clearly visible in regards to PMCs and PSCs.

The second aspect of the proscriptive norm stems from the weak controls placed over mercenaries by sovereign entities. Mercenaries have been feared across time and place simply because they threaten the ability of other actors, in particular sovereign states and other sovereign entities, to control the use of force. As they are not under the control of these actors, mercenaries are feared because they might run amok, ravaging the countryside without accountability to any other organization. When states hire mercenaries, they cannot be assured that their control over their employees is complete. As mercenaries possess the means and methods of warfare, and do not share the same motivation as their employers, they might work to undermine state interests, mutiny, or change sides. What is especially interesting is that national troops may be equally likely or even more likely to mutiny or desert, as we see in later chapters. However, the perception that mercenaries are the more disloyal troops has remained even in the light of contrary evidence.

Attention to the norm against mercenary use, and the definition of 'mercenary' from which it arises, can help us explain why there have been two distinct shifts away from mercenary use. The first shift, the ground for which was laid in the twelfth, thirteenth, and fourteenth centuries and was largely completed by the end of the seventeenth, was essentially a shift in control. Mercenaries during this period were brought under legitimate control, and accordingly became less objectionable, if they could be considered mercenaries at all by the standards of the day.

By the nineteenth century, however, the notion of 'cause' had changed, throwing mercenaries under the harsh glare of moral disapprobation once more. Even though the practice of buying and selling mercenaries from state to state, or the related practice of a 'selling' state granting a 'hiring' state permission to recruit on the hiring state's territory under strict conditions was relatively effective, ideas about the appropriate cause for fighting had changed. The increasingly pronounced belief that only citizens ought to fight for national glory meant that the old, relatively accepted, arrangements had changed once again. In fact, objections to the use of mercenaries on the basis of cause that originated with Machiavelli and the Italian humanists persisted even when the controlled arrangements for mercenary exchange were at their height.

The second shift away from mercenary use, in the nineteenth century, was a shift that occurred on the basis of cause. Dislike of mercenaries on the basis that they do not fight for an appropriate cause is all the more remarkable considering the degree to which mercenary practices of the day conformed to the control aspect of the norm. States felt so strongly that mercenaries were mercenaries, and immoral, because they did not fight for a cause, that they rejected the accepted system of private force and turned entirely to their own citizens to provide military personnel.

These two aspects of the proscriptive norm are generally present whenever mercenaries are present, taking different forms over time. The motivational objections shift because of prevailing shifts in beliefs about war. The objections centred on control shift depending on the nature of the actor in control, from lords or kings to the modern sovereign state. With the development of the sovereign nation state in the nineteenth century, control obligations shifted towards a belief that the state ought to have the sole control over the use of force and its citizens the sole right to wield it as members of national armies. By the nineteenth century, the belief that only citizens could have the proper motive for fighting solidified the norm against mercenary use and mercenaries all but disappeared for nearly a century.

Having identified the main aspects of the proscriptive norm, Chapter 3 turns to examining its origins.

3

The Origins of the Norm against Mercenary Use, 1100–1600

The early origins of the norm against mercenary use are best examined through three major cases of mercenary use, broadly covering the twelfth through sixteenth centuries: first, mercenaries in France and England from the twelfth to the fourteenth century, with a particular focus on the *routiers*[1] and *écorcheurs*[2] of fourteenth century France; second, Swiss mercenaries from the thirteenth to the sixteenth centuries; and finally, Italian mercenaries in the same period. An additional case will be examined in less depth: the military enterpriser system in the German states during the Thirty Years War. These cases represent nearly all the mercenary activity in Western Europe between the twelfth and the nineteenth century.

This chapter first examines the 'cause' aspect of the norm through each of the three main cases outlined above and second analyses the control aspect of the proscriptive norm through the same cases, and also through the case of the German military enterprise system. As the military enterpriser system is unique and not conventionally 'mercenary', it will be examined as a counterpoint in relation to the control aspect of the norm. Attention to these four cases reveals that the anti-mercenary norm ultimately led to a major shift away from mercenary use by the end of the seventeenth century. Rulers brought the mercenary trade entirely under the control of the state, eliminating the independent, entrepreneurial mercenary from the international stage. After the seventeenth century, states bought and sold units of mercenaries or allowed the recruitment of individual mercenaries on their territory under strict licence. The norm against mercenary use not only pre-dates the nineteenth century, but rulers had already effectively eliminated independent and entrepreneurial mercenaries.

---

[1] The term 'routier' refers to a freelance mercenary (Housley 1999: 115). It indicates a small number of men and derives from the Latin 'to break' (Saunders 2004: 30).

[2] The term 'écorcheur' means 'skinner' (Contamine 1984: 123), and reflects the violent nature of mercenary activity. Its use is common throughout the period 1100–1600.

3.1. ATTACHMENT TO A CAUSE

Dislike of mercenaries on the basis of their motivation has four different manifestations, each present at different times. First, there was an increasing distinction between native and foreign soldiers, and an increasing dislike of the latter. Second, there were two strong ideas about just cause operating in this period. In the twelfth, thirteenth, and fourteenth centuries causes were considered just if they were deemed so by the nobility and the Church, and so unattached mercenaries could not have just cause. In renaissance Italy, a growing body of work suggested that citizens ought to fight for the cause of the state, and mercenaries could not fight for this cause in the same way as citizens. Third, there was a growing sense that a community's own people ought to fight, for the strength and good of all, and by replacing citizens mercenaries tore apart the community's fabric. Fourth, as we see, contemporary commentators believed that because mercenaries were not attached to a just cause, they would be more likely to behave badly on the battlefield. These ideas about the dangers mercenaries pose because of their lack of attachment to a cause and therefore their inappropriate motivation indicate that notions of citizen responsibility to the state and a sense of *patrie* existed before the nineteenth century, and that mercenary dislike is an old phenomenon.

France and England from the Twelfth to the Fourteenth Centuries

England and France between the twelfth and the fourteenth century illustrate the difficulty of depending on financial motivation and foreign status to define a mercenary, and demonstrate that mercenaries were marked out as different from, and more problematic than, other fighters because they did not fight for an appropriate cause.

If a purely financial motive is the defining indicator of a mercenary, then many different medieval fighters might at first glance appear to be mercenaries. Armies in this period were a mixed bag of different types of soldiers fighting for different reasons. The Norman English army, for example, might include the king's household retainers, which incorporated knights hired on a permanent basis to serve on behalf of vassals unable to fill their required quota; mercenaries hired for a particular campaign, usually but not always foreign; and the armies of loosely allied lords. It is a moot point whether this last category could be considered feudal or mercenary.[3] As early as the beginning of the twelfth century, fighting for money was a regular part of war.[4]

[3] Hollister (1965: 169). [4] Chibnall (2000: 17).

Changes in military organization also made the motivations of soldiers difficult to discern. There was no clean break between a feudal system in which obligation was the main way to obtain troops and a monetary system in which remuneration secured soldiers,[5] with the result that it is extremely difficult to tell whether soldiers were serving out of obligation, for pay, or both.[6] Contamine points out that it is astonishing that the authorities preserved the 'system of obligations, when this system had resulted more and more frequently in the payment of wages and various indemnities comparable in every sense to wages, as well as other recompense to volunteers'.[7] It was difficult to differentiate between mercenaries and soldiers in the medieval period, because fighters of all varieties fought for pay.[8]

The distinction between mercenaries and regular soldiers is also unclear. Mercenaries were often the preferred choice of sovereigns because of the problems caused by the feudal system. Feudal armies were of notoriously poor quality, and 'indescribably undisciplined'.[9] Mercenaries had the advantage of training and experience, often in specialist fields.[10] Long campaigns were stymied by short periods of service,[11] a function of feudal obligations. English knights were only required to serve forty days a year, and wanted to avoid service abroad.[12] It was often more practical to hire an army at the theatre of war than to transport it overseas.[13]

Financial systems were developed to override feudal obligations and allow the hire of foreign troops, an example of the overlap between feudal and mercenary forms of military organization. The system of *scutage*, whereby a knight could buy himself out of military service, was used in England as early as 1100[14] and was further developed by Henry II.[15] *Scutage* became a form of taxation, the proceeds of which were used to fund paid armies.[16]

Despite the omnipresence of financial motivations and the practical military expertise of mercenaries, there is evidence that mercenaries were widely disliked because they were outsiders, and were not motivated by loyalty or duty in the same way as native troops. In the thirteenth and fourteenth centuries, as states became increasingly centralized and independent, and therefore more sharply differentiated from each other, distinctions between 'local, "national", "own" troops and "foreign" troops became gradually apparent', with suspicion increasingly directed at foreigners.[17]

[5] Hollister (1965: 190) and Housley (1999: 125).   [6] Brown (1989: 38).
[7] Contamine (1984: 93).
[8] Mallett (1974: 13), Corvisier (1979: 41), Hale (1985: 146), and France (1999: 71).
[9] Preston and Wise (1979: 80).   [10] Hindley (1971: 82).   [11] Kaeuper (1988: 18).
[12] Mockler (1969: 26), Preston and Wise (1979: 80), and Mallett (1999: 213).
[13] Hollister (1965: 177).   [14] Contamine (1984: 79).
[15] Hollister (1965: 195) and Prestwich (1996).
[16] Mockler (1969: 26) and France (1999: 131).   [17] Mallett (1999: 210).

In the *Gesta Stephannii*, a chronicle of the reign of King Stephen, the chronicler commented that the mercenary bands brought by Henry II to England in 1153 were disliked at least in part because they were foreign:

[T]he profane scoundrels...were so shamelessly guilty of murder and pillage and various abominations, and so savagely and brutally did their reckless and unblushing presumption rage without pity against all...that the barons of England shuddered in utter loathing of their company, and being unable to endure their bestial and brutal presumption any longer suggested to the duke that he should allow them to go home.[18]

At the signing of Magna Carta in 1215, explicit criticisms were made of mercenaries because they were foreign, and because of the damage they caused. King John was required to expel his foreign mercenaries as soon as the treaty was signed.[19] Magna Carta states that the King will 'remove from the kingdom all the foreign knights, bowmen, their attendants, and the mercenaries that have come to it, to its harm, with horses and arms'.[20]

The native population's growing dislike of mercenaries meant that rulers began to use them abroad rather than at home, which had the associated advantage of not flooding one's own country with demobilized and unemployed armed men at the end of a war.[21] Native troops had the advantage of being 'more faithful, more conscious that they were fighting for fatherland, family, and possessions; less—in a word—mercenary'.[22]

There was a distinction between a sovereign's own troops and foreign troops hired as mercenaries on the basis of nationality, and the former were preferred to the latter. The categories of nationality, while they existed, were not hard and fast distinctions until at least the fifteenth century, even though a sense of patriotism existed in the fourteenth.[23] As a result it is hard to see that nationality was the defining characteristic of a mercenary in the medieval period, even if it was important. A financial motivation is similarly unable to mark what made a mercenary. It 'was not the taking of pay that was reprehensible. Payment of fees and wages was central to the military organization of the period, and was not a matter for criticism'.[24] The real mark of a mercenary in the medieval period, and what made the difference between an unacceptable and an acceptable paid fighter, is the idea of appropriate cause. Medieval mercenaries were marked out as different from, and problematic because, they did not fight for an appropriate cause.

The medieval laws of war took the position that only wars fought for a just cause were just. In turn, the justness of a cause depended on the sanction of

---

[18] Gesta Stephanii and Regius Anglorum (1976: 223).   [19] Holt (1992: 356).
[20] Text of Magna Carta. Edited and translated by Davis (1963).   [21] Mallett (1999: 214).
[22] Hale (1985: 73).   [23] Barnie (1974: 97).   [24] Prestwich (1996: 152).

authority, provided by the nobility or the Church.[25] Mercenaries fighting for themselves did not have 'just cause' because they were not fighting for, and under the direction of, the noble classes or the Church; their actions were 'seen as criminal, and in some cases, traitorous, treasonable and even heretical'.[26] Keen notes that mercenaries went to great lengths to ensure they had just title; one mercenary even claimed he was fighting on behalf of a lunatic who *thought* he was the King of France and tried (and, needless to say, failed) to claim just authority on this basis.[27]

The distinction between a war fought under just authority and a war fought outside it had significant practical ramifications. A *routier* captain on trial in 1391 pointed out that he had 'done all those things which a man can and ought to do in a just war, [such] as taking Frenchmen and putting them to ransom, living on the country and despoiling it, and leading the company under his command about the realm of France, and burning and firing places in it'. The captain was executed not for committing the acts, but because he did not have just authority to commit them.[28] The 'justice of war could...render acts, which would otherwise be crimes, legitimate'.[29] A just cause separated criminals from warriors.

The medieval view of just authority excluded the lower orders from warfare between 1000 and 1200.[30] Mercenaries were considered to be legal so long as they were in the employ of, and so fighting for, the nobility. Nobles did not always themselves have just cause to wage war, as cause depended on Church sanction and also on the specifics of the war being fought. Unlike the nobility, the humbly born could never pursue their own goals, but only the goals of their employers.

Medieval chroniclers noticed the fact that mercenaries fought only for themselves and were somehow different from regular fighters. The chronicler Jordan Fantosme[31] wrote that mercenaries 'do not know how to bear arms like knights, and why they had come was to pick up plunder and the spoils of war',[32] indicating that pillaging mercenaries could not fight as knights did. Jean de Venette[33] referred to 'those...men of iniquity, warriors from various lands who assailed other men with no right and no reason other than their own passions, iniquity, malice, and hope of gain'.[34]

Church punishment of fighters relied on the notion of cause. Those who served for personal gain, rather than for a lord, had greater penance to serve.[35]

---

[25] Russell (1975: 2). [26] Fowler (2001: 1). [27] Keen (1966: 85).
[28] Quoted in Kaeuper (1988: 85).
[29] Keen (1966: 65). The ability to engage in these activities, even under just authority, only lasted as long as the hostilities. They were also illegal in peacetime (Keen 1966: 83).
[30] Contamine (1984: 31). [31] Fantosme wrote in the twelfth century.
[32] Fantosme (1981: 73). [33] Ca.1308–ca.1369. [34] de Venette (1953: 106).
[35] France (1999: 71).

Independent, roving bands of mercenaries of common birth, like the *routiers* and *cotereaux*[36] of the twelfth and thirteenth centuries, fought for themselves rather than a lord or king, and therefore did not fight for a just cause. For 'relatively humble men in the form of mercenary bands to take power was entirely unacceptable'.[37]

This period provides further evidence for the argument that it is not necessarily financial motivation or foreign status which distinguishes mercenaries from other fighters, but the presence or absence of some kind of appropriately sanctioned cause. From the twelfth century to the fourteenth century, the only appropriate, or 'just', cause could come from fighting for the nobly born under Church-granted authority.

Swiss Mercenaries from the Thirteenth to the Sixteenth Centuries

The first references to Swiss mercenaries come in the thirteenth and fourteenth centuries. Some of these mercenaries were organized into companies and some were not.[38] Between the fifteenth and sixteenth centuries the Swiss fought for Louis XII of France, themselves, and for the French again in wars in Italy. By 1516, the groundwork for a long-standing arrangement whereby Swiss mercenaries served the French crown was set.[39] The Swiss served the French crown until 1793.

The service of Swiss mercenaries abroad led to criticism at home, because mercenary service was seen as practically and morally detrimental to Switzerland. In 1503, there was agreement at a Swiss diet that 'foreign service and foreign bribery were objectionable and were to be avoided' in part because of extensive battlefield losses.[40] The Swiss continued with the practice because it was financially necessary, and their 'balance of payments could be maintained only by an export policy of armed men'.[41] However, the 'more thoughtful Swiss saw the disadvantage of foreign service' and 'the lowering of Swiss moral standards resulting from too intimate an acquaintance with violence and plunder'.[42]

Swiss religious leaders, like Zwingli,[43] were deeply uncomfortable with what amounted to a trade in able-bodied young men fighting for money. In 1513, Zwingli accompanied a group of Swiss mercenaries as chaplain on

---

[36] The term 'cotereaux' is another common way to refer to mercenaries in the medieval period. It derives either from the word 'cotter' indicating the poor, rural origins of mercenaries or 'couteau', dagger, indicating that mercenaries, unlike knights, did not use swords (Mallett 1999: 213).

[37] France (1999: 71).   [38] McCormack (1993: 38).   [39] Ibid. 44, 62.
[40] Potter (1976: 30).   [41] Ibid.   [42] Gilliard (1955: 36).   [43] 1484–1531.

campaign in Italy.[44] The Battle of Marignano, where the Swiss lost 10,000 men, reinforced the extent to which the Swiss mercenary trade was essentially the sacrifice of young men for financial gain. Zwingli came away from the Battle of Marignano with the conviction that 'mercenary service, the sale of flesh and blood for gold, was immoral'.[45]

The idea that Swiss mercenaries were motivated by a foreign cause led to criticism that this devotion distracted attention from Switzerland, which ought to be the motivating factor for soldiers. Zwingli's argument against mercenaries was framed as 'an eloquent appeal to Swiss patriotism'[46] and reflected 'his love of his country and his desire for its liberty'.[47] By fighting for foreigners, the Swiss were neglecting their own cause, which should surely be the preservation and strengthening of Switzerland. Zwingli argued that 'the acceptance of foreign money for military service had brought corruption, division and greed in return for lost lives'.[48] While the appeal did not meet with much response,[49] Zwingli argued that fighting abroad for 'lucre' had caused the Swiss to neglect their homeland and ignore Swiss needs.[50] Fighting for foreign causes prevented the Swiss from tending to their own community.

Moreover, fighting for a foreign cause was inherently immoral. 'How do you explain the fact,' wrote Zwingli, 'that you take money from a foreign lord to aid him wantonly destroy, damage and ravage countries innocent of guilt?'[51] In other words, the Swiss were morally culpable for the violence they inflicted in the name of their foreign employers. By the eighteenth century, the seeds sown by Zwingli had taken root, and recruitment was made difficult by 'the increasingly outspoken opposition to the mercenary system led by articulate writers and churchmen'.[52]

Italian Mercenaries from the Thirteenth to the Sixteenth Centuries

Throughout the thirteenth century, Italian city-state militias were reinforced with mercenaries[53] on an individual basis and by the end of the century they were recruited as units.[54] The *condottiere* system in Italy was built around

---

[44] Potter (1976: 34). While the Swiss fought in their own right at Marignano, they fought against a French army which contained Swiss mercenaries. See Potter (1976: 38–9).

[45] Potter (1976: 39). See also Stephens (1986: 8) for how the defeat at Marignano coloured Zwingli's response to the mercenary problem.

[46] Potter (1976: 139).   [47] Stephens (1986: 7).   [48] Potter (1976: 139).

[49] Ibid.   [50] Ibid.   [51] Zwingli, quoted in Stephens (1986: 284).

[52] McCormack (1993: 139).   [53] Mallett (1974: 13).   [54] Ibid. 13, 16.

the hire of these companies. Contracts, or *condotta*, were signed between cities and mercenary captains (*condottieri* or *condottiere* in the singular). Italy was flooded with mercenaries looking for work between 1360 and 1369, a pause during the hostilities of the Hundred Years War. Some of these mercenaries formed companies which dominated the country.[55] The companies were attracted by the possibility of rich prizes in the wealthy environment of the Italian city-states,[56] and they 'spread terror and destruction from the northern reaches of Savoy to the southern limits of the kingdom of Naples'.[57]

Even outside the problems created by the pause in the Hundred Years War, the large number of *condottieri* in Italy meant that the system was not perfect. When mercenaries were unemployed, during peacetime and truces, they wreaked havoc.[58] One of the primary sources of money was the payment of protection money, which modern eyes would recognize as 'mafia-style extortion'.[59] The amount of 'purely wanton damage the mercenaries committed before moving on...depended largely on what inducement they were offered'.[60] The extent of the extortion was substantial. The mercenary captain Sir John Hawkwood sent the Sienese city officials a polite letter suggesting that he would not put the city to the sack if they would pay him an appropriate sum.[61] He extorted from Siena in a few days an amount five times the biannual salary of two of the most important Sienese city officials,[62] and the depredations of mercenaries almost certainly hastened Siena's decline in power from a 'position rivalling Florence in the fourteenth century to provincial backwater by 1400'.[63]

Italian humanists were concerned, as Zwingli was, that using mercenaries would undermine civic spirit, which ought to be devoted to the preservation of the city itself. They condemned the *condottieri* because 'both classical tradition and current preoccupation with active civic participation ran counter to the practice of employing mercenaries'.[64] The poet Petrarch's 'vituperation for the mercenary forces of his time was picturesque and unrestrained' and he saw them as 'cohorts of thieves and murderers'.[65] The use of mercenaries was not just immoral because mercenaries were not fighting for the cause of their employers, but because the fact of their existence prevented citizens from having to support the cause of the state. Bruni and Guicciardini feared what would happen when:

---

[55] Ibid. 27.   [56] Mallett (1999: 216).   [57] Caferro (1994: 219).
[58] Mallett (1974: 27).   [59] Armstrong (2000: 293).   [60] Trease (1970: 36).
[61] Saunders (2004: 178).   [62] Caferro (1994: 221).   [63] Armstrong (2000: 294).
[64] Mallett (1974: 3).   [65] Bayley (1961: 187).

a city ceased to use its own citizens in its armies and employed mercenaries instead. The citizens would be corrupted because they permitted inferiors to do for them what should be done for the public good; the mercenaries would be agents of that corruption because they performed a public function without regard for the public good; and any ambitious individual could set himself above the republic and destroy it, by bringing the unthinking mercenaries to do for him what should only be done for the republic.[66]

Because mercenaries could not fight for the cause of the public good, they brought the republic into grave danger. The humanist concerns about mercenary use reached their apotheosis in the work of Machiavelli.

Machiavelli believed that mercenaries lacked *virtú*, including the 'willingness to set aside all considerations of personal safety and interest in order to defend the liberties of one's native land'[67] that would be present in native troops. Mercenaries fighting for themselves are dangerous for leaders because 'they have no other passions or incentives to hold the field, except their desire for a bit of money, and that is not enough to make them die for you'.[68] Mercenaries do not fight for the cause of the common good; Machiavelli argued that 'the republic is the common good; the citizen, directing all his actions toward that good, may be said to dedicate his life to the republic; the patriot warrior dedicates his death'.[69]

Machiavelli's concerns about mercenary use revolve around a deep-seated feeling that native sons *should* fight for the republic, to ensure its health and success at war. Part of what made a republic strong was having its citizens fight for its preservation and perhaps expansion. Hiring foreigners to fight thus diminished the strength of the republic.[70] 'Experience teaches', writes Machiavelli, 'that independent princes and well-armed republics accomplish great things but mercenary armies do nothing but lose; and a republic with its own armies holds out longer against the tyranny of one of its citizens than does a republic with foreign armies'.[71] Machiavelli asserts 'the present ruin of Italy is caused by nothing else than its having trusted for so long to mercenary armies'.[72] A foreigner, not motivated by the republic, will only undermine it.

It is important here to note that some of the facts Machiavelli uses to support his general argument—that mercenaries undermine the republic by preventing citizens from fulfilling their duty to serve it, and because they can never be effective fighters because they are not motivated by the cause of the common good—are inflated. He substantially downgraded the number of casualties in mercenary battles,[73] which he argued were few because

---

[66] Pocock (1975: 204).   [67] Skinner (1981: 74).   [68] Machiavelli ([1513] 1992: 34).
[69] Pocock (1975: 201).   [70] Mallett (1974: 133, 197).
[71] Machiavelli ([1513] 1992: 35).   [72] Ibid. 34.
[73] Trease (1970: 325), Mallett (1974: 196), and Contamine (1984: 258).

mercenaries were insufficiently motivated to be bloodthirsty. Skinner argues that Machiavelli's 'vehemence of tone' on the mercenary question 'stands in need of some explanation, especially in view of the fact that most historians have concluded that the mercenary system usually worked quite effectively.'[74]

It must be emphasized that, while Machiavelli's *facts* are inaccurate, his argument still stands as an example of Renaissance humanist thinking about mercenaries. The whole point about normative discomfort over the use of mercenaries is that it has frequently existed at the same time as the activities of mercenaries were not causing practical problems at all, or not guilty of the abuses of which they were accused. It is possible that Machiavelli believed so strongly that mercenaries, because they were not motivated by the common good, would undermine the republic that he was willing to distort the facts. As Mallett argues, 'above all Machiavelli was a rhetorician seeking to convince ... that good infantry should be the core of every army, and that, ideally, those infantry should be citizens defending heart and home'.[75] Machiavelli's arguments against mercenary use, whatever their factual accuracy, have had a direct impact on subsequent anti-mercenary thought. As we will see, there is a direct line of opposition to mercenaries on the basis that they do not fight for the appropriate cause that can be traced from Machiavelli and the Renaissance humanists through the eighteenth and nineteenth century republican traditions and through to the anti-mercenary norm of today.

From the period 1100 to 1600, the belief that mercenaries did not fight for an appropriate cause made them problematic actors. In Switzerland and Italy, the appropriate cause was deemed to be the common good of the state or republic. A warrior not motivated by the common good would undermine the polity. A native soldier, fighting for homeland, contributes to the strength of that homeland; a mercenary, fighting for himself, undermines that contribution in two ways. First, a mercenary is simply less effective because he is not motivated in the same way a national soldier would be. Second, by replacing a native soldier, a mercenary actively undermines the duty to homeland vital for a strong state. Republican norms about civic duty contributed directly to the norm against mercenary use by emphasizing the fact that because mercenaries do not fight for the appropriate cause, they undermine the republic. Examining this period reveals that 'cause' is defined differently in different times and places, and that mercenaries are objectionable because they do not fight for the appropriate cause, whether or not it is defined as something which is decided upon by the church or nobility or simply defined as the common good.

---

[74] Skinner (1981: 32).   [75] Mallett (1999: 229).

The next section turns to outlining the challenges mercenaries posed to control, and how these challenges resulted in significant ill-feeling towards mercenaries.

3.2. THE NEED TO CONTROL MERCENARY FORCES

The ravages of independent fighters and the challenges they posed to order caused sovereigns to attempt to bring the right to use force under their exclusive control during the period from 1100 to 1600. The need to control mercenaries was not divorced from the sense that mercenaries were dangerous because they were not fighting for the appropriate cause. Because independent mercenaries were fighting for themselves, they did not take into consideration the needs of the sovereign. The solution was to bring them under tight control and attempt to make mercenary interests coincide with those of the sovereign. Sovereigns attempted to control mercenaries in an effort to persuade them to adopt the cause of their employers as their own.

Mercenaries unquestionably caused practical problems for leaders in France and in Italy. In France, the period of truce during the Hundred Years War, 1360–1369, left many unemployed mercenaries on French soil. With entrepreneurial zeal, they took to ravaging the countryside in companies, demanding protection money from towns and cities. Independent mercenaries 'were the scourge of western Europe before the emergence of standing armies in the fifteenth century'.[76] As noted above, Italy was threatened by mercenaries spilling over from the conflict in France.

These practical difficulties were underscored by the belief that mercenaries were not fighting for the appropriate cause. In France, unattached mercenaries were morally problematic because by fighting without just title, they upset the social order. In Italy, mercenaries were morally troublesome because they undermined the increasingly common belief that citizens owed a duty to the republic.

Mercenaries caused two more general problems for their employers. First, the need for mercenary use often exceeded the capacity to control it, and at times when state capacity for control was weakest, the scourge of wandering mercenaries was most severe. Independent companies of mercenaries posed a grave threat, and by the sixteenth century, were no longer commonly used. Second, even when under firm control, the sense that mercenaries were

[76] Fowler (2001: ix).

self-motivated rather than motivated by a cause remained. It was not until the nineteenth century, as we see in Chapter 5, that states shifted away from the use of mercenaries in a controlled fashion on the basis that an improper motivation was morally problematic.

States wanted to control mercenaries both to minimize the practical difficulties caused by mercenary rampages and to attempt to make mercenaries less morally problematic by trying to make them adopt an appropriate cause for fighting. The effect of such control mechanisms was to remove many of the problems that made mercenaries objectionable in the first place. Indeed, it is arguable that by the end of this period Italian mercenaries ceased to be mercenaries at all, and that the only mercenary arrangements which persisted were the tightly controlled sale of units from state to state and the granting of permission by a state to recruit for mercenaries on its soil. These arrangements did not, as we see in Chapter 5, avoid the mercenary label because foreign fighters were still deemed not to share their employers' cause.

France and England from the Twelfth to the Fourteenth Centuries

The notion that unattached mercenaries were inappropriate fighters because they were not motivated by the goals of the nobility is of course a notion intimately tied to the idea of control. Because mercenaries used force without just cause, they challenged the strongly normative world view based on the Church-sanctioned[77] idea that only the nobly born were granted, and ought to have, the right to use force.[78] Non-nobles could only use force when working for nobles. Mercenaries, fighting for themselves, upset the feudal order, creating wide dislike.[79] A group of lower order individuals did not have the right to take up arms for themselves or any other cause they selected. Only when a mercenary was *under control* were his actions considered legal. As long as 'they did not threaten the accepted social order, mercenaries were such an accepted part of contemporary armies that they were often not clearly distinguished from others'.[80] In other words, it was the fact that mercenaries did not have just cause that marked them as unacceptable.

As much as independent, self-motivated mercenaries lying outside the control of their masters were a threat to a social order, they also constituted a

---

[77] France (1999: 75).   [78] Contamine (1984: 238) and Keen (1999a: 4–5).
[79] Prestwich (1996: 153). See also Kaeuper (1988: 19).   [80] France (1999: 73).

practical threat to lands and lives. In twelfth century France, *routiers* and *cotereaux* pillaged the countryside, particularly the Limousin and the Auvergne, and were known for attacking churches; their names recalled 'their purpose as destroyers and pillagers and their wandering, rootless way of life'.[81]

The *routiers* were condemned because of 'their cruelty, the lack of respect they showed for churches (an excellent source of booty), and the fact they seemed all to often to be quite uncontrollable'.[82] The medieval chronicler Walter Map, writing in the twelfth century, described 'bands of many thousands...armed cap-à-pie with leather, iron, clubs, and swords, lay monasteries, villages, and towns in ashes...saying with all their heart, "There is no God"'.[83]

The damage caused by *routiers* was symptomatic of the fact that rulers could not prevent other actors from using force within their territories. The 'more or less prolonged weakness of normal political structures'[84] explains why the mercenaries were able to have such a devastating effect. The routine destruction of the countryside in peacetime was a consequence of the inability of rulers to maintain armies in peacetime as well as in war.[85]

The Church did, however, attempt to control the use of force by bringing mercenaries to heel. In 1179, the Lateran Council excommunicated mercenaries because of the *routiers* and their attacks on the Church. The decree explicitly associated mercenaries with the heretics of south-west France and promised those who fought against them all the privileges of a crusader to Jerusalem.[86] The Lateran Council condemned only those mercenaries fighting for themselves, and out of control, leaving mercenaries fighting under just title unaffected.[87] Again, the difference between acceptability and excommunication lay in whether or not a mercenary was under control of someone with the right to use force, and so had just cause to fight. Mercenaries were accepted as useful tools for lords and kings, but not as fighters in their own right.

The regulations in the laws of war and the attempts of the Church to control mercenaries by excommunication and the threats of the Lateran Council indicates that strong efforts were made to control the problem of independent mercenaries in this period. By the 'thirteenth century the Western state was launched on its remarkable course as the agency defining and practising legitimate violence while working to suppress the illicit violence of private persons at every social rank within its boundaries'.[88]

---

[81] Ibid. 71, 72.
[82] Prestwich (1996: 152). See also Corvisier (1979: 10), and Kaeuper (1988: 1).
[83] Map (1983: 119). [84] Contamine (1984: 247). [85] Mallett (1999: 214).
[86] France (1999: 70). [87] Russell (1975: 2). [88] Kaeuper (1988: 381).

The mercenaries who found themselves out of work after the peace of 1360 during the Hundred Years War were quick to create their own prospects for employment. During the entire pause in hostilities, France 'was never to be free of the horrors inflicted by the "Free Companies", ravaging bands of mercenaries from all over Europe, whose contracts had expired and who owned no master'.[89] At one point, the Free Companies controlled sixty fortresses and a large part of central and eastern France.[90] Bands of mercenaries could number up to 10,000 men, and local authorities had to tax a countryside already impoverished by the actions of the mercenaries in order to pay protection money.[91]

The difficulties caused by the Free Companies constituted 'one of the major problems facing those responsible for government and the rule of law in western Europe, and churchmen in particular spoke out against their actions'.[92] As in the twelfth and thirteenth centuries, the problems caused by the Free Companies were made worse by the weak control exercised by rulers. The French state had degenerated after strong growth in the previous centuries[93] and its weakness caused the situation to spiral out of control.[94] The free companies 'were an affront to order, and especially to the royal authority, which feebly did its rather limited best to rid France of this affliction'.[95] The existing framework did not have much of an effect; the mercenaries did not feel bound by the laws of war as they stood outside the social order upon which it was based.[96] Rulers had to develop the capacity to control the unsanctioned use of force within their territories in order to bring the mercenary problem to an end.

There were essentially three different solutions to the problems caused by the free companies, all of which were designed to reassert control over mercenaries: moral condemnation in the form of excommunication; attempts to send mercenaries on crusade under control of various rulers; and finally, incorporating mercenaries into a ruler's forces. The final solution was ultimately the most successful, as the 'real answer to this problem of the freelance soldier was only found at the end of the Hundred Years War, in the organisation of standing armies'.[97]

Pope Urban V was instrumental in the fourteenth-century attempts to regain control over the mercenary problem. The depth of the problem is exemplified by Urban's comments in the bull *Cogit nosi* of 27 February 1364, one of three he issued:

---

[89] Preston and Wise (1979: 89). [90] Fowler (2001: 109).
[91] Keen (1966: 95) and Fowler (2001: 21). [92] Fowler (2001: 1).
[93] Kaeuper (1988: 121). [94] Fowler (1971: 12). [95] Ibid. 171.
[96] Contamine (1984: 291). [97] Keen (1966: 96).

The wickedness of our age, in which the sons of iniquity have multiplied, and fired by the flames of their own greed, are dishonestly attempting to gorge themselves on the labour of others, and for that reason rage more cruelly against the innocent peoples, compels us to draw on the resources of the apostolic power to counter their evil stratagems.[98]

Urban's bulls excommunicated mercenaries, granted indulgences to those who fought against them, forbade assisting mercenaries, and tried to restrict the payment of protection money to get the mercenaries to leave various areas.[99] These moral condemnations did have some effect, and 'with the whole range of spiritual and material sanctions pitted against them, a significant number of mercenary captains took the opportunity to secure absolution for their past misdeeds'.[100]

Urban also organized the second solution, the attempt to rein in mercenaries by sending them on crusade, which brought them under papal authority and the authority of the leader of the crusade; the Church in this period was one of the entities that could justifiably wage war in the form of crusades. This effectively made mercenaries no longer mercenary, as it will be recalled that the difference between a mercenary and another fighter rests in whether or not they are fighting for just cause. A crusade was, of course, the most glorious just cause.

Two crusade attempts were made. The first was to send the mercenaries overland to the Balkans from France. This crusade was an abject disaster, as it was insufficiently financially appealing for the mercenaries, and almost no preparations were made to ensure that they would behave themselves en route.[101] The net effect of the overland crusade was to create the danger of spreading the problems caused by mercenaries in France to the rest of Western Europe.[102] The second crusade, against the Moors in Spain, was more popular as the opportunities for plunder were good, and it was much better organized.[103]

The problems caused by the free companies persisted until the resurgence of hostilities in 1369 and the re-employment of mercenaries by the warring parties.[104] They were finally solved by the development of more organized permanent forces, which brought violence under control and an end to the roving mercenary. As early as 1420, the English were attempting to keep records of every man at arms,[105] bringing their troops under tighter control. After the Treaty of Arras in 1435, a new wave of *écorcheurs* appeared; to end the crisis, Charles VII of France needed to end the 'uncontrolled errant way of life'

---

[98] Quoted in Fowler (2001: 119). [99] Ibid. 119–20. [100] Ibid. 144.
[101] For details see Ibid. 129–43. [102] Ibid. 130. [103] Ibid. 143.
[104] Ibid. 285. [105] Keen (1966: 96).

The Origins of the Norm against Mercenary Use

of soldiers and 'to claim for himself alone the right to wage war and control all soldiers in the kingdom'.[106] He created the *compagnies d'ordonnance*, a prototype standing army, to deal with the problems of the free companies.[107] Charles appointed captains to select the best troops from the companies to form the nucleus of the new *compagnies*, and then to disband the rest.[108] As Mockler puts it, 'the wheel had turned full circle: the bands that had originally sprung up as free companies ended up as tightly controlled royal companies'.[109] Mercenaries brought under control of the state were considered to have just cause; as such, they were no longer mercenaries at all.

The attempts to control mercenaries during the Hundred Years War reflected the danger self-employed mercenaries posed and how much they were disliked. The Hundred Years War also demonstrates how much rulers wanted to control private force, and the different strategies they used to do so. One of the main solutions was to take fighters fighting for an unjust cause, and provide them with a just one—and the control of a ruler leading the crusade. The challenges posed by independent companies of mercenaries were overcome by bringing the use of force under centralized control and creating more permanent armies.

Swiss Mercenaries from the Fourteenth to the Sixteenth Centuries

Swiss mercenaries followed a very similar pattern. In the fourteenth century, they were disreputable, disorganized and dangerous; by the sixteenth century they were tightly controlled, nationally organized forces loaned out as part of an alliance agreement with the French.

The Swiss in the fifteenth century were 'more a turbulent band of marauders than an organized military formation'.[110] After the capture of Burgundy in the fifteenth century, the Swiss celebrated their victory by drowning some bound prisoners and throwing others out of a tower onto a bed of pre-prepared lances.[111] The Swiss were renowned for their ferocity. In 1444, it was considered necessary to create a regulation which forbade them from tearing out the hearts of their dead enemies.[112]

In the sixteenth century, Swiss mercenaries enhanced their disreputable image at the Battle of Novara, scene of the 'famous, or infamous, *Trahison de Novara* which did so much to lower the already low reputation of the Swiss'.[113] At Novara, two groups of Swiss mercenaries faced off against each other, one in

[106] Contamine (1984: 169). [107] Mallett (1999: 216). [108] Keen (1999b: 283).
[109] Mockler (1969: 69). [110] McCormack (1993: 38–9). [111] Mockler (1969: 83).
[112] Rogers (1999: 145). [113] Mockler (1969: 98).

the employ of the French and the other employed by Ludovico il Moro, Duke of Milan. A stand-off ensued, and the Swiss refused to fight each other.[114] The stalemate was resolved by a ceasefire whereby the French-employed Swiss would leave the city alone in exchange for the Duke of Milan. Chaos ensued when the Swiss colluded with each other to free the Duke, disguising him as one of their number, and passing him from side to side during a feverish French search. Only at the last moment was the Duke revealed, by a mercenary tempted by (of all things) bribery.[115] The events at Novara were responsible for enshrining the poor reputation that led to Racine's now famous saying, 'no money, no Swiss'.[116]

The Swiss mercenaries rehabilitated their reputation, but only when they were placed under tighter central control. Subsequent arrangements for Swiss mercenaries were governed by strict contracts on the Swiss side and controls on the side of the hiring state. Until the end of the seventeenth century, the Swiss were primarily employed by the French, and afterwards expanded to other employers.[117] Both sides had an obvious interest in controlling the Swiss mercenaries.

The Swiss Confederation faced social and political problems because of the mercenary question. The 'problem facing the Swiss states in the sixteenth century was not how to get young men into the army but how to keep them out of it'.[118] The loss of too many young men to mercenary service was bad for the economy, and foreign recruiters working in Switzerland might recruit young Swiss men to opposing sides of a conflict.[119] This, combined with the understanding that 'mercenary service was an important national asset that the Swiss authorities felt it their duty to control'[120] and the fact of poverty and overpopulation,[121] which led to large numbers of unemployed young men who could be kept out of trouble through military recruitment, led to tightened restrictions on the export of Swiss mercenaries. The first regulations about foreign service appeared in the diets in the late fourteenth century, and in 1422 Zurich prevented its citizens from fighting for other powers.[122]

The French motives for control were much simpler. The Swiss were brave fighters, but unreliable; control would make them more useful. Under the Perpetual Peace Treaty of 1516, specific rules were set about the number of troops the French king could recruit; where and under which circumstances Swiss

---

[114] Bonjour, Offler, and Potter (1952: 142).
[115] For details on the Battle of Novara, see Mockler (1969: 96–8) and McCormack (1993: 45). On the bribery point see Mockler: 98.
[116] McCormack (1993: 45).   [117] Ibid. 96.
[118] Bonjour, Offler, and Potter (1952: 142).   [119] McCormack (1993: 39).
[120] Ibid.   [121] Bonjour, Offler, and Potter (1952: 177).
[122] Contamine (1984: 136).

troops could be used; and when the Swiss could recall their troops, which was only in times of war.[123] It is interesting to note that under this treaty the Swiss had to be paid at all times, regardless of whether or not they were fighting.[124] These were, effectively, permanent troops. By the 1540s, the system was tightly organized, down to a tribunal with two judges from each country to arbitrate pay disputes.[125] The degree of control was *so* tight, however, it is perhaps better to understand the Swiss/French relationship in most of the sixteenth century as an alliance rather than a purely commercial arrangement.[126] The permanence of the arrangement, its exclusivity, and its status as part of an alliance suggests that the Swiss fighting for the French in the sixteenth century were far removed from their mercenary ancestors, with their enthusiasm for drowning Burgundians and disguising dukes. Indeed, it is striking that despite multiple arrears of pay, the Swiss were extremely loyal.[127] By making the arrangement permanent, the Swiss and the French each brought the problems caused by mercenaries under control, and the Swiss became far more like permanent foreign troops than mercenaries. However, as we have seen, moral concerns about mercenary use persisted. By the nineteenth century, tight control was no longer enough to ameliorate the absence of shared cause between the Swiss and their employers.

Italian Mercenaries

The *condottieri* system in Italy followed a similar pattern of increasing control over mercenaries. The first companies were collectives of individual mercenaries, which later coalesced under specific leaders;[128] they began as temporary associations and became 'permanent coherent military organisms' employed by or seeking employment with the Italian city-states.[129] These companies were mainly composed of foreigners, including the famous Werner von Urslingen, whose breastplate bore words that surely encapsulated the perceived problems with mercenaries: 'Enemy of God, Enemy of Piety, Enemy of Pity'.[130] During the fourteenth century, permanent mercenary arrangements became much more common than roving bands of mercenaries.[131] However, as we have seen, periods of truce and demobilization created the same problems as those caused by the Free Companies in France. Italian mercenary

---

[123] McCormack (1993: 62). Another agreement in 1521 granted Francis I the right to recruit in Switzerland. Gilliard (1955: 38).
[124] McCormack (1993: 62). [125] Ibid. 68. [126] Ibid. 96.
[127] Ibid. 77. One answer lies in the fact that the poor Swiss economy still meant there were few alternatives (Redlich 1964a: 140).
[128] Mallett (1999: 217–18). [129] Contamine (1984: 158). [130] Ibid.
[131] Mallett (1974: 26).

companies were regarded by their contemporaries as 'a scourge on a par with the plague'.[132]

Attempts were made to bring the mercenaries to heel. In Florence, a code of conduct regarding mercenary use was created in 1337 and revised twice afterwards.[133] Later on, Florence developed an elaborate contractual structure for mercenary hire, with different types of contracts depending on the state of war or peace; in an indication of the trustworthiness of potential *condottieri*, one of the contracts was essentially a pay-off against future attacks.[134] Fourteenth-century Siena employed two officials to deal with mercenary contracts.[135] By the fifteenth century, the arrangements between states and *condottieri* were becoming increasingly permanent, with the *condottieri* identified with particular states.[136] Contracts usually contained clauses preventing mercenaries from going to war with their former employers for a certain period,[137] and mercenaries were offered land, citizenship, or palaces in capital cities to try and bind them to the employing state.[138] By the late fifteenth century, Milan's army was typical in that 'certain mercenary institutions survived but the overall impression was one of a large standing army which could be expanded rapidly when needed'.[139] Permanence afforded the Italian city-states the opportunity to resolve some of the problems with disloyalty inherent in a system whereby soldiers fight on temporary contracts.[140] Moreover, the system whereby mercenaries were given citizenship effectively rendered them no longer mercenaries; as citizens, they shared the cause of the defence of the common good.

The medieval and early renaissance worlds saw mercenaries as a dangerous force which required control. Even when control tightened, concerns remained about the morality of killing for a selfish reason. Further concerns stemmed from the idea that people *ought* to fight for their own countries, and that hiring out foreigners to do the job undermined the community. All this suggests that mercenaries were considered reprehensible long before the nineteenth century, and that concerns about the morality of mercenary use and its dangers set the stage for the series of decisions that led to the end of mercenary use during that century.

The German Military Enterpriser System

This chapter has examined most of the major forms of mercenary action before the seventeenth century. The most significant exception is Germany,

---

[132] Armstrong (2000: 293). [133] Bayley (1961: 9). [134] Ibid. 14.
[135] Caferro (1994: 240). [136] Mallett (1974: 83). [137] Ibid. 86.
[138] Ibid. 92–3 and Mallett (1999: 222). [139] Mallett (1999: 225).
[140] Mallett (1974: 102) and McNeill (1983: 75).

which had two prominent usages of private force. First, German mercenaries called *landsknechts* arose in imitation of and competed with the Swiss in the fifteenth and sixteenth centuries.[141] Second, during the period of the Thirty Years War, the capital for war, and armies themselves, were raised and supplied by contractors commonly referred to as military enterprisers.[142] The most famous of these enterprisers was Albrecht von Wallenstein, who financed and led the army for the Holy Roman Emperor Ferdinand II between 1625 and 1630, and again between 1631 and 1634, when he was murdered.

The German military enterpriser system is worth a brief examination, because it is the most prominent example of private force in the seventeenth century. An in-depth discussion is not necessary. The military enterpriser system was not clearly mercenary; it is unique in Europe and associated only with one or two individuals over a very short period; and finally, despite its other differences, it follows the same pattern of being brought under tighter state control and ultimate replacement with a state-to-state-based exchange.

The German military enterpriser system was, at its apotheosis, unique in Europe. There was a tradition of captains and colonels recruiting and in many cases equipping their own regiments, and this continued after the end of the Thirty Years War and well into the eighteenth century.[143] The system reached its greatest height, in the person of Wallenstein, between 1625 and 1634. Wallenstein was unique because of the size of the forces he supplied, the credit system he could provide alongside the troops, and his ability to support and supply his forces on the battlefield.

Unlike most other military enterprisers, Wallenstein was able to raise an entire army as opposed to a regiment of men.[144] Only a small number of other enterprisers were able to do the same: Bernhard von Weimar, the Marquis of Hamilton (for Sweden), and Count Mansfield (for Ferdinand V).[145] Military enterprisers raising entire armies only existed in the latter stages of the Thirty Years War, after 1625.

Part of the reason for the unique character of the German military enterpriser system was that it existed because of the particular finances of the Holy Roman Empire. The Empire needed to use military enterprisers because it was not financially solvent enough to raise the large sums necessary to finance its troops. Spain, for example, had healthier finances and did not need to rely on enterprisers.[146] By 1625, the Holy Roman Empire was suffering a financial

---

[141] Mockler (1969: 99–101) and Singer (2003a: 27).   [142] Redlich (1964a, 1964b).

[143] Redlich (1964a, 1964b). The system of raising regiments for a sovereign is not mercenary, even if a profit is made, as the sovereign retains control over the force and the regiments are deemed to fight for the cause of their employers. Independent raising of regiments will be discussed in Chapters 4 and 5.

[144] Redlich (1964a: 231).   [145] Parker (1997: 175).   [146] Asch (1997: 156).

crisis. Ferdinand first attempted to bring his finances under control by debasing the value of coins, which led to heightened inflation. At this time Wallenstein manipulated the system to buy estates at rock-bottom prices.[147] Wallenstein was already a man of great wealth, thanks to a rich and conveniently deceased wife.[148] The additional wealth he accrued during the financial crisis allowed him to offer both his services in recruiting an army and also the ability to raise credit on behalf of the Empire,[149] and he could also use his vast estates to supply his troops.[150] Using Wallenstein also meant that Ferdinand could have troops under his own control, as opposed to having to share control with the Catholic League.[151] Military enterprisers like Wallenstein were thus both entrepreneurs recruiting their own forces and financiers who made fighting sustained wars possible.

Wallenstein was unique even among the other military enterprisers who also had the capacity to raise entire armies. He became a prince in his own right, and controlled a vast fortune and an equally vast amount of territory.[152] Mortimer argues that the other enterprisers never fully realized their ambitions,[153] and did not reach the same heights of success as Wallenstein. Wallenstein also differed in his ability to support his troops. Not only could he supply them from his own estates, he also enhanced the use of contributions from occupied territory common at the time. He did so to such a degree that the ability to tax in these areas was fundamentally altered, and even after the war areas under Wallenstein's control were accustomed to, and therefore paid, significantly higher taxes.[154]

The military enterpriser system, although a clear instance of the use of private force, is not a genuinely mercenary system. It is actually an early step on the way to total state control over the trade in mercenaries. Military enterprisers never recruited troops and commanded them outside the control of a sovereign, as was the case in the Hundred Years War.[155] Wallenstein and the other enterprisers worked directly for the sovereigns who hired them, and so are not pure entrepreneurial mercenaries.

Military enterprisers capable of raising and commanding entire armies were few in number, and operated only for a short period. By the 1640s, the military enterpriser system had virtually disappeared, and by the end of the Thirty Years War, it had disappeared entirely. Military enterprisers disappeared because of the political threat they posed to the sovereigns that hired them.

---

[147] Ibid. 157. [148] Redlich (1964a: 228). [149] Asch (1997: 157).
[150] Ibid. 160. [151] Mortimer (2002: 6). [152] Asch (1997: 160).
[153] Mortimer (2002: 12). [154] Asch (1997: 158). [155] Parker (1997: 176).

The Origins of the Norm against Mercenary Use 89

Military enterprisers, and especially Wallenstein, were as politically dangerous as they were militarily useful. Wallenstein's command of resources was so great that after he was fired, his refusal to supply the troops under his successor Tilly's command greatly contributed to Tilly's failure.[156] Concentrating such resources in the hands of one man could lead to the creation of a dangerous rival to the ruling powers.

Wallenstein's self-aggrandizing and occasionally bizarre behaviour suggested that he was beginning to see himself as beyond the control of any sovereign, and perhaps as a sovereign in his own right. He began to demand complete silence in his presence, and it was alleged that when arriving in new towns he ordered dogs and cats to be killed, and refused to allow the wearing of boots in his presence.[157] He had 100 horses, and 50 grooms to deal with them, all for his personal use.[158]

The Catholic Electors of the Holy Roman Empire had been concerned about Wallenstein's personal power as early as 1630, when they demanded that Ferdinand dismiss him. He was re-hired in 1631, because of military necessity, but by 1634 the concerns rose dramatically. Wallenstein's egomaniacal behaviour reached new and treacherous heights. In 1634, he demanded that his colonels swear an oath to obey him over all others; this was the last straw for the Electors, who conspired to murder him.[159] The military enterpriser system came to an end because sovereigns feared the degree of political power that flowed from the military and financial power these private generals wielded.[160]

Ultimately, just as in the other cases outlined in this chapter, military enterprisers were brought firmly under sovereign control and sovereigns themselves took the profits from raising and selling regiments. The military enterpriser system was dead by the end of the Thirty Years War.

It persisted, however, in two forms. First, the notion that individual captains and colonels could raise and equip their own regiments persisted for many years. Often, these smaller-scale enterprisers were responsible for raising troops within a state for service to the crown. Small-scale enterprisers, however, did not always fight alongside the troops they recruited. Women were often colonels (in order to make money) but entrusted the actual recruiting and fighting to a deputy.[161] In order to make additional money, captains and colonels diversified into a number of other businesses, including spinning cloth; this was so common that German infantry corporals were still known as 'spinners' in 1914.[162] Second, princes increasingly took on the role of

---

[156] Asch (1997: 160).   [157] Parker (1997: 124).   [158] Redlich (1964a: 348).
[159] Ibid.   [160] Ibid. 36, Asch (1997: 160).   [161] Asch (1997: 161).
[162] Redlich (1964b: 83).

military enterprisers themselves. Recruiting and selling military power abroad allowed a small state to finance a larger army than it would otherwise be able to afford.[163] Sovereigns replaced their subjects in the trade in force, bringing it completely under state control. The state-to-state-based exchange of troops through a variety of mechanisms became the norm in the mercenary market. The 'age of the great independent...military subcontractors faded with the Thirty Years War (1618–48)...the whole business was now officially controlled by governments'.[164] The disappearance of these two practices are discussed in Chapters 4 and 5.

The German military enterpriser system was particular to the Holy Roman Empire, short-lived, and associated with only a handful of individuals. It was not a purely mercenary system, but even so, it follows the same pattern of increasing state control identified in the other cases in this chapter. The independent or quasi-independent use of force by private individuals disappeared by the seventeenth century.

3.3. CONCLUSION: REVELATIONS

Part of the origins of the proscriptive norm against mercenary use clearly lie in the interests of those entities, whether they were states, kings, lords, or popes, who attempted to assert the exclusive right to use force within their territories. It was simply untenable to try to maintain power and control at the same time as armed bands of mercenaries roamed the country. At the same time, sovereigns sometimes needed mercenaries because of the difficulties of the feudal system, or later, the pressures of economics. As a result, a compromise was struck. Mercenaries, while out of control (and at their most dangerous) were outlawed, and when placed under the control of a 'right authority' were considered to be an unobjectionable part of an army.

It would be a mistake, however, to ignore how normative this compromise really is. The language and mechanisms used to ban mercenaries were often religious in nature. It was not merely that it was *impractical* to allow mercenaries to ravage the countryside, it was that it was inherently wrong for them to do so. Mercenaries did not have the right to fight, and threatened the medieval social order. The increasingly permanent relationships created between states and mercenaries, and states and their allies who provided mercenaries, suggest a strong relationship between the motivational, 'cause' aspect of the norm and the 'control' aspect. By bringing mercenaries under control a ruler would

[163] Ibid. 89. [164] Hobsbawm (1965: 13).

reduce the chances of bad behaviour while retaining a useful tool, and at the same time restore the social order. The divine right of kings and the belief that the nobility held its exalted social place because of God's will meant that any rule that suggested only nobles and kings could control force had moral overtones. Even if arguing that mercenaries were morally problematic because of the challenge they posed to social order was merely a cloak for the desire of sovereigns to retain the sole control over force, it is vital to recognize that this argument was couched in religious, not necessarily practical, terms. The 'effort to downscale the phenomenon of mercenarism therefore has a strong moral and legal side'.[165]

As states were bringing mercenaries under tighter control, reducing practical fears about violence and moral fears about who ought to use violence, concerns surrounding mercenary motivations remained. Political philosophers like Machiavelli and religious reformers like Zwingli were each concerned about the prevalence of mercenaries in their homeland, because their inappropriate motivation would make them inefficient. Zwingli argued that the sending state, Switzerland, would be corrupted by the sale of its young men to fight for a cause that was not Swiss. The Italian humanists feared that as hiring states, Italian city-states would be damaged by the presence of mercenaries who would prevent citizens from performing their necessary duties to the state. There were voices arguing all along during this period that mercenaries were morally dangerous because of their improper motivations.

The state had effectively stopped the use of independent mercenary companies by the sixteenth century and completely ended it after the Thirty Years War. The mercenaries remaining were no longer independent and were generally hired out from one state to another in situations of tight control and even as part of an alliance. According to the standards of the day, the medieval mercenaries incorporated into prototype standing armies, as in France, or sent on crusade, were simply no longer mercenaries as they were now under just authority and so were fighting for a just cause. Italy no longer used mercenaries, because it had placed its former mercenaries under tight control and made them literally a part of the city-states which shared its cause. In Switzerland, the Swiss mercenaries pursued the Swiss cause in a tightly controlled alliance with the French and appeared to be alliance troops rather than mercenaries. In Germany, the new principalities created with the end of the Thirty Years War raised and sold troops themselves, rather than entrusting the duty to independent military enterprisers. To put it in modern terms, we do not consider a nation that sends troops as part of an alliance agreement to be

[165] Joenniemi (1977: 189).

dealing in mercenaries. Nor do we consider small nations whose contributions to UN peacekeeping missions occur essentially for financial gain to be in the mercenary business. The first shift away from independent mercenary use occurred long before the nineteenth century.

But the story of the anti-mercenary norm did not end with the seventeenth century. The arrangements which made mercenaries 'normal' soldiers were only temporary, because by the nineteenth century ideas about what constituted a proper motivation for warfare had changed. The 'cause' aspect of the norm became extremely powerful as it became associated with the idea that war should be fought only by states, and using only their citizens. Even though the controlled exchange of foreign troops was a relatively effective practice, states considered these troops to be mercenaries because they were not motivated by the national cause, and so sought to abandon the use of foreign mercenaries. Indeed, as we see in Chapter 4, the nineteenth century changes might be better understood as a shift away from the use of foreign troops hired in another state. States had already largely stopped using mercenaries by this point.

The motivational or 'cause' and control aspects of the proscriptive norm set the stage for explaining how the proscriptive norm evolved in later years. Our 'view of mercenaries as deeply hated presences in Christian society'[166] begins in the period *before* the development of standing and national armies. To understand why citizen soldiers were considered to be more appropriate and better fighters than mercenaries requires understanding that they have been assumed to be so long before the nineteenth century. Part of the reason that it became so easy to make the transition from mercenary to standing armies is that there was already a history of preferring one's own soldiers because of a distrust of mercenaries and a belief that a native soldier's superior motivation was not only morally beneficial but would result in greater loyalty and so in more effective fighting.

While it at first seems that the idea of appropriate cause in the period outlined above is less important than the desire to control private force, it is quite significant. The idea that warriors ought to be properly motivated by an appropriate cause meant that medieval mercenaries were regarded with distaste and suspicion. The desire to control force clearly played a role in state policy during this period. Rulers were faced with practical problems caused by uncontrolled mercenaries, and sought to end these problems via a variety of mechanisms. The relative weight of each component ebbs and flows with the changes in historical context. In the nineteenth century, the idea of cause developed extraordinary strength.

[166] France (1999: 72).

Chapters 4 and 5 discuss the second shift away from mercenary use, which was based almost entirely on the 'cause' component of the norm. States began to adopt citizen armies because it was increasingly believed that mercenaries did not share the state's cause for war, and that this improper motivation would undermine the state and lead to ineffective action on the battlefield.

4

Competing Explanations for the Nineteenth-Century Shift Away from Mercenary Use

> Just as darkness was falling, I and my companions had formed a circle.... Most stayed silent, a few spoke, but no one could come up with an opinion or verdict on the day's events. Eventually, they turned to me and asked me what I thought about it, for in the past I had usually cheered them up and stimulated them with pithy epigrams; but on this occasion I just said: 'From here and today there begins a new epoch in the history of the world, and you can say you were there.'
> —Goethe, after the inconclusive Battle of Valmy in 1792 where initial Prussian gains were offset by French patriotic fervour.[1]

The years following the French Revolution led to a remarkable change in the conduct of European warfare. For the first time in at least several hundred years, states began to fight wars using their own citizens exclusively, and foreigners disappeared from the armies of Europe. The significance of this shift is clear. The stage was set for the nationalist wars of the nineteenth century and the bloody struggles of the twentieth; even today, despite monumental changes in technology and the nature of war, states still fight wars with armies composed of their citizens.[2]

What is less clear, and more interesting, is why that shift occurred. As we have seen, a huge first step away from the common use of private fighters had been taken in the control of mercenary forces. Independent military contractors with their own armies selling their services to the highest bidder or working for their own interests no longer existed. The long history of moral dislike of mercenaries, and attempts to control them, makes the nineteenth-century shift away from mercenary armies even more puzzling. On a practical level, states had successfully *controlled* the mercenary problem. The benefits

---

[1] Quoted in Blanning (1996: 78).
[2] The wars of the French Revolution were a major turning point in military history, ending a period which had begun about 1500 and marking the beginning of a period that continued until the 1980s (Palmer 1986: 95) and arguably still continues.

of using foreign soldiers persisted with few of the disadvantages caused by the presence of independent mercenary companies. States seemed to be fixing a system that was not broken.

This chapter focuses on the three existing arguments that seek to explain why, after years of success with one system, states shifted to another. The first argument is largely realist, making the case that material changes pressured states to adopt citizen armies.[3] The second argument is based more on the role of ideas, arguing that the developing relationship between states and citizens and the increasing role of neutrality in international law combined to render the use of mercenaries obsolete.[4] A third argument suggests that while ideas and material pressures are important antecedent conditions the change to a citizen army is best explained by domestic politics and path dependency.[5]

It is important for this book to be able to counter these three arguments, because all of them provide explanations that discount the existence of a norm against mercenary use as one of the influences which might have been responsible for the disappearance of mercenaries. If a plausible explanation of why citizens replaced mercenaries in the armies of Europe can be made *without* reference to the anti-mercenary norm, it would be a serious blow to the argument that a norm against mercenary use has shaped state policy towards mercenaries and so influenced opportunities available to mercenaries themselves. In explaining some of the problems with these three approaches, this chapter sets the stage for the next, which examines the shift away from mercenary use in America, France, Prussia, and Great Britain, and the argument that for citizen armies to become more popular, the use of mercenaries had to become less popular. Chapter 5 argues that the norm against mercenary use played a large role in influencing states to adopt citizen armies, and ideas about the moral superiority of citizen soldiers persuaded states to make the change in the first place.

This chapter argues that all three of the current explanations of the shift away from mercenary use share a common problem: the inability to explain why the option of a citizen army was so much more appealing than a mercenary force. Because none of these explanations focuses on the norm against mercenary use, or the related norm of citizen duty to the state, none can provide a compelling explanation of why a citizen army was so attractive to the leaders of Europe. In this chapter, I address each of the three alternative explanations for the decision to set aside mercenaries outlined above. The first section examines the realist explanation; the second section focuses on the explanation offered by Avant; and the third section considers the argument

---

[3] Posen (1993) most clearly identifies his position as realist. McNeill (1982) relies heavily on material pressures in explaining change.
[4] Thomson (1994).   [5] Avant (2000).

proposed by Thomson. The fourth section concludes by proposing that all of these explanations fail to explain why citizen soldiers became such an appealing alternative, and mercenaries lost their appeal. It sets the stage for Chapter 5 by arguing that it is not possible to understand why states adopted citizen armies without understanding two norms: the anti-mercenary norm and the norm that the use of citizens in national armies was moral.

4.1. MATERIALIST OR REALIST EXPLANATIONS OF THE SHIFT AWAY FROM MERCENARY USE

Realist and materialist explanations of the decision to adopt citizen armies argue that material changes, like population growth, and military changes, like new tactics, produced pressures best responded to by the creation of a citizen army. Increases in population meant that states had enough citizens to create large armies, and enough wealth to keep them supplied.[6] Population growth, social dislocation, and urbanization meant that the devil was finding predatory work for idle hands, and incorporating troublemakers into the army was one solution to the problem.[7]

As armies became larger, and military tactics changed, the question of how to keep troops motivated became more important. Eighteenth-century armies containing mercenaries had been held together by strict discipline. Only 'iron rule could make into a unified force men who had no cohesion in themselves' and rulers and aristocrats did not expect to find appropriate moral qualities for fighting, like courage, loyalty, group spirit, and independence in the lower classes which composed the bulk of the army.[8]

Realists argue that patriotic motivation became more useful around the French Revolution because of changes in the nature of war. War increasingly required troops who could be trusted to make independent decisions or travel away from the group, and so strict discipline on its own was no longer as useful to keep troops in order. After 1740, military thought encouraged the use of light troops and skirmishers,[9] used to harass enemy armies operating mainly under their own initiative and often required to forage for their own supplies. Commanders had to trust that these troops would not desert while operating far from the main body of the army, and their inability to do so constrained the conduct of war.[10] Citizen armies, motivated by more than the desire for

---
[6] Posen (1993: 83). [7] McNeill (1982: 145–6). [8] Palmer (1986: 93).
[9] Starkey (2003: 53).
[10] Rothenberg (1977: 14); Posen (1993: 93). On territorial expansion see Avant (2000: 45).

pay, would arguably be less likely to become demoralized.[11] Patriotism could keep troops cohesive while allowing them to be more independent.

Once a state had created a mass army, Posen argues that patriotically motivated citizen soldiers were vital to sustain it. A large army is successful because it can maintain its size despite the loss of troops, but replacement soldiers must be willing to fight and care about winning, and must be able to fit in quickly, making political motivation a key element of the mass army.[12]

The realist or materialist argument points out that the combined pressures of the desire for a larger army with more independent soldiers capable of functioning farther from home and at the end of long supply lines forced states to adopt citizen-based armies. Changes in material factors like technology would bring states into conflict with each other, and force the less technologically developed or organized state to adopt the tactics of the more developed, or face defeat.[13] States could not ignore this systemic pressure without failing; successful states adopted a citizen army and others had to follow suit. The 'mass army is a successful practice from the point of view of state survival in international politics'.[14]

Problems with the Realist/Materialist Approach

There are four problems with a realist explanation of the shift to citizen armies in the nineteenth century. First, the pressure of population growth may not have been as significant as realists argue it was, and contemporary practice did not suggest that a mass army was the best response either to population growth or a change in tactics. Second, military necessity cannot explain the different times at which states adopted a citizen army. Third, systemic pressures did not lead states to favour mass armies staffed by citizens. It was by no means obvious that a citizen army *was* a successful model, and so by no means clear that states should follow this practice to avoid failure themselves. Fourth, the kind of nationalism that would be useful on the battlefield did not really exist prior to the creation of a citizen army, so states were taking a leap of faith that citizens would suddenly behave patriotically while at war.

The Pressure of Population Growth was Less Significant than Realists Argue

Despite significant population growth in the eighteenth century, the proportion of the population serving in the military between 1670 and 1790 was

---

[11] Palmer (1986: 94).   [12] Posen (1993: 83).   [13] McNeill (1982: viii).
[14] Posen (1993: 83).

similar to and often greater than that of the nineteenth century, and remained so until the mobilization of reserves in 1914.[15] The change in recruiting created by the *levée en masse* was neither an abrupt nor a revolutionary increase in numbers, as armies had steadily increased in size during the sixteenth and seventeenth centuries[16] and particularly dramatically in the period 1660–1720, especially between 1680 and 1710.[17] In 1768, before the transition to citizen soldiers, the French army was the largest army on French soil since Imperial Rome, which pressured other European states to similarly increase the size of their forces.[18]

The argument that states favoured mass armies, which would in turn require citizen mobilization, also falls down when contemporary practice is examined. Guibert was opposed to the idea of a large army, believing that good generals would simply be held back by large numbers and that size was an indicator of weak authority.[19] Paret argues that Guibert's inability to understand the problems with the small armies of the day was typical of eighteenth-century theorists.[20] Montesquieu shared Guibert's views about the size of European armies, arguing that 'a new disease has spread across Europe; it has afflicted our princes and made them keep a number of troops' and damaged economies. The ideal army for Montesquieu was not a mass army but a small militia.[21] Enhancing the size of the army was not necessarily the obvious response to the demands of warfare and the increase in population growth.

The Napoleonic Wars demonstrated that mass armies 'outgrew their nervous systems'[22] and were less effective than the smaller strike forces used in Lodi, Marengo, and Austerlitz.[23] Large forces came with large problems of supply, training and leadership, and without effective structures, large numbers on their own were ineffective.[24] After Waterloo, some of Napoleon's marshals argued for 'developing a quality army, smaller than its predecessors but susceptible to the kind of precise operational control that would avoid the costly gridlock characteristic of modern large-scale battles'.[25] Even if states believed reform to be necessary, it did not need to take the form of a citizen army.

The largest difficulty with the argument that states wanted mass armies is that after the Napoleonic Wars concluded, the states of Europe returned to small armies which did not require mass mobilization, as will be argued below.

---

[15] Black (1994: 221). [16] Guerlac (1986: 64). [17] Black (1994: 9).
[18] Ibid. 94. [19] Palmer (1986: 109). [20] Paret (1992: 58).
[21] Montesquieu ([1748] 1989: 224). On the militia see n.14.
[22] Showalter (2002: 32–3). [23] Ibid. 32–3. [24] Black (1994: 62).
[25] Showalter (2002: 33).

The desire to use citizens, then, cannot have been because of the pressures of surplus population or the desire to have a mass army.

The Timing of the Adoption of Citizen Armies Is Not Explained by Systemic Pressure

The realist position suggests that states will adopt a citizen army when placed under pressure by the international system. Posen argues that states will change to a citizen army when they have been defeated by, or expect to meet, one on the battlefield.[26] But states adopted conscription without military necessity as an impetus, and at remarkably different times. Spain adopted conscription in 1704 and abandoned it as unworkable by 1766.[27] The French shifted towards a citizen army in 1790, *before they had been defeated*, but the British did not stop using foreigners until the 1860s.[28] If the pressures in the system were pushing states towards adopting citizen armies, why did some states take so much longer than others?

One possible realist response is that Britain's powerful status in the system, combined with her isolation, allowed her to avoid the pressure to convert to a citizen army for longer.[29] However, the simple fact of the matter is that the British multinational mercenary army was not a failure, and so the pressure which was allegedly coming from the international system was absent. Not until the Crimea did the British suffer a military setback, and it is hard to argue that this setback was the result of mercenary action, as the mercenaries recruited for the conflict had not even arrived by the time the war ended. The problems of the Crimea indicated difficulties with the British method of *recruitment*, but there was nothing to indicate that the solution should be the wholesale abandonment of foreign troops.

The Prussian adoption of a citizen army cannot be explained with reference to systemic factors. French forces were not the only successful model to copy; and, in fact, had been defeated by Wellington's old-style multinational force. Neither was Prussia defeated by a purely citizen-based military. In 1805–7, no fewer than a quarter of Napoleon's troops were foreign, brought in from the territories which France occupied, including Belgians, Germans, Italians, and

---

[26] Posen (1993: 87).   [27] Black (1994: 222).

[28] While the use of foreigners in Britain persisted, in the form of the Gurkhas and Indian sepoys, they were considered to be part of the Empire and not foreign in the same way as the mercenaries used previously. See Chapter 4 for further explanation.

[29] Paret points out that Britain's size, alliances, naval power, and operational requirements allowed her to continue using an eighteenth-century-style force (Paret 1986: 136).

Poles,[30] and this was the army that smashed Prussia at Jena and Auerstädt. So, why would Prussia adopt a citizen army?[31]

Citizen Armies Were Not Necessarily the Best Response to Systemic Pressure

It is by no means clear that a citizen force was the obvious solution to the pressures of the eighteenth century, and nor was it obvious that a citizen army was the best solution and so the route to success in the international system. There are two specific problems with the argument that systemic and material pressures would have influenced states to adopt a citizen army. First, the realist model leaves unexplained the fact that beliefs about citizens would have had to change before a citizen army could be adopted. Second, it was not obvious that citizen armies were superior to the multinational, mercenary-based forces they replaced, and nor did the outcome of the wars after the French Revolution dictate that any reforms should take the shape of a citizen army.[32] The realist explanation's plausibility rests on the fact that states will imitate a successful model. Why states should want to imitate an unsuccessful model, or adopt an untested one, is not straightforward.

Contemporary observers were not convinced that citizens were superior. Guibert, who had argued for a citizen army in his 1772 *Essai général de la tactique*, had reversed his position seven years later in *Défense du système de guerre moderne*. In *Défense*, Guibert insisted that the citizen armies like those of the Americans during the American Revolution could never fight against professionals, and that that the American success had to do with British failures, as opposed to the nature of American troops.[33] This was not an unusual position; Frederick the Great 'would have been the last to seek new ideas on the war in the American campaigns. The political incompetence of the British government impressed him more strongly than the military abilities of the colonists'.[34] In his final book, *De la force publique*, Guibert argued that a citizen army is impossible as the differences between what makes a civilian and what makes a soldier are insuperable.[35]

Citizens were not perceived to be better behaved than their mercenary counterparts. Frederick the Great argued that his army was 'for the most part composed of the dregs of society—sluggards, rakes, debauchees, rioters, undutiful sons, and the like, who have as little attachment to their masters or

---

[30] Addington (1994: 27–8).
[31] Avant offers one explanation, which is addressed in the next section.
[32] This latter point is central to Avant's argument and is addressed in depth in the next section.
[33] Palmer (1986: 107, 111). [34] Paret (1966: 43). [35] Paret (1992: 58).

concern about them as do foreigners'.³⁶ As late as the mid-nineteenth century Austrian officers called their enlisted men 'an army of pigs'.³⁷ It is hard to imagine that such profound disrespect for citizen soldiers coexisted with a belief in their superiority. For a citizen army to be adopted, these beliefs would have to change.

Changes in the nature of war did not necessarily favour the citizen over the professional. Even if warfare did require a better disciplined, more loyal soldier than it had previously, it is far from clear that a civilian would be either disciplined or loyal. In fact, it was commonly argued that effective troops were created by training and experience; 'professionalism would trump patriotism'³⁸ on the battlefield. Even the American revolutionaries were concerned about the professionalism and expertise of British mercenaries.³⁹

The problems of the eighteenth-century army were not limited to mercenary soldiers. Desertion, for example, was rife in all armies and among all types of troops. No matter the nature of the army, discipline was seen to be the only solution.⁴⁰ Tight discipline was a normal part of eighteenth-century armies, and contemporaries regarded it as desirable. Adam Smith puzzled over the behaviour of 800 Prussian soldiers, who bravely held off several thousand Austrian troops for a whole day only to become cowardly and run away at night. Smith believed that their apparent courage could not be based on 'a principle of honour, nor love to their country, nor a regard to their officers, for these still would have detained them; it was nothing but the dread of their officers, who were hanging...over their heads, and whom they durst not disobey. This...shows the governableness of our nature and may also shew how much that manly courage we so much boast of depends upon external circumstances'.⁴¹

Even entirely citizen armies struggled with desertion. George Washington continued with practices common in the British army, such as running the gauntlet and the liberal use of the lash, because he could see no other way to discipline his troops—despite their strong patriotic motivation.⁴² The thing that would save an army from desertion was not bravery or patriotism, but discipline. Its use in all types of armies undermines the argument that those including mercenaries required an unusual level of discipline.

French citizen armies were also affected by cowardice and desertion. Early French citizen troops panicked because of lack of training. In 1792, the French General Dillon, who foresaw the problems of poor training, was killed by his

---

³⁶ Quoted in Cohen (1985: 45).   ³⁷ Showalter (2002: 39).
³⁸ Ibid. 34.   ³⁹ See Chapter 5.   ⁴⁰ Black (1994: 226).
⁴¹ Smith ([1766] 1978: 543). As pointed out below, this is especially remarkable considering Smith believed citizen armies to be superior to mercenary forces.
⁴² Royster (1979: 79).

own troops, who shouted, ' "we are betrayed" and "every man for himself!" as they fled in utter rout'.[43] The immediate impact of the French Revolution was to triple the rate of desertion during the first half of 1789; by the end of 1790 the regular army of 130,000 had lost 20,000 men.[44] Many of these soldiers were volunteers in the purest sense, and had responded out of a sense of duty rather than because of conscription, which was not introduced in France until 1793. Desertion, then, could have more to do with inexperience and poor training than with motivation and the type of soldier used.

Far from possessing unbridled national enthusiasm which could be embodied in military service, citizens avoided it wherever possible. A purely volunteer army was impossible to achieve, even in revolutionary France, which ultimately had to opt for conscription. Paret points out that the myth of the *levée en masse* is that it expressed the people's defence of revolutionary France when it had only been achieved by political skill[45] and conscription. The *levée en masse* allowed men with disabilities and married men to stay home, and as a result there were numerous marriages and mutilations.[46] By 1810, Napoleon faced a situation where 80 per cent of the annual quota failed to respond to conscription and 40,000 troops were devoted to seeking out the missing conscripts.[47]

All of the citizen armies created in Prussia, Great Britain, Russia, and France retained the popular option for citizens to buy themselves out of service in one way or another, and most who could afford to do so did. In Prussia, only 12 per cent of the army of 1813 were middle class,[48] indicating the number using various forms of exemptions to avoid service. In Britain, militia insurance allowed for the purchase of a substitute.[49] Substitution only disappeared in France in 1905,[50] and in Prussia preferential class treatment persisted until the First World War,[51] demonstrating that leaving the door open for civilians to avoid military service guaranteed its use. 'Everywhere', writes Paret, 'men were alike in rejecting the ethical imperative of military service that was held out to them by party propagandists, army reformers, and political theorists'.[52] It must have been hard to believe that a groundswell of popular and patriotic enthusiasm would fill armies and create effective soldiers when citizens were so keen to avoid fighting.

Not every observer of the late eighteenth century assumed that citizens, by virtue of superior motivation and education, would be more easily able to take the initiative and therefore function as more effective skirmishing troops. If the British found a model for the skirmishing light infantryman in the

---

[43] Lynn (1984: 186).   [44] Gooch (1980: 27).   [45] Paret (1992: 63).
[46] Schama (1989: 762).   [47] Gooch (1980: 36).   [48] Paret (1992: 71).
[49] Ibid. 44.   [50] Cohen (1985: 145).   [51] Paret (1992: 72).   [52] Ibid. 44.

Revolutionary Wars, it was 'not the American rifleman but the Hessian Jäger. Light infantry tactics were not for amateurs. They required a higher training and were an even truer discipline than the tactics of the line. These qualities were found at their best, not in free Americans, but in the docile subjects of a German despot'.[53] French success in the area of light infantry during the French Revolutionary and Napoleonic Wars cannot be attributed entirely to the increased trustworthiness of the citizen soldier; in fact, the French success in skirmishing was a happy accident resulting from poor training, which caused conventional formations to break up, while superior numbers and mobility obviated the need for conventional tactics and allowed for light infantry movement.[54] Light infantry troops, then, could be created rather than born; and given the tradition of using foreigners as elite troops,[55] their use was not necessarily a reason why citizens would need to replace foreigners.

The first French Revolutionary armies did not use patriotism to consistently successful effect against their *ancien régime* opponents. There was no reason to assume that patriotically motivated armies would yield superior results. The initial response of many states was to assume that wholesale change was not necessary, and this belief was reinforced by the fact that the French armies were often defeated.[56]

Nationalism, revolutionary spirit, and military success did not always go hand in hand.[57] T. C. W. Blanning makes a strong case against the idea that the French army relied on patriotism for their successes. On the occasions where the French were defeated, 'it would be absurd to suppose that when the citizen-soldiers were defeated they were somehow having an off-day and were not feeling very revolutionary'.[58] Just as French patriotism was not responsible for France's successes or losses, lack of patriotism cannot explain why their opponents were successful. The soldiers France faced were 'capable of feats of heroism, both individual and collective, which cannot be explained simply in terms of iron discipline making the soldiers fear their officers more than the enemy. Two awful possibilities loom: either that ideological commitment had little to do with fighting effectiveness or that the values of the old regime were just as powerful motivators as the ideals of the Revolution'.[59]

Blanning argues that when the two sides met on the battlefield, success was determined by who marshalled the largest numbers of troops, and that the total mobilization of French society ultimately made it easier to have a mass army.[60] But, as we will see, while other states in Europe adopted a citizen army,

---

[53] Mackesy (1984: 198). [54] Ibid. 209. [55] Rothenberg (1977: 12).
[56] Paret (1986: 135). [57] Cohen (1985: 44). [58] Blanning (1996: 119).
[59] Ibid. [60] Ibid. 120–1.

they did not adopt a revolutionary one and nor did they adopt the French system of complete social mobilization.

The defeats of citizen armies by multinational opponents provided further disincentive to adopt a citizen army. Citizen armies were not ultimately successful in the Napoleonic Wars. In fact, Wellington's victorious British army was notoriously multinational, and in April 1813, had 75,000 troops, 26,000 of whom were Portuguese, 5,000 were German, and 1,000 French.[61] Later armies also relied on foreign troops successfully. In Spain, the British Legion recruited to assist the Queen Regent's armies during the Carlist wars 'may be regarded as having made a small but definite contribution' to the ultimate success of their side.[62]

A belief that citizens were not necessarily worthy, evidence that problems existed in citizen armies, an understanding that good troops were created by training and professionalism rather than motivation, and the mixed record of civilian army success combine to demonstrate that a citizen army was not the obvious solution to systemic pressure, and not a clear option for states seeking military reform.

Nationalism was Created by Citizen Armies; Citizen Armies Did Not Arise from Nationalism

The realist approach fails to consider that motivated soldiers were not floating around Europe merely waiting to be incorporated into citizen armies, which would take advantage of their national sentiment to achieve great victories on the battlefield. The 'great majority of Englishmen saw no difficulty in reconciling national awareness and national pride with a profound distaste for military service'.[63] In eighteenth-century France the situation was similar, with nationalism 'unaccompanied by a sense of general military obligation among Frenchmen' who 'resisted this duty toward the greater, abstract whole of the French state'.[64] Prussia, whose army became the model for Europe in the mid-nineteenth century was in the eighteenth the 'least animated by the spirit in its people'.[65] Conscription did not reflect 'attitudes already widely held in 1793 or 1814—loyalty to a cause, hatred of the foreigner, patriotism—conscription helped create and diffuse these attitudes. It constitutes one of several channels through which ideas, feelings and energies flow to give substance to the new concept of the state and eventually to nationalism'.[66] In France, the men raised by the *levée en masse*, 'as long as they remained civilians, protected by the comfortable traditions of their community, the Revolution had little means

---

[61] Cohen (1985: 53).   [62] Holt (1969: 167).   [63] Paret (1992: 44).
[64] Ibid. 42.   [65] Palmer (1986: 96).   [66] Paret (1992: 73).

of educating them in citizenship, of installing newfangled notions of civic obligation'; the army was necessary for this type of education.[67] Patriotism alone did not make effective troops. Rather, it had to be channelled into a useful form.

Posen recognizes that the army was the source of nationalist feeling, and argues that preparations for war incubated nationalist tendencies and reinforced them among the people.[68] But an important question remains: how did Europe's leaders know that creating a mass army would create nationalism, a school for the nation? To abandon an effective system in favour of an untested one requires confidence.

4.2. AVANT: DOMESTIC POLITICS, PATH DEPENDENCY, AND THE TRANSITION FROM A MERCENARY TO A CIVILIAN ARMY

Deborah Avant[69] argues that the decision to use citizens as soldiers can only be understood with reference to the role of Enlightenment ideas, domestic politics in France, Prussia, and Britain, and the logic of path dependency. After an exogenous shock, such as a military defeat, differences in the nature of domestic politics influenced whether or not a state would adopt the Enlightenment ideal of civilian service. In particular, states with a strong conservative belief in the status quo of military organization were less open to new ideas about citizen armies, and states without such a consensus had room to debate the citizen alternative. This explains why Prussia, with divided politics, was the first to adopt the citizen army on a large scale, and Britain, with a strongly united conservative position on the military, was the last.

Once the citizen army was adopted by one state, the logic of path dependency took hold. Path dependency tells 'us that an initial outcome, even if it is only one of many potentially successful possibilities, is privileged in subsequent interactions' in part due to sunk costs.[70] Institutions, like the citizen army, 'which have met with success (even by sheer luck or accident) become a "past practice" and are thus more likely to become models for reformers in other countries'.[71] The ultimately successful Prussian adoption of a civilian-based mass army after the Napoleonic Wars set the standard for other states, influencing them to also adopt a citizen army, even if it was not the only available option. Avant argues that a small, professional army that

---

[67] Forrest (1990: 88).   [68] Posen (1993: 81).   [69] Avant (2000: 42–3).
[70] Ibid. 51.   [71] Ibid. 51–2.

would not necessarily preclude the use of mercenaries was compatible with some Enlightenment ideas and presented an equally plausible choice for states in the nineteenth century.[72] Avant rejects the realist approach as well as the approach taken by Thomson, which is discussed in the next section, on the basis that neither adequately explains the timing of the decision to stop using mercenaries.[73]

Difficulties with Avant's Approach

Avant's discussion of the decision to stop using foreign troops fails to give sufficient weight to the complex role that norms can play. She limits the role of norms acting on states in the nineteenth century to norms associated with the Enlightenment, and in particular rationality and a new relationship between state and citizen, where each was responsible to the other and states were responsible for the actions of their citizens abroad.[74] While Avant does recognize that norms can play a role,[75] she sees them only as antecedent conditions.

Assuming that Enlightenment norms were the only important norms during this period creates two problems in Avant's analysis, which I address in turn. First, Avant sees Enlightenment norms as universal, and does not recognize that they manifested themselves differently in different states. She also does not discuss the presence of other norms which preceded but were reinforced by the Enlightenment, like the anti-mercenary norm. Second, Avant does not take into account that path dependency is an inherently normative process. I argue that neglecting the role of norms in path dependency makes it difficult to explain the logic of how a particular path becomes the standard and remains appealing to other actors.

Enlightenment Norms were neither Universal nor the only Important Norms

Avant implicitly assumes that policies based on Enlightenment ideas were similar across Europe. In fact, there was significant variation in how the relationship between citizen and state was conceived. She writes, 'many people (myself included) are interested in explaining why Britain—the dominant state in many ways and far more liberal than Prussia—lagged behind others in institutionalizing liberalizing reforms in its army'.[76] A deeper analysis of normative factors reveals, as we will see, that Prussian reconfiguration of the

[72] Ibid. 42. [73] Ibid. 65, n. 109 and 48, n. 31. [74] Ibid. 45. [75] Ibid. 41.
[76] Ibid. 48 n. 31.

relationship between the citizen and the state did not take a liberal form, and moreover, that Britain's liberal conception of the same relationship actually prevented 'liberalizing' reforms.[77] A more thorough discussion of normative factors would have allowed the recognition that Enlightenment ideas were neither universally shared nor implemented in the same way in different states.

While the development of Enlightenment thinking on the social contract and the relationship between the state and the citizen are undoubtedly important for understanding how reformers came to advocate abandoning the use of foreign troops, these beliefs existed alongside far more explicitly moral beliefs about the appropriate motive for fighting. Enlightenment thinking reinforced an existing dislike of foreign troops on moral grounds, which in terms of political thought went as far back as Machiavelli, if not to the teachings of the medieval Christian church. Europeans were becoming increasingly, and explicitly, uncomfortable with the morality of using foreign troops to fight wars.[78]

Avant dismisses the importance of motive, pointing out that in reality French troops were not necessarily more motivated than the armies they faced.[79] But if motive was not responsible for the French victories, why did people assume it was? Why did the myth about the *levée en masse* become so compelling, and how did confidence in citizen soldiers result? The Enlightenment ideas to which Avant refers say very little about motivation. Rationality, natural law, and human rights were unquestionably influential in shaping the direction of military reform in the nineteenth century.[80] These aspects alone, however, do not explain why it was that the superior *motivation* of citizen soldiers was so valued by military leaders, even when evidence suggested that citizens might not be motivated at all. We must understand why, given all the evidence to the contrary, much of which Avant cites, Prussian reformers were convinced of the merits of a citizen army. The moral appeal of these fighters was as great for Prussian reformers as was its practical appeal. The idea of a patriotically motivated force was appealing *on its own merits*, regardless of the success that force might have on the battlefield.

Path Dependency Depends on Norms

Avant does not recognize that understanding the logic of path dependency itself requires an explanation of how norms are adopted and spread. Why does having a citizen army seem to have precluded a return to a mercenary army, even though post-Napoleonic leaders did not trust their citizens?

---

[77] See Chapter 5.   [78] See Chapter 5.   [79] Avant (2000: 55).
[80] Starkey (2003: ch. 2).

Why did states follow France's, and then Prussia's, lead? As Avant points out, 'The Prussian successes, for whatever reason, made the citizen army the international model'.[81] But surely this 'whatever reason' is crucial to explain why states with successful multinational armies, like Britain, adopted the Prussian system rather than reforming in a different direction as well as why the citizen option was victorious over the evidence and over other alternatives. For example, why did the Prussians interpret 'the French victories at Auerstädt and Jena as a testament to the value of citizen soldiers rather than the consequence of poor leadership or bad strategy'?[82] If reformers won the struggle over conservatives, how were they able to do so over the evidence that citizens were not responsible for the French victories?[83]

Even if the argument that European states adopted the citizen army because of path dependency is true, the addition of normative influence provides a far more thorough explanation of the mechanism of path dependency. Simply stating that 'a particular way of doing things may become the commonsensical starting point and may be considered best even though other equally good (or better) solutions are possible'[84] does not explain why states reject the other equally good or better solutions. Surely the fact that a particular way of doing things is *first* does not explain why it has been adopted.

Part of the answer might lie in the role of norms. If a state adopts a particular path, and that path is perceived by other states as successful, then the dynamic becomes normative. Successful states, the logic works, have citizen armies; therefore, to be considered a successful state, our state must also adopt a citizen army. The identity of 'successful state' begins to include the component of 'citizen army' regardless if in reality citizen armies are the most successful or if there are other alternatives. Gong's argument about the standard of civilization can be applied here. To be considered civilized states had to adopt a particular set of rules and institutions.[85] In the increasingly militaristic and nationalistic world of the late nineteenth century, the identity of 'great power' was associated with a citizen army. Prussia's military successes meant that to be taken seriously as contenders on the European stage, states had to adopt the Prussian model. The role of norms provides a more profound explanation for how path dependency works than merely stating that the first option somehow becomes the best, regardless of the competition. The first option can become the best if it is seen as a component of a particularly desirable identity.

---

[81] Avant (2000: 43). [82] Ibid. 59.
[83] Avant herself illustrates the ways in which the Prussian defeat had little do with the superiority of the French citizen army (ibid. 47).
[84] Ibid. 52. [85] Gong (1984).

The idea that 'sunk costs' explain why states are reluctant to reverse changes can also be better explained on normative grounds. While Avant recognizes that sunk costs can be cognitive, she does not delve into how a cognitive, or a normative, cost might make it difficult for states to reverse course. I will argue below that part of the 'sunk cost' in adopting a citizen army is that the norms that attend it are utterly incompatible with any other sort of fighter. Once patriotism is used to remind citizens of their duty to fight and the army becomes the 'school for the nation', the belief that only citizens can fight for the state becomes more widely spread and ultimately impossible to reverse unless the citizen duty argument is abandoned entirely.

Another problem with Avant's depiction of path dependency is that without understanding the role of norms, it is hard to understand why states initially preferred mercenaries. As we have seen, to choose a citizen army was a leap of faith. Avant never explains why the option of a citizen army was so attractive, and why it could become the international model. This is problematic because for Avant's argument to work the attractions of a citizen army had to be powerful enough that they would outweigh the lack of evidence that they were successful, counteract the prevalent belief that citizens were unreliable and that arming them could be dangerous, overcome the fact that replacing the military system was a socially and politically costly decision[86] and swing support away from the option Avant suggests was plausible and possible: the small professional army, which could have contained mercenaries.

Moreover, Avant never explains why the first states to adopt a civilian army did so. Why did the American colonists and the French revolutionaries choose to use citizens in the first place? An inability to explain the first step in the path all states eventually followed is a significant problem in explaining military change.

Why States Did Not Take Other Paths

Understanding the role norms play in path dependency allows us to understand why once states chose the path they did, it foreclosed the option of other paths or a return to the old system. A crucial component of Avant's argument about path dependency is that there was another path for states to take. Domestic 'conditions in key states influenced the selection of citizen armies (which precluded the use of mercenaries) rather than small professional forces (which did not preclude the use of mercenaries)'.[87] Why was the option of a small, professional army, which could have incorporated mercenaries, and which was 'quite consistent with the portion of Enlightenment ideas focused

[86] Paret (1986: 135). [87] Avant (2000: 43)

on rationality'[88] not adopted? States could have returned to the *status quo ante* and used mercenaries once more. The claim that domestic politics, in particular the absence of a dominant conservative lobby advocating the status quo, does not go far enough to explain the shift.

One aspect of the shift away from mercenary use which Avant's discussion of domestic politics cannot explain is that the use of foreign officers, who were often a critical part of military victories and in some cases military reformers in their adopted states, did not continue. Even if all the worst fears about mercenary members of the rank and file were true, surely these fears could not apply to the officer class. Many of the officers making military reform decisions were foreign themselves. Scharnhorst, one of the leading lights of Prussian military reform, was from Hanover and served in Saxony before ultimately serving in Prussia.[89] General Yorck, a Prussian, served in the Dutch army and gained expertise from his international adventures which greatly added to his cachet.[90] Gneisenau, another Prussian reformer, had fought in Canada.[91] Napoleon installed Bernadotte as King of Sweden and he managed to keep the job, even fighting against his mentor.[92] Baron Rottenberg, a Prussian, was a crucial element of Wellington's army.[93] The French minister of war, Narbonne, attempted to enlist the Duke of Brunswick, a bold plan considering the German Duke had just led the Allied army against the French.[94] His foreignness presented no obstacle for the revolutionaries.

Given the fact that so many of the international figures around the time of the Napoleonic War either had valuable international experience or were actually foreign, and most made an effective contribution, we must consider why this useful aspect of foreign service was abandoned. In an era when military genius was prized, states no longer hired the best from abroad.

Another difficulty with Avant's argument stems from the fact that states *did* return to the use of small, professional forces that she argues could have accommodated foreigners after the Napoleonic period. With the exception of Prussia, 'continental European powers... returned to the *armée de métier*, the long-service, professional army, after 1815. Most of these armies were somewhat like those of the pre-1789 era, though more national in character'.[95] Though the 'methods by which armies were raised underwent some changes, their fundamental nature was not transformed either by the French Revolution or by the wars that followed it.'[96] In France after Napoleon, the Bourbons,

---

[88] Ibid. 46.   [89] Kitchen (1975: 37).   [90] Paret (1966: 48–51).
[91] Ibid. 43, Dupuy (1977: 21).   [92] Rothenberg (1977: 131).
[93] Paret (1966: 205).   [94] Blanning (1996: 63).
[95] Addington (1994: 44). Even the Prussian army arguably returned to the old system, as Chapter 5 argues.
[96] van Creveld (1991: 38).

Orleanists, and Bonapartists all had severe reservations about the concept of a 'nation in arms'.[97] Despite 'the new power that revolutionary idealism and the administrative implementation of liberty and equality had conferred upon the French between 1792 and 1815', writes McNeill, 'the rulers and military men of Europe clearly and emphatically preferred the security of old routines. Consequently, the traditions and patterns of Old Regime armies and navies survived the storm of the revolutionary years relatively intact'.[98]

But the militaries of the *ancien régime* did not survive intact; they survived with one essential difference: they were no longer staffed by foreigners in France and in Prussia. If security and sameness were valued above novelty and difference, why was there no return to the familiar mercenary soldier in Europe? Avant herself recognizes this and argues that professional armies could have remained open to mercenaries.[99] But these armies were *closed* to mercenaries, and even with domestic agreement about a return to the old system, they remained closed. The question ought not to be, 'could mercenaries have been incorporated in the armies of Europe after 1815' but rather '*why* were mercenaries not incorporated?'.

4.3. THOMSON: IDEAS CAN EXPLAIN THE SHIFT AWAY FROM MERCENARY USE

Thomson provides a third explanation for the shift away from mercenary use in the nineteenth century. She argues that norms, in particular the norm of neutrality, explain why states adopted citizen armies. The combination of two normative changes led to the disappearance of mercenary use. A new relationship between citizen and state, whereby each had responsibilities to the other, had appeared at the same time as the growth of the concept of neutrality in international law. The growth of neutrality forced states to take further responsibility for their citizens' actions abroad, because a citizen fighting in a war in which his home state was neutral could in theory draw the state into conflict. The question became, 'could a state claim neutrality in a particular armed conflict while people within its jurisdiction chose to serve in the armed forces of one of the belligerents?'.[100] Thus, changes in international law allowed states to enhance control over their citizens, and combined to encourage states to eliminate the practice of using foreign soldiers in their armies.[101]

[97] Showalter (2002: 33).   [98] McNeill (1982: 220).   [99] Avant (2000: 45).
[100] Thomson (1994: 55).   [101] See Ibid. Chapter 4.

Mercenaries disappeared from the international system because once states began to control their citizens, there were fewer and fewer candidates for mercenary recruitment. As 'more and more states place restrictions on foreign military service, it becomes increasingly difficult for a state to simply buy an army from the international system'.[102] In essence, the supply of mercenaries dried up.[103]

Problems with Thomson's Approach

There are three central problems with Thomson's argument. First, there are difficulties associated with making an argument about the disappearance of mercenaries based on supply, including an inability to explain some inconsistencies in the timing of when states stopped using foreign troops. Second, there are problems with the neutrality argument, some of which Thomson herself recognizes, and others of which reside in the absence of evidence and the timing and substance of neutrality legislation. Third, there are problems with the argument that states sought to control their citizens and that the disappearance of mercenaries was an unintended effect of this decision.

A Supply-Based Argument Explains the Behaviour of Selling States but Not Necessarily that of Buying States

The crux of the problem with Thomson's supply-based argument is that it only recognizes one of *two* ways states consciously shifted away from mercenary use. One way, which Thomson identifies, was for states to restrict the movements of their own citizens and prevent either recruitment for foreign wars on domestic soil or, in some cases, going abroad to enlist in another state's forces. The second way was for states to decide to stop hiring foreigners themselves, and rather insist on exclusively recruiting their citizens for military service. A large part of the story about why states abandoned the use of mercenaries and adopted citizen soldiers stems from the states who bought mercenaries in the international system, not the states that sold them.

Thomson argues that the supply of mercenaries dwindled and eventually disappeared as a result of restrictions on foreign recruitment and enlistment. For Thomson to be right, 'we should see countries trying to buy mercenaries and failing; but there is little evidence of this phenomenon'.[104]

---
[102] Ibid. 84.
[103] Avant also recognizes that Thomson's argument focuses on questions of supply (Avant 2000: 67 n. 112).
[104] Ibid.

In fact, both supply of and demand for mercenaries dwindled in the nineteenth century. While Thomson might be right about the reasons for the decline in supply, she does not entirely explain the change in state demand. Even if supply was restricted and the price of mercenaries went up, it remains difficult for Thomson to explain why states simply no longer seemed interested in hiring mercenaries in the first place. States went from being enthusiastic employers of foreigners to employers actively seeking to avoid foreign troops in the space of less than 100 years.

States had moved to restrict hiring foreigners at totally different rates from their decision to prevent their own citizens from fighting for other states. France no longer hired foreigners long before the enactment of foreign recruitment legislation. Prussia never adopted such legislation despite having stopped hiring foreigners by 1815. And Britain passed foreign enlistment legislation in 1819, long before the government decided to stop hiring mercenaries. Moreover, neither Britain nor America was a source of mercenary recruitment, and yet both enacted neutrality legislation early on. Moves to restrict citizens, which should have had the effect of reducing the number of mercenaries, appear to be chronologically disconnected from the times when states stopped hiring mercenaries. The question of demand (state interest in using foreigners) and supply (states preventing their own citizens from becoming mercenaries) are not as connected as Thomson argues.[105]

Thomson does not explain why states were no longer interested in hiring foreign soldiers to fight in their armies. This is, in part, because she argues that the practice of states hiring mercenaries from other states was well established and reduced many of the problems associated with mercenarism.[106] If this is true, it poses an important (and unanswered) question. Why did states abandon a commonly used and well-established practice? Why did states no longer *want* mercenaries? The problems with Thomson's supply-based argument are made worse by the fact that neither the mechanics of neutrality law nor an increased desire to enhance state control over citizens can explain the change in supply, and so cannot explain the decision to abandon the practice of hiring foreign soldiers.

Neutrality

A second problem with Thomson's argument is her reliance on neutrality legislation as the mechanism that allowed states to gain control over their

---

[105] Avant makes the same argument about the different timing of the decision to stop using mercenaries at home and the decision to prevent citizens from enlisting in foreign armies (Ibid).
[106] Thomson (1994: 54–5).

citizens. Thomson outlines, and rejects, the explanation that new expectations about how neutral states ought to control their citizens during war became universal, because states did not create neutrality laws when a conflict occurred during which they wished to remain neutral.[107] For example, only two of the twenty Latin American states entering the international system adopted neutrality legislation at the same time as a war.[108] While recognizing these problems, Thomson goes on to argue that states sought to control their citizens and neutrality became the mechanism they chose to use to accomplish that control.[109]

Significant problems remain with arguing that neutrality legislation was the primary mechanism that controlled, and therefore diminished, the supply of mercenaries ultimately leading to their disappearance. The first of these problems is that the eighteenth- and nineteenth-century mode of mercenary trade would not necessarily be affected by implementing neutrality laws. Agreements where one state hired an army from another state could fall outside neutrality laws, and these arrangements were certainly the most significant in the eighteenth and nineteenth centuries. In the eighteenth-century Holy Roman Empire, individual princes of the Empire's component states could enter into contracts with states at war against the emperor, without being considered belligerents themselves.[110] Legal opinion in the nineteenth century concurred that providing soldiers 'under an agreement made between a non-belligerent sovereign and a country at war, or about to enter into war, was not incompatible with neutrality. It was, of course, open to the belligerent against whom such "treaty" mercenaries were operating to regard the arrangement as an unneutral act amounting to a *casus belli*'.[111] Vattel, Wolff, and other Continental lawyers all concurred that the practice of sending auxiliaries to other states—the state-to-state system—did not violate international law.[112]

And, in fact, Hessen-Kassel was not considered to be a belligerent in the American Revolution despite the presence of thousands of Hessian troops on American soil. The Americans could also have hired troops from the Landgraf.[113] State practice indicates states were not drawn into conflict merely because some of their citizens were fighting for another state; technically, they were so unencumbered by the actions of their citizens that they could supply both sides of a conflict, although of course most parties insisted on contractual safeguards to prevent this situation from arising. States could decide whether

---

[107] Ibid. 84–5. [108] Ibid. 85. [109] Ibid. 86. [110] Atwood (1980: 30).
[111] Green (1979: 210). Redlich concurs that these agreements were treaties between sovereigns (Redlich 1964*b*: 94).
[112] Atwood (1980: 15, 23).
[113] Indeed, the joke was made that when John Adams was staying next to the Landgraf in Paris during the American Revolution, he could have done so (Ibid. 31).

or not status as a neutral was important, and accordingly decide whether or not to supply an interested state with soldiers.

Arguing that neutrality legislation was the main instrument used to control citizen movements, and therefore eliminate the practice of mercenary use, leads Thomson into another predicament. The evidence simply does not suggest that neutrality legislation adopted in various states represents 'the globalization of antimercenarism laws'[114] because *mercenaries* were responsible for very few problems with which neutrality law was designed to deal. Neutrality law became global, but this body of law only dealt with mercenaries incidentally. To call neutrality laws 'anti-mercenarism legislation' is misleading, because it suggests that states were using neutrality law with the purposeful intent to eradicate mercenaries,[115] when in fact neutrality law was designed primarily to deal with other problems caused by non-state actors.[116]

Thomson's argument that states were trying to create national armies in the nineteenth century, and that doing so required new legislation banning citizens from serving abroad[117] has some merit. Thomas Jefferson, when he was Secretary of State, argued that 'no citizen has any right to go to war on his own authority.... Indeed, nothing can be more obviously absurd than to say that all citizens may be at war and yet the nation be at peace'.[118] States needed potential military personnel at home, and certainly not in the armies of other states.[119] Neutrality legislation may indeed have been the mechanism they used to ensure that this was the case.

However, there were very few international problems caused by foreign enlistment. The 'real purpose of the [American] neutrality laws is to prohibit the commission of unauthorized acts of war by individuals *within* the United States',[120] such as bases for privateers or the launching of armed bands. The American legislation was created in response to an incident sparked by privateering rather than mercenary enlistment. An American citizen was acquitted

---

[114] Thomson (1994: 81).

[115] It is also inconsistent, because Thomson argues (as quoted above) that states did not purposely attempt to eradicate mercenaries. If it was not a purposeful attempt, how could the legislation be 'anti-mercenary'?

[116] The major states discussed in this book enacted neutrality legislation at different times. In America, the US Neutrality Act was created in 1794; Britain created two foreign enlistment acts, one in 1819 and one in 1870; Prussia never created such legislation; France's legislation was created in 1804. For a full table of legislation, see Thomson (1994: 80).

[117] Ibid. 86.

[118] Letter from Jefferson, 17 August 1793, collected in Moore (1906: 917).

[119] Early foreign enlistment acts were designed to deal with just this problem. Britain's early attempts were 'inspired not so much by the desire to enforce duties of neutrality as to avoid depletion of the nation's man power by the enlistment of British subjects in the military service of other nations'. Dumbauld (1937: 258 n. 5).

[120] Ibid. 260. Emphasis added.

after serving aboard a French privateering ship called the *Citizen Genet*,[121] violating American claims to neutrality during the French Revolutionary Wars.[122] Legislation was created to deal with this situation, and cases which came to court under its auspices involved privateers recruited on US soil, or American filibustering expeditions, in which individual Americans engaged in a kind of international vigilantism and involved themselves independently by attacking Cuba and Canada,[123] and other attempts to raise bands for hostile action outside the United States. Privateering was a particular concern. In practice, the US Foreign Enlistment Act 1794 'was primarily concerned with the fitting out of raiding naval vessels, a matter which was eventually dealt with by the *Declaration of Paris*, 1856, having over centuries been regarded as an act of extreme infamy and akin to piracy.'[124]

The only instance of problems of foreign enlistment reaching the courts before the turn of the twentieth century was the case of *Wiborg* v. *United States*, where the Supreme Court found that it was lawful for an American to leave the country and enlist in another state's armed forces,[125] reiterating that the law only made recruitment within the United States illegal. *Wiborg* demonstrates that the US neutrality law was not primarily concerned with ending the practice of foreign enlistment, merely recruitment on US soil. This is an important distinction because the provisions dealing with recruitment were also designed to deal with the raising of armed bands and filibustering, and not exclusively with the problems caused by mercenaries. And of course recruitment on US soil violates sovereignty in a way that the decision of an individual American to leave the country would not.

British legislation followed a similar track. The Foreign Enlistment Act 1819 was designed to deal with armed raiding bands and the fitting out of ships, although it also banned foreign enlistment outright.[126] The major problems encountered by the law were also caused by fitting out ships, especially the *Alabama*, a ship fitted out in England for the Confederacy during the American Civil War. The Law Officers found that such an action clearly

---

[121] Ibid. 262.
[122] Privateering was a problem on a completely different scale, and an international agreement was needed to eliminate it. For details see Thomson (1994: chs. 3 and 4).
[123] Dumbauld (1937: 263–4).
[124] Green (1979: 211). A major instance of this sort of problem was the case of *The Three Friends*, where the Supreme Court upheld the legality of seizing a ship which had been fitted out to assist Cuban insurgents (Cesner and Brant 1977: 356).
[125] Cesner and Brant (1977: 356). A second case, *Gayon* v. *McCarthy*, upheld the conviction of a Mexican who recruited an American to fight with revolutionary forces in Mexico. This conviction deals only with recruitment rather than enlistment. See Cesner and Brant (1977: 356) and Taulbee (1985: 345).
[126] Green (1979: 214).

violated the Foreign Enlistment Act.[127] As a result of this experience[128] and the additional experience of the Franco-Prussian War, Britain passed a new Foreign Enlistment Act in 1870. While this Act prohibits recruitment on British soil, it does not ban enlistment abroad, and mercenary service itself is not illegal.[129] Lord Diplock, in his report analysing the mercenary problems of the 1970s, argues that many of the 'provisions of the act of 1870 deal with the building and fitting out of ships for foreign belligerent forces and the preparation and equipment of naval and military expeditions against friendly states'.[130]

For Thomson to be right, we would expect that states required neutrality law because their citizens' foreign enlistment was causing them difficulties. What we see is that states banned foreign enlistment almost as a side effect of their attempts to control other types of force, such as privateering and filibustering. Neutrality law, in its earlier guises in the United States, 'prohibited mercenary activity by implication',[131] rather than directly. If the law was actually designed to deal with a different problem, it provides further evidence for the argument that the disappearance of mercenaries from the international system was not the result of state attempts to enhance control via the creation of new legislation. Legislation governing foreign enlistment did not stop states from using mercenaries; it was mainly intended to deal with other problems, and would not have stopped states from exchanging troops in the way they had done during the eighteenth and nineteenth centuries. Mercenaries must have disappeared for another reason. And, as we will see, states actively attempted to remove foreigners from their armies.

Interestingly, Prussia had no laws on foreign enlistment or recruitment, which Thomson calls 'anti-mercenarism laws' and nor did the other nineteenth-century German states.[132] Nonetheless, each of these states stopped selling mercenaries and stopped using foreign troops. One of the central problems with Thomson's neutrality-as-control-mechanism argument is that even in states without neutrality laws, the practice of selling or using mercenaries stopped. And it is in these German states that the decision is in many ways especially significant. Both Hesse and Wurttemberg developed large armies in the eighteenth century for the express purpose of selling soldiers to other countries.[133] In the absence of legislation, why did these states stop selling their soldiers? It cannot have been the lack of supply, because they were the suppliers. Indeed, Redlich argues that the nineteenth-century

[127] Ibid. 215.   [128] Ibid. 215, Diplock, Walker-Smith, and de Freitas (1976: para. 24).
[129] On the latter point, see Burmester (1978: 50).
[130] Diplock, Walker-Smith, and de Freitas (1976: para. 24).
[131] Taulbee (1985: 344).   [132] Thomson (1994: 83, Table 4.3).
[133] Childs (1982: 33, 46–7).

international market for mercenaries was characterized by vast oversupply.[134] A lack of demand provides one explanation as to why mercenaries disappeared in the German states. Another reason might have been that later in the nineteenth century industrialization meant that there were fewer mercenaries to be recruited; however, previous consumers of mercenaries, like France and Prussia, had stopped buying long before industrialization.[135] The only option remaining within the bounds of Thomson's argument is that these states also wished to enhance their control over their citizens, and so stopped selling them to other states. These problems, however, were not severe enough to prompt legislation (which was common in the rest of Europe), and the desire to control citizens alone cannot explain why states abandoned using mercenaries.

The Desire to Control Citizens Would Not Necessarily Lead to the Disappearance of Mercenaries

The third difficulty with Thomson's argument is that the connection between control over citizens and the disappearance of mercenaries is not as tight as she suggests. A state's decision to enhance control over its people by restricting foreign recruiters from operating on its territory would not necessarily lead to the end of the mercenary era. Such a decision affects neither a situation where a state recruits an army itself and sells it to another state, nor a situation whereby a state invites in a recruiter from another state. Mercenaries disappeared because states stopped selling their armies and stopped granting permission to other states to recruit on their soil, neither of which is incompatible with legislation aimed at foreign recruitment. States refused to allow the recruitment of their citizens without their knowledge, but also refused to grant permission for this sort of action when in the past they had allowed it.

A second problem with the argument that states increasingly wanted to control the movements of their citizens in order to monopolize force lies with the fact that they were notably dilatory about enforcing the legislation they had created. The United States has only ever prosecuted three people for violations of its various acts.[136] Great Britain has never prosecuted anyone, resulting in the suggestion that the legislation be reformed entirely.[137]

---

[134] Redlich (1964*b*: 94).
[135] France stopped the recruitment of mercenaries after the revolution and Prussia in 1808. See Chapter 5.
[136] Thomson (1994: 83, Table 4.3).
[137] In Chapter 6, I discuss the Diplock Report, which attacks the 1870 and 1819 Foreign Enlistment Acts as unenforceable.

A final problem brings us back to the entrepreneurial German states of Hesse and Wurttemberg. These states were very successful at selling their citizens to fight abroad, and had no legislation which they could use to control the problem. Why did states decide that the lucrative practice of selling soldiers to other states was no longer useful, and without neutrality legislation, how did they stop? There are two possible answers, neither of which Thomson proposes. First, the demand for buying such soldiers might have disappeared, which presupposes that states changed their opinion on the merits of a mercenary army. As we will see, the reasons for this decision were never entirely material. Second, states could have decided that the practice of selling troops to other states was essentially immoral and ought to be banned.

4.4. A COMMON PROBLEM: WHY DID STATES PREFER CITIZEN ARMIES, AND WHY WERE THEY WILLING TO TAKE A LEAP OF FAITH TO ADOPT THEM?

The three approaches outlined above share a central problem. None is really able to explain why states preferred citizen armies over a force containing foreigners. The fact that states favoured citizens over mercenaries is crucial to explain why citizen armies became the standard. And this favouritism is not easily explained without reference to norms.[138]

The realist approach cannot explain why, in the light of evidence to the contrary, leaders assumed that citizens would make effective and reliable troops. There was not necessarily a correlation between the degree of nationalism and motivation, cohesion and increased effectiveness of troops. There was no past evidence of striking success among citizen forces. When Prussia adopted a citizen army, her leaders were taking an extraordinary leap of faith. They had to hope that a standing army would create nationalism in a people notably lacking in it, and that nationalism would lead to better and more unified soldiers. If states did not adopt a citizen army when defeated by states using their citizens to fight, what explains the different timing of the shift away from mercenary use in different states? Neither material pressures nor changes in the nature of war can explain why European and American leaders came to believe their future rested on citizen soldiers. Nor can it explain why states which shifted to the use of citizens later, like Britain, decided to do so when they had many other possible alternatives to consider.

---

[138] The evidence for this argument comes from Chapter 5.

Avant's argument is similarly unable to explain the attractions a citizen army held for the leaders of Britain, France, and Prussia. She argues that domestic politics under certain conditions made it possible for the idea of a citizen army to take root and be implemented. She does not, however, explain why citizens were so strongly preferred, and nor does she explain how the alternative posed could carry any weight given past experience and the evidence of the Napoleonic Wars. Fractured domestic politics cannot explain why the idea of a citizen army was so compelling, and why reformers were taken seriously. What was it about a citizen army that was so attractive or contained such possibilities that leaders took a chance and rejected the old system, rejected the alternative of a small, professional army, and opted for citizen soldiers? How did the adoption of a citizen army effectively close the doors on other alternatives?

Thomson's approach also fails to explain the allure of a citizen army. She disregards the fact that states were as interested in purging foreigners from their own armies as they were in banning their citizens from enlisting abroad. In not recognizing the decline in demand for mercenary services, Thomson does not recognize that part of the reason mercenaries disappeared from the international system is that states preferred to use citizens to staff their armies. And once again, the question returns: why did leaders in Europe put all their eggs in the new basket of a citizen army? States stopped using foreigners in their own armies, and this decision had to rely on the belief that citizen armies were, at the very least, potentially better, if not clearly superior. Where did this belief come from? If neither material factors nor changes in the nature of war necessarily dictate the adoption of the citizen army, what was it about a people in arms that was so attractive?

None of the three approaches above can explain why citizen armies were such a good proposition that states were willing to reject a stable, established, and effective practice in favour of one which was untested, potentially unstable, and had existed only in theory. And surely we cannot understand why states rejected mercenaries without understanding why they preferred citizens. If performance on the battlefield cannot provide enough compelling evidence, then the choice must be at least in part moral. A strong element of the decision to adopt citizen armies was that they were considered the morally superior alternative. States were persuaded to take a leap of faith and use citizens to fight their battles not necessarily because it was the *best* thing to do, but because they began to believe it was the *right* thing to do.

5

How Citizens Became the Standard: A Normative Explanation of the Shift Away from Mercenary Use

The norm against mercenary use, in particular the argument that mercenaries are morally undesirable because they do not fight for an appropriate cause, is crucial to understand why states abandoned the use of foreign soldiers and took a great leap of faith in opting for citizen armies. As the concept of citizen duty to the state grew, and as patriotism and nationalism became increasingly seen as desirable and practical for armies, a selfish and financial motivation became morally inappropriate and practically inferior.

A norms-based explanation is able to highlight three important factors in the decision to stop using foreign soldiers. First, although Avant and Thomson are correct to argue that a changed relationship between citizen and state is in part responsible for the shift away from mercenary use, they pay insufficient attention to the fact that this was a *moral* change as much as it was a theoretical or practical transformation. Attention to the norm against mercenary use and how it was bolstered by changing beliefs about citizens can provide a sharper explanation of the decision to adopt citizen armies. Without attention to the norm against mercenary use and the attendant belief in the superiority of citizen armies, it is impossible to see the variation in practice among states. In different states, the relationship between state and citizen took on new, and different, forms and attention to these differences reveals why states adopted a citizen army at different times.

Second, the decision to turn to citizens to staff armies was a moral as well as a practical decision. When states reformed their armies, the reason a citizen army seemed preferable was in part because it was understood to be morally superior to an army containing foreigners, even though there were few practical reasons why foreign officers if not foreign soldiers could not be retained. A strong citizen army came to indicate something about the state for which it fought. If citizens were willing to die for their state, it suggested that the state was a powerful and glorious entity that took care of its people, who returned the favour. Civilized states, furthermore, were not inclined to engage in the trade of able-bodied men, and warfare became something that could only be honourably fought by someone with a personal stake in the matter. The development of nationalism and patriotism as appropriate motives for war enhanced the idea that to fight for a mercenary motive was wrong. A citizen army became tied up in the normative concept of state identity, and began to be a requirement for states wanting to be taken seriously on the world stage. Norms provide a better explanation for one of Avant's key questions. The path on which the world became dependent, that of the citizen army, was a desirable path because 'good' states, as well as successful states, fought their wars using their own people.

Third, attention to the norm against mercenary use provides us with a clear picture of why, in a reactionary era where leaders in Europe attempted to put the French Revolutionary genie firmly back inside its lamp, they did not return to the use of foreign soldiers at the same time they returned to the use of small, professional armies. At the end of the Napoleonic Wars, Europe had essentially returned to the *ancien régime* system of military service,[1] but with one crucial difference; foreigners had already disappeared from the Prussian and French armies and began to disappear from other European armies. Why was the return to the old system only partial?

America, France, Prussia, and Great Britain abandoned foreign soldiers and adopted citizen armies in chronological order. In all four cases, a pre-existing normative tradition against mercenary use was buttressed by normative beliefs about the nature of the state and of its military organization, setting the stage for the decision to abandon the mercenary system. France and the American colonies are important cases for analysis because they were the first states in the modern era to adopt a citizen army, and took the decision on faith alone, with little or no evidence it would be successful. In these two cases, I demonstrate that France and America adopted a citizen army as an organic part of a revolutionary ideology which precluded the use of foreigners and reinforced the existing intellectual tradition suggesting that mercenary use was problematic.

Conversely, Prussia and Britain needed to experience a change in normative outlook before they could adopt a citizen army. Existing intellectual traditions laid the theoretical groundwork for the decision in both cases. In Prussia, beliefs about the nature of the citizen's relationship to the state changed, and so beliefs about the morality of foreign troops also changed, resulting in military reforms which stopped the use of mercenaries. The norm against mercenary use became so strong that even when most of these reforms were abandoned, Prussia's refusal to use foreigners continued. In Britain, the existence of a

[1] Cohen (1985: 55).

very strong norm against standing armies, which relied on the belief that the citizen–state relationship would be *preserved* by the absence of a standing army prevented the change to a citizen army for some time. But as the norm against mercenary use grew stronger, the belief that civilized states did not use mercenaries spread around Europe, and the norm against standing armies was shattered in the Crimea, Britain joined the ranks of states who fought wars using only their own citizens.

As I examine the shift away from mercenary use in each of these four cases, I will demonstrate that an intellectual tradition of dislike of mercenaries provided the framework for the subsequent changes in the relationship between citizens and states, and the effect that having (or not having) a citizen army had on state identity, ultimately leading to the end of mercenary use.

5.1. AMERICA

The American Revolution was the first major case in the modern era where a citizen army motivated by duty and patriotism fought an old-style army that included the use of foreign mercenaries. Britain, as she had done throughout the eighteenth century, relied on troops provided through a subsidy or auxiliary arrangement, where one state paid another for the use of its troops.[2] Using the subsidy system, Britain supplemented 65,000 of her own troops with 30,000 Germans. Most came from Hessen-Kassel but a mix of troops came from other German principalities, and they were collectively, if incorrectly, referred to as Hessians.[3] George III, because he was Elector of Hanover, was also able to borrow Hanoverian troops, who replaced British garrisons in Minorca and Gibraltar and so freed up more soldiers for service in America.[4]

The American Revolution was not only a meeting of two differently composed armies; it was a clash of different beliefs about war. The revolutionaries understood their project in explicitly moral terms, and these terms made the use of mercenaries by the other side heinous, and made the option of using mercenaries for the revolutionary cause unthinkable. To demonstrate that America's adoption of a citizen army had a strong moral element, I first examine how the moral position against mercenaries had its roots in

---

[2] For the definition, see Atwood (1980: 1).

[3] Addington (1994: 12). The American army had 35,000 troops. Bayley and Conway put the number of German troops at 18,000 (Bayley 1977: 6 and Conway 2000: 16). French points out that German troops constituted 45% of Britain's total strength in America (French 1990: 68). The spelling of Hessen-Kassel is often anglicized as Hesse-Cassel.

[4] Conway (2000: 16).

the republican tradition, which created a worldview suggesting that liberty could be gained only by those willing to fight for it themselves. Second, I examine how Americans explicitly expressed their dislike for the British use of mercenaries. Third, I argue that the American moral preference for citizen troops is illustrated by the fact that Americans were not convinced about the quality of citizen troops and thought that mercenaries might be more useful on the ground. Despite a recognition that professionalism was useful, and difficulties with creating a volunteer army, America continued to use citizen rather than mercenary troops.

The Republican Tradition and Moral Dislike of Mercenaries

Republican ideology suggested not only the ultimate goal of the revolution, but also how to go about achieving that goal. When the revolutionaries examined their strategic position in the war, they did so through the lens of republicanism, which was most likely based on the English theorist Harrington's gloss on Machiavelli.[5] According 'to this theory, a republic at war had one important advantage over monarchical or aristocratic states: it could call upon the services of free citizens who had a stake in their society, hence more incentive to fight than soldiers procured only with the money or under the compulsion of less happy governments'.[6] One of the crucial aspects of citizenship for Harrington, as it was for Machiavelli, was the bearing of arms in the defence of the republic.[7] It is important to emphasize fighting for the republic is not merely the duty of the citizen, but a necessity to secure his freedom. The idea that citizens should fight for themselves is so important that the citizen's 'liberty is guaranteed as much by his right to be the sole fighter in his own defence as by his ultimate right to cast a vote in his own government'.[8]

This profound belief in the morality and necessity of citizen soldiers is wholly incompatible with the use of foreign mercenaries, who would prevent citizens from fulfilling the duty that would bring them freedom and secure the republic. Its direct descent from Machiavelli, who disapproved of mercenaries for the same reasons, demonstrates the long lineage of the appropriate cause aspect of the norm. Defending 'liberty and moral rectitude' rested on 'the individual citizen's eagerness to fight for them in person'.[9] Americans were putting into practice a republican programme descended from Machiavelli, and so could not possibly approve of the use of inappropriately motivated fighters. Moreover, the American republican tradition had

[5] Buel Jr. (1984: 142). [6] Ibid. See also Bonwick (1991: 51).
[7] Pocock (1965: 556). [8] Ibid. 566.
[9] Royster (1979: 28). See also Carp (1987: 22).

at its centre a concept of liberty that included distrust 'for the large, permanent military establishments' on which European governments relied.[10] These military establishments, of course, contained a large number of foreign troops.

The revolutionaries also hoped that Americans would be strongly motivated by the project of liberty. Most 'revolutionaries expected the citizen-soldier to surpass his mercenary, brutalized enemies. Since he fought to preserve his standing as a citizen against those who would make him a slave, his pride in civil society would help to make him stronger than his opponents in combat'.[11] Americans saw citizen armies as honourable, decent, and brave, and potentially as practically successful as they were morally superior.

It is important to note briefly that the use of *foreigners* is not incompatible with the American revolutionary tradition and its republican background. Indeed, the Americans were assisted by foreigners. The use of troops who are not interested in republican ideals, or who fight only for money rather than ideals, is problematic. Support by an individual soldier sympathetic to the American cause did not cause difficulties. The appropriate cause element of the norm is at work here. Fighters are morally suspect if they do not fight for the appropriate cause, and in revolutionary America, and as argued below, revolutionary France, the appropriate cause came to be defined in terms of liberty and freedom, terms which made a mercenary motivation especially awkward.

Explicit American Opposition to the Use of Mercenaries

All this added up to an America adamantly and explicitly opposed to the use of private force. The Declaration of Independence highlighted King George III's use of mercenaries as one of the prime grievances of the newly declared republic against its monarchical progenitor:

He is, at this time, transporting large armies of foreign Mercenaries, to compleat the works of death, desolation and tyranny, already begun with circumstances of cruelty and perfidy scarcely paralleled in the most barbarous ages and totally unworthy the Head [sic] of a civilized nation.[12]

The Declaration of Independence explicitly associates the hiring of foreign troops with uncivilized behaviour. The revolutionary identity was at once opposed to and devolved from Britain. Britain was the hirer of mercenaries,

---

[10] Whiteclay Chambers II (2003: 76).   [11] Royster (1979: 39).
[12] Declaration of Independence. Text available at <http://www.law.indiana.edu/uslawdocs/declaration.html>

the seat of tyrannical monarchy, and the denier of liberty, while America was a 'purer and freer England'.[13]

Britain's insistence on using immoral foreign fighters, men 'such as have neither property nor families to fight for, and who have no principle, either of honor, religion, public spirit, regard for liberty or love of country' indicated to the Americans that she was interested in conquest and not reconciliation.[14] The news 'that foreign mercenaries were to be used seemed to make the breach irreparable. If the British intended to treat the struggle as a foreign war, as foreigners themselves they should be treated'.[15] The use of mercenaries demonstrated to the Americans that the British were not about to treat the dispute as an internal one, and would respond forcibly, using troops that they had bought because they did not or could not inspire their own men. The British use of Hessians was so disliked that it convinced both neutral citizens and even citizens with loyalist inclinations to support the rebels,[16] and provided a useful source of propaganda.[17]

American revolutionaries, having trumpeted the belief that in fighting for their nation citizens preserved their own liberty and the ultimate freedom of the country itself, could only associate the use of mercenaries with the barbarity of states clinging to old ways. If the Americans saw themselves as free and civilized not only because of their cause but because of the way they used citizens to fight for it, then it is not surprising that they saw the British as barbarians tightening the shackles of tyranny.

Americans Recognized Problems with a Citizen Army and Practical Advantages of Mercenaries

What is especially interesting about the American position is the degree to which it started life as something that had the potential to be more morally correct than it was practically useful. Despite their hopes for the enthusiasm of citizen soldiers, Americans were concerned about the professionalism of the British mercenary troops. Their 'celebration of the fighting virtues of freemen could not dispel their fear that the freemen's conduct might prove less reliable than the discipline of mercenaries. The soldier who had the freedom to hide behind fences and trees also had the freedom to flee. Tyrants used professional armies because professionalism had proven its effectiveness in destroying liberty'.[18] And, in fact, the action of American civilian soldiers demonstrated that patriotism and duty alone could not make a good army.

---

[13] Bailyn (1967: 83). [14] Moore (1859: 213–14). [15] Mackesy (1964: 72).
[16] Cogliano (2000: 75). [17] Ellis (1973: 47). [18] Royster (1979: 12).

How Citizens Became the Standard 127

The Americans struggled to maintain a purely volunteer militia. American leaders' belief in the moral superiority of the citizen fighter and the necessity of his fighting caused them to overestimate wildly the number and quality of men who would volunteer,[19] and the length of time they would be prepared to offer their services. By March 1777 American numbers had dwindled to 3,000 men; among those who left were men who had accepted a bounty to serve.[20] Washington's biggest challenge as a general was holding the army together, given refusals to volunteer, or volunteers who came only for short periods.[21]

The moral difficulty of creating a professional army to solve the difficulties caused by the unwillingness of the people to volunteer for long periods was directly tied to the concern about mercenaries. Americans, like the British, as we will see below, grappled with their discomfort over the use of standing armies, which they explicitly associated with mercenaries, because of the fact that both types of soldier pursued war as a profession.[22] The revolutionaries 'clung to the conviction that a professional soldier was dangerous, vicious and damned. He killed for money. He made war a trade and preferred long, easy-going wars that yielded him the largest gains for the smallest inconvenience. These gains came at the expense of both taxpayers and civil government, which a professional soldier necessarily corrupted'.[23] The Americans struggled with the problem of a standing army, and finally gave in, creating a more professional army with longer terms of service.[24] But the American belief in the superiority of the citizen soldier and the essential nature of citizen military service persisted despite the problems with translating it into reality. They did not introduce universal service, preferring to cling to 'their own figurative ideal'[25] of the citizen soldier rather than creating a system that might be more efficient.

American moral apprehension of private force cannot be understood without understanding the normative context provided by the republican tradition. The entire American project relied on the contribution of citizens to the war effort, and totally foreclosed the possibility of using mercenaries in the revolutionary army. It also made the decision of the British to employ Hessian troops reprehensible.

Understanding the American normative dislike of mercenaries is crucial to understanding the background to the change in the British position much later on. Harrington's ideas about the republic and against mercenaries had crossed the Atlantic,[26] and now American ideas about the immorality of private fighters returned back to Britain. Critics of the British decision to fight

---

[19] Buel Jr. (1984: 142).   [20] Middlekauf (1982: 364). See also Mackesy (1964: 121).
[21] Ropp (1959: 72).   [22] Carp (1987: 22).   [23] Royster (1979: 46).
[24] Mayer (2000: 309).   [25] Royster (1979: 43).   [26] Buel Jr. (1984: 142).

the Americans had new grist for their mill. Part of the reason the war was morally problematic is that Britain had to use mercenaries to fight it. The misgivings about the Revolution many held in Britain became tied in with misgivings about mercenaries.[27] Moreover, American rhetoric associating citizens with freedom and mercenaries with tyranny took hold. Debate about the morality of the subsidy system also flowed back to the German states that had supplied the troops; because of the perceived moral superiority of the American cause, subsidy treaties like the one supplying the Hessians to Britain became reprehensible, and public opinion began to diverge on the issue.[28]

The American case sets the stage for the other cases we will examine. America was the first modern state to adopt a citizen army, and American beliefs about the appropriate relationship between the citizen and the state precluded the possibility of using a mercenary army. Similar republican ideals were put into practice in France, but Prussia argued for a citizen army on a different basis. Britain shared the American distaste for a standing army, but with notably different effects.

5.2. FRANCE

Like their American revolutionary predecessors, the French adopted a citizen army because the idea of the citizen soldier grew organically from the general ideals of the revolution. The 'citizen turned soldier—indeed, conscript service as both the badge and moral consequence of citizenship' was a major component of the French Revolution.[29] The philosophy of the revolution and the strength of the intellectual tradition arguing against mercenary use on moral grounds made the use of mercenaries untenable. A shift in norms made the notion of a foreigner fighting for money repugnant, and the idea of the citizen fighting for the state morally ideal.

Enlightenment discussions of the citizen's military obligation to the state were accompanied by specific denigrations of mercenaries. It was not just that Enlightenment thinkers believed citizen soldiers to be the best option, morally and practically, but that they believed that mercenaries were not and could not be morally and practically viable. A small professional army, potentially

---

[27] Mockler (1969: 126).
[28] Atwood (1980: 227, 229). Interestingly, the Hessians were also tainted in American eyes because of an earlier iteration of the norm against mercenary use: the fact that German mercenaries were allowed to plunder during the Thirty Years War predisposed Americans to see them as looters (Atwood 1980: 171).
[29] Challener (1965: 4).

staffed with mercenaries, would have gone against the grain of French thinking so completely that it would have been unthinkable. Norms, much more so than domestic politics or path dependency, are necessary to explain why the French adopted a citizen army and then stuck with it despite extreme reaction to the idea in the nineteenth century. This section begins by outlining the Enlightenment view on mercenaries and citizen soldiers. It then turns to a discussion of how French revolutionary ideals shaped the French army in a way that made mercenary use very unlikely. It concludes by arguing that the fact that the French did not return to the use of mercenaries during a period of reaction suggests how strongly the anti-mercenary norm was held.

The French Enlightenment Tradition and Mercenaries

Jean-Jacques Rousseau is at the centre of the Enlightenment view of war, representing the shift from cosmopolitanism to patriotism, civic virtue, and republicanism.[30] Rousseau argued that patriotism is an essential part of a good polity. If 'we want people to be virtuous', he writes, 'let us begin by making them love their country'.[31] Rousseau describes a new relationship between citizens and the state. 'A country cannot subsist without liberty', he writes, 'nor can liberty without virtue, nor can virtue without citizens. You will have everything if you train citizens; without this you will merely have wicked slaves, beginning with the leaders of the state'.[32] The development of a stronger relationship between citizen and state, with the former closely identifying with the latter, will preserve liberty and virtue.

But if citizens have to be created, and if they must love their country, their country cannot use foreigners to perform the functions of citizens. A polity that relies on mercenaries is a polity suffering from more than one problem. The citizens, 'no longer considering themselves interested in the common cause, would cease to be the defenders of the homeland'. Magistrates will prefer mercenaries to free men 'if only to use the former at a suitable time and place to subjugate the latter more effectively'.[33]

Mercenaries pose a grave threat to the liberty of the people, because they do not have a proper relationship with the state; they submit to the orders of the leadership of the state, rather than thinking of the needs of the polity itself.

---

[30] Starkey (2003: 8).
[31] Rousseau ([1755] 1987: 122). Rousseau's *Discourse on Political Economy* was originally a contribution to Diderot's *Encyclopédie* in 1775 and was published on its own in 1778.
[32] Ibid. 124.   [33] Ibid. 131.

Mercenaries in Rome, whose value could be determined on the basis of the price at which they sold themselves, were proud of their debasement, held in contempt the laws by which they were protected, as well as their comrades whose bread they ate, and believed it an honour to be Caesar's satellites rather than Rome's defenders. And given as they were to blind obedience, their task was to have their swords raised against their fellow citizens, ready to slaughter them all at the first signal. It would not be difficult to show that this was one of the principal causes of the ruin of the Roman Empire.[34]

Rousseau believed that these mercenaries, because they sold themselves and saw no shame in doing so, respected neither their non-mercenary comrades nor the laws of the community that hired them; aside from all these problems, the use of mercenaries put Rome in danger of despotism because any loyalty the mercenaries owed was to Caesar rather than to Rome.

Rousseau had good reason to suspect that introducing foreigners into the state led to tyranny, because foreigners could not have the true needs of society at heart in the same way as citizens. The King's Swiss mercenaries, kept apart from the people and hated by them, were used to quell civil unrest before the French Revolution.[35] The ideal army, recruited from and at one with the people, would prevent tyranny because citizens would not act to subjugate other citizens in the way a mercenary might be persuaded to do.

Rousseau's fellow contributors to the *Encyclopédie* shared his mistrust of mercenaries. Saint Lambert, Jaucourt, and others 'regarded a standing mercenary soldiery with a mixture of fear, disgust and even pity'.[36] The other encyclopedists disapproved of mercenaries on two grounds. First, like Rousseau, they believed that the use of mercenaries could lead to despotism.[37] Second, they argued that patriotism ought to animate the French army and that soldiers who lacked it were unreliable. 'Mercenary troops who have no attachment to the country they serve', wrote Montlovier, 'are those who fight with the greatest indifference and desert with the most facility'.[38] Montlovier's entry, entitled *Voleur, maraudeur*, explicitly associates mercenaries with thieves and marauders and emphasizes the degree to which they were held in disrepute.

Voltaire argued against mercenaries in the *Dictionnaire philosphique*. He contends that at first war 'was cultivated by nations who mobilized for their

---

[34] Ibid. [35] McCormack (1993: 155). [36] Lynn (2001: 138).
[37] See Jaucourt's entry *Deserteur* in the *Encyclopédie*, Vol. 4: 881, available at <http://portail.atilf.fr/encyclopedie/>
[38] Translation in Lynn (2001: 138). The original reads 'Les troupes mercenaries qui n'ont aucun attachement pour le pays qu'elles servent, sont celles quicombattent avec le plus d'indifférence, & qui désertent avec la plus de facilité' and can be found in the *Encyclopédie*, Vol. 17: 452, available at ibid.

common good' but that 'it's not this way today'. Instead, in modern war princes make 'far-fetched claims' to distant provinces, which in turn know nothing of the prince and do not wish to be governed by him. The prince 'at once assembles a large number of men who have nothing to lose; he dresses them all in coarse blue cloth... makes them turn right and left, and marches to glory'. Other princes are inspired to join, 'each according to his strength and cover a small space of land with more mercenary murderers than Genghis Khan, Tamerlane or Bajazet ever had in their train'. Modern princes employ more murderous mercenaries than the famous despots of history. More problematic still is that 'distant nations hear that there is going to be some fighting and they can make five or six *sous* a day if they want to join in' and right away they 'sell their services to anyone ready to employ them'.

The net result of this type of war is that the cause and its fighters are profoundly divorced from each other. Neither mercenary nor nation selling its services does so with the motivation of the common good. 'The marvelous part of this infernal enterprise,' writes Voltaire, 'is that every murderer's chief has his flags blessed, and solemnly invokes the Lord before he goes out to exterminate his neighbours'.[39] War is hypocritical; these murderers who are detached from the cause for which they fight have their flags, for which they are not really fighting at all, blessed by the church before they move on and violate religious teachings. War fought in this manner is furthermore especially devastating.

Voltaire's polemic rages against the nature of war in his day as well as the mercenaries who fought it, because no longer were wars fought with the justification of the common good.

The anti-mercenary beliefs of French Enlightenment thinkers did not just set the stage for the abandonment of mercenaries in France. The pan-European influence of these thinkers meant that their anti-mercenary, pro-citizen views were disseminated around Europe and to America. Frederick the Great corresponded with Voltaire, who had lived in the Prussian court, and the movement of Enlightenment ideas through Europe was commonplace. Just as British and American ideas influenced each other, so too did French ideas about mercenaries spread to other states. The Prussians, for example, were influenced by some, but not all, of the Enlightenment positions on the relative merits of different types of military service.

This intellectual context sets the stage for the abandonment of foreigners in the French army after the Revolution. Enlightenment ideas about the reprehensible nature of mercenaries and the moral superiority of citizens were available to the revolutionaries when they took power.

[39] Voltaire ([1764] 1962: 304–5).

French Revolutionary Ideas and the French Revolutionary Army

The French Revolution, by its very nature, meant that at the same time the monarchy was overthrown and replaced the military would similarly be disbanded and reconfigured.[40] France's ideological war shaped the nature of the military. The new revolutionary army needed to reflect the new French social and political order,[41] which raised particular questions about how to make recruitment and discipline compatible with ideas of liberty and equality.[42] The old army was suitable for conquest, while the new needed to be able to promote the new ideas associated with the Revolution. Moreover, the *ancien régime* armies 'depended on foreign mercenaries to a degree that the nationalist ideology of the Revolution could not accept'.[43]

There was, however, some debate about what kind of army the French should design to replace the military of the old regime. The minister of war in the immediate post-Revolution period, La Tour du Pin, proposed that the army should be a small, professional mercenary force supported by a militia composed of propertied men. Dubois Crancé rejected this notion, arguing that the extreme danger faced by France required different, and radical action. 'And so I say that in a nation which seeks to be free...', he said, 'every citizen should be a soldier and every soldier should be a citizen, if France does not wish to be utterly obliterated'.[44]

The French decision to adopt Dubois Crancé's proposal eventually went a step further. By 1793, *all* French citizens were required to assist with France's war effort, not just men of fighting age. The Convention of 23 August 1793, which initiated the *levée en masse,* read 'young men shall go to battle; married men shall forge arms and transport provisions; women shall make tents and clothes and shall serve in the hospitals; children shall turn old linen into lint; old men shall repair to the public places, to stimulate the courage of the warriors and preach the unity of the Republic and the hatred of kings'.[45] French men recruited under the *levée en masse* were required to carry a banner which read '*The French people risen against the tyrants*'.[46] The war was an effort of all French people, and they had a duty to participate in exchange for their French citizenship.[47] The use of mercenaries in this context would have been

---

[40] Blanning (1996: 31).   [41] Best (1982: 76).   [42] Forrest (1990: 12).
[43] Forrest (2003: 9). There were twenty-three regiments of foreigners in the French army in 1789. Paret (1992: 54).
[44] Ellis (1973: 83) and Blanning (1996: 83).
[45] Decree of 23 August 1793 collected in Stewart (1951: 473).
[46] Rothenberg (1977: 101).   [47] Forrest (1989: 20) and Forrest (2003: 8).

impossible, because to bring in outsiders would have demeaned the project of total national defence. Foreigners 'were not wanted any more...and pure professionals likewise became very suspect. The new ideology looked down on men who served for money, calling them hirelings and mercenaries. Soldiering was only respectable when it was done voluntarily by citizens from love of their country, under which circumstances it became morally admirable'.[48]

France, and the French military, functioned on the basis of new norms. Reforms in all areas reflected the idea that the soldier's duty was to serve the nation.[49] Indeed, the basic idea of enlistment changed from a contract between two individuals to a contract between the individual and the state.[50] The 'prime motivation of volunteers and conscripts was perceived to be their concern for the nation's welfare' and salary was no longer supposed to be an incentive.[51] The French army tried to replace regional attachments with national enthusiasm, with the ultimate goal of creating a 'fighting force that would reflect the character of a revolutionary society and which could be entrusted with the task of defending a revolutionary state'.[52] Indeed, patriotism and republicanism had become so morally powerful it obscured the fact that conscription was inherently coercive.[53]

Arguments which relied on the primacy of the citizen and the citizen's duty to the state were incompatible with the use of foreign troops, because bringing in foreigners would undermine the new relationship between the citizen and the state. The army had to maintain revolutionary spirit to protect it from foreign recruitment; 'an effective revolutionary army had to be an army of revolutionaries who believed in the justice of the cause in which they were fighting'.[54] In France, for the first time, the army and the people were joined together; 'now that the government was responsible to the people, the soldier was their servant—no longer an enemy but an ally'.[55]

The army had to function along new normative lines to be effective. Military discipline had to change now that the citizen was motivated by a duty to the state and the army was designed to reflect liberty and equality. Normative control rather than harsh discipline was necessary to reflect the fact that soldiers were now free citizens.[56] By serving in the army, citizens were fulfilling their obligation, but their service was also explicitly designed to teach them about the nature of civic obligation.[57] France's military was a school for the nation, but a normative school, which would teach the values of the new France to her people.

---

[48] Best (1982: 77).   [49] Forrest (1990: 44).   [50] Bertaud (1988: 46).
[51] Lynn (1984: 43).   [52] Forrest (1990: 29). See also Ellis (1973: 88–9).
[53] Moran (2003a: 2).   [54] Forrest (1990: 101).   [55] Lynn (1984: 64).
[56] Ibid. 43.   [57] Forrest (1990: 89).

Why Did Reaction in France Not Lead to the Return of Mercenaries

The initial French enthusiasm for citizen soldiers did not last forever, and a more interesting normative question arises. Why, given the period of reaction that was to consume France after the Napoleonic Wars, did the French not return to the old system and use mercenaries?

The volunteer army was not without challenges. Volunteers came with significant drawbacks; they 'could volunteer their way into an army, but they could also volunteer their way back out again'.[58] In 1792, the generals had to struggle with a disappearing army, as the volunteers assumed that their enlistment only lasted until the beginning of winter.[59] The volunteers, once treated as free and equal individuals, behaved autonomously rather than as automatons. One French general remarked, 'it is a terrible job trying to get the [Paris] volunteers to obey orders—they challenge them all the time.'[60]

France struggled to recruit soldiers. A year after the great *levée en masse*, the army had already shrunk by 350,000 men, because of desertion and the general unpopularity of service.[61] Genuine volunteers were few and, by the end of the 1790s, so rare that their appearance attracted comment, and desertion increased, growing from an individual problem to a problem plaguing entire units.[62] Desertion led to brigandage, and by 1798 the problem was so serious that the Directory's local authority was unenforceable, more troops could not be recruited, and local government had collapsed.[63] Ellis goes so far as to argue that the *levées en masses* of 1793 actually demonstrated the end of France's status as a nation-in-arms, because of the degree of coercion necessary for conscription.[64] And as we have seen, citizen enthusiasm was not necessarily responsible for French battlefield success.

It did not take long for patriotism to cease being the driving force of French armies. The Napoleonic army abandoned the attachment to *patrie* which had characterized the Revolutionary spirit, and replaced it with an attachment to the military unit. French political leaders 'abandoned an Army of Virtue that emphasized selfless dedication to a republic and embraced an Army of Honour that encouraged the self-concerned pursuit of honors awarded by...Napoleon'.[65] Revolutionary banners exhorting the defence of the people were replaced with banners that referred to Napoleon.[66] It is hard to see how mercenaries could not be compatible with this kind of system, and indeed, foreigners were prevalent in the Napoleonic army.

---

[58] Blanning (1996: 88). [59] Bertaud (1988: 116). [60] Blanning (1996: 87).
[61] Best (1982: 89). [62] Forrest (1989: 26, 170). [63] Esdaile (1995: 50).
[64] Ellis (1973: 950). [65] Lynn (1989: 155). [66] Ibid. 165.

After Napoleon, in the ensuing period of reaction, the French leadership became justifiably concerned about liberal ideas taking root in the army, and the persistence of old revolutionary ideas. In the war against Spain in 1823, the French were concerned that soldiers would be unwilling to fight because of republican sympathy with the Spanish.[67] Also in 1823, the reserve, the last remaining element of the French nation-in-arms, was abolished, and until 1870 French conservatives argued for a small, tightly organized professional army immune to political troublemaking.[68] This is precisely the type of army Avant argues could incorporate foreigners with some ease.[69] It is also the sort of army that is easily controlled by the state; relying on *esprit de corps* rather than patriotic enthusiasm 'emphasizes loyalty to an institution of the state'.[70] In particular, mercenaries might have been desirable because they would be less likely to indulge in the sort of political agitation in which French citizens might engage.

But the French did not consider a return to the use of mercenaries, even as conservatives lobbied for the sort of army compatible with the use of foreign troops and even as the British persisted in using foreigners to assist their military forces. In 1832, France passed the Soult Law, which reiterates a principle outlined in an earlier 1830 law: that foreigners should not serve in the French army, a measure so uncontroversial that it was adopted without discussion. The Soult Law goes a step further, and argues that 'no one will be permitted to serve in the French forces if he is not French'.[71] Of course, foreign service in France continued in the form of the French Foreign Legion. However, as argued earlier, the fact that service in the Legion leads to citizenship after five years indicates that foreign service was allowable when predicated on integration with France. The absence of mercenaries in the French army after Napoleon cannot be explained in materialist terms, as the French military organization would not have precluded the use of mercenaries. Nor can it be explained by the decline in supply, because at this time Britain was still using foreign mercenaries.

The presence of a norm against mercenary use, however, can explain why France did not return to the old system despite some good reasons and a general reaction against Napoleonic reforms. During debate on the Soult Law, Deputy Teste argued that the bill was 'based on the French *idea* that the army must be a national one. It is not only a question of the defence of the country and its interests. It is also a question of defending national institutions. For this

---

[67] Porch (1974: 10).
[68] Ibid. 61. On the desirability of small armies in France, see also Best (1982: 217) and Griffith (1989: 8).
[69] See Chapter 5 and Avant (2000: 45).   [70] Lynn (1989: 164).
[71] Porch (1974: 64).

reason it is both *moral* and politically expedient to insist that the French army be exclusively French'.[72] The idea that a national army was the best choice was a French idea, so returning to a foreign army would be a decision that undermined, in a way, Frenchness. The Deputy saw the decision to use citizens as morally correct.

Norms can explain why states pursued a particular path when it came to the composition of their armies, and why they continued to pursue it once they had begun, even when other alternatives might have made sense or been more desirable. The idea of the glory of the French national army became part of French national identity, and what it meant to be French. As a result, even when the political currents in France drifted in directions that might have been amenable to the use of foreigners, there was no going back without fundamentally threatening French identity itself. Without understanding the role of norms, we can understand neither why France adopted a citizen army in the first place, nor why she clung to it despite the fact that a mercenary army could have performed the same job.

5.3. PRUSSIA

Prussia's decision to adopt a citizen army must be understood in the light of the development of the notion that citizens owed military duty to the state, which mercenaries could not fulfil. This section begins first by outlining the problems of the pre-nineteenth-century Prussian military and its defeat at Jena and Auerstädt. Second, I outline the intellectual tradition of mercenary dislike and the growing idea of the duty owed by the citizen to the state. Third, I argue that the Prussian military reforms were based on a transformation of the relationship between the citizen and the state and the expectations the latter had of the former. This transformation precluded the use of mercenaries. Fourth, I demonstrate that the social cost of the decision to abandon mercenaries and the fact that Prussia did not return to mercenaries emphasize the degree to which the shift away from mercenaries was normative.

Prussian Military Problems and the Defeats of 1806

The Prussian decision to adopt a citizen army is extraordinary in the light of the high proportion of mercenaries in its eighteenth-century armies and the prevailing belief that Prussian subjects were better off not serving the state. Frederick the Great, who argued that his subjects ought to be protected

---

[72] Quoted in ibid. Emphasis added.

and best served the nation by contributing to the economy from their own hearths,[73] first increased the proportion of foreigners to nearly half the army's total size[74] and by the time of his death, there were twice as many foreigners as natives in the army.[75] By the early nineteenth century, 35 per cent of the Prussian army were mercenaries.[76]

The Prussian army was forced to reform after its great defeats in 1806 at Auerstädt and Jena, at the hands of Napoleon and his army. The Prussian army was composed of the lower orders of society[77] and foreigners who were often surrendered enemy troops or deserters from other armies.[78] It was led by an officer class restricted to the nobility,[79] which at senior levels was not only elderly but pursued outmoded tactics.[80] It was plagued by desertion and had to operate under strict discipline.[81]

In addition to these problems, all of which reared their heads on the battlefield against Napoleon, the Prussian campaign was plagued with errors and disorganization. The Prussians did not mobilize all of their available soldiers, so they could not begin to match Napoleon's numbers,[82] and moreover, diplomatic mistakes caused by Prussia's inability to decide how or when to attack made a defeat inevitable.[83] To make matters worse, the army's complex administration confused decision-making.[84] Boyen, one of the Prussian military reformers of the period following the defeats, wrote 'there have been few campaigns in which such numerous, and often, such incomprehensible blunders piled up on top of each other'.[85] After the battles were over, the Prussian army collapsed into disorganization,[86] while Prussian society was passive.

The Prussian losses of 1806 were catastrophic, and a nation that had believed itself to be unbeatable had been beaten easily. Reform was vital, but it was not immediately clear which direction reform would take. To understand the Prussian military reform debate, it is necessary to examine the intellectual history alongside the military history just examined.

Intellectual Background

Within Prussia, a debate flourished on the relative merits of citizens and mercenaries. This debate forms the backbone of the intellectual tradition of dislike of mercenaries, and can be divided into two main categories: before

---

[73] Craig (1964: 21), Paret (1966: 16), Rosinski (1966: 33), and Rothenberg (1977: 17).
[74] Rosinski (1966: 33).
[75] Rothenberg (1977: 17).   [76] Paret (1966: 16).   [77] Ibid. 133, Simon (1971: 146).
[78] Rosinski (1966: 35).   [79] Rothenberg (1977: 19).
[80] Craig (1964: 26) and Gooch (1980: 23).
[81] Kitchen (1975: 22) and Rothenberg (1977: 19).   [82] Rosinski (1966: 51).
[83] Craig (1964: 3) and Kitchen (1975: 34).   [84] Craig (1964: 29).
[85] Ibid. 33.   [86] Rosinski (1966: 51).

and after the defeats of 1806. The majority of the debate occurred after, as Prussia was forced into examination of its problems and discussions about reform. However, arguments about the moral superiority of citizen soldiers pre-dated Jena. And, as we see in the next section, a defeat did not suddenly cause Prussians to believe that mercenaries were morally incorrect actors; a large number of Prussians clung to the belief that the old system had been satisfactory and would require only small reforms.

While most of the German jurists of the eighteenth century did not disapprove of mercenaries on moral grounds, the philosopher Immanuel Kant took a moral position against their use. He differentiates between mercenaries and civilian soldiers. Mercenaries represent 'the practice of hiring men to kill or to be killed' and using them implies that they are 'mere machines and instruments in the hand of another (namely, the state) which cannot easily be reconciled with the right of humanity'.[87] Citizens are a different matter, because they 'seek to secure themselves and their country against attack from without'.[88] Kant disapproves of mercenaries because they are inappropriately motivated; they are merely machines hired to kill by the state. Treating men in this instrumental sense is immoral, and citizens seeking to defend themselves are neither morally problematic nor do they challenge humanity.

In the 1790s, reformers like Berenhorst were already concerned about the absence of patriotic enthusiasm in the Prussian army. The 'revolutionary *élan* of the French—even though it had faltered often enough—convinced Berenhorst that change was needed, since in the long run the enthusiastic and patriotic fighter would always defeat that "soulless automaton", that "lifeless work of art," the mercenary'.[89] Berenhorst preferred citizen soldiers to mercenaries because he believed their potential for enthusiasm would be more effective, but this was not a purely instrumental belief. Berenhorst 'placed more stress upon the moral and spiritual values of the army than a formal drill learned by repetition'.[90] In other words, if moral values could be instilled in the army, such that its members would recognize their status as citizens and the moral duty that entailed, the army would be more effective.

While Frederick the Great was perfectly happy to buy foreigners to serve in his own army, a paternalistic attitude towards his subjects made him reluctant to sell them. As inconsistent as it seems, Frederick the Great himself spoke out against the mercenary trade in moral terms. He wrote to Voltaire that the British acquisition of Hessians for the American Revolution was the Landgrave of Hessen-Kassel's decision alone:

---

[87] Kant ([1795] 1917: 110).   [88] Ibid. 111.   [89] Paret (1966: 75).
[90] Shanahan (1966: 66).

If he had come out of my school... he would not have sold his subjects to the English, as one sells cattle to have their throats cut. This last act is no way compatible with the character of a prince who poses as the preceptor of monarchs. The pursuit of a sordid interest is the sole cause of this unworthy proceeding. I pity those poor Hessians who will terminate their careers unhappily and uselessly in America.[91]

Indeed, the events of the American Revolution were a turning point in German public opinion on the mercenary question; subsidy treaties in the German states were no longer accepted but disreputable.[92]

Prussian Military Reform and the Transformation of the Relationship between the Citizen and the State

There is no question that the Prussian collapse at Jena and Auerstädt forced a debate on the merits of the Frederican system.[93] To ignore the pressures created by the defeat would be foolish. The argument that Prussia's domestic politics made it especially open to reform may also be valid, although the degree of the defeat might have made any country militarily introspective. The interesting question is *why* the reform took the path it did, and in particular, why Prussians believed that a thorough overhaul of the relationship between citizen and state was necessary for effective military reform. The overhaul of this relationship was cast in thoroughly moral terms, that would undoubtedly have felicitous practical effects. The reformers took the evidence of the problems in the Frederican army evidenced at Jena and Auerstädt and interpreted them through an existing ideological lens: that citizen soldiers were morally, and therefore practically, superior to mercenaries.

There were 'inseparable links... between the old army and the entire social edifice of *ancien régime* Prussia'[94] and reformers argued that the two combined to crush Prussian citizens and prevent the good in them from coming out. Frederick the Great's decision to exclude the bourgeoisie from the officer class, and recruit the rank and file from the lowest orders of society meant that the Prussian army was essentially feudal. Inhabitants of the Prussian state were seen as 'objects of government rather than participants in it; in the activities of the state their share was the right to obey'.[95] A good people during the *ancien*

---

[91] Translation quoted in Atwood (1980: 230). The letter reads: 's'il était sorti de mon école... il n'aurait vendu ses sujets aux Anglais, comme on vend du bétail pour le faire égorger. Ce dernier trait ne s'assimile point avec le caractère d'un prince qui s'érige en précepteur des souverains. La passion d'un intérêt sordide est l'unique cause de cette indigne démarche. Je plains ces pauvres Hessois qui termineront aussi malheureusement qu'inutilement leur carrière en Amérique'. Letter from Frederick II to Voltaire, 18 June 1776 (Besterman [1776] 1964: 155).

[92] Atwood (1980: 228).   [93] Simon (1971: 145). See also Parkinson (1970: 99).

[94] Simon (1971: 145).   [95] Craig (1964: 18).

régime needed only to be loyal; 'it need have no sense of its own identity as a people, or unity as a nation, or responsibility for public affairs, or obligation to put forth a supreme effort in war'.[96] The state's response after Jena illustrates the degree to which this social relationship was reflected in the military. After the battle, a proclamation appeared, which read, 'The King has lost a battle; calm is the first duty of the citizen!'.[97] The proclamation neatly sums up the relationship between citizen and state: the army was the King's, not the people's; it was the King who had lost the battle. The citizen's only role was to stay calm.

To change the army thus required fundamental social change. The reformers wished to make Prussian society more liberal, but not necessarily democratic; to free individuals from the artificial shackles of the Frederican state by creating a 'certain limited field for the development of initiative and responsibility'.[98] Prussia's reforms thus differed from the French Revolutionary project, 'not only because they were proclaimed by the monarchy, but because they were born not of a desire to secure the rights of man but to regenerate the state as a better instrument for national defence under dynastic leadership'.[99] Prussia's reforms were designed to build a better monarchy better able to defend itself rather than demolish the old system.

The defeat at Jena demonstrated the terrible flaws of the old political and military system. The Prussian people, facing the defeat of their army and government, showed a 'deplorable absence of a popular sense of duty and sacrifice', which proved, reformers believed, that the people 'regarded the state as a mere instrument of oppression' and the army as 'an alien establishment serving the king' rather than the people.[100] The political philosophies of the reformers 'required the destruction, or at least the reduction, of every barrier that limited the participation of the people in military affairs'.[101]

The recognition that society needed to change in turn rested on a belief that individual Prussians had merit and worth, characteristics that were suppressed in the military. Until this changed, the army could not change. Reforming the state would, Scharnhorst argued, 'raise the spirit of the army and of the nation and…give it direction towards its great and important destiny'.[102] Berenhorst believed that 'by turning the soldier into a mindless robot his true soldierly nature and his dignity as a human being were denied and his effectiveness as a soldier was greatly diminished.'[103] Stein argued that the chief idea behind the reforms was 'to arouse a moral, religious, and patriotic

---

[96] Palmer (1986: 92).
[97] Craig (1964: 18). Ford (1965: 241) and Parkinson (1970: 70) also cite the proclamation.
[98] Rosinski (1966: 66).   [99] Ford (1965: 221).
[100] Craig (1964: 18).   [101] Paret (1966: 134).   [102] Quoted in Kitchen (1975: 47).
[103] Ibid. 32.

spirit in the nation...to instill into it again, courage, confidence, readiness for sacrifice'.[104] Prussian military reformers believed that men were rational and capable of sacrificing themselves for a just cause.[105]

First among the factors crushing the independent spirit and inherent worth of the Prussian soldier was military discipline, especially corporal punishment. Corporal punishment was not compatible with a belief in the worth of the individual citizen[106] and Prussian military discipline restricted a soldier's ability to think for himself.[107] The selection of officers from the aristocracy had to change, and to do so required an attack on the idea that the middle classes were unsuited to war.[108] But admitting that the individual could think for himself and that individuals from all classes were capable of sacrifice in military terms meant that Prussia's social system would have to change. A social system that denied the equal rationality present in all humans could not exist alongside a military system that accepted it.

The Prussian military reform movement, then, rested on social reform that in turn relied on a new belief that citizens were worthy and required more liberal treatment. Improving society to improve citizens would create better soldiers, better aware of their duty to the state. A free citizen 'was expected to take upon the cause and defence of his country—if need be by the sacrifice of his life—as an act of his own free will...as the simple and unconditional duty of every member of the community'.[109] Prince August and Carl von Clausewitz wrote in a memorandum sent to the Commission that 'it is every citizen's duty to defend the state'.[110]

The changes proposed by the Prussian military reformers reinforced the norm against mercenary use. If society changed in the way the reformers wished it to, the use of foreigners to fight would be untenable. The citizen's duty to the state was exalted, and the reformers attempted to transform military service from a 'despised occupation reserved to foreign mercenaries and the "lower orders" into the highest honor of every citizen'.[111] Scharnhorst was worried that the patriotism and spirit of a Prussian militia would be threatened by enforced proximity to mercenaries,[112] who were not motivated by the same glorious duties. Once the citizen owed service because of his status as citizen, and that service became an honour, the use of foreign soldiers was impossible.[113]

While the Prussian way of thinking about the individual changed, the general position of the individual in the political system remained the same.

---

[104] Quoted in Parkinson (1970: 100).   [105] Kitchen (1975: 44).
[106] Anderson (1939: 184), Paret (1966: 129), and Rosinski (1966: 68).
[107] Kitchen (1975: 44).   [108] Gooch (1980: 39).   [109] Rosinski (1966: 66).
[110] Quoted in Parkinson (1970: 86).   [111] Rosinski (1966: 67).
[112] Shanahan (1966: 121).   [113] Rosinski (1966: 67).

Respect for the individual was a 'self-evident moral necessity' but that respect did not mean that individuals qualified for political rights.[114] The citizen received only recognition, not rights, but was nonetheless expected to sacrifice his life freely in the cause of his country, 'not merely as the result of external compulsion, nor in exchange for political rights conferred upon him, but as the simple and unconditional duty of every member of the community'.[115] The Prussian position was explicitly moral; the citizen was expected to defend the community because he *ought* to, not because of political change nor because of military threat. And, of course, this line of moral thinking hearkens back to the Machiavellian tradition with its emphasis on the morality of citizen duty, even if it deviates from the republican vision by not assuming the state owed the citizen anything other than respect in exchange for the citizen's duty.

Once military duty to the state is seen in moral terms, both reflecting the individual's worth and the worth of his sacrifice, the use of mercenaries is morally difficult. The mercenary cannot make a worthy sacrifice, because he does not belong to the state; and, in fact, the mercenary's worth is diminished by the fact that he kills for money rather than a sense of duty.

The Prussian reformers transformed the relationship between the state and the individual from one of state and subject, where the subject was treated as a chattel, to one of state and citizen, where the citizen was believed to be worthy of respect and the state's institutions were reformed to reflect that respect. It was not a democratic revolution, but a moral overhaul of the way individuals and their duties to society were perceived. Social change caused by a change in moral beliefs about citizenship in Prussia explains the adoption of a citizen army and the refusal to return to the mercenary system during subsequent conservative reaction.

While the defeats at Jena and Auerstädt forced Prussian military reform, it was not obvious that a citizen army was the solution to the nation's military woes. Conservatives defended the old army and were convinced minor changes and better leadership were all that was needed for improvement.[116]

Citizens were not necessarily effective, and some believed unleashing citizen enthusiasm on the battlefield was dangerous. Before the defeats at Jena, the soldier Friedrich van der Decken argued that the French-style citizen soldier fighting with enthusiastic patriotism was not necessary. The skills admired in the French 'could be developed by professional training, with a minimal amount of general social reform involved' and instilled through 'careful instruction'.[117] Decken and other conservatives were not convinced that patriotism was useful and worried that it might be dangerous.[118] Adopting a

---

[114] Ibid. [115] Ibid. 66. [116] Simon (1971: 179) and White (1989: 134).
[117] Showalter (1980: 58). [118] Paret (1966: 88, 92).

citizen army might lead to political revolution. Indeed, as late as 1794 Frederick William II rejected conscription on the grounds that 'it was infinitely dangerous to assemble such a mass of men'.[119]

There was, then, a body of opinion in Prussia which suggested that patriotic fervour was not necessary, that training and professionalism could match French tactics, and that revolutionary enthusiasm was dangerous. If this were true, then surely mercenaries could still fight for Prussia, either as members of the rank and file or as officers. An elite corps of foreigners would also be perfectly compatible with conservative desires.

So why did the conservatives fail? Part of the answer comes from the Military Reorganization Commission set up in 1807 by Frederick William III in response to Napoleon's devastating victories. Frederick William asked a group of experts to examine all of Prussia's military problems, including the question of recruitment and the use of foreigners.[120] In the early stages, conservative members of the Commission argued for the minimal change approach outlined above.[121] The reform contingent, led by Scharnhorst and Gneisenau, ultimately took control of the Commission, in part because of Scharnhorst's effective manoeuvring.[122]

Even though the use of foreigners would have been perfectly compatible with the kind of army the conservatives advocated and, as we have seen, Avant suggests that this option was on the table, the conservatives do not appear to have suggested it. In December 1807, an official Cabinet Order prohibited foreign recruitment. Shanahan argues that the move happened for two reasons: first, French domination of Europe was drying up the supply of foreigners to recruit, but second, and more important, was the fact that 'nationalism had sealed the bond between citizens and the army' and so soldiers were more easily obtained.[123]

The Cabinet Order may sound as though it was responding merely to practical pressures: a lack of foreigners coincided happily with the increased availability of soldiers. The 'bond between the citizens and the army', however, is crucial. Once the reformers changed the army to reflect the citizen's worth, and the citizen was tied to the nation's army by a moral duty, the use of mercenaries was impossible. In 'one of its first acts, the Reorganization Commission announced that "all inhabitants of the state are its born defenders"'.[124]

In 1808, a report by the Commission reasserted the duty of the Prussian citizen to the state, and 'large mercenary armies were admitted ... to be best for

---

[119] Gooch 1980: 38.
[120] For details on the Military Reorganization Commission, see Paret (1966: 122–7), Simon (1971), and Kitchen (1975: 40).
[121] Paret (1966: 127). [122] Ibid. 125. [123] Shanahan 1966: 124.
[124] Paret (1966: 134).

prosperous states with ambitious policies. But when small states were threatened with conquest' they had a superior resource, the 'voluntary sacrifice of popular rights and personal property for the state'.[125] The Commission recognized that mercenaries might be useful in some circumstances, but mercenary use was incompatible with the complicated social/military edifice of reform. Moreover, the Commission argued that the patriotism of national soldiers would be depressed by the presence of mercenaries.[126] The reformers believed that the sacrifice of the citizen in defence of the state was a moral good, and in its morality, was also practical.

Mercenaries may have been abandoned because Prussia's domestic divisions allowed the reformers to win. But that assertion does not really answer the question of *why* the reformers won on the question of abandoning foreigners in the army. We can only understand why mercenaries were discarded if we understand that the reformers 'won' with a programme with the citizen, his worth, and his duty at its core; the abandonment of mercenaries had to be a first step along that path because of the dangers posed to the citizen's pure patriotic duty by the presence of mercenary greed. Scharnhorst, as argued above, was explicitly concerned about the taint mercenaries might spread among volunteers.

The decision to stop using mercenaries was taken very early. The Cabinet Order 1807 occurred on 17 December, and most of the Commission's work took place in 1808. Still more interesting is that the reformers did not take control of the Commission until 1808.[127] At the time of the Cabinet Order, 'five months of work had not brought any other important reforms, if one may except the substitution of grey trousers for white'.[128] In other words, the reformers 'won' on the question of mercenaries before they had 'won' about anything else.

And, in a sense, they would have had to. To argue that citizens had a special duty to the state, that they would be superior soldiers, would not work if it could be demonstrated that mercenaries were perfectly capable of duty and just as good as citizens. By 1813, the shift was complete. While after Jena, it was the King who had lost the war and the people who needed to remain calm, when Prussia took on France in 1813, a decree establishing the *Landsturm* or militia said 'a people united with its King can never be defeated' and that 'every citizen is obligated to resist the approaching enemy with every kind of weapon'.[129] The unity of king and people and the obligation of resistance could not have made sense, because foreigners could never be united with a

---

[125] Shanahan (1966: 120).   [126] Ellis (1973: 127).   [127] Shanahan (1966: 127).
[128] Ibid. 124.   [129] Quoted in Simon (1971: 169).

Prussian king, and nor could they be obliged to resist on any other basis than the financial.

The Influence of Norms Is Demonstrated by the Social Cost of Reform and the Persistence of the Ban on Mercenaries during the Period of Reaction

What is especially remarkable about the Prussian decision to glorify the citizen and abandon the mercenary is its huge social cost. Creating a citizen army would require 'deep social and political changes'.[130] Although the blows of Jena and Auerstädt struck with such force they made reform inevitable, conservatives in Prussian society quickly recovered and offered formidable resistance.[131] Further evidence for the argument that Prussia's decision to abandon mercenaries was a moral, rather than a practical, decision comes from the fact that it would have been far easier for Prussia to retain the old system, or at least some version of it, than to replace it.

Accepting citizen soldiers meant that Prussian society had to reverse a tradition of thinking about the military as a specialized community, a tradition which went back to the twelfth century.[132] The notion of a mass army populated by thinking soldiers and with the possibility of promotion on the basis of ability was 'repugnant to the aristocratic officers of the Prussian army'.[133] Reversing the old system was thus a difficult task; uniting the people and the state was novel and the old system entrenched.[134] Opposition to the reform programme came from all parts of society. The nobility feared the loss of their privileges, while bourgeois civil servants preferred an absolutist state.[135] The King 'and most of those around him regarded universal military service as a unwarranted revolutionary step, whose social costs would render any subsequent victory empty'.[136] But Prussia was willing to adopt a citizen army, which would require a complete overhaul of society *and* threaten the position of elites, and we must consider why.

The catastrophic losses to Napoleon unquestionably provide part of the explanation. The old system had clearly failed and its defenders could not be taken seriously.[137] But as we have seen, many of the problems of Jena and Auerstädt could have been solved without resorting to wholesale social change and the exclusive use of citizens to staff armies. The rest of the answer might lie in a confluence of factors: the defeat; the presence of able and powerful

---

[130] Paret (1966: 90).   [131] Simon (1954: 305).   [132] Gooch (1980: 7).
[133] Kitchen (1975: 33).   [134] Gooch (1980: 38).   [135] Simon (1971: 11, 13).
[136] Moran (2003b: 53).   [137] Simon (1971: 149).

reformers; and the fact that these reformers managed to get the ear of the King, perhaps because of domestic divisions. But none of these on their own, or even in combination, is sufficient.

When we add the moral component of the argument the situation is clearer. The moral belief that citizens were not only potentially superior fighters, but that their utilization required some basic changes in Prussian society was relatively uncontroversial. The presence of mercenaries could only undermine this project. The normative lens meant that the reformers picked a particular path and stuck with it. The disappearance of mercenaries was an early casualty of the decision, and one of the few early points of agreement. And, as noted above, the Prussian state was not suggesting democracy or even particularly liberal reforms, but rather a state that would enable the citizen to perform his duty, for which he would receive only minimal rights in exchange.

The continued use of citizen soldiers and exclusion of foreigners is also interesting in the light of the return to a professional army and socially conservative values in Prussia after 1815. The sort of army Prussia ended up with could have, in theory, very easily included foreigners. After all, it was essentially the same sort of army that the conservatives had advocated in 1807—small, professional, and held together with honour and devotion to the unit. The Prussian army that became the envy of Europe was not successful because of passionate nationalism, but because of professionalism, which persisted long after France's revolutionary élan had declined.[138] Even if the Prussian economy were able to support a mass army in the French style, 'the Prussian government was unwilling to accept the domestic risks of creating one'.[139] Europe at large had become less convinced about the powers of enthusiasm on the battlefield after 1815, and 'soldier and citizen sank, or were pressed, back in to the passivity most suitable for a subject'. Even the liberal reformers did not maintain the popular nationalism which sprang up during the final stage of the war against Napoleon, and if they could have done so, they might have been able to resist the strong reactionary trend in Prussia.[140] The forces of reaction ultimately won. By 1819, Prussia had successfully undone the new military reforms[141] and returned to a system that not only 'bore no relation to the nation-in-arms' but contained nothing 'that would have been startling to any of the monarchs of the eighteenth century'.[142]

The critical question about Prussia's military reforms, then, is not why the conservatives lost, because they were ultimately successful, but why they were unable to reverse all of the reforms and return to an old-style army. By 1819, France was no longer in control of wide swathes of European territory and

---

[138] Gooch (1980: 42).   [139] Showalter (2002: 36).   [140] Simon (1954: 320).
[141] Craig (1964: 38) and Paret (1966: 220).   [142] Esdaile (1995: 216, 215).

the mercenary export states were back in business. There were foreigners to be had, if Prussia were interested in hiring them. There was indeed nothing about the sort of army that became the model for Prussia that would have excluded the presence of foreigners. But as we have seen, the conservatives agreed that the army should be composed of citizens, and only disagreed about which kinds of reform were necessary for citizens to develop feelings of duty and enthusiasm for the state.

The new citizen–state relationship in Prussia was not one that Enlightenment theorists would have embraced. The common note of the Prussian reforms 'is not one of revolutionary ferment, but of social discipline: a *levee* [sic] *en masse* rendered safe for the consumption of liberals and conservatives alike'.[143] The conservatives did not wish to stop citizens from fighting because of a sense of duty and sacrifice to the state, because they too had come to believe in the morality of citizen duty to the state, just differently from the way the reformers had. The disappearance of the mercenary system was complete. By 1853, open recruiting for mercenaries within the major German states was no longer possible, and Prussia was not only obdurately opposed but 'fully prepared to take the most drastic measures against violators'.[144]

In short, both conservatives and reformers in Prussia believed that the citizen had some kind of moral duty to the state. The state did not return to the use of mercenaries, even when it could have, because mercenaries would have undermined the new relationship between citizen and state. Even when the conservatives abandoned the concept of universal service and clung to the use of exemptions, they simultaneously stuck to the idea that some citizens could be called on to sacrifice themselves for the state.

A belief in the morality of citizen military duty (and hence the immorality of hiring foreigners) became part of the Prussian identity. German and Prussian historians overemphasized the role of the *tirailleurs* because of their belief in the superiority of the citizen soldier and the difficulties of the mercenary. The historians Freytag-Loringhoven and von der Goltz were influenced by 'aggressive patriotism and a fervent belief in large, standing armies [which] could not but color their judgement of the revolutionary past'.[145] German accounts of the American Revolution were also coloured by a passionate belief in the merits of the citizen army. Nineteenth-century accounts of the performance of Hessians dwell on arguments of '"blood money" and "trade in human beings"'.[146] The transformations of the French and American revolutions and the consequent changes in the public's opinion of the use of foreign

---

[143] Moran (2003*a*: 5). [144] Bayley (1977: 45, 78).
[145] Paret (1966: 96). v.d. Goltz wrote in 1906 and Freytag-Loringhoven in 1911.
[146] Atwood (1980: 6).

troops meant that 'every aspect of the Hessians—the morality of the subsidy treaties, recruiting, desertion rates, their performance in war, their princes' private lives—became a subject of historical, and indeed political, debate in Germany'.[147] The belief that citizen armies were morally superior to mercenary forces was so ingrained in nineteenth-century Prussia that objective analysis of the past was no longer possible.

The decision to adopt a citizen army cannot be understood without examining the norm of citizen service, which was inherently incompatible with the use of foreign troops. Once the army had been restructured, the exclusive use of citizens was never abandoned. In fact, many of the reforms that sought to protect the basic dignity of the soldier were never repealed: the Prussian army permanently stopped its system of drastic corporal punishment. The concept of citizen duty outlived the reality of citizen zeal by many years. The *Landwehr* militia did not train its recruits, expecting that their call to duty would allow them to pick up what they needed; by the 1850s, Prussia's army 'had the worst of two worlds. Its operational effectiveness was open to serious doubt because of a dependence on men neither trained nor motivated'.[148]

5.4. BRITAIN

The British decision to opt, belatedly by European standards, for an army composed of citizens cannot be understood without reference to the role of norms. The British hired contingents of mercenaries for the last time in the Crimea, but to understand why Britain took so long to abandon mercenaries and why she adopted a citizen army when she did requires an examination of the intellectual history of anti-mercenary feeling and the competing norm that standing armies are morally and politically dangerous. The norm against standing armies was more powerful than the anti-mercenary norm, until the American Revolution began to increase dislike of mercenaries. By the time of the Crimea, the decision to hire mercenaries was seen not only as indicative of the British military's failings and the necessity to create some kind of regular recruitment, but as a moral failing that suggested that Britain was not one of the great states of Europe. To demonstrate the importance of norms and ideas in the British decision to exclude foreigners from the military, I examine first the intellectual origins of both the anti-mercenary and the anti-standing army norms. Second, I argue that anti-mercenary sentiment was expressed over the use of German mercenaries in the American Revolution, which increased as the Revolution became increasingly unpopular. The third

[147] Ibid. 2.   [148] Showalter (2002: 36).

section demonstrates that the use of mercenaries in the Crimea created great criticism on normative grounds. The Crimean debacle at once eroded the norm against standing armies and allowed anti-mercenary feeling to take hold more permanently. The anti-mercenary norm ultimately led to a policy change, in part because of the problems in the Crimea and in part because Britain could no longer be taken seriously as a civilized nation as long as she traded in mercenaries. The final section considers why it took Britain so long to adopt a standing army.

Two Strong Norms: The Norm against Mercenary Use and the Norm against Standing Armies

Britain commonly used foreigners to fight abroad during the seventeenth, eighteenth, and nineteenth centuries. During the 1690s, foreign mercenaries composed on average nearly half of the English army in Flanders, and by the first decade of the eighteenth century, their numbers had risen to 60 per cent.[149] By the time the American Revolution began, there was no question that Britain would send foreign troops as part of its army, because foreigners had always been used in the past.[150]

Even if the use of foreign troops was commonplace in eighteenth- and nineteenth-century Britain, it does not mean that there was no dissent about the morality of their use, or no discussion that a citizen army would be morally superior because of motivation. As we have seen above, Harrington made a strong case for the idea of civic military duty. Adam Smith believed that a society based on commerce would have its military spirit weakened, because defence of the community would rest on a specialized few and the obligation would not extend to the community at large. Commerce 'sinks the courage of mankind and tends to extinguish the martial spirit...the defence of the country is therefore committed to a certain sett of men who have nothing else ado; and among the bulk of the people military courage diminishes'.[151] Smith believed that 'the security of every society must always depend, more or less, upon the martial spirit of the great body of the people' and that a society where every citizen possessed such a spirit would succeed in diminishing 'the dangers to liberty'.[152] Without military exercise, martial spirit would decline and the 'mental mutilation, deformity, and wretchedness' which resulted from cowardice would spread throughout society.[153] Even at the height of mercenary use in England, the idea that citizens might be the most moral way to defend the nation existed.

[149] Bowen (1998: 13). [150] Atwood (1980: 2). [151] Smith ([1766] 1978: 540).
[152] Smith ([1776] 1976: 307). [153] Ibid. 308.

William Blackstone likewise argued that 'in a land of liberty it is extremely dangerous to make a distinct order of the profession of arms'. Such a profession is necessary in absolutist states that rule by fear, but not in free states, where 'no man should take up arms, but with a view to defend the country and it's [sic] laws: he puts not off the citizen when he enters the camp; but it is because he is a citizen, and would wish to continue so, that he makes himself for a while a soldier'.[154] The army ought to be a body of and for the people. It 'should be wholly composed of natural subjects; it ought only to be enlisted for a short time; the soldiers also should live intermixed with the people; no separate camp, no barracks...should be allowed'.[155] To ensure the total interchangeability of the lives of citizens and soldiers, military service should be rotated among the population, 'by dismissing a stated number and enlisting others at every renewal of their term'.[156] For Blackstone, military duty is what makes the citizen, and the right kind of army ensures that all citizens can perform this duty. He explicitly states that only 'natural-born' subjects ought to be in the army, because mercenaries would clearly be incompatible with a duty based on citizenship and required in order to defend that citizenship.

The opposition between fear of conscription and hopes for the morality of citizen service leads us into the next phase of the argument. At the same time the British advocated the potential merits of citizen armies, they believed that standing armies were inherently dangerous. This belief was to prevent the preference for citizen soldiers from reaching its obvious conclusion, and leading to the creation of a standing army and the exclusion of mercenaries on the basis of their incorrect and immoral motivation.

The British dislike of standing armies had its roots in the English Civil War, during which the crown had controlled the army; this legacy meant that royal control of standing armies was associated with the denial of civil liberties.[157] A strong norm against standing armies resulted, which associated standing armies with loss of freedom. The Bill of Rights, created after the Glorious Revolution, stated 'that the raising or keeping of a standing army within the kingdom in the time of peace, unless it be with the consent of Parliament, is against law'.[158]

The question of whether to defend the nation with a militia or with a standing army was one of the 'few genuine political issues that distinguished factions in opposition and factions in power' and was based on a pamphlet war waged between 1697 and 1699.[159] A seventeenth-century pamphlet

---

[154] Blackstone ([1765] 1979: 395). [155] Ibid. 401. [156] Ibid. 401–2.
[157] Mead Earle (1986: 226) and Ropp (1959: 60).
[158] Text of the Bill of Rights available at <http://www.britannia.com/history/docs/rights.html> and also quoted in Ropp (1959: 60).
[159] Barnett (1970: 167).

asked 'whether standing forces, Military, and Arbitrary Government came not plainly in by the same steps'.[160] Another pamphlet pointed out that 'if we look through the World, we shall find in no Country, Liberty and an Army stand together'.[161] Pamphlets, political writers, and recent history gave birth to a norm against standing armies in the late seventeenth century 'with Harrington playing at least an umbilical role'. It was the 'bogey of the standing army which was to figure so prominently among the political ideas of the next century'.[162] In 1713, the Tory Francis Atterbury contrasted Whig and Tory views in a pamphlet: while the Tories would fight against a standing army, the Whigs would seek 'an augmentation of troops for the better suppressing of mobs and riots'.[163]

The norm against standing armies had become a bogey that no longer had basis in reality.[164] The tradition of avoiding standing armies meant that Britain could not rely on a core of trained men, and it also led her to turn abroad in searches for recruits to staff the temporary army. After the Seven Years War, the army shrank in size from 203,000 (including mercenaries) in 1760 to 45,000 in 1764.[165] Yet it is important to remember that fear of a standing army coexisted with the idea that citizens could make effective soldiers. Throughout the eighteenth and nineteenth centuries attempts were made to reform the militia system and make it more effective.[166]

In peacetime 'during the eighteenth century the army as a combined organized and fighting force hardly existed.... barracks... were opposed in Britain as smacking of European modes and standing armies'.[167] The fundamental prejudice against a standing army made it impossible for Britain to develop the institutions necessary to create a more effective militia. Without creating a more permanent army structure Britain was left with severe recruitment problems, and the uncertainty surrounding recruitment at home made the nation reliant on foreign soldiers.[168] Moreover, it led to a situation by the late eighteenth century where English patriotism co-existed with distaste for military service, and 'the constitutional monarchy, though its political controls over the army and navy differed from those on the continent, relied as much on the mercenary soldier and impressed sailor as did absolutist regimes'.[169] The structure of the British state was not incompatible with the use of mercenaries; in fact, seeking to preserve British liberty by preventing a standing army created a situation where foreign soldiers were vital.

[160] Quoted in Pocock (1965: 560).   [161] Quoted in Hoppit (2000: 157).
[162] Pocock (1965: 560).   [163] Quoted in Hoppit (2000: 285).
[164] Pocock (1965: 562) and Barnett (1970: 167).   [165] Barnett (1970: 202).
[166] Ibid. 171–4.   [167] Ibid. 176.   [168] Bayley (1977: 4).
[169] Paret (1992: 44).

Reliance on foreigners was not a popular way out of Britain's recruitment problems, even though it remained an effective strategy. During the American Revolution, noises began to be made about the dangers and the morality of relying on foreigners to fight.

The American Revolution and War of Independence

As we have seen, the army Britain sent to America to deal with the colonial rebellion included German mercenaries. The British were able to recruit from Hessen-Kassel, Brunswick, and Waldeck with relative ease, although schemes to recruit from other nations came to naught when recruitment was forbidden.[170] In contrast, recruitment at home was unsuccessful, with only 8,620 men found for the regular army in 1777. To make up the numbers the following year the parish quota was revived and troublesome social problems were shipped from the parishes to America. This effort raised 1,000 men, 'who took the first opportunity to desert *en masse*'.[171] Recruitment of foreigners to fight the Americans was a necessity.

But it was not automatically popular. There were those who felt that Britain 'had once more made gold take the place of men'.[172] The decision to hire the mercenaries gained attention when the treaties signed between Britain and the various German princes were debated in the House of Lords. Mockler argues that 'it is unlikely that at any time or in any place were the principles of mercenary soldiering and the right of a government to hire mercenary soldiers submitted to such searching and profound criticisms'.[173] Four specifically normative concerns marked the debate about the use of German mercenaries in the war with America.

Buying Mercenaries Was a Trade in Human Flesh

First, the practice of hiring mercenaries from another state was damned as an immoral trade in human beings. The Duke of Camden concurred, arguing that that 'the whole is a mere mercenary bargain for the hire of troops on one side, and the sale of human blood on the other; and that the devoted wretches thus purchased for the slaughter, are mere mercenaries, in the worst sense of the word'.[174] The Duke of Richmond believed that the treaties were

---

[170] Attempts to recruit from Russia and to recruit the Dutch Scotch brigade failed (Atwood 1980: 24).

[171] Bayley (1977: 6).   [172] Barnett (1970: 218).   [173] Mockler (1969: 121).

[174] Cobbett (1776: 1203). Cobbett is the pre-nineteenth-century version of Hansard, and contains the transcripts of parliamentary debates.

a 'downright mercenary bargain, for the taking into pay a certain number of hirelings, who were bought and sold like so many beasts for slaughter. There was no common interest which mutually bound the parties'.[175] The treaties with the German princes were based purely on finance, rather than on a coincidence of interest that would make them more palatable. Even the King had concerns about the use of mercenaries, remarking 'this giving commissions to German officers to get men...in plain English amounts to making me a kidnapper which I cannot think a very honourable occupation'.[176] To make matters worse, men were being kidnapped or bought and sold specifically to kill, and to kill in a conflict that they had no proper motive for joining.

Mercenaries Did Not Have the Right Motive to Fight against America

Second, concerns were raised that mercenaries, as outsiders, could not have a just motive for fighting the war. Because the war was one between England and her colony, the use of mercenaries was inviting foreigners into an intimate family dispute. As Mr Alderman Bull exhorted the House, 'let not the historian be obliged to say that the Russian and the German slave was hired to subdue the sons of Englishmen and of freedom'.[177] The Duke of Chandos argued that mercenaries were being brought in to fight because 'the British troops...shew an honest backwardness to engage against their fellow-citizens'.[178] The decision to hire mercenaries was disreputable in part because the concept of English fighting English was disreputable; but to do so with foreign troops seemed utterly immoral.

The disapproval over the fact that mercenaries were both foreign to the conflict and financially motivated led to problems on the ground as well as in the debates in the House of Lords. The officers could not countenance the financial motivation of their Hessian colleagues while the loyalists especially disliked the idea that foreigners should fight to restore British rule.[179] And it was recognized that fighting the Americans with morally distasteful foreigners could indeed make the resistance obdurate. William Pitt, the Earl of Chatham, argued that 'If I were an American as I am an Englishman, while a foreign troop was in my country, I never would lay down my arms; never, never, never'.[180] Mr Hartley also recognized that bringing in foreign troops

---

[175] Ibid. 1193. [176] Mockler (1969: 115). [177] Cobbett (1776: 1185).
[178] Ibid. 1203. [179] Atwood (1980: 153).
[180] Mockler (1969: 129). It will be recalled that the Americans felt that the use of mercenaries signalled that the British were not interested in reconciliation.

would utterly destroy the connection between Britain and her American colony.[181]

Mercenaries Were Part and Parcel of What Made the War against America Wrong

Third, the use of mercenaries was another nail pounded into what some believed was the coffin of an unfair and unnecessary war. The Duke of Richmond, in a written address to the King, remarked that 'if the justice and equity of this unnatural war was not questioned by so large a part of your Majesty's subjects... yet a reconciliation with the colonies... would be more agreeable to sound policy, than to entrust the prosecution of hostilities to foreigners'.[182] Mr Hartley argued that the Americans were not even rebelling, as the British had been the aggressor in all cases.[183]

The war was unpopular because many believed that the Americans' cause, liberty, was just. In this context, mercenaries, motivated by money, were especially appalling. Lord Irnham argued that the sale of men to fight as mercenaries was wrong, but believed it worse for a prince to send his subjects to the slaughter in 'such destructive wars, where he has the additional crime of making them destroy much better and nobler beings than themselves'.[184] Part of Bull's objection was that foreign 'slaves' were being used to subjugate the sons of freedom.[185] To 'support a cause in no shape whatever connected with the empire' and in which they had no interest would render the German states 'vile and dishonourable in the eyes of all Europe, as a nursery of men reserved for the purposes of supporting arbitrary power'.[186] To use disinterested outsiders with an inappropriate motivation to quash a rebellion which was about freedom seemed profoundly wrong.

Once the Hessians had been sent, British failures in the American Revolution further tainted the whole notion of using foreign troops. When the British war effort began to flag and it became increasingly apparent that the Americans would win the war, the blame was on the Hessian side, especially for the sort of abuses with which mercenaries were typically charged: plundering and a cowardly (and profitable) interest in self-preservation.[187] Negative opinion about the war in general enhanced negative views about mercenaries,[188] and Britain's use of foreign troops became a major controversy.[189] The growing ill-feeling against mercenaries was reinforced by their failure in a war that

---

[181] Cobbett (1776: 1174–5).　[182] Ibid. 1189.　[183] Ibid. 1170.
[184] Ibid.　[185] See above.　[186] Lord Irnham (Cobbett 1776: 1169).
[187] Atwood (1980: 107).　[188] Mockler (1969: 126).　[189] Conway (2000: 150).

many felt Britain should have won, and many others felt Britain should not have fought at all.

Mercenaries Undermined Britain's Greatness

Fourth, Britain could hardly count herself as a great state if she relied so heavily on foreigners to provide for her. In the Duke of Richmond's written address, he pointed out that the decision to hire mercenaries was attended by 'danger and disgrace' and that Britain's decision to subjugate her colonies with foreign mercenaries would signal to the rest of Europe that 'these kingdoms are unable, either from want of men, or from a disinclination to this service, to furnish a competent number of natural-born subjects to make the first campaign'.[190]

Not only did the decision to hire mercenaries reflect the fact that British subjects were disinclined to serve the Crown, Britain's very identity as a free state was threatened. 'For should that time ever arrive', Lord Camden argued, 'in which our existence as a nation depends on the assistance of foreign hirelings, from that instant I should deem our consequence as a sovereign state, and our liberties as a free people, no more'.[191] Lord Camden's argument summarizes the two great blows that the decision to hire mercenaries might strike at British identity. Free states would be threatened by foreign troops, *and* states could not be sovereign states of consequence so long as they relied on mercenaries. The idea that Britain should rely on foreign soldiers was increasingly incompatible with the nation's sense of itself as a free state, which protected liberties, and of a sovereign state in Europe.

These four normative arguments were repeated more vehemently during the debate that was to take place over whether or not to send mercenaries to the Crimea. They were to combine and gain strength because of the increasing unpopularity and disrepute of the war against America. The use of mercenaries came to be explicitly associated with the opposition of freedom. The early fears that were expressed in the Lords about how the use of foreign troops could damage the country's good name abroad were brought up again, and in no uncertain terms. Many of these concerns were washed away by Wellington's victories in the Napoleonic Wars, but the seeds of mercenary dislike had been sowed during America's revolution. The decision to abandon mercenaries cannot be understood by examining the Crimean War alone, because mercenaries had not been an uncontroversial part of British history, and distaste for mercenaries pre-dated the failure at Crimea by decades.

[190] Cobbett (1776: 1189). [191] Ibid. 1224.

It is also important to recall that while foreigners fought in large numbers under Wellington (as noted in Chapter 4), these foreigners were not recruited using a subsidy or auxiliary system. Many of them were members of states which had fallen to Napoleon, or of British allies. They were not considered by contemporary observers to be mercenaries, as argued below. The Napoleonic Wars were important because British success unnaturally preserved an ineffective system, the implications of which will be discussed later.

The Crimean War

By the time of the Crimean War, Britain had faced one defeat with a multinational army, and one glorious success. Wellington's magnificent victory at Waterloo unquestionably preserved the British system of foreign recruitment. Troops from the Wellington era were still involved in the British army decades later, and had preserved the army 'like a garment in a bottom drawer, sentimentally loved, but rotted and rendered quaint by the passage of time. Even its uniforms in 1854 were essentially those of Waterloo'. Only the disgrace of the Crimean War shattered the Wellingtonian illusion.[192]

At the outset of the Crimean War, Britain began to look for the foreign soldiers that customarily formed part of the army. But it was no longer an easy task. Post-Napoleonic Europe was, as we have seen, increasingly opposed to the use of mercenaries on normative grounds and states had closed the doors to foreign recruiting. At home, the usual problems with recruiting for the militia continued. Even if men could be recruited, the government believed it would take between six and eight months to train them to a useful standard.[193] Only within the peripheral and weak states of Germany, Italy, and Switzerland, without sufficient authority to close tightly the door on foreign enlistment, was even the attempt at recruiting possible.[194] Troops were eventually recruited from Sardinia, and more problematically from the German states, where Prussia remained strongly opposed to the recruitment and the British operated under the watchful eye of the police.[195] Spectacularly unsuccessful attempts were made elsewhere, including one in the United States which caused a serious diplomatic incident.[196]

---

[192] Barnett (1970: 282, 271).
[193] Speech by the Duke of Newcastle (Hansard 1854–7: 287).   [194] Bayley (1977: 79).
[195] Ibid. 69, 76, 84. French also points out that British recruiting in the German states was illegal (French 1990: 130). The Prussian police were interested because a soldier could not serve for the British unless he had completed his term of service for his home state; British zeal meant that recruiters were not always careful about the letter of the law.
[196] Dumbauld (1937: 259) and Bayley (1977: 88, 91).

Before the recruiting missions could begin, legislation needed to be passed. The Enlistment of Foreigners Bill went before Parliament in December 1854. The debates in both the Commons and the Lords were ferocious. Bayley argues that the government was well aware of the furore that would result from the attempt to recruit mercenaries for the Crimean War, and so introduced the bill in the Lords, where it would have a smoother passage than the Commons.[197] The Opposition, sensing weakness, believed that the bill was explosive enough to bring down the Government, and indeed lobbied for extending debate past Christmas in an effort to build the negative public opinion they felt sure would result from the bill.[198] But it was not to be, and the debate was restricted to December. The Aberdeen ministry stated that it would resign if the bill failed. Its passage, however, was anything but smooth. Four explicitly normative concerns about mercenaries shaped the debate.

Mercenaries Were Inappropriately Motivated

First, those who opposed the sending of mercenaries to the Crimea did so with a series of arguments that centred around the idea that mercenaries, because they are foreign, are not motivated to fight by an appropriate cause. There were two variations of the argument based on appropriate cause.

Crimean Mercenaries Were Not the Same as Wellington's Foreign Troops

The first variation was that the mercenaries now being recruited for the Crimea were a different proposition from the foreigners who had fought gallantly with Wellington at Waterloo. The Government argued that the German Legion's honourable history set a precedent for using foreigners.[199] Those who opposed the bill pointed out that use of foreigners in the past was different, and perfectly all right, because in all cases these foreigners had some stake in the conflict themselves. Under Wellington, 'the foreigners who gave their services to England were men whose sympathies were as fully, if not more so, [enlisted] than those of our own countrymen'.[200] The troops which assisted England 'fought under the banners or with the sanction of their respective Sovereigns, or they were fighting in a national cause, or in a cause which was to them of national interest'.[201] Disraeli summarized the situation: 'our objection is, that our countrymen should be fighting by the side of foreigners who are *condottieri* and mercenaries, but we do not object to their fighting by the side of foreigners who are our allies'.[202]

---

[197] Bayley (1977: 48). [198] Ibid. 52.
[199] Speech by Duke of Newcastle (Hansard 1854–7: col. 254).
[200] Earl of Clancarty (Ibid., col. 290). [201] Earl of Derby (Ibid., col. 445).
[202] Ibid., col. 594.

The Times echoed this position in an editorial, pointing out that Wellington's German Legion was acceptable because 'we always associated it with the fact that the war was especially German, fought on German soil and by German sovereigns and people, who were, indeed, more immediately *interested* in it than ourselves'.[203] In other words, the foreign assistance rendered to England in the past had been morally different, because the soldiers in question *had* been motivated by something other than financial gain.

The response of the Government and those in support of the bill to the argument that the troops hired for the Crimea might not be motivated to fight by an appropriate cause demonstrates the degree to which both sides believed that a proper cause for fighting was important for soldiers. Supporters of the bill pointed out that all Europeans had an interest in British and French success against Russia in the Crimea. Lord John Russell pointed out that to argue that the foreign recruits would not be interested in the war would be to say that 'you are engaged in a purely British quarrel, and not, as we have maintained, in the cause of Europe'.[204] Under these circumstances, Mr Phillips 'could not see that we were justified in having recourse to the assistance of persons, who, according to the theory of war, had as immediate an object in the results of the war as the English nation could pretend to have'.[205] The foreigners, Britain sought to hire, did indeed have an interest in the outcome of the war, and so were not mere mercenaries at all.

Queen Victoria disliked the idea of referring to the troops eventually recruited as Foreign Legions; she suggested, successfully, that they be called the British-German, British-Swiss, and British-Italian Legions,[206] a decision that emphasized their commonality with those who hired them rather than their differences. Supporters of the bill did not seek to challenge the idea that mercenaries are immoral because they are improperly motivated; rather, the choice to argue that the foreigners to be recruited for the Crimea did have a stake in its outcome, and therefore an appropriate cause, demonstrates that they believed cause to be as important for morality as the opposition.

The only exception to the opposition's acceptance of the morality of Britain's previous use of foreign troops was the use of the Hessians in America, because this too represented a case where the mercenaries could make no claim that it was in their interest to fight abroad. Disraeli called it 'a shameful page' in British history.[207] Even the Government disavowed the use of mercenaries in America.[208] German historians, who had argued against the decision to use mercenaries in moral terms, influenced their British counterparts Trevelyan

---

[203] Emphasis added. Editorial in *The Times*, 15 December 1854, page 6.
[204] Lord John Russell (Hansard 1854–7: 515).   [205] Ibid., col. 678.
[206] Bayley (1977: 109).   [207] Hansard (1854–7: col. 595).
[208] Lord John Russell (Ibid., 510).

and Gooch, who took the position that the German princes', and by implication the British leaders', crime 'was not merely to have trafficked in the blood of their subjects, but also to have opposed the realization of the liberal democratic state, the highest form of human government'. [209]

Mercenary Motivation Was Immoral, Making It a Danger to British Troops
Arguments that centred around the immorality, pure and simple, of a mercenary motivation were the second type of cause-based argument. The opposition's arguments on cause rested on the idea that soldiers should have some kind of unselfish motive to kill. 'For what could be baser than the trade of a mercenary soldier', asked Mr Phillimore in the House of Commons, 'without one feeling that could embellish his calling or "make ambition virtue"?'.[210] The belief that a mercenary cannot be moral because of his motivation is summed up by Richard Cobden, in a way that echoes exactly the appropriate cause component of the anti-mercenary norm:

... it is assumed that men fight for a cause, that they are actuated by a love of home, devotion to the country, or attachment to a Sovereign; these are the sentiments that are considered to hallow the pursuit of arms. But what motives have these men whom you endeavour to hire out of the back slums of the towns of Germany? They can have no pretensions to fighting from any moral motive whatever; *they are deprived of every ground upon which you can justify war*, and, as they want the motives which I have described, there is just the difference between them and an ordinary soldier fighting for his country that there is between a hero and a cut-throat. It is wholesale assassination to employ them.[211]

Members of both Houses argued that the base motivation of a mercenary led in turn to base behaviour. Again, the kinds of behaviour those against the bill expected of mercenaries echoes the charges levelled at mercenaries in the past. Mercenaries were only interested in money,[212] would change sides for higher wages and did not care for whom they fought as long as the price was right.[213] Mr Drummond provides a succinct and colourful summary of the opposition's concerns: 'These men are nothing but men-butchers; they fight and murder for 1s. a day and, of course, if anyone will give them 2s. a day they will turn round and murder you in turn'.[214]

Mercenaries, and their dangerous selfish motivation, might taint either the proud spirit of the British people, or the spirit of her soldiers already in the Crimea, or both. The Earl of Derby warned the government that if they told

---

[209] Atwood (1980: 2).   [210] Hansard (1854–7: cols. 544–5).
[211] Ibid., col. 668. Emphasis added.   [212] Mr Gibson (Ibid., 551).
[213] Mr Gibson (Ibid); Mr E. Ball (Hansard 1854–7: 546); and Mr Disraeli (Hansard (1854–7: 597).
[214] Hansard (1854–7: 640).

the British people that the means of recruiting British troops were exhausted, 'then you extinguish the feeling of the country and damp the whole national spirit, which is now entirely and altogether with you'.[215]

In the Crimea itself, brave British soldiers might be undermined by the presence of unmotivated troops. The dubious morality of the foreigners, once recruited, meant that if 'you value the moral character of your soldiers, you are to some extent endangering that moral character by placing beside them, and in connection with them, troops for whose moral character you have no security'.[216] An editorial in the *Illustrated London News* urged its readers to 'guard against the illusion that a mercenary force would display patriotism and a sense of devotion to its adopted country. These qualities could be expected only in British troops'.[217] Mercenaries could cause a sort of immorality by association, with their lack of national enthusiasm degrading the enthusiasm of the soldiers on the field with them and the nation which hired them.

Mercenaries Were Equated with the Sale of Humanity

The second normative argument raised in Parliament was the idea that the practice of hiring mercenaries was simply a trade in flesh, and therefore immoral. This argument had appeared in the debate in 1776 and was reinforced by the anti-slavery movement. By the nineteenth century Britain was leading an international crusade against slavery, and British delegates had brought up the need for an anti-slavery convention at the Peace of Paris (1814–15) and Congresses of Vienna and Verona (1815 and 1822, respectively) while individual Britons set up what we would today consider non-governmental organizations (NGO) to pressure for change on slavery.[218] Efforts to control slavery were the first international attempt to 'criminalize international commerce in a particular "commodity"'.[219] It is hardly surprising that the debate over the international sale of mercenaries would highlight the similarities between the trade in the commodity of slaves and in the commodity of soldiers.

Sir Edward Bulmer-Lytton spoke with scorn of 'the princes who thus sell the blood of their subjects' and his grief 'at the degradation of England in the blood-money she pays to the hirelings'.[220] The Earl of Ellenborough drew a conclusion that seems obvious once the discussion turned to accusations of trading in human flesh, and asked if there were any difference between paying the German princes for their subjects and 'the consideration which the buyer of slaves gave to the King of Dahomey for the bodies of his subjects'. He 'did

---

[215] Ibid. 369.   [216] The Earl of Ellenborough (Ibid. 260).
[217] Quoted in Bayley (1977: 58).   [218] Nadelmann (1990: 492–98).   [219] Ibid. 497.
[220] Hansard (1854–7: 525).

not see how, if they repudiated the detestable practice of slave dealing, the principle could be different on the banks of the Elbe from that which took place on the banks of the Congo'.[221]

Britain Was Degraded by Hiring Mercenaries

The third normative argument raised against the decision to hire foreigners to reinforce British troops in the Crimea was that Britain was undermined or degraded as a state by doing so. It is important not to underestimate the role played by Britain's humiliating contribution to the Crimean War in the abandonment of mercenaries in future wars. Britain's identity as the glorious military nation which had defeated Napoleon at Waterloo had been threatened by her inability to get enough troops to the Crimea. In 1854, French conscription brought 140,000 men to the Crimea,[222] while Britain hoped to use reinforcements to build her troops up to 35,000.[223] There 'was no way of getting around the fact that the British army was now the junior partner and that it was the French General...who made the crucial decisions'.[224]

The humiliation was in some ways simply practical. Lord Stanley asked the House how Englishmen would feel 'if they were to hear that the Emperor of Russia was advertising for soldiers in every European city? Why, there would be a shout of triumph from one end of the country to the other. Every newspaper would be saying, "Oh! The Emperor is beaten; his cause is so unpopular his own subjects will not fight for him; he is driven to the last resource of a feeble Government and an unwarlike people, that of seeking aid from foreigners"'.[225] *The Times* concurred in an editorial, pointing out that 'the people are clear, and whatever mistake the Government has committed, it cannot go to the Emperor of Russia that the British people, slow to take arms, chary of their lives, and flagging in their zeal, will no longer fight for themselves and are inviting German adventurers to fight for them'.[226]

The shame of hiring foreigners went far beyond the fact that it publicly aired Britain's dirty recruitment laundry. Opting for mercenary assistance was no longer a common and accepted alternative. Both Houses used the language of humiliation[227] and degradation[228] to describe Britain's use of foreigners. In a war for freedom and the interests of Europe, England had been shamefully reduced to reliance on foreigners.[229] The Government, by seeking to hire

---

[221] Ibid. 433.   [222] Bayley (1977: 34).
[223] Conacher (1987: 110). Conacher puts the number of French troops at 120,000.
[224] Ibid. 111.   [225] Hansard (1854–7: 577).
[226] Editorial in *The Times*, 15 December 1854, page 6.
[227] Duke of Richmond (Hansard 1854–7: 267).
[228] Lord Wodehouse (Ibid. 357).   [229] Lord Wodehouse (Ibid).

foreigners, had 'proclaimed the moral and physical weakness of England by the advocacy of the mercenary system, which has long been condemned by the policy of every enlightened State in Europe'.[230] *The Times*, which supported the bill after the Aberdeen ministry staked its future on the bill's passage, nonetheless argued that the use of mercenary troops was no longer acceptable in Europe 'partly because in almost every country the practice of foreign enlistment has been discouraged by municipal law; partly because the rules of international law now recognized by civilized Powers regard with great suspicion breaches of neutrality of this nature; and still more because the sense of personal and national dignity condemns the custom'.[231]

Hiring mercenaries did not only signal that Britain had problems with recruitment. It signalled that Britain had problems *as a nation*. Just as Rousseau feared that the use of mercenaries would lead to corruption and collapse, so too did British parliamentarians. At 'all times, and in all countries, the hiring of mercenaries has been the surest mark of the weakness of a nation, and the certain sign of approaching decay' and even if Britain were not in that state,[232] others might think she was. And 'the fact was, that wherever mercenaries were introduced there were found to be corrupt governments—there civil and religious liberty were crushed, and universal national demonisation prevailed'.[233] Hiring mercenaries would show the world that Britain was struggling not only with recruitment, but as a nation.

The rest of the world perceived the British army the way members of parliament feared they did. De Tocqueville pointed out that Britain's inability to raise an army was problematic because 'according to continental notions, a nation which cannot raise as many troops as its wants require, loses our respect. It ceases, according to our notions, to be great or even to be patriotic'.[234]

What is interesting here is that normative considerations still operated at a time when the British military was in fairly dire straits. The necessity of sending *some* soldiers to reinforce the British in the Black Sea was clear, and yet debate raged on the issue. The public, and the opposition, could not accept the use of foreigners even if it was necessary to fill an obvious, and pressing, military need. In practical terms, the Government's argument was above reproach. Suggesting that Britain ought to rely on its own men, as yet untrained, was foolish. 'You might as well say, "Do not go to Liege for Minié rifles, for there is plenty of ore and coal in the country, and in time we may obtain the rifles"', pointed out Lord John Russell, who introduced

---

[230] Mr Murrough (Ibid. 760).   [231] Editorial in *The Times*, 22 December 1854, page 7.
[232] Earl of Derby (Hansard 1854–7: 368).   [233] Mr Laing (Ibid. 853).
[234] Letter from Alexis de Tocqueville to Nassau William Senior, 15 February 1855. Collected in Simpson ([1855] 1872: 93).

the bill to the Commons, 'no doubt this would be the case if sufficient time were afforded, and just in the same manner these men would be converted to soldiers if sufficient time were given'.[235]

Why Did Britain Take So Long to Adopt a Citizen Army?

All this leaves us with the question of why, if it were necessary, and if it had been common in British history, there should be such strenuous opposition to the notion of foreign recruitment. In other words, why did Britain wait so long to adopt a citizen army, and why did the normative concerns aired in 1776 and again in 1854 not prevent foreign recruitment?

One answer is, of course, Wellington's great success at Waterloo. The second is more practical. Peace between 1815 and 1854 meant that a generation of British people no longer had any direct experience with foreign recruitment.[236] And indeed, the Victorian sense of self had probably been shaped by the fact that foreigners, rather than British soldiers, were sent off to fight. Thanks 'to their mercenary army, the British people as a whole never felt the burdens of world power during the Victorian age' and 'the mercenary army made possible Victorian pacifistic optimism'.[237] While the British navy resorted to impressing men, the country had never had to fight its own land wars in large numbers. But, perhaps more significantly, a very strong norm against the creation of a permanent army created problems in the British military that could only be solved by opting for foreign recruitment. Britain's belief that the liberties of citizens were best safeguarded by the absence of a standing army explains why mercenary use persisted for so long in a very liberal state.

The Crimea struck a devastating blow at the norm against standing armies. The Duke of Newcastle, who introduced the measure in the House of Lords, himself recognized that Britain's military system made recruitment at the outset of a war difficult, because the country had 'no immediate system for bringing into the field a large and trained force. The military systems of other countries give much greater facilities in that respect'.[238] It was clear that Britain's recruiting problems required solutions, and that one of these solutions would be some kind of standing army. That said, it was not until ten years later that the Cardwell Reforms formally established a permanent standing army and not until the First World War that conscription was introduced. The timing of the Cardwell Reforms is crucial, because Britain did not begin to consider the attractions of the Prussian army until those reforms,

[235] Hansard (1854–7: col. 614). [236] Bayley (1977: 64). [237] Barnett (1970: 274).
[238] Hansard (1854–7: col. 254).

ten years after the Crimea. Abandoning mercenaries had little to do with emulating the Prussians, as Avant argues. During the Indian Mutiny in 1857, the norm against mercenary use was clearly at work. Cambridge suggested that Legions be raised from foreigners residing in England, having already abandoned the idea of recruiting abroad. Panmure, however, stated that the cabinet had decided against raising foreign troops because of the distaste for foreign recruits shown by Parliament. This 'formal rejection by the cabinet of the proposals of the commander-in-chief in a moment of extreme military crisis' indicated growing prejudice against foreign troops.[239] Foreigners in the British army only continued to be used if they had colonial or imperial ties, like the Gurkhas or Indian sepoys. These troops were not really 'foreign' in the sense they were considered to be part of an imperial project.[240] If anything, once the mercenary option had been closed after the Crimea, Britain had to adopt military reforms. Britain stopped using foreigners in her armies because of normative dislike *and* the failure of the system; but dislike was enough, because mercenaries disappeared before reforms were made.

The anti-mercenary norm has a long history in Britain. Arguments about appropriate cause led to a belief that mercenaries were morally suspect actors, and remind us that the mere fact of mercenary use does not indicate that it is accepted, and nor does it indicate that norms are not playing a role in state decisions about the use of force. Attention to norms clears up the picture of the British delay in adopting a citizen army. The norm against standing armies was strong enough to create a situation where recruitment problems, and so the use of foreigners, would be inevitable. But moral outrage at the spectacle of using foreigners with no interest and therefore no natural motive to reinforce British troops helped contribute to the sense that the Crimea was a debacle, and that Britain could no longer claim to be a glorious state if patriotism could no longer earn her enough troops to fight. Continuing to use mercenaries was incompatible with the kind of state Britain was, and wanted to appear to be. The norm against mercenary use began to undermine the norm against standing armies, which was permanently put out of commission by the practical problems and the visible horrors of the Crimea. Norms alone, of course, cannot explain the British shift entirely, but they do go a long way to helping us understand why Britain retained the option of using foreign soldiers for such a long time.

---

[239] Bayley (1977: 141–2).
[240] Of course these troops may not have been considered to be the 'equal' of their British counterparts, but they were nonetheless believed to be pursuing the same project.

5.5. CONCLUSION

Mercenaries disappeared from the armies of Europe because states began to question the morality of their use. New ideas about the relationship between states and citizens reinforced the existing notion that the use of mercenaries was immoral, and the use of mercenaries became impossible. To use foreign fighters in Europe after the nineteenth century would have undermined the entire system of military service used in all states, and challenged the underlying beliefs about how war and killing could be justified. To use mercenaries would also undermine national identity, as the willingness of citizens to fight and die for the state was one indicator of that state's success and status as a great player on the world stage. To ignore the importance of norms in the nineteenth century shift away from mercenary use is to ignore the fact that war itself became deeply normative. As the battlefields of Europe were increasingly crowded with ideologically or patriotically motivated soldiers, the presence of financially motivated mercenaries became more glaring. The debates in the British parliament demonstrate that by mid-century there was a belief that *civilized* states did not use foreigners to fight their wars.

The intellectual traditions of the eighteenth century laid important groundwork for the subsequent shift away from mercenary use. Practical pressures, like the growth in population and increasing reliance on tactics, were undeniably important factors in the decision to adopt a citizen army. But they cannot tell the whole story, for as we have seen, the first states to adopt a citizen army, America and France, did so because any other sort of army would have been incompatible with the norms of the Revolution. The pressures of the war, and the necessity of raising troops, may have dictated the use of citizens, but the whole normative programme of each revolution relied on the belief that the citizen had a duty to the state, and that hiring foreigners would have had drastic effects on the moral fibre and practical performance of the military.

In Prussia and Britain, the decision to abandon mercenaries in favour of citizens was not a natural outgrowth of a newly formed government ideology. In each case, the desire to use citizens had to come from a change in existing policy, and it is in these debates that we can clearly see the influence of norms. In Prussia, a particularly Prussian view of the citizen's duty to the state led Prussia to act on dislike of mercenary armies and create a system whereby the citizen owed a duty to the state and the state owed the citizen very little in return. This conception of the citizen–state relationship in part explains why Prussia did not return to the use of mercenaries during the period of reaction after Napoleon's defeat. The citizen–state relationship, as understood by the reformers, was radical, but as actually implemented, was deeply conservative. The norm against mercenary use in Prussia combined with a norm that the citizen owed the state unquestioning service, and the combination was so successful that no change was needed.

In Britain, the norm against mercenary use combined with a different understanding of the relationship between citizen and state. There was a strong tradition opposed to the creation of a standing army, on the basis that citizen liberty was best served without one. The strength of this norm created a situation where Britain was forced to rely on foreigners because of problems with domestic recruitment. This norm needed to erode, or the norm against mercenary use needed to strengthen, before Britain could use only citizens to fight her battles. As it happens, both norms had changed by mid-century. Anti-mercenary feeling had begun with the American Revolution and by the time of the Crimean War was strongly in place, reinforced by the influence of Europe, where mercenaries had already largely disappeared. What is interesting about the defeat in the Crimea is that it was not a defeat of mercenaries themselves; mercenaries were not demonstrated to be weak or cowardly or ineffective fighters, because they never actually fought. And the problems of the British army in the Black Sea once and for all demonstrated that some kind of standing army would be necessary for Britain. The demise of one norm and the strength of another can explain why Britain finally let go of the foreigners that had served her for so many years.

6
The Norm against Mercenary Use and International Law

Mercenaries largely disappeared from the international system after the Crimea. Developing neutrality laws made it even more difficult to hire mercenaries, even if they did not cause the disappearance of mercenaries from the international system.[1] The shift away from mercenary use in the nineteenth century was so absolute that mercenaries did not appear on the international stage again until the 1960s, when they made a spectacular and controversial re-entry. Mercenaries became involved in multiple African civil wars following decolonization, but first and most famously in the Congo in the early 1960s. The role of these mercenaries garnered such a huge amount of attention that attempts to create new international law preventing the use of mercenaries quickly followed.

The international law created to control the mercenary problem in the 1960s, 1970s, and 1980s presents a particularly tough case for a normative approach to explain. The law itself is both ambiguous and ineffective, which might suggest that the influence of the anti-mercenary norm had waned by the twentieth century. If the law were indeed problematic because of a lack of commitment to the underlying norm against mercenary use, it would be extremely difficult to make the argument that the norm continued to influence states in the twentieth century. Examining the creation of international law on the mercenary question while paying close attention to the anti-mercenary norm, however, reveals that the norm's influence was far from declining. It is misguided to assume that unwieldy law signals that the international community was unenthusiastic about the creation of a legal regime governing a particular issue. The law's problems result from the fact that the underlying anti-mercenary norm was particularly difficult to translate into legal terms, and particularly strongly held. Other tensions in the law are explained by the presence of conflicting norms rather than the disinterest of states. The fact that

---

[1] van Creveld (1991: 40) and Price (1995: 95). Neutrality laws and the 1907 Hague Convention implicitly banned mercenaries. See Chapter 4 for a discussion of these laws and below for a discussion of the Hague Convention.

the law in question was especially supported by African states does not indicate that an anti-mercenary norm was specific rather than universal, but rather suggests that the norm against mercenary use drew strength from association with norms of national liberation.

This chapter argues that understanding why international law on the mercenary question is flawed is impossible without understanding the role of the norm against mercenary use and the influence of other norms. The chapter is composed of three sections, each of which takes one of the arguments that the norm against mercenary use was declining in influence as its starting point, and then moves on to demonstrate that in fact the norm's power remained strong. Each section also reveals a different facet of the way norms operate.

The first section examines the argument, made most forcefully by the international lawyer Antonio Cassese,[2] that the international law on mercenaries, particularly the definition found in Article 47 of Protocol I of the Geneva Conventions, is full of loopholes intentionally left by states, who were uninfluenced by any moral dislike of mercenaries and who could and did pursue the creation of law that was more about preserving advantage than enshrining concern over mercenaries. Cassese argues that the law on mercenaries is ambiguous because states were not particularly committed to it. I argue that in fact these loopholes exist because the anti-mercenary norm was very strongly held but could not be effectively translated into law. The first section reveals that the relationship between norms and law is not always as clear as we might imagine, in particular because strongly held norms do not always lead to the creation of effective law.

The second section takes a close look at the argument that only states directly affected by mercenaries, those in Africa, had any interest in dealing with mercenaries through the creation of international law. In other words, there was no universally held moral belief that mercenaries ought to be controlled. However, it is clear that not only was a moral belief that mercenaries ought to be controlled shared by states outside of Africa, within Africa this belief gained strength from its close association with the norm of national self-determination. This section demonstrates how norms can draw strength from the support of related norms and provides an interesting depiction of how norms evolve.

The third section examines a different facet of the argument that anti-mercenary sentiment was not universal. The assertion that only African states were interested in creating law of course suggests that Western states were not interested in creating law and felt no moral compulsion to control mercenaries. I argue that in fact Western states did agree that mercenaries ought to

[2] Cassese (1980).

be controlled, but strongly disagreed about how to go about doing so. Laws regarding freedom of movement and limited state responsibility prevented Western states from agreeing to a legal regime controlling mercenaries, and so the third section demonstrates that conflicts between two norms can be responsible for weak law. States can be torn between two or more conflicting norms and must decide between them.

6.1. STRONG NORMS DO NOT LEAD TO THE CREATION OF STRONG LAW: HOW THE LAW'S WEAKNESSES ARE EXPLAINED BY THE ANTI-MERCENARY NORM

The international law on mercenaries takes four main forms: first, General Assembly[3] and Security Council resolutions proscribing or condemning the use of mercenaries; second, the Organization of African Unity Convention for the Elimination of Mercenaries in Africa;[4] third, Article 47 of Protocol I additional to the Geneva Conventions;[5] and fourth, the United Nations International Convention against the Recruitment, Use, Financing, and Training of Mercenaries,[6] which closely follows the definition supplied by Article 47.

The international law scholar Antonio Cassese makes a forceful argument that the first three of these, in particular Article 47, are a concrete demonstration of a situation in which states use law to preserve their interests. He contends that states, especially African states, have used the process of the creation of international law to protect themselves from mercenary attacks while retaining the option to use mercenaries themselves.[7] As the primary impetus for developing international law came from African states,[8] Cassese's argument is potentially damning. If the main actors promoting the law were doing so in essence to protect their interests, it suggests that the underlying norm against mercenary use has lost its strength.

---

[3] General Assembly resolutions are an indication of state practice and are not, in themselves, a source of international law. In context of the other sources examined, they provide further evidence of law.

[4] Hereinafter referred to as the OAU Convention. Created in 1977 and came into force in 1985.

[5] Hereinafter referred to as Article 47. Created in 1977.

[6] Hereinafter referred to as the UN Convention. The General Assembly created an Ad Hoc Committee on Recruitment, Use, Financing, and Training of Mercenaries in 1979 (hereinafter referred to as the Ad Hoc Committee or Committee) which made its first report in 1980 and created the UN Convention in 1989. The UN Convention came into force in 2001. The UN Convention retains essentially the same definition of a mercenary as Article 47, which can be found in Appendix 1.

[7] Cassese (1980: 11).

[8] The significance of African states' enthusiasm for regulating private force is addressed below.

Article 47 states:

1. A mercenary shall not have the right to be a combatant or a prisoner of war.
2. A mercenary is any person who:
   (a) is specially recruited locally or abroad in order to fight in an armed conflict;
   (b) does, in fact, take a direct part in the hostilities;
   (c) is motivated to take part in the hostilities essentially by the desire for private gain and, in fact, is promised, by or on behalf of a Party to the conflict, material compensation substantially in excess of that promised or paid to combatants of similar ranks and functions in the armed forces of that Party;
   (d) is neither a national of a Party to the conflict nor a resident of territory controlled by a Party to the conflict;
   (e) is not a member of the armed forces of a Party to the conflict; and
   (f) has not been sent by a State which is not a Party to the conflict on official duty as a member of its armed forces.

Article 47 does appear to contain two problems, which would suggest that Cassese is correct to argue that states were attempting to retain the option of using private force themselves rather than acting under the influence of any pre-existing moral dislike of mercenaries. First, Article 47(2)(e) appears to allow significant 'wiggle room' for states to use private force *themselves* while making sure it remained illegal for other actors. Second, Paragraphs (2)(b) and (f) seem to be an intentional loophole in the law that would allow states to continue to use foreign technical advisers, which some critics argue demonstrates a striking lack of enthusiasm for genuine anti-mercenary legislation. In this section, I explain that apparent loopholes and evident weaknesses in the law reflect the fact that the norm against mercenary use was strongly influential but impossible to translate into legally sensible terms. I examine each supposed loophole in turn, demonstrating that the documentary evidence does not suggest that any gaps in the law were the result of intentional state attempts to preserve the right to use private force. I then demonstrate that another major weakness in the law, the difficulty of demonstrating financial motivation, in fact directly reflects the influence of the anti-mercenary norm. The documentary evidence strongly suggests that the inconsistencies and loopholes were nearly all the side effects of state attempts to deal with particularly thorny issues, in ways consistent with the norm, rather than purposeful attempts to create law that might be easily circumvented.

The First 'Loophole': Incorporation into a State's Armed Forces

Cassese points out that Article 47(2)(e) indicates that states are allowed to use private force as long as it is integrated into their own forces, so avoiding the 'mercenary' label.[9] A private fighter hired by a state would not legally be considered a mercenary, and so states themselves could use mercenaries with impunity. States could manipulate the situation so that an individual, who by any other estimation would be called a mercenary, cannot legally be called a mercenary at all.

Paragraph (2)(e) of Article 47 is one of the most criticized aspects of a heavily criticized article. Only 'the most foolish or unlucky'[10] could ever be considered mercenaries under it, as surely all intelligent private fighters would avoid it by making integration into their employers' armed forces a condition of employment.[11] Cassese believes that state interests are responsible for these loopholes and flaws in the law. 'Incompleteness, reticence, ambiguity', he writes, 'this is the price that must be paid by forward-looking States to the forces in favour of the *status quo* and the protection of vested interests'.[12]

Attention to the *travaux préparatoires* reveals, however, that states were not trying to use paragraph 2(e) to ensure that they retained the right to use mercenaries themselves. Rather, the inclusion of this paragraph serves to protect fighters not considered to be mercenaries from the punitive elements of Article 47, which could lead to 'life or death consequences for a person charged with being a mercenary'.[13] States were trying to exclude actors they did not perceive to be mercenaries from the definition, and so inserted paragraph 2(e) to protect regular soldiers and foreign fighters permanently enrolled in the armed forces of a state.

During the creation of Article 47, states were firmly committed to the idea that mercenaries are financially motivated, and there was very little debate on this point.[14] Once that commitment was made, it created a further problem: how could soldiers, who might be fighting for financial gain, be distinguished from mercenaries? The delegates all agreed that the definition must be framed so that a soldier who enlists 'because he is attracted by the good pay is not on that account deemed to be a mercenary'.[15] States were also explicit about the

---

[9] Cassese (1980: 24, 29).   [10] Hampson (1991: 29).
[11] As we will see in Chapter 7, one of the first steps taken by PMCs like Sandline and EO is integration into the hiring nation's armed forces.
[12] Cassese (1980: 29).
[13] Doc CDDH/236/Rev.1, para. 98, 405. Article 47 paragraph 1 removes the protection of combatant and prisoner of war status from mercenaries.
[14] See below for a longer discussion about the financial motivation component of Article 47.
[15] Doc CDDH/236/Rev.1, para. 99.

fact that they did not consider permanently incorporated foreigners, like the Gurkhas or the French Foreign Legion, to be mercenaries. During discussions at the Diplomatic Conference on International Humanitarian Law, which led to the creation of Protocol I,[16] states reached 'general agreement'[17] on the idea that 'the mercenary may be a career fighter or killer, but if a person makes a career of fighting in support of one and only one State, it seems rather difficult to regard him as a mercenary'.[18]

States came up with a single solution to this dual problem. They would exclude 'from the legal category of mercenaries those who are members of the armed forces of a party to the conflict. The addition of this criterion would exclude from the legal status of mercenary such troops as Gurkas [sic] ... and the French Foreign Legion.'[19]

Some delegations noted that this paragraph created a potential loophole. States could use mercenaries themselves and avoid the consequences by incorporating them into national forces, and so some delegations 'opposed excluding members of the armed forces from the category of mercenaries'.[20] But these delegations did not suggest that states *were* trying to do so by including the paragraph, just that it might present a future problem.

And indeed, the protection afforded to national soldiers on the basis of this paragraph alone suggests that states saw it as a protective device rather than a loophole. Moreover, it seems clear that states did not consider foreigners *permanently* incorporated into the armed forces, foreign soldiers who made a career of serving 'one and only one State', to be mercenaries.

Further evidence for the fact that states did not consider foreigners permanently incorporated into their armed forces as mercenaries comes from other sources. In practice, the Gurkhas and the French Foreign Legion are generally not considered to be mercenaries. Even Cassese asserts that the French Foreign Legion are an integral part of the French Army and represent the *disappearance* of mercenaries from the international stage.[21] In 1982, Britain differentiated Gurkhas from mercenaries on the basis of their permanence and their long and distinguished record of service to the British crown, and emphasized that they did not fall under the definition of Article 47.[22] Without paragraph (2)(e), venerable military traditions, like the British use of Gurkhas,

---

[16] The *Conference Diplomatique de Droit Humanitaire* was held in 1974–6, and resulted in the two Additional Protocols. Hereinafter referred to as the Diplomatic Conference.
[17] Doc CDDH/236/Rev.1, para. 100.   [18] Doc CDDH/236/Rev.1, para. 100.
[19] Van Deventer (1976: 813).   [20] CDDH/236/Rev.1, para. 102.
[21] Cassese (1980: 1).
[22] United Kingdom Materials on International Law, in Marston (1982: 418). While it could be argued that Britain had an interest in making this argument and protecting its use of Gurkhas, it is important to note that the argument was made in terms of long and loyal service, which implies that the Gurkhas were deemed to share the cause of their employers.

the Vatican's Swiss Guards, and the French and Spanish Foreign Legions would be considered mercenaries when they previously had not been so considered. These arrangements persisted throughout the period in which mercenary use was deemed to have largely disappeared from the international stage; institutionalized use of foreign troops was not perceived as mercenary behaviour by the international community.

Finally, the perception that permanently incorporated foreigners are not mercenaries is perfectly in line with the norm against mercenary use. The norm against mercenaries relies on the fact that mercenaries are outside state control *and* that they are not motivated by an appropriate cause. There is nothing inherently objectionable about foreign fighters, and indeed, states fight alongside foreigners and are often commanded by foreigners as a matter of routine, either through alliance arrangements or during UN peacekeeping missions. What makes a British soldier from NATO working in the Pentagon a soldier rather than a mercenary is that he is part of state forces and has not enlisted specifically for financial gain. Fighters operating *outside* the legitimate control of sovereign states are regarded with suspicion, but those operating inside it are acceptable. There is nothing unusual about excluding permanently incorporated foreigners from the definition of a mercenary.

Without the inclusion of paragraph 2(e), both regular soldiers and foreigners employed under long-standing arrangements would be in danger of losing their rights as combatants and the right to prisoner-of-war status.

The Second 'Loophole': Excluding Foreign Advisers, Technicians, and Trainers

A second argument that states left behind a 'loophole' that would allow them to use private force comes from evidence suggesting that states were not opposed to the use of private force in the form of trainers or advisers.[23] Two parts of Article 47 indicate that trainers and advisers would be excluded from the definition of a mercenary. Paragraph 2(b) states that mercenaries must actually take part in the fighting while 2(f) excludes soldiers sent by states not party to the conflict on official duty. An adviser who does not fight and is sent by one state to another would thus not be considered a mercenary.

At the Diplomatic Conference, there was disagreement about the exclusion of advisers and trainers,[24] but the reasons for the disagreement were not revealed.[25] Taulbee argues that the earlier OAU Convention suggests that African states purposefully created space for assistance to sovereign states,

[23] Cassese (1980: 3, 29).   [24] CDDH/236/Rev.1, para. 103.
[25] Van Deventer (1976: 814).

the result of 'careful drafting which came from the desire...to give support to "national liberation movements" without creating conditions which might encourage dissident groups within their own borders'.[26]

A strong interest in continuing to use foreign trainers and advisers, and so excluding them from international legal instruments on private force, has far less effect on the norm than it first appears. The debate over advisers and trainers has its roots in the question of whether or not these actors can be considered to be mercenaries. Practically speaking, there may be very little difference between a trainer and a fighter. As Kwakwa puts it, 'in terms of the consequences of their actions, however, there is not much difference between the expert who advises the combatant on how to do the killing, and the combatant who does the actual killing'.[27]

Surely, however, the logic of a distinction between actual combatants and non-combatants is clear, as is a distinction between official and unofficial foreign assistance. Sending advisers and trainers is common practice among states of all kinds. There is a free flow of foreign troops between NATO countries, and this sort of shared military expertise would not normally be regarded as mercenary activity. The sending of foreign advisers by both superpowers during the Cold War was common,[28] as was assistance provided by former colonial powers to newly independent states.[29] The problem with describing the practice of foreign technical assistance as mercenary is that it would have criminalized a common international practice.

While there was debate over the inclusion of trainers and advisers during the Diplomatic Conference,[30] only one state mentions the exclusion of these actors from the definition as a point of concern at the Plenary Meetings at the end of the Conference in 1977, where states brought up a number of other concerns, including worries about the need to demonstrate higher material compensation than regular troops and the absence of state liability provisions.[31] And, in fact, there does not seem to have been substantial disagreement about the exclusion of non-combatant military assistance.

---

[26] Taulbee (1985: 341). [27] Kwakwa (1990: 71). [28] Clapham (1996: 153, 155).
[29] Lee (1969: 61) and Clapham (1996: 82). [30] CDDH/236/Rev.1, para. 103.
[31] See CDDH/SR.41. Of the twenty-five states that mentioned Article 47 in their reasons for voting, the only state referring to either paragraph 2(b) or (f) was Mauritania, at p. 190, whose main concerns were that the idea of financial motivation did not capture the range of mercenary motivations or the fact that some mercenaries were imperialist tools. The twenty-four other states mentioned five concerns, none of which deals with trainers and advisers: eight were concerned that the fundamental guarantees of Article 65 should apply to mercenaries; four were concerned that it would be practically difficult to demonstrate that mercenaries received a higher rate of pay; five believed that the article should have included those states supporting or facilitating mercenary action; three mentioned general support; three were concerned that the definition remained unclear; and three believed that the article regarding mercenaries was out of place in a document of international humanitarian law.

The large number of examples of foreign military assistance in the form of trainers, instructors, and advisers during the period leading up to the Conference suggests that states in no way saw this sort of aid as an abnormal practice. Conversely, the presence of mercenaries was emphatically regarded as subversive. Not a single state disputed the need to have an article dealing with mercenaries.[32] States believed that mercenaries needed to be controlled, and the exclusion of trainers and instructors from the definition demonstrates that foreign military aid was a common practice, not that states were purposely excluding trainers and instructors to allow themselves the possibility of using mercenaries.

The most compelling evidence that states were not attempting to create room for manoeuvre in an otherwise tight provision against the use of private force is best seen through the lens of the norm against mercenary use. The idea that mercenaries are normatively troublesome because they lie outside state control and because they are not properly motivated can help make sense of the apparent loopholes in Article 47.

Even if the question of foreign military advisers was a furiously debated and significant point of argument—and as we have seen it was neither—this does not indicate a violation of the norm against mercenary use. Similarly, even if states did purposely exclude foreign troops incorporated into a state's armed forces from the definition, it does not necessarily constitute a violation of the proscriptive norm.

The debate over trainers and advisers is essentially a debate about whether or not controlled forms of state-to-state assistance can be considered 'mercenary'. There was consensus in the debate at the Diplomatic Conference that uncontrolled mercenaries ought to be bound by the law, as article 47 paragraph (2)(e) excludes foreign fighters in a state's armed forces and all other types of mercenary are included. There was also agreement that mercenaries are mercenaries because they are motivated by financial gain, as evidenced by paragraph (2)(c).

Advisers are not mercenaries on two grounds. First, they have been invited by the receiving state and sent with the blessing of the sending state. If foreign advisers are mercenaries, then so too are troops serving in an alliance arrangement. Second, they are presumably not motivated by private gain if they are sent by their home state for a cause deemed by the home state to be important. States at the Diplomatic Conference were dealing with trainers and advisers in this sort of situation exclusively, as the phenomenon of independent training companies did not exist. It is unclear that Article 47, even if it excluded paragraph (2)(b), would be able to penalize foreign troops sent by one state

---

[32] CDDH/SR.41.

to another in an advisory capacity, without penalizing troops sent as part of a regular alliance arrangement.

The lack of consensus over the inclusion of trainers and advisers does not conclusively demonstrate that states were attempting to keep their options open by allowing the use of private force in some forms. If anything, it suggests that states were reluctant to criminalize a common international practice and in fact behaving in line with the proscriptive norm, which proscribes mercenaries when they are outside state control and permits them otherwise.

An uncontrolled influx of foreign troops arriving to assist in a war against the state is one thing, and the arrival of foreigners invited by the state to work with that state, either as an adviser or as a member of its armed forces, is another thing entirely. As the framers of Article 47 were *not* dealing with independent PMCs providing training and instruction, as these companies had not yet appeared, they could only have been dealing with state-to-state assistance. Exclusion of this type of assistance is completely in line with the norm, and indeed is common state practice. The provision of Article 47 relating to trainers and advisers does not suggest that the anti-mercenary norm's influence was waning; rather, it suggests that states were very clear about which types of fighters they considered to be mercenaries, and which they did not.

And indeed, the UN Convention keeps the exclusion of foreign assistance and expands upon it. Article 1 paragraphs 2(d) and (e) state that a mercenary has not been seen by a state on official duty and is not a member of the armed forces of the state on whose territory the conflict occurs. Discussions in the Ad Hoc Committee further emphasize that states believed that such arrangements could not be considered mercenary.[33] The exclusion of fighters not normally considered to be mercenaries from international agreements which very clearly proscribe the activities of mercenaries does not suggest that anti-mercenary feeling was on the decline.

The Problems of Article 47 Represent Strong State Agreement on the Anti-Mercenary Norm

There are two further frequently cited problems with Article 47. First, it is legally difficult to rely on motive as the defining factor of a mercenary. Second, there is an argument that Article 47, which seeks to punish mercenaries for their motivation, is out of place in Protocol I, which as a document of international humanitarian law ought to be concerned with governing war as it actually occurs and not with governing the motives of those who fight. These

---

[33] See comments of France and Australia. UN Doc A/C.6/35/SR.23, paras. 62, 44.

problems exist purely because of strong state agreement about the definition of a mercenary, and the legal impracticality of implementing that definition. Article 47 demonstrates that law can be weak because of a very high level of agreement, that states are unwilling or unable to water down.

Legal Problems with Relying on Motivation

One of the main concerns about the definition of a mercenary adopted in Article 47 and the very similar definition adopted later in the UN Convention is that both rely so heavily on personal motivation. The Working Group at the Diplomatic Conference charged with creating Article 47 had an area of 'core agreement' in their definition of a mercenary. A 'mercenary is a person who is motivated to fight essentially or primarily by the desire for... "hard cash"'.[34] This definition reflects the anti-mercenary norm: mercenaries are objectionable because they are not motivated by an appropriate cause, but by financial gain.

Converting the belief that mercenaries are financially motivated into a workable legal document is fraught with obstacles. Such a motivation, as many commentators have pointed out, is at best difficult or at worst impossible to prove.[35] In 1976, several UK nationals were among thirteen mercenaries charged and put on trial in Angola,[36] prompting the UK government to commission an enquiry led by Lord Diplock to examine relevant British law. The resulting Diplock Report pointed out that fighters may have a variety of mixed motives ranging from 'sheer desire for private gain accompanied by indifference to the cause which that force is supporting, to a conscientious conviction that the merits of the cause are so great as to justify sacrificing his own life'.[37] It would be impossible to prove 'to the standard of proof called for in a court of law' that any one of these motives is dominant.[38] The report concluded that any definition relying on positive proof of motivation would 'either be unworkable or so haphazard in its application as between comparable individuals as to be unacceptable'.[39]

The Working Group that created the draft of Article 47 at the Diplomatic Conference foresaw that 'the establishment of a person's motivation may pose some problems of proof'[40] and tried to account for this problem by suggesting that mercenaries must be paid substantially more than regular soldiers,[41] in

---

[34] CDDH/236/Rev.1, para. 99. [35] Burmester (1978: 39) and Kwakwa (1990: 71).
[36] See Lockwood (1976), Cesner and Brant (1977), and Hoover (1977) for details.
[37] Diplock, Walker-Smith, and de Freitas (1976: 2).
[38] Ibid. [39] Ibid. [40] CDDH/236/Rev. 1, para. 99. [41] Article 47 (2)(c).

order to provide a practical test for mercenary status.[42] If it is legally difficult to argue that a soldier is a mercenary on the basis of motivation, and the framers of various international legal instruments recognized and tried to account for this difficulty, why retain the criterion of motivation at all?

The debate at the Diplomatic Conference was coloured by the norm against mercenary use to such an extent that delegates included an article they knew might be legally problematic because it reflected what they believed was the defining characteristic of a mercenary.

Article 47 Is Out of Place in a Document of International Humanitarian Law

The incompatibility of Article 47 with the rest of Protocol I provides further evidence of the influence of the anti-mercenary norm. Article 47 undermines the basic thrust of the rest of the Protocol, which is predicated on the idea that fighters should not be discriminated against on the basis of their motivation[43] and undermines the idea that international humanitarian law ought to be universal and apply to all those in a theatre of war.[44] The Holy See, Switzerland, the Netherlands, and Colombia all expressed a specific concern about this aspect of Article 47.[45] By insisting on relying on motivation as the defining mark of a mercenary, states created a fundamental inconsistency in the Protocol.

International legal regulation of mercenaries could have gone down two different paths. The first path would have been to regulate mercenary actions using existing international law. Under this approach, mercenaries would be accountable for breaking the laws of war as would any other combatant. Mercenaries could be punished for what they do, rather than for why they do it.[46] The second path, the one ultimately taken in Article 47, is to regulate mercenaries on the basis of their status. This approach required a definition of a mercenary sufficiently clear to differentiate mercenaries from other fighters, a solution to the problems inherent in defining actors on the basis of their motivations, and a way to provide evidence for those motivations. It is more difficult to regulate mercenaries on the basis of their status than on the basis

---

[42] CDDH/407/Rev.1, para. 26.

[43] International Committee of the Red Cross (1987: 573) and Kwakwa (1990: 89).

[44] Burmester (1978: 56). According to this argument, spies, who are excluded from protection in Article 46 might also be an awkward fit with the overall thrust of the treaty. However, spies are condemned on the basis of what they do (espionage) rather than why they are motivated to do it.

[45] CDDH/SR.41.

[46] The Diplock Report recommends this approach. Diplock, Walker-Smith, and de Freitas (1976: 2).

of their actions, prompting the question of why states took the less efficient path. The answer can only be that it is the *fact of being a mercenary* which is repugnant, as much as any actions undertaken by that particular mercenary. Mercenaries 'are being penalized for the fact of being mercenaries and nothing else'.[47]

The law's focus on motivation may well be practically unworkable, but it reflects a profound belief that it is wrong to be motivated by money rather than an appropriate cause, and that an inappropriate motivation is what makes a mercenary. If the factor of motivation were removed from the definition, the definition would be meaningless.[48] Bad law on mercenaries indicates substantial agreement among states that mercenaries are motivated by financial gain, and this agreement was made into law despite concerns about practicality. The depth of agreement that mercenaries are actors that must be controlled, and can be distinguished by their inappropriate motivation, has resulted in unworkable law.

6.2. THE HEIGHTENED AFRICAN INTEREST IN LAW DEMONSTRATES THAT THE NORM WAS NOT UNIVERSAL

There is another argument which, if correct, would suggest that the norm against mercenary use was no longer influential. The fact that the law on mercenaries was driven by African states and closely tied to national liberation and self-determination might suggest that mercenaries were only considered to be problematic because they threatened self-determination, not because they were considered problematic actors in and of themselves. Furthermore, if only states affected by questions of self-determination, and states which had a vested interest in supporting self-determination in other parts of the world, were interested in controlling mercenaries it might suggest that the norm against mercenary use was far from universal.

In fact, the influence of the anti-mercenary norm is still strong in this period, and it gained strength because of its similarity with the project of national self-determination. The influence of the proscriptive norm against mercenary use on its own remains clearly visible in the debate on how to define a mercenary at the Diplomatic Conference leading to the creation of Protocol I. Unquestionably, the proscriptive norm's influence was affected by the existence of powerful norms of national liberation and anti-colonialism, but the strength of the latter does not obscure the impact of the former. The coincidence of these two norms provides us with an opportunity to examine

[47] Kwakwa (1990: 88). [48] Taulbee (1985: 353).

how norms can interact with each other. In this case, the core aspects of the norm of national liberation and the anti-mercenary norm are very similar, even if the concept of national liberation is far broader. The power behind national liberation gave strength and new direction to the proscriptive norm.

To demonstrate that the proscriptive norm against mercenary use retained a great deal of influence during this period, I proceed in five sections. First, I explain some of the documentary evidence and scholarly work supporting the argument that African states only saw mercenaries as problematic because of their negative effect on national liberation, and not because of any underlying anti-mercenary sentiment. Second, I point out that the powerful influence of the national liberation norm pushed the General Assembly into condemning the problems caused by mercenaries with the language of national self-determination, and that General Assembly debates do not reflect universal state practice, which retained a more broadly anti-mercenary thrust.

In the final three sections, I turn to making the argument that this period demonstrates the interesting effects of two norms that share core characteristics and so support and strengthen each other. In the third section, I explain how the proscriptive norm and the norms of national self-determination and national liberation are closely associated. Fourth, I argue that the strength of the two norms working in tandem led to an especially vehement reaction to the actions of mercenaries. If African states were only worried about the threat mercenaries posed to the success of national liberation, the strength of their reaction makes no sense. Only by assessing the conjoined influence of the two norms it is possible to explain why the African response was so intense. Finally, the simultaneous African pursuit of national liberation and anti-mercenary legislation, and the close relationship between norms underlying both, demonstrates the difficulty of separating norms from interests. The argument that states were only interested in mercenaries in so far as they affected the success of national liberation falls down on the documentary evidence, but it also fails to take into consideration the extent to which the interest in national liberation is itself a normative interest.

Evidence Supporting the Argument that State Interest in Mercenaries Only Existed in the Light of Concern over National Liberation

Elements of the documentary record seem to support the argument that African states opposed any action threatening national self-determination, and they sought to regulate mercenaries for this reason, rather than because of a particular fear of or problem with the use of private violence. Evidence for this argument comes in part from statements of states in the developing world. The Cuban delegate at the Diplomatic Conference wished that Article 47 had clearly reflected 'the truth of mercenary activities, the aims of which are to hamper and thwart the struggle of people to free themselves'.[49] The delegate from Mozambique argued that 'to kill for money a people struggling for its complete independence, a people fighting to put an end to racial, colonial and neo-colonial domination is, indeed, the most odious crime known to mankind'.[50] The article, according to Libya, 'can be construed as an implicit recognition and a real consciousness of the dangerous violations carried out by mercenaries against human rights and the right of self-determination'.[51]

The basic tenor of UN General Assembly and Security Council resolutions on mercenaries appears to provide further evidence for the argument that mercenaries were only considered to be negative actors in the context of national self-determination. There is general agreement that the spate of General Assembly resolutions that deal with mercenaries in the 1960s and 1970s really only deal with them in the context of decolonization and national liberation,[52] and that the international community is especially concerned with mercenary action because of its effects on national liberation.[53] Sandoz summarizes the argument that national liberation, not mercenaries, was the real concern of states, pointing out that 'it was not so much the phenomenon [of mercenaries] itself that came under attack as the support that was given by mercenaries to colonial governments intent on remaining in place—and hence opposed to the struggle for national liberation'.[54]

The states most challenged by mercenary action, or most afraid of it, were also the states that pursued international legal regulation. The first attempt to regulate mercenary action was made by the Organization for African Unity,[55] and the trial of mercenaries in Angola[56] brought international attention to the problem and led to the creation of a draft Convention against mercenaries. Nigeria, itself a victim of mercenary action, took the lead in creating

---

[49] Statement of Cuba, CDDH/SR.41, 184.
[50] Statement of Mozambique, CDDH/SR.41, 193.
[51] Statement of Libya, CDDH/SR.41, 199. The statement of the delegate from Ukraine echoes these sentiments: CDDH/III/SR.33–36 p. 498, para. 10.
[52] Cassese (1980: 9), Kwakwa (1990: 83), and Major (1992: 1). The resolutions dealing with mercenaries in the context of national self-determination are: A/Res/2465 (XXIII) 1969, which declared the use of mercenaries against national liberation movements to be a criminal act; and A/Res /2708 (XXV) 1970 and A/Res/3103 (XXVIII) 1973 which reiterate A/Res/2465.
[53] Yusuf (1979: 127).   [54] Sandoz (1999: 203). See also Green (1979: 229).
[55] The OAU made resolutions condemning mercenaries in 1964 [ECM Res. 5 (III) Addis Ababa], 1967 [AHG Res. 49 (IV)], and 1970 [ECM Res. 17 (VII) Lagos]. The OAU made a Declaration on the Activities of Mercenaries in Africa in 1971 [CM/St.6 (XVII) Addis Ababa].
[56] See below.

both Article 47 of Protocol I and the UN Convention. Repeated leadership by African states suggests that the most affected (or potentially affected) states were the most interested in dealing with the mercenary question.[57]

General Assembly Resolutions Do Not Reflect an Accurate Picture of Existing Anti-Mercenary Sentiment

Relying on General Assembly resolutions to make the point that mercenaries were only considered to be in need of control in the context of national liberation is problematic. Green suggests that after events in Angola and other Portuguese territories, the General Assembly 'carried its prejudicial discrimination to its logical conclusion'[58] and declared that the act of being a mercenary was criminal. He is surprised that such a conclusion took so long, given the numerical advantages of African states in the General Assembly.[59]

As Green recognizes, the General Assembly's 'definition of colonialism, imperialism, foreign rule, racism and the like, is highly subjective'.[60] It is vital to take General Assembly resolutions with a grain of salt because during this period they tended to reflect a preoccupation with national liberation, whereby many issues possibly unrelated to independence were parcelled into the rhetoric of anti-colonialism. The General Assembly's association of mercenaries with national liberation may not represent the opinion of all states.

Statements in the Security Council and in other bodies outside the General Assembly indicate that international concern over mercenary use existed because of the problems caused by mercenaries on their own terms, and not simply because of their association with national liberation movements. Green argues that the Security Council resolutions on the Congo crisis in the 1960s deal with mercenaries only as a particular manifestation of foreign intervention, all types of which were considered equally problematic.[61] Relying on Security Council Resolution S/5002, Green argues that mercenaries were condemned 'solely on the basis that they formed one of the resources being employed to secure Katanga's secession and thus to thwart the resolutions of the Council'.[62]

The wording of the resolution tells a slightly different story. In Resolution S/5002, mercenary action is highlighted by receiving its own paragraph, separate from other forms of foreign intervention. The resolution calls for 'the immediate withdrawal and evacuation from the Congo of all foreign military, para-military, and advisory personnel not under the United Nations

---

[57] As discussed below, African states were also not alone in their advocacy of anti-mercenary laws.
[58] Green (1979: 231).   [59] Ibid.   [60] Ibid.
[61] Ibid. 225. The resolutions are S/4741 (1961) and S/5002 (1961).   [62] Ibid.

Command, and all mercenaries' and concludes with the authorization to use necessary force to deal with foreign personnel in the same terms. It is crucial to note that the problem of mercenaries gets three consecutive paragraphs on its own, without the inclusion of other forms of foreign intervention. The resolution goes on to state that the Security Council '*strongly deprecates* the secessionist activities illegally carried out by the provincial administration of Katanga, with the aid of external resources and manned by foreign mercenaries'.[63] This specific mention of mercenaries is notable because in the next two paragraphs the Security Council '*further deprecates* the armed action against United Nations forces and personnel in the pursuit of such activities' and '*insists* that such activities cease forthwith'. An independent mention of mercenaries suggests that there were some particular problems with mercenaries not associated with other forms of foreign intervention, and that the UN was especially concerned with mercenaries.

Brian Urquhart, who held several different senior UN positions, including that of the Secretary-General's special representative during the Congo operation, suggested that mercenaries were a new problem in the 1960s, and that at first no one took them seriously. Later, however, the mercenaries were seen as 'grotesque'[64] and Urquhart argues that the presence of mercenaries provided the justification for the Security Council to use force in the Congo, as mercenaries were very largely responsible for the round of fighting against UN personnel.[65]

Clearly, dislike of mercenaries on their own terms existed within the UN. Mercenaries were differentiated from other fighters and considered to be especially problematic, and it is unsurprising that inside the General Assembly the debate about mercenaries was cast in terms of national liberation, as were many other debates.

The Relationship between the Norm of National Liberation and the Anti-Mercenary Norm

Even if critics are right to suggest that anti-mercenary feeling in the 1960s and 1970s stemmed from concerns about national liberation rather than concerns about mercenaries, it does not mean that the anti-mercenary norm had lost influence. The norm of national self-determination supported rather than undermined or displayed the irrelevance of the proscriptive norm against mercenary use. African states were not interested in banning mercenaries merely because it was in their interests to do so, but rather because mercenaries

[63] SC Resolution S/5002. [64] Interview with Brian Urquhart.
[65] Ibid.

were particularly incompatible with the norms inherent in the project of self-determination.

National self-determination can be defined as 'the belief that each nation has a right to constitute an independent state and determine its own government' while a nation is a 'community that is, or wishes to be, a state'.[66] National self-determination is a recognized international legal right,[67] and an influential international norm. It is related to the concept of national liberation, which is also about the development of a state. National liberation is about 'not only political independence, but also economic independence and self-reliance, profound internal social change, and cultural regeneration. Social change was to be both "anti-feudal" and "anti-capitalist" '.[68] The related norms of national self-determination and national liberation share certain core characteristics.

First, national self-determination and national liberation are centred around a cause—the project of building the new state. This project entails a spirit of nationalism, and as a result, the two norms rely heavily on delineation between 'self' and 'other'. The self is the new nation, and the other is the entity preventing self-determination, or the entity from which independence must be gained for self-determination to be successful.

Second, the cause of national self-determination, or the development of a new state, also requires the new state to be more than superficially independent. As Mayall argues, newly decolonized states tried to avoid 'substituting one form of subordination for another' and sought 'the abolition of colonialism and racism to insure against the possibility that the major powers might try to put the clock back...and modernization and development necessary to give reality to political independence and to enable the new states to maintain themselves in a self-help system'.[69] The projects of national self-determination and national liberation thus share an emphasis on self-reliance, and a belief that for independence to be genuine, a state must be able to stand on its own two feet and have the ability to choose freely how it interacts with other states and external entities.

National liberation and national self-determination are tied to the norm against mercenary use in two ways. First, both norms centre around a sense of cause. The use of mercenaries is objectionable because they do not share what

---

[66] Cobban (1969: 39, 108).
[67] Higgins (1994: 113), Roberts (1999: 93), and Falk (2002). There is some dispute about to whom the right of self-determination applies. This dispute is not relevant to the argument of this chapter. The states and minorities (like Biafra) discussed believed themselves to be engaged in the process of national self-determination and sought to protect that right for others, regardless of its international legal status.
[68] MacFarlane (1985: 112).   [69] Mayall (1990: 127).

is deemed to be an appropriate cause for fighting within a society. National self-determination and national liberation clearly define what the appropriate cause is: the independence of the nation-state. National liberation and national self-determination also suggest which kinds of cause are not appropriate motivations: capitalism, colonialism, and imperialism. White mercenaries fighting for money in this context were profoundly divorced from the kind of cause deemed to be appropriate.

Second, mercenaries challenge the element of self-reliance at the core of the two concepts. The presence of white mercenaries represented the racial and colonial domination new states were seeking to end. More problematically, mercenaries suggested that foreigners still had influence over the newly decolonized state and that the state was not strong enough to run its affairs without external interference. Soviet or Cuban advisers, foreign sympathizers, and other volunteers might fight for national liberation because they shared a belief in the overall project; mercenaries, because they were fighting for pay and frequently employed by former colonial interests, were simply fighting for the wrong cause.

Without understanding the degree to which norms of national self-determination enhanced the proscriptive norm against mercenary use, it is impossible to understand why African states reacted so strongly to the activities of mercenaries in wars of national liberation.

The African 'Overreaction' to the Mercenary Problem

The extremity of the African response to the mercenary problem is puzzling.[70] The Congo represents the only case where mercenaries caused significant problems, with their interference on both sides between 1960 and 1968.[71] Ralph Bunche, who held several UN offices relating to the Congo, complimented a French article about mercenaries 'since it shows that they are a group of incompetent and fanatical psychopaths who completely failed in what they were trying to do and did an immense amount of damage to Katanga in the process' and went on to suggest that the article demonstrated the 'depths of silliness, destructiveness, and sheer irresponsibility' that the Congo mercenaries had.[72] Brian Urquhart holds a similar opinion, and believes that the mercenary soldiers fighting for Katanga in 1960–1 were ineffective soldiers.

---

[70] Taulbee (1985: 362).
[71] See Hempstone (1962), Mockler (1969, 1985), Burchett and Roebuck (1977), and Tickler (1987a).
[72] UN Archive. Office for Special Political Affairs, UN Operation in the Congo (ONUC) Box S-0219-006-13. Letter dated 15 March 1963 from Ralph Bunche to Mr Jean Beck.

Despite a 'flamboyant' approach, they were essentially a 'complete fraud'.[73] The presence of mercenaries was a blow to the Congo's identity as well as a problem for its political progress, as the problem of white mercenaries symbolized the state's continued reliance on external assistance.[74] How could the Congo claim to be free with the intervention of white mercenaries?

After the Congo, mercenaries were simply not particularly successful. In Angola in 1975 and 1976, mercenaries again drew international attention for their participation in the three-way civil war which erupted between the three groups which had fought for independence against Portugal: UNITA (National Union for Total Independence of Angola) under Jonas Savimbi, Holden Roberto's FNLA (National Front for the Liberation of Angola), and the MPLA (Popular Movement for the Liberation of Angola). A previously court-martialled, Cypriot-British, ex-paratrooper named Costas Georgiou, or 'Callan', was selected as the leader of an operation to assist the FNLA. Recruiting went on in London through advertisements in newspapers, and a small number of men were recruited, some of whom had 'positively unmilitary' backgrounds.[75] The mercenaries were only active between 20 January 1976 and 17 February 1976, and only faced action for part of that time.[76] Some of the recruits from London refused to fight and deserted; some of these men were executed and the mission deteriorated into a bloodbath without having much military effect. The mission was 'a shambles, a text-book [sic] of military bungling and inefficiency which no ruthlessness of method could offset'.[77]

Thirteen mercenaries were captured by the MPLA and put on trial, charged with the crime of being a mercenary. Arguably, only two of these soldiers had committed any criminal acts,[78] aside from the crime of being a mercenary, which did not even exist under Angolan law.[79] The mercenaries in Angola had made no military gains and succeeded in killing only each other. And yet the Angolan government not only prepared an elaborate trial, but invited experts from around the world to form an International Commission of Enquiry

---

[73] Interview with Brian Urquhart.   [74] Lee (1969: 6).   [75] Mockler (1985: 172).

[76] Ibid. Some questions were raised in the American Congressional hearing as to whether the Americans involved had been funded by the CIA, an allegation which George H. W. Bush, the Director of the CIA, categorically denied. The Assistant Secretary of State for African Affairs, however, was unable to provide an answer to the question of whether or not American funding for UNITA and FNLA was used to recruit mercenaries in the United States. See the letter by Bush appended to the Report of the Special Subcommittee, and the Report itself. Special Subcommittee on Investigations of the Committee on International Relations (1976: 22, 33).

[77] Burchett and Roebuck (1977: 83). See also Thomas (1984: xi).

[78] Cesner and Brant (1977: 346). The mercenaries Callan and McKenzie were charged with homicide, the other eleven with offences relating to mercenarism. All thirteen were found guilty; four were sentenced to death, including Callan and McKenzie, and executed, and nine were given prison sentences (Tickler 1987a: 95).

[79] Hoover (1977: 338).

on Mercenaries to observe it and make recommendations, which included a draft convention against mercenary use.[80] Why did the Angolans have such a severe response to these foreign troops, if they were caught before they had even really begun intervening in the civil war? Even if the trial was intended to have a deterrent effect on future mercenaries, the manner in which it was conducted, discussed below, suggests that the problems the mercenaries caused were viewed as normative.

Elsewhere, the deeply angry rhetoric of African states about the problems caused by mercenaries was out of proportion to the threat they actually posed. Throughout the late 1960s and 1970s, mercenary action was generally short-lived and not particularly successful. For example, mercenaries in Biafra in the civil war between 1967 and 1970 were largely useless,[81] despite all the attention paid to them by the international media. De St. Jorre argues that mercenaries in Biafra performed 'one useful service in destroying what remained of the legendary invincibility of the white soldier of fortune in Africa'.[82]

Later on, mercenary action occurred most frequently in states considered weak and peripheral even by African standards, like Benin, the Comoro Islands,[83] and the Seychelles. Even then, these operations were almost comically badly executed. In 1977 in Benin, the mercenaries, led by Bob Denard, were eventually driven away by a machete-wielding crowd.[84] In the Comoro Islands, Denard was more successful, but changed sides during the course of his work. The islands are so remote that it took the outside world some time to realize that Denard had organized a coup and was ensconced in disguise as Colonel Said Mustapha M'Hadju, the Minister of Defence.[85]

In the Seychelles in 1981, the legendary mercenary Mike Hoare, who had been deeply entangled in mercenary operations in the Congo, headed a botched coup better described as amusing than appalling. Disguised as a rugby team known as the Ancient Order of Frothblowers, the mercenaries were meant to carry their weapons, hidden inside Christmas gifts for local children, in their 'kitbags'. One of the mercenaries accidentally went through the 'Something to Declare' line at customs, his gun was discovered, and the mercenaries seized the airport, where they remained essentially trapped. They

---

[80] See Lockwood (1976), Cesner and Brant (1977), and Hoover (1977). The resulting convention was the Luanda Draft Convention for the Prevention and Suppression of Mercenarism, the text of which can be found in Cesner and Brant (1977: 29).
[81] De St. Jorre (1972: 312). See also Mockler (1985: 123) and Arnold (1999: 21).
[82] De St. Jorre (1972: 313).   [83] Mockler (1985: ch.11).   [84] Ibid. 246.
[85] Ibid. 253, 256. Denard's first involvement was in 1975. By 1978, he had changed sides and become Minister of Defence. He made one last coup attempt in 1995, and was removed through French intervention. In 2000, the *Guardian* exposed Denard's latest exploit, the apparent takeover attempt of a nudist colony in the South of France (Henley 2000).

ultimately escaped to South Africa in a hijacked plane. The South African authorities tried and imprisoned Hoare for the hijacking.[86]

Mercenaries did not cause a prolonged problem in Africa after the Congo, and did not engage in operations on a similar scale until the 1990s. African states were effective at stopping mercenaries in their tracks, albeit in some cases as a result of the combination of their own efforts and mercenary incompetence. But if mercenaries did not pose a significant threat to African states, why was the response of African states, and later of the world at large, so extreme?

Only attention to the combination of the anti-mercenary and national self-determination norms can really explain the intensity of the African response. The negative reaction to mercenaries 'seems to derive more from a perception of the mercenary as a symbol of racist and colonial domination than from the actual substance of mercenary accomplishments.'[87] The Angolan response to the captured mercenaries in 1976 was severe because 'having endured the participation by white mercenaries in their struggles for independence, Black African countries were ripe to make an example of them'.[88] In short, mercenaries represented everything African states were fighting against: capitalism, in the sense that mercenaries were fighting for money, and colonial domination.

The trial of the captured mercenaries in Angola demonstrates the extent to which African states saw the problems caused by mercenaries as normative. The trial was deeply political,[89] and one of the main pieces of evidence was a film which interspersed footage of an interview with US President Ford, military troops in action in Angola, mass graves, and scenes of devastation.[90] George Lockwood, a Canadian member of the Commission of Enquiry, believed that the use of the film was 'prejudicial and inflammatory' and introduced for political reasons.[91] The trial indicates what African states believed (or at least wanted to portray) mercenaries as representing: vicious foreigners fighting for themselves and disrupting the cause of national liberation, who had devastated the people and their land. An observer of the trial would have been surprised to find out that the mercenaries mainly fought each other.

Mercenaries stood in direct opposition to the great project of self-determination, not only because they often literally fought against it but also because the idea of fighting for money was disturbing in an environment

---

[86] Mockler (1985: 297–309) and Tickler (1987a: 100–16).
[87] Martin (1977: 52) and Taulbee (1985: 340).   [88] Hoover (1977: 349).
[89] Cesner and Brant (1977: 349).   [90] Hoover (1977: 336).
[91] Lockwood (1976: 193).

where the other players were deeply motivated by a belief in national liberation. The disapproval that greeted mercenaries fighting in Biafra provides an excellent example of this type of thinking. White mercenaries were hired by the Biafrans to assist them in their effort to secede from Nigeria, a national liberation project supported by many,[92] even if it was not supported by Nigeria. In fact, the Biafran leadership used mercenaries only out of absolute desperation, recognizing the political dangers of using forces held in such low esteem by other African leaders.[93] But even when they were hired by an entity with a relatively well-recognized claim to national self-determination, the Biafran decision to use mercenaries was considered to be problematic. Little had happened to 'alter the unflattering image which "Les Affreux" had originally created for themselves in Katanga and has remained with them ever since'.[94] Mercenaries were not there to support the Biafran cause, but rather were there to fight for their own gain.[95]

Mercenaries were condemned because they fought for the wrong cause in wars which were defined by belief in a 'right' cause: national liberation and self-determination. The appearance of mercenaries seemed to indicate an attempt to reassert external control over nations striving for freedom. Mercenaries represented exactly the phenomenon newly independent states were fighting against.

The belief that mercenaries, by virtue of their external status, were upsetting the project of national self-determination provides some evidence for the reluctance of African states to promote the use of private force for themselves. Newly independent states were focused on creating nationalist armies consistent with the spirit of independence,[96] able to fight for the new cause of the state. The African interest in national liberation directly reinforced the norm against mercenaries, and made mercenary action seem even more reprehensible. The relationship between that one strongly held norm can intensify the effect of another. As we see in Chapter 7, the relationship between a strongly institutionalized norm like self-determination has also made the anti-mercenary norm more resilient.

---

[92] The Biafrans had 'in favour...their Catholicism which won them the instinctive sympathy of much of Western Europe' (Mockler 1985: 125). Even though European states were sympathetic, only five countries recognized Biafra: Gabon, Tanzania, Zambia, Haiti, and the Ivory Coast.

[93] De St. Jorre (1972: 314).   [94] Ibid. 329.

[95] There is one notable exception—Count Carl Gustav von Rosen, a Swedish pilot, deeply identified with the Biafrans and flew on missions with them throughout the war. The nature of his motivation would exclude him from the definition of a mercenary (Ibid. 338, Mockler 1985: 133–8).

[96] Lee (1969: 115).

International Concern Evolved beyond Preoccupation with National Liberation

The claim that states were only interested in the mercenary problem if it affected national self-determination can only be made in the 1970s. The norm began a clear evolution during this period which culminated, in the late 1970s and the early 1980s, with a very general acceptance that mercenaries in and of themselves, even when not damaging the prospects for independence, were problematic actors. While the debate may have begun within the General Assembly, as we have seen it was not exclusive to that body. As soon as the debate moved out of the General Assembly, and accordingly into organizations without such a marked interest in anti-colonial measures, it became more general. By the mid-1970s, the exclusive relationship between anti-mercenary feeling and anti-colonial feeling was beginning to erode.

Article 47 of Additional Protocol I seeks to control mercenaries of all types, rather than those working against independence and self-determination. Some delegates to the Diplomatic Conference noted 'that they would have preferred' a definition of a mercenary which included the idea 'that the activities of mercenaries are directed to the frustration by armed violence of the process of self-determination'.[97] No compromise was achieved in this direction and the final document makes no mention of self-determination. Even between 1974 and 1976, the international consensus was beginning to reflect a norm against mercenaries that was no longer explicitly associated with the problems mercenaries cause for national liberation movements.

The Security Council strongly condemned mercenary action by the late 1970s. Although the condemnation could have come in terms of thwarting national self-determination, as mercenaries were still exclusively a problem for African states, it did not. Rather, the language remained general and mercenaries were broadly associated with a threat to international peace and security. In 1977, in relation to the attempted mercenary coup in Benin, a Security Council resolution called upon states 'to exercise the utmost vigilance against the danger posed by international mercenaries and to ensure that their territory and other territories under their control, as well as their nationals, are not used for the planning of subversion and recruitment, training and transit of mercenaries designed to overthrow the Government of any Member State'.[98] In a second resolution later that year, adopted without vote or objection, the Security Council stated that it was '*deeply concerned* over the danger which international mercenaries represent for all States, particularly

---

[97] CDDH/III/369 at 510. [98] UN SC Res. 405 (1977) S/12322.

the smaller ones'.[99] This Security Council resolution recognizes that *all* states are threatened by mercenary activities, underlining the point that concern about mercenaries was not totally tied up in concern over the success of national self-determination.

Similarly, by the 1980s, while some General Assembly resolutions associated the problems caused by mercenaries with their effect on national self-determination, many others did not. Continued concern over the role mercenaries played in subverting national self-determination was sensible, because mercenary operations remained a problem exclusive to states which had recently gained their independence. But mercenaries had clearly moved into a situation where they were condemned more generally. The UN Convention proscribes mercenaries and mercenary activities in general, and not only in relation their subversion of national self-determination movements.[100]

The development of the anti-mercenary norm is an interesting example of how norms evolve, in this case from specific to general. Thinking back to Finnemore and Sikkink's discussion of the evolution of norms, we can see the role of norm entrepreneurs in creating international law on the mercenary question. In this case, the main norm entrepreneurs were the first states who faced the mercenary problem. There is also a clear tipping point, and the beginning of a norm cascade, whereby many states agree to the norm.[101] The anti-mercenary norm reached its tipping point between 1975 and 1979, when African leadership, specifically Nigerian, introduced the norm to a worldwide forum and general acceptance occurred. However, at several junctures, state interests were important, alongside the norm, as engines of state behaviour.

The anti-mercenary norm presents an interesting variation on Finnemore and Sikkink's model. First, the main entrepreneurs in the case of this norm were the interested parties. In other words, the initial process of spreading a norm may be a manifestation of state interest.

Second, the proscriptive norm against mercenaries changed in substance to become generally accepted, and so moved beyond the original interest of the entrepreneurial states. A specific norm, by nature, would only engage the interests of specific states; to become internationally accepted, a norm must display more universal characteristics. In the case of the anti-mercenary norm, there is no question that heightened African interest in the situation—even though that interest was sharply tied to norms of national self-determination—led to very effective advocacy of the norm. The anti-mercenary norm was brought to international bodies, where other states make their voices heard.

---

[99] UN SC Res. 419 (1977) S/12454/Rev. 1.   [100] See Appendix 1.
[101] Finnemore and Sikkink (1998: 901).

Third, and perhaps most interestingly, although the anti-mercenary norm reached a tipping point and was generally accepted by states, this development was not reflected by successful international law controlling mercenaries. A strong international regime did not result and so could not provide the legitimating function Finnemore and Sikkink see as part of the process of spreading a norm.[102] This failure, as we will see, has more to do with competing norms than competing interests, but nonetheless demonstrates that reaching a tipping point does not necessarily result in formal international action. And as we see in Chapter 7, it is not always necessary to have effective formal institutionalization for a norm to persist.

6.3. THE PROSCRIPTIVE NORM AGAINST MERCENARY USE IS MOST CHALLENGED BY OTHER NORMS

The flip side of the charge that only African states were interested in pursuing anti-mercenary legislation, and then only because mercenaries threatened national self-determination, not because mercenaries are inherently problematic, is that Western states were uninvolved in the process. The norm against mercenary use was not universally held, this argument would run, because it was advocated only by African states with support of the Soviet bloc in a particular context. Western states during this period indeed advocated a very different position on the mercenary question from that of non-Western states. If the norm against mercenaries were universally held, then we would expect that states of all varieties would agree that mercenaries ought to be controlled.

Once again, attention to the norm and its component parts reveals that the differences between these two groups of states are not as dramatic as they first appear. In fact, an examination of the record reveals that there was very little debate over *whether* mercenaries should be banned, but a great deal of debate surrounding *how* they ought to be banned. And, interestingly, this debate largely hinged on competing normative views about how states ought to treat their citizens, and about whether or not states could be held responsible for the actions of their citizens abroad. There was agreement on the norm against mercenaries, but competing norms prevented anti-mercenary sentiment from becoming effective international law.

I demonstrate the continued salience of the norm despite an apparent lack of universal consensus by first outlining the evidence suggesting that Western and non-Western states had different positions on the mercenary question. Second, I point to other aspects of the documentary record which indicate

---

[102] Ibid. 903. For further discussion see Percy (2007*a*).

that Western states were in fact supportive of attempts to regulate mercenaries. I then turn to the argument that disinterest on the part of Western states did not lead to disinterest in the law. On the contrary, Western states were interested in creating law against mercenaries, but only if it did not contradict existing norms of freedom of movement and state responsibility. I address these norms in the third and fourth sections, respectively. Fifth, I conclude by arguing that an approach that takes norms seriously can recognize that the fundamental conflict preventing international agreement, and so the effective legal regulation of mercenaries, was between two norms. In turn, this leads to important questions about how states adjudicate between different norms and whether or not concrete legalization of norms renders them more powerful.

Evidence Suggesting that the Norm Against Mercenaries was not Universally Held

As we have seen, the impetus for much of the international law on mercenaries came from developing states who feared that mercenaries might undermine 'their hard-won political independence, sovereignty, territorial integrity, national unity and security',[103] or their political ideals. In the early 1970s, Schwarzenberger argued that dislike of mercenaries came out of 'quarters susceptible to third world pressure'.[104]

By the end of the 1980s, the UN Convention on mercenaries had only been signed by African states. In 2002 and 2004, Belgium and New Zealand, respectively, became the first Western states to ratify the Convention.[105] Additional Protocol I was not ratified by, among others, the United States, and contains Article 47. It would seem that when African states called for attention to the mercenary problem, only other African states and the politically sympathetic Soviet bloc really responded. The only Western interest in the mercenary question came from states directly affected in some way. For example, both the United States and the UK engaged in governmental enquiries and reports after their nationals were caught up in the Angolan mercenary trials of 1976.[106] During the American hearing the Assistant Secretary of State for African Affairs explicitly stated that the number of Americans involved in mercenary

---

[103] Layeb (1989: 466). [104] Schwarzenberger (1971: 280).
[105] The Convention came into force in 2001. As of 2007, there are seventeen signatories and twenty-eight parties.
[106] The Americans responded with a Congressional hearing: Special Subcommittee on Investigations of the Committee on International Relations 1976. The British called an enquiry that culminated in the Diplock Report (Diplock, Walker-Smith, and de Freitas 1976).

activity did not pose a particular problem for Africa, even though the Africans viewed the situation differently.[107]

All this might seem to provide significant evidence that interests on their own can explain state behaviour on the mercenary question, and that states were not adhering to a norm against mercenaries. Closer examination reveals, however, that there was a large degree of international consensus on the mercenary question, and the debate that occurred was not about *whether* mercenaries ought to be regulated, but *how,* and the method of regulation led to disagreement about the resulting international legal instruments.

Evidence Suggesting Western States were Interested in Legal Regulation of Mercenaries

The first piece of evidence demonstrating a coincidence of interests among states on the mercenary question comes from debates in the UN Security Council. As we have seen, the Security Council condemned mercenaries outside the context of national self-determination and its interest indicates that the mercenary question was not seen as purely about national self-determination.

The debates in the Ad Hoc Committee suggest that other Western states were interested in controlling the mercenary problem even when their national interests were not at stake. Countries like Canada,[108] Sweden,[109] Norway,[110] and the Netherlands[111] all actively supported international legal instruments controlling mercenaries, even though none of them faced problems caused by their citizens acting as mercenaries.

Closer examination reveals that there was an international consensus on the mercenary question. Western states actively participated in the creation of legal instruments dealing with mercenaries. The Americans worked with the Nigerians to create the draft article put before the Diplomatic Conference in the mid-1970s.[112] None of the Western states involved disputed the basic idea that mercenaries ought to be controlled.[113]

---

[107] Special Subcommittee on Investigations of the Committee on International Relations (1976: 28).
[108] See below. [109] CDDH/SR.41 at 198.
[110] CDDH/III/SR.33-36, Annex, 548, para. 16. [111] CDDH/SR.41, para. 194.
[112] Cassese (1980: 23) and Gasser (1987: 916).
[113] The Western delegations present at the Summary Meeting which discussed Article 47 included Switzerland, Italy, Portugal, Australia, Canada, Sweden, the Netherlands, and France. None of these countries suggested that an article was unnecessary and the Netherlands and Sweden explicitly refer to their support for the article. The Holy See was also present and supported the article. CDDH/SR.41.

From the beginning of the Ad Hoc Committee's meetings in 1980, there was widespread agreement about the necessity of creating a convention. The Committee's chairman reported in 1981 that 'the use of mercenaries had been unanimously condemned and no one questioned the advisability, utility or importance of the Ad Hoc Committee's mandate'.[114] The statements of the Western members of the committee reinforce the Chairman's point.[115] The UK delegate, speaking on behalf of what were then the EEC members, stated that they 'strongly condemned the use of mercenaries, shared the concerns of African States and others in Asia and Latin America in that regard, and were very conscious that the involvement of mercenaries could make the settlement of internal disputes more difficult by introducing an international dimension'[116] and the American delegate noted that his country 'totally opposed the use of mercenaries and had long since enacted legislation to deal with certain aspects of the problem'.[117]

An examination of the specific concerns of Western states, as brought forward during the Ad Hoc Committee debates, demonstrates that while Western states agreed in that mercenaries required control, they did not approve of the mechanisms proposed to do so. The discussions in the Ad Hoc Committee were promoting a view of the law which would have had serious consequences for the norms of freedom of movement and state responsibility.

Freedom of Movement

From the Western perspective, the norm against mercenary use was not trumped by state interest, but rather reshaped by the necessity of adhering to different norms. Western states argued through the course of creating the UN Convention that preventing nationals from leaving the country to enlist abroad was a violation of their fundamental right to freedom of movement. The resolution which first proposed the creation of a Convention calls upon member states 'to ensure by both administrative and legislative measures that their territory and other territories under their control, as well as their nationals, are not used for' mercenary activities.[118] The United States indicated that it did not agree 'with the wording of the operative paragraph by which States were urged to consider measures to prohibit transit of persons within their territories'.[119] The argument that freedom of movement would be restricted

---

[114] UN Document A/C.6/36/SR.15, para. 19.
[115] UN Document A/C.6/36/SR.18, para. 16.
[116] UN Document A/C.6/36/SR.18, para.19.
[117] UN Document A/C.6/35/SR.22, para. 25.   [118] UN GA Res. 34/140.
[119] Yearbook of the United Nations (1979: 1151).

by anti-mercenary legislation is cited as one of the stumbling blocks to anti-mercenary legislation.[120]

There were genuine practical difficulties with creating legislation to restrict mercenary movements. Legal instruments to ban foreign enlistment existed (and continue to exist) in several Western countries. They are rarely used, mainly because they are impossible to enforce. The large numbers of Americans who enlisted abroad as volunteers during the First World War drove a significant hole in the legislation, as they were not prosecuted.[121] The movements of volunteers during the Spanish Civil War presented another challenge to foreign enlistment legislation. Some argue that the American legislation is not really designed to deal with individuals leaving the country, but rather to prevent recruitment on US soil.[122]

State experience in Africa suggested that even with the strongest will in the world, it was impossible to prevent citizens from becoming mercenaries if they were committed to doing so. Most of the mercenaries active in the Congo were active in the early 1960s and again in 1968. Despite having their passports taken, and despite being permanently banned from the Congo, many returned. Mockler notes the constant reappearance of mercenaries in different conflicts, pointing out the futility of 'passports stamped "Not Valid in Africa"'.[123] The Diplock Report argues that removing mercenaries' passports is a 'minor obstacle to departure'.[124]

These practical arguments cut no ice with the non-Western states. First, they argued that in some of the cases of repeated mercenary action, active Western collusion was to blame.[125] There is certainly evidence to show that the repeated return of Westerners to the Congo was a problem for the UN. A report on mercenaries in the UN operation in the Congo ONUC files of the UN Archive points out that Tshombe 'has continually permitted, even if he has not arranged for, the renewed recruitment of mercenaries including a large number of those repatriated by the UN last year'.[126] However, countries which

---

[120] See Burmester (1978: 46). Burmester believes that at some point individual rights need to be set against the threat mercenaries pose to humanity.

[121] Mourning (1982: 597).

[122] Ibid. Indeed, this was the position taken by the Department of Justice official in his testimony before the Special Subcommittee. Special Subcommittee on Investigations of the Committee on International Relations (1976: 5).

[123] Mockler (1985: 127 n).   [124] Diplock, Walker-Smith and de Freitas (1976: 5).

[125] Layeb (1989: 466–7). The delegate from Sierra Leone pointed out that it was perfectly possible for states to deny passports. UN Doc A/C.6/36/SR.23, para. 14. The delegate from Libya pointed out that the argument that mercenary activities could not be controlled without 'infringing human rights and democratic freedoms' was a 'mere excuse and was worse than the acts themselves'. UN Doc A/C.6/35/SR.23, para. 16.

[126] UN Archive. Office for Special Political Affairs, UN Operation in the Congo (ONUC) Subject Files. Box S-0129-006-7. Memo to Ralph Bunche.

were trying faced similar problems. The conclusions of the Diplock Report 1976 suggest that practical problems with banning mercenaries indeed existed.

The normative conflict between the right of a citizen to move freely and the desire of the state to control that movement had proved to be a problem as early as 1907. During the debate leading to the Hague Conventions 1907, an attempt to ban mercenaries outright failed because of concerns about violating freedom of movement. As de Bustamente puts it, the prohibition of foreign service by states was an 'innovation' which 'departed from established usage up to the present time and seriously threatened individual liberty'.[127]

The right to freedom of movement is also protected in the 1948 United Nations Universal Declaration of Human Rights, in article 13(2). The International Covenant on Political and Civil Rights, 1966, with 160 parties,[128] similarly safeguards the right to freedom of movement. Both these documents have the status of customary international law.[129]

Western states were not making a new argument during the deliberations of the Ad Hoc Committee. Rather, they were working within the parameters of a long-standing approach to deal with the problems of foreign service, and were governed by an equally long-standing belief in the importance of individual liberty. The Western approach was far from a cynical manoeuvre designed to protect Western interests in the particular circumstances of the 1980s, but an old approach reflecting a settled debate.

Given the practical problems with preventing foreign enlistment, any legislation to prevent citizens from enrolling as mercenaries would have to be strict to the point of being draconian and possibly go far beyond the removal of a passport. If an individual left the country to take a holiday and signed up as a mercenary abroad then states could do very little, beyond the measure of checking all passports on the way out of the country at all border crossings, to control the problem. While this type of passport control has been common in dictatorships and was a feature of the Eastern bloc nations during the Cold War, it is not common practice for democratic states to prevent their citizens from leaving. Moreover, to do so would violate the UN Declaration on Human Rights and the International Covenant on Civil and Political Rights.

The Diplock Report considered the problem of freedom of movement at some length, and concluded that the prospect of a mercenary's damage to himself could not justify the prohibition of foreign enlistment.[130] Lord Diplock and his colleagues took the right to freedom of movement very seriously. To restrict freedom of movement would require a compelling public interest. The Report argues that no such domestic interest exists, and the interests of good

---

[127] De Bustamente (1908: 100). [128] As of December 2004.
[129] Higgins (1994: 105). [130] Diplock, Walker-Smith, and de Freitas (1976: 3).

international relations would require case-by-case attention. Any attempt to prohibit a citizen from leaving the country or volunteering abroad would involve 'a deprivation of his freedom to do as he will'.[131] Finally, even removing a passport constitutes a serious violation of the right to freedom of movement, specifically the right to leave a country unhindered, as British law and the UN Declaration on Human Rights concur.[132]

The argument that Western states were adhering to an old approach to the problem of foreign service which in turn attempted to protect the norm of individual liberty draws strength from the debates in the Ad Hoc Committee. Western states took the position that holding states responsible for the movements of their citizens abroad would be both impractical[133] and a violation of the rights of citizens to move freely.[134] Even Nigeria, which had proposed the Convention, recognized that the UNDHR meant that 'it could be argued that it might not be practicable for a State to prevent the departure of any of its nationals intending to take part in mercenary activities'. The fact that the Nigerian delegate then pointed out that 'the maintenance of international peace and security must have primacy over individual rights and freedom of movement and association'[135] illustrates the fundamental point of contention between Western and non-Western states over freedom of movement. If Western states had agreed to placing controls on their citizens in the UN Convention, they would have been reversing at least seventy years of state practice which protected the right to freedom of movement and trampling upon an important democratic right. Clearly, Western states were seeking to protect a different norm rather than protect their own interests.[136]

State Responsibility

The norm of state responsibility, or the extent to which, if at all, states can be held to be responsible for their citizens' private actions at international law, created the most significant problems during the Convention's creation.

---

[131] Ibid. 4. [132] Ibid. The right is enshrined in Article 13(2) of the UNDHR.
[133] Belgium, UN Doc A/C.6/35/SR.24, para. 54. Portugal, UN Doc A/C.6/36/SR.24, para. 56.
[134] The United Kingdom refers specifically to the problems of passports and the protection of freedom of movement in the International Covenant on Civil and Political Rights. UN Doc A/C.6/35/SR.21, para. 44.
[135] Nigeria, UN Doc A/C.6/35/SR.51, para. 70.
[136] It is interesting to examine the Western championing of the right to freedom of movement in the 1970s and 1980s in today's climate. Western states seem to have lost their distaste for restricting free movement from a country and have considerably tightened their approach to granting and removing passports. This about-face represents a shift away from a very long established practice in international relations and at international law and deserves some examination.

The question of state responsibility, which became the sticking point during the Ad Hoc Committee's deliberations, created two responses. Most of the non-Western states in the Ad Hoc Committee concurred that states must be held responsible for their citizens' actions for the law to work. These states argued that there were two crimes associated with mercenaries: the crime of being a mercenary, and the crime of 'mercenarism'. Mercenarism includes state support for mercenary action, and includes state *failure* to bring the mercenary problem under control.

The Western states in the Ad Hoc Committee argued that the crime of mercenarism should not be included in the UN Convention, and that states could not be held responsible if their citizens became mercenaries, for both practical and legal reasons. These states contended that agreeing to a Convention that explicitly held states responsible for their citizens' actions, even if it also achieved the desirable goal of controlling mercenaries, was simply not worth the threat it would pose to international law.

Holding states responsible for crimes committed by mercenaries challenged the way international law had dealt with state responsibility in the past. States had previously been held responsible for the private actions of their citizens only when they were aware of those actions and did not seek to prevent them. The issue during the Ad Hoc Committee debates, however, was over 'absolute' state responsibility, or whether a state could be held responsible for the mercenary acts of its citizens *even in situations where it did not have knowledge of those acts*. The Canadian delegate pointed out that absolute state responsibility only existed in international law in specific circumstances: in multilateral treaties concerning nuclear installations, nuclear powered ships, and damage caused by space objects.[137] This type of absolute state responsibility applied to specific treaties dealing with situations that would have massive international consequences, like the explosion of a nuclear reactor, and had very specific application in international law.

The difficulty with making absolute state responsibility an international rule was fourfold. First, the International Law Commission (ILC) had been considering the problem of state responsibility since the early 1970s and Western delegates felt that any decision they made about state responsibility would pre-empt the work of the ILC.[138] By the mid-1970s, the ILC had already concluded that states could not be held responsible for their citizens' acts unless they supported, directed, or otherwise approved of those acts.[139] The existence of ILC draft articles making this statement about responsibility meant that the

---

[137] A/C.6/36/SR.22, para. 25.   [138] See Japan, UN Document A/C.6/36/SR.19, para. 23.
[139] See Rosenne 1997, which contains the ILC's report to the General Assembly and supporting documents on the subject of state responsibility.

Ad Hoc Committee's decision to include state responsibility could indeed have undermined the ILC's work.

Second, absolute state responsibility for individual criminal activities (as opposed to negligence under a treaty regime) simply did not exist. As early as the nineteenth century, arbitration bodies dealing with the question of state responsibility were advancing the principle 'that the conduct of a private person could, never, by itself, justify holding the state responsible in international law'[140] and that the private person's actions must involve some sort of wrongful conduct or approval on the part of the state.[141] The ILC concluded that 'the act of a private person not acting on behalf of a State cannot be attributed to the State and cannot as such involve the responsibility of the State' and that this rule 'meets the needs of contemporary international life and does not need to be altered'.[142]

Third, Western states were specifically supported by the authority of previous conventions and international legal decisions. Several similar UN Conventions[143] do not suggest that states can be held responsible for their citizens' private actions. If the mercenary convention took this approach, it was argued, it would suggest that the other conventions did not establish responsibility for wrongful acts.[144] Decisions in the International Court of Justice, particularly the *Corfu Channel Case*, suggest that states had limited responsibility for individual actions. *Corfu* concerned a British ship damaged by mines placed in Albanian waters by unknown persons. The International Court of Justice found that merely because the mines were in Albanian waters did not indicate that Albania 'necessarily knew, or ought to have known, of any unlawful act perpetrated therein, nor yet that it necessarily knew, or should have known, the authors'.[145] The mere organization of an illegal activity within a state's territory does not indicate that the state knew or should have known about the activity, which would make it difficult for states to be held responsible for simply being the ground on which mercenaries organized their activities. Other tribunals have tended to minimize absolute state responsibility, suggesting that a state ought to have had knowledge of the individual act in question and the capacity to control it; tribunals have been reluctant to hold states responsible in areas where they could not have controlled the act.[146]

---

[140] Ibid. 117.   [141] Ibid. 118.   [142] Ibid. 126.
[143] The Convention for the Suppression of Unlawful Seizure of Aircraft (1970), International Convention against the Taking of Hostages (1979), and the Vienna Convention on Diplomatic Relations (1961).
[144] Layeb (1989: 481).
[145] *Corfu Channel Case (UK v. Albania)*, ICJ Reports, (1949), 18.
[146] Taulbee (1985: 358).

Fourth, Western states were clear from the beginning that the most significant problem with including absolute state responsibility in the UN Convention was that Western states would not and could not sign it, which would prevent the creation of an important and necessary legal instrument.[147]

Needless to say, non-Western states, including those from the developing world and in the Soviet bloc, saw Western arguments about state responsibility as an attempt to dodge responsibility for the actions of their citizens.[148] While it is true that state responsibility provisions would only affect South Africa and the West, the principal sources of recruitment,[149] which would make the stakes for Western states particularly high on the question of responsibility, Western states were not merely trying to avoid negative legal consequences. Some of the Western states advocated this position despite never having been sources of mercenary recruitment.[150]

Nor was the argument that state responsibility should not have entered into the UN Convention an indication that Western states felt that mercenaries should go unpunished at international law. Western states proposed an alternative solution: the harmonization of existing domestic and international law in order to control mercenaries. There was a precedent for the harmonization solution in dealing with other types of internationally wrongful acts, for example, in conventions on hijacking, diplomatic protection, and hostage-taking. As the UK delegate put it, the approach 'adopted in those Conventions had been not to create crimes to be judged by an international criminal court or to lay down rules on state responsibility, but to intensify international cooperation with a view to ensuring that individuals' could be brought to justice.[151] Western states were advocates of an approach that would punish mercenaries, but would not undermine the existing norm of state responsibility. During the 1970s, Western states were on the receiving end of hijacking and hostage-taking efforts, and yet promoted conventions that would punish individuals, rather than holding their home states responsible. Finally, Western states also recognized that states *could* be held responsible for the mercenary actions of their nationals if and when they failed in their treaty obligations.[152]

---

[147] Japan, UN Document A/C.6/36/SR.19, para. 23, and the United Kingdom, A/C.6/36/SR.18, para. 17.
[148] Libya, UN Document A/C.6.36/SR.18, para.14. The USSR argued that the majority of the members of the Committee, including the non-aligned states and the socialist states, were in favour of establishing state responsibility while the minority Western states suggested instead the harmonization of domestic and international laws to deal with the problem. UN Document A/C.6/36/SR.19, para. 31.
[149] Taulbee (1985: 359).
[150] e.g., the Scandinavian countries; Japan also advocated this position.
[151] UN Doc A/C.6.36/SR.18, para. 16.   [152] UN Doc A/C.6.36/SR.18, para. 17.

The apparent split between Western and non-Western states on the mercenary question does not represent a challenge to the idea that the law on mercenaries reflects a norm against mercenary use. Western and non-Western states were agreed that mercenaries ought to be controlled, but differed in the methods by which they proposed to do so. In seeking to implement the proscriptive norm against mercenary use, Western states were prevented from agreeing to provisions of the Convention because they were attempting to protect the norm of state responsibility. Western states universally agreed about the importance of these long-standing norms, suggesting that the disagreement between the two groups of states during the creation of the UN Convention was a conflict between norms, rather than a conflict created by differing interests.

Conflict between Norms was the Most Significant Conflict Preventing Effective Law

The apparent split between Western and non-Western states on the mercenary question does not represent a challenge to the norm against mercenary use. Western and non-Western states agreed that mercenaries ought to be controlled, but differed in the methods by which they proposed to do so. In seeking to implement the proscriptive norm against mercenary use, Western states were guided by two related and powerful norms. The norms of freedom of movement and state responsibility prevented the West from agreeing to provisions of the Convention which would have violated these norms. The universal agreement among Western states on these norms, and the long histories of both, suggests that the disagreement between the two groups of states during the creation of the UN Convention was a conflict between norms, rather than a conflict created by differing interests; moreover, it was a debate more about how best to deal with the mercenary problem rather than a discussion about whether to deal with it at all.

If the international law dealing with mercenaries was undermined by the presence of other norms, then it follows that some states must have considered the norm against mercenary use to be less important than state responsibility and freedom of movement norms. This raises the question of how states rank norms in importance. If Western states decided that state responsibility and freedom of movement were more important than the norm against mercenary use, does this indicate that the latter was insignificant? One answer might be that in this particular case a norm that was relatively uncodified at international law (the anti-mercenary norm) was coming up against a norm that was well codified (the state responsibility norm). To disrupt codified norms is more difficult and has more striking effects than failing to incorporate a new norm.

As Lowe points out, state responsibility is a fundamental, primary norm, upon which other norms are built.[153] Tinkering with state responsibility for the sake of creating law on mercenaries would have disrupted the entire system of international law. It is important to emphasize that a solution—the harmonization of existing domestic and international law—was on the table and would have controlled mercenaries without threatening this norm. The conflict of norms does not signal that the anti-mercenarism norm was unimportant.

6.4. CONCLUSION: THE SIGNIFICANCE OF THE NORM AGAINST MERCENARY USE IN INTERNATIONAL LAW

The formal attempts to create international law regarding mercenaries in the 1960s, 1970s, and 1980s can be clarified through attention to the proscriptive norm against mercenary use. The appropriate cause aspect of the norm had a great deal of influence because of the strength of similar norms of national self-determination, and the control aspect of the norm played a role in suggesting to African states that the sort of independent state they wished to become was a state in control of its own armed forces, unmenaced by external forces and unlikely to use such forces outside the context of a formal arrangement.

The translation of the norm against mercenary use into formal international law was profoundly influenced by the existence of other norms. The question of state responsibility and the defence of freedom of movement each prevented agreement on how to ban mercenaries during the debates of the Ad Hoc Committee, created to design the UN Convention. But the norm against mercenary use, the basic belief that mercenaries are undesirable because they threaten state control and do not fight for an appropriate cause, remained strong. There was no question that mercenaries needed control, and there was grave concern about their selfish and financial motives.

The influence of the norm against mercenaries highlights some important aspects of the interplay between norms and international law. Tensions and weaknesses within a particular law do not necessarily point to weaknesses in the underlying norms. In the case of the international legal regime on mercenaries, the weaknesses of the law may indeed point to the *strength* of the underlying norm. The law focuses on motive as a crucial aspect of the definition of a mercenary, despite its legal unworkability. Here the strength of

[153] Lowe (2001: 208).

the norm and the belief in the importance of a correct cause for fighting pulled the law into an unworkable direction. The norm was put into place in a UN Convention, despite quite intense disagreement on how to do so.

The international law on mercenaries also demonstrates the practical difficulties of how to translate norms into law. Sometimes, elements of a norm may be widely accepted but simply impossible to put into law, because they are not really logical. The selfish motivation element of the anti-mercenary norm, for example, has clear philosophical and practical difficulties and yet is a commonly accepted element of what defines a mercenary. Law cannot encapsulate this norm without running into practical difficulties. Norms with a long history can be pushed and pulled by other influences in such a way that law is difficult to create, even though states might be interested in doing so.

Ambiguous law, then, does not necessarily demonstrate that there was really no underlying norm. In reference to the debate at the Diplomatic Conference, Van Deventer asks 'why, in the presence of such enthusiasm for drastic measures against mercenaries, it was impossible to achieve a consensus on a definition and a statement of the legal consequences of the status remains something of a mystery'.[154] There was an underlying norm, but debate over how best to realize the norm in international law led to disagreement, and ambiguity. And as we have seen, in some ways, the strength of the norm pulled the law in directions which made it hard to implement.[155]

Even though norms and interests remained intertwined during this period, attention to normative influence is crucially important. A first glance at the documentary evidence and the evolution of international law suggests that direct state interest in the law is responsible for its problems. States were either disinterested or interested in the law, and their position affected their enthusiasm; alternatively, states were keen to create law which would protect them while enabling them to use private force themselves. Without some attention to how norms influence states, and how the anti-mercenary norm in particular shaped state response to international law, it is impossible to cut to the heart of debates which resulted in the creation of international law.

Attention to norms in general is necessary to understand the vehemence of the African response to the mercenaries problem and the cause of Western opposition to the UN Convention. Close analysis of the proscriptive norm against mercenary use can explain the flaws in the law more coherently than an approach which argues for a clear state interest in retaining the option to use private force. The 'appropriate cause' component of the norm can

---

[154] Van Deventer (1976: 815).
[155] For a longer discussion of the relationship between law and norms, see Percy (2007a).

explain why in the context of national self-determination mercenaries seemed so egregious. The 'control' component of the norm can explain why states were willing to exclude forces like the Gurkhas and the French Foreign Legion from the definition.

A focus on norms provides a richer and more complete picture of international law on mercenaries. It demonstrates that law can be undermined and weakened by conflicting norms, and strengthened by complementary norms. As we have seen, such an approach does not have to discount the importance of interests or the fact that norms and interests are related. But if other critics suggest that state policy has been created by the pursuit of interests, it is important to counteract these critiques by pointing out the strength of norms. Moreover, it is important to recognize that in some cases norms gained strength because of a congruence with interests. The interest-based approaches outlined above are incomplete in part because without attention to norms, they are unable to explain why states held particular positions and pursued their interests so strongly in some cases. A normative lens provides a sharper picture of a complex debate.

7

New Model Mercenaries: PMCs, PSCs, and the Anti-Mercenary Norm

The appearance of PMCs in the mid-1990s and PSCs a few years later appeared to herald a new world of mercenary assistance. Where the mercenaries of the 1960s, 1970s, and 1980s were loosely organized and extremely colourful, the new PMCs were tight outfits without even the pretence of old-fashioned seedy mercenary glamour. With anodyne names like Executive Outcomes (EO) and Sandline, these companies promised business-like solutions to entrenched civil conflicts. PMCs worked hard to distance themselves from *les affreux* of the 1960s and cast themselves as honourable solutions to problems ignored by the rest of the world. Involvement in several international scandals quickly revealed that seedy mercenary glamour was not as far in the distant past as EO and Sandline had hoped, and by 2004 both companies had closed their doors.[1] PSCs, which had existed in various incarnations and on a very small scale since the 1970s,[2] expanded enormously after 2001. During the first Gulf War, American troops were assisted by private security forces: one in fifty personnel were PSC employees. During the invasion of Iraq in 2003, that number jumped to one in ten. In Iraq in 2006, it was estimated that at least 20,000 PSC employees assisted American and British troops.[3] PSCs insist that they do not engage in any type of active combat, and that not only are they not mercenaries, they are also not PMCs.

The appearance of the new breed of mercenary might seem to herald the demise of any lingering adherence to a norm proscribing mercenary use. The commonplace use of private force by major states seems to disprove Thomson's argument that today's 'real' states do not hire mercenaries.[4] And yet, despite best efforts of first PMCs and later PSCs to present themselves as legitimate business concerns free from the mercenary label, they have been tainted by it. The norm against mercenary use continues to influence state policy, despite evidence of the successes of PMCs engaged in active combat, and despite the fact that it is probably impossible for the United States military to go to war today without the assistance of PSCs.

---

[1] EO closed in 1999 and Sandline in 2004.   [2] Kinsey (2006).
[3] Some estimate the number to be 40,000 or even 60,000.   [4] Thomson (1994: 96).

The emergence of new types of private force does not, on its own, invalidate or diminish the norm against mercenary use. It is not surprising that the private sale of military force takes on new forms; in fact, given its long tradition it would be surprising if it disappeared. Norms do not have to result in the complete end of a practice to remain influential. Social and legal norms against the taking of illegal drugs are not invalidated by the appearance of new drugs. Initially, it might even appear that the new drug is acceptable; the test for the norm is whether or not society ultimately reacts to the new drug by either accommodating it within the existing norm or, perhaps, changing the norm itself. The emergence of PMCs and PSCs does not necessarily suggest that the international climate is newly receptive to the use of private force. Rather, the reaction to these companies, and the evolution of the industry from one that openly promoted the use of active combat to one that actively avoids it, demonstrates that the anti-mercenary norm is still influential. I argue that the anti-mercenary norm not only played a crucial role in shutting down the private military industry, but that it continues to plague the private security industry and influence the prospects for PSCs.

This chapter first demonstrates the continued influence of the norm against mercenary use by examining the development of PMCs and PSCs starting in the mid-1990s. Second, the chapter argues that the shift away from the provision of combat services can only be explained by the anti-mercenary norm. The third section traces the continued relevance of the anti-mercenary norm to the private security industry, looking at state control and regulation and the persistence of the cause aspect of the norm. The final section considers the future of the norm against mercenaries.

7.1. THE ANTI-MERCENARY NORM IN THE 1990s: PMCs

A quick glance of the facts about PMCs and the international attitude towards private force in general in the early 1990s might suggest that private force was becoming increasingly accepted and efforts to control it had failed. The alacrity with which companies like EO and Sandline found clients and notoriety, and the marked decline of enthusiasm for the UN Convention, suggested that the prospects for the future use of private force were good, and the influence of the norm against mercenary use was weak.

This section begins by outlining the international context of the early 1990s, and providing a brief glimpse into the growth of the UN Convention. It turns to an examination of the operations of PMCs in Angola, Sierra Leone, and Papua New Guinea (PNG). These three cases have been selected because they are the three examples of a PMC contracting with the state to provide services including combat activities. I then examine the allegations made against these companies and how they demonstrate the persistence of the norm against mercenaries. The final section examines the fact that PMCs were only ever used in peripheral areas, suggesting they did not really challenge the norm, and the degree to which the norm has become 'puritanical', as evidenced by international hostility to PMCs at the UN.

The UN Convention

The UN Convention seemed to be a non-entity soon after it was signed. Because it shares so many of the loopholes of Article 47, critics remained concerned about its utility as an instrument of international law.[5] To make matters worse, most states were showing a distinct lack of enthusiasm for ratifying the Convention, which itself had taken nine years to create. In 1989, the year it was finalized, only African states who had had a particular problem with mercenaries had signed it. By 1993, when EO appeared on the scene, these states had been joined by very few others.[6] It did not come into force until 2001, meaning that its influence was minimal throughout the 1990s.

While the UN Convention was undoubtedly not a roaring success in terms of ratification, in the context of the 1990s this perhaps indicates more about events and less about the norm. The appearance of PMCs so soon after the Convention was signed dealt it a serious blow.[7] Legal commentators analysing the PMCs phenomenon all agree that not only is the Convention (and Article 47, which it closely follows) fatally flawed, but it does not apply to PMCs because their whole design takes advantage of one of the major loopholes identified in Chapter 6. Because Executive Outlines and Sandline both asserted they would work only for sovereign states, and because of their incorporation into the structure of the armed forces of the state which hired them, they were not considered to be mercenaries.[8] By 1994, Angola, one of the signatories of the Convention, had already used a PMC.

In some ways, this is a blatant display of state interest. Angola spent the 1970s and 1980s decrying the existence of mercenaries and, when it was in a desperate situation in the early 1990s, was the first state to hire a PMC on a large scale. However, as we see, the problems of the UN Convention and the

---

[5] Hampson (1991: 30) and Singer (2004a: 531).
[6] In 1993, the following states were parties to the Convention: Angola, Barbados, Belarus, Cameroon, Congo, Croatia, Democratic Republic of the Congo, Germany, Italy, the Maldives, Morocco, Nigeria, Poland, Romania, Suriname, the Seychelles, Ukraine, and Uruguay.
[7] Singer (2004a: 531).
[8] Shearer (1998a: 18), Zarate (1998: 124), and Singer (2004a: 532).

stark demonstrations of state interest by the signatories of the Convention, while real problems, do not indicate that the norm is no longer influential.

Angola: The Debut of the New Dogs of War

EO was created in the early 1990s by Eeben Barlow, a former South African Defence Forces officer. It incorporated members of the Buffalo 32 Battalion, known for its covert operations in Mozambique and Angola. In the early 1990s, a situation in Angola was brewing that would lead to EO's big break as a player in the private military industry. Each side of the Angolan civil war had been funded by opposing superpowers during the Cold War, and were abandoned by them at its end.[9] Having contributed greatly to the terrible security situation in Angola, the superpowers had effectively left the Angolans to solve the problem themselves.

In 1993, UNITA forces had captured the Soyo oilfields, marking another chapter in the long Angolan civil war. The oilfield was owned by Sonangol, the state oil company, and Branch-Heritage Oil.[10] EO was hired to take back the Soyo oilfield,[11] and did so successfully. In September 1993, EO was offered a contract worth $40 million to train the Angolan army[12] EO's main project was the retraining of the army's 16th Brigade, which began to have increasing success.[13] EO's training programme came to fruition when the 16th Brigade defeated a large UNITA force outside the Angolan capital, Luanda.[14] EO's personnel fought with the army they had trained,[15] and some were killed in combat.[16] By 1994, PMC's assistance had forced UNITA back to the negotiating table, and a peace accord was signed in November.[17] The terms of the peace agreement included the repatriation of private fighters; however EO stayed on for over a year.[18]

EO's actions in Angola were widely considered a success. The company's assistance brought the civil war to an end at a lower political and economic cost than could have been accomplished through aid to the Angolan military,[19]

---

[9] Howe (1998: 312) and Singer (2003a: 108).
[10] Singer (2003a: 108). The alleged relationship between EO and Branch-Heritage is discussed below.
[11] Shearer (1998a: 46), Howe (2001: 198), and Smith (2002–3: 108).
[12] Howe (1998: 312), Smith (2002–3: 109), and Singer (2003a: 109)
[13] O'Brien (1998: 86). [14] Smith (2002–3: 109). [15] Ibid.
[16] Howe (1998: 312).
[17] Singer (2003a: 109). Cleary (1999: 159) questions the degree to which EO can take credit for bringing the parties to the table, citing the influence of other factors, like the Lusaka peace talks.
[18] Howe (1998: 313). [19] Reno (2000: 62).

and its assistance was of great benefit to the Angolan government.[20] Indeed, the resurgence of the conflict after EO left in 1995 might demonstrate the importance of their involvement to the government's success.[21]

Sierra Leone: EO Continues Its Work, and Sandline Enters the Game

Like Angola, Sierra Leone had been embroiled in a long and complex civil war by the time EO appeared on the scene. In 1991, Foday Sankoh's Rebel United Front (RUF) began fighting against the government, with the support of Charles Taylor's regime in neighbouring Liberia. Sierra Leone has significant diamond deposits, many of which are alluvial. Alluvial diamonds can be mined by hand, which makes them a ready source of income.[22] The RUF began to use these easily obtainable diamonds to finance its war effort. The war was soon recognized as particularly senseless and intractable. In 1992, Valentine Strasser, a young military officer, seized power in a coup and established the National Provisional Ruling Council (NPRC), but the civil war continued and Strasser's new government struggled to be considered legitimate. In 1995, the security situation became acute, and in January Strasser hired Gurkha Security Guards (GSG) to assist his regime. The following month GSG's leader was captured in an ambush, killed, and possibly eaten by his captors, leading to the withdrawal of the company. In April, Strasser's government turned to EO.

EO had a quick and decisive impact on the conflict. They pushed back the RUF, which had come within 20 kilometres of the capital, Freetown. Further victories came when the rebels were pushed out of the diamond areas of Koidu and Kono. In January of 1996 EO's contract was renewed, with an increase in the number of personnel. As they had done in Angola, EO engaged in combat. By February of 1996, despite an internal coup replacing Strasser with Brigadier General Julius Maada Bio, the country was stable enough to hold multiparty elections, which were won by Ahmed Tejan Kabbah. Kabbah continued EO's contract and by November the RUF had been brought to the negotiating table. In early 1997, Eeben Barlow and another senior leader of EO resigned from the company. In January 1997, Kabbah terminated EO's contract. EO had predicted that if they left Sierra Leone, the Kabbah government would fall within a hundred days. Their predictions proved correct, as ninety-five days later the government fell and Kabbah fled amid bloody fighting.

[20] Howe (1998: 331) and Singer (2003a: 108).   [21] Singer (2003a: 110).
[22] Resources, Primary Industry, and Conflict in Sierra Leone (1997).

EO's operations in Sierra Leone were generally considered to be successful.[23] In both Sierra Leone and Angola, EO brought stability from insecurity. With 'less than 20 total casualties, including those from accidents and illness, the private firm had succeeded in bringing stability to two endemically conflict-ridden states'.[24]

The collapse of the Kabbah government set the stage for a second PMC to become involved in the conflict. Sandline, a British company very similar to (if not a sister company of) EO, offered its services to Kabbah's government-in-exile. Sandline's major service was to help plan a counter-coup designed to restore Kabbah to power. However, a delivery of arms arranged by Sandline and destined for Kabbah's supporters was captured in Nigeria, resulting in accusations that Sandline was in violation of the UN arms embargo on Sierra Leone. The ensuing scandal worsened when the British Foreign Office was accused of having full knowledge of Sandline's work in Sierra Leone, a charge a government enquiry was to find true. The 'Sandline Affair' received massive media attention in the UK and put the Labour foreign minister, Robin Cook, under intense scrutiny.

Sandline's Second Mission: PNG

A prolonged civil war, as it had in Sierra Leone and Angola, provided an opportunity for an enterprising PMC in PNG. The island of Bougainville had been the scene of disputes through the 1980s between local landowners and the Australian operators of the Panguna copper mine, and these disputes came to a head with the outbreak of civil war in 1988.[25] Prior to its closure in 1989 (due to the war), the Panguna mine accounted for 8 per cent of gross domestic product, 35 per cent of export earnings, and 12 per cent of government revenue in PNG.[26] The PNG government was a part-owner, holding 19 per cent of the shares in the mine.[27] The loss of the mine caused financial difficulty for the government, and by February 1997, 10,000 people had been killed in the conflict.[28]

After talks between the government of Prime Minister Sir Julius Chan and the Bougainville Revolutionary Army (BRA) broke down in April 1996, Tim Spicer, head of Sandline, held meetings with Chan to discuss the possibility of PMC assistance to end the war. In January 1997, Sandline and Chan agreed

[23] Howe (1998: 315) and Coker (1999: 197). Douglas (1999: 182, 183) comments that EO's use of air power was particularly successful.
[24] Singer (2003a: 114).   [25] Dinnen (1999: 279).
[26] Ibid. Shearer puts the export earnings figure at 30%, Shearer (1998b: 78), and Singer at 45%. Singer (2003a: 192). Copper exports were a significant part of PNG's export revenues.
[27] Dorney (1998: 39).   [28] Arnold (1999: 76).

to a contract whereby the PMC would train the PNG special forces, and use intelligence it collected to neutralize the BRA and retake the mine.[29] Sandline subcontracted EO to provide training, aircraft, and equipment for PNG troops.[30] Spicer began preparations and was in PNG when the international media got hold of the story that Chan was going to use mercenaries against rebels in Bougainville. By the middle of March, Defence Force Commander Jerry Singirok came out publicly against the plan. The army became mutinous at the prospect of PMC involvement.[31] Large street demonstrations occurred in Port Moresby, the capital city. Singirok's comments led to a government enquiry into charges of corruption over the deal between the Chan government and Sandline. The first enquiry, operating with limited time, concluded there had been no wrongdoing but a second indicated that there had been improper conduct.[32] The affair wound up with Sandline's departure before its weapons had even arrived; left unpaid, Sandline successfully sued the PNG government for violating the terms of its contract.[33]

Allegations about PMC Operations in the Early 1990s

The PMC operations in Angola, Sierra Leone, and PNG garnered a great deal of international attention. Three specific allegations have been commonly made about all these operations: first, that there was a complex network of relationships between mining companies, the contracted PMC, and other PMCs; second, that PMCs were attracted by the presence of natural resources in the host state; and third, that some kind of international pressure influenced the termination of the PMC's contract by the host state. These allegations, particularly the first two, are contentious and difficult to prove. However, for the purposes of a book concerned with tracing the impact of a norm against mercenary use, it is more important to note that these allegations were made rather than to attempt to get to the truth behind them. The *perception* that these claims are true has coloured state behaviour and the response of the international media, even if the facts upon which the allegations are based are shaky. The allegations, once made, contributed to a sense that PMCs were, like mercenaries, morally problematic; the fact that they have persisted, in some cases without a great deal of evidence, further demonstrates that there is a predisposition to looking at private fighters in a negative fashion. Moreover, the allegations against PMCs are important because they directly

---

[29] Singer (2003a: 193).   [30] Arnold (1999: 79). See also Dinnen (1999: 279).
[31] Dorney (1998: 289–90) and Arnold (1999: 81).
[32] Dinnen (1999: 279). On the first enquiry see Dorney (1998: 27, 333–4).
[33] Singer (2003a: 195).

support the norm against mercenary use. I examine each of these allegations in turn, before turning to discussing how the history of PMCs in the 1990s demonstrates the continued influence of the anti-mercenary norm.

Alleged Relationships between EO, Sandline, and Natural Resource Extraction Companies

First, the tangled relationship between EO and Sandline, and these two companies and natural resource extraction companies, supposedly played a role in all three cases. Critics argue that Sandline was merely a new incarnation of EO, and that each company is a member of the Branch-Heritage Group.[34] The Branch-Heritage Group allegedly included the mining companies Branch Energy and Branch Minerals, Heritage Oil and Gas, and three others. It also included Sandline and partly owned Ibis Air, an air support company. There were apparent links between EO and the Branch-Heritage Group through another company called Strategic Resources Corporation.[35] While the links between EO and Branch were never conclusively proved, there is general agreement among journalists and scholars that the relationship existed.[36]

Howe argues that Branch introduced EO to the Angolan government, while others argue that different oil companies of various nationalities played a role.[37] Tony Buckingham, an executive of Branch, had mining interests in Sierra Leone, and he may have introduced EO to the Strasser government, just as he had acted as intermediary in Angola.[38] There is circumstantial evidence suggesting that the contract between the Strasser government and EO included diamond concessions to be paid to Branch-Heritage. Although the companies concerned deny this charge, Branch-Heritage did receive concessions in Koidu and Kono, worth an estimated US $1 million,[39] shortly after the contract between EO and the NPRC regime was signed.[40] Neither company disputes the grant of concessions, but both dispute the argument that the two companies, and consequently their respective contracts with Sierra Leone, were related.

---

[34] Shearer (1997a: 203).
[35] Ibid, Shearer (1998a: 45) and Singer (2003a: 104–5). See Pech (1999) for an in-depth analysis.
[36] Shearer (1998a: 72), Arnold (1999: 84), Pech (1999: 86), and O'Brien (2000: 67).
[37] Howe (1998: 312). There is disagreement about how EO came to be offered the contract. Various oil companies have been suggested and some suggest that it was the Angolan government. For a summary of the various viewpoints see Smith (2002–3: 118 n. 19).
[38] Singer (2003a: 112). [39] Vines (1999: 53).
[40] The Branch/Sierra Leone agreement was signed in July 1995, granting the former a 25-year concession in Kono. Francis (1999: 331). Sandline presents a refutation of some of these allegations on its website: <http://www.sandline.com/comment/list/comment22.html>.

The same web of companies, some argue, were responsible for the complex contract arrangements and side payments in the form of concessions were also implicated in PNG, this time with Sandline taking the PMC role. Branch Energy representatives are said to have been present at the original meeting between Chan and Spicer, at which mining arrangements associated with the contract were discussed.[41] There is speculation that arrangements similar to those made in Sierra Leone and Angola were made in PNG, with Branch-Heritage receiving a share in the Panguna mine in exchange for bribes paid to key PNG officials.[42]

PMC involvement in Sierra Leone, if the argument that EO and Sandline are related is correct, is the sustained involvement of one company with an interest in government stability to ensure the continued extraction of valuable natural resources, rather than two separate interventions by two companies. The PNG mission also apparently demonstrates a relationship between Sandline and EO. Commentators suggest, as pointed out above, that Sandline subcontracted EO to fulfil the terms of the contract with PNG. Singer argues that 'the majority of the actual troops Sandline delivered to PNG were later discovered to be employees of EO'.[43]

The Presence of Extractable Natural Resources

The relationship between the two PMCs and natural-resource extraction companies is tied to the second allegation made about the three cases of PMC involvement: that the PMC was only involved because of the presence of extractable natural resources. It has been argued that EO arrived in Angola for the purpose of protecting oil interests, rather than solving Angolan security problems. Only after their original mission did they begin to work for the Angolan government. EO's official earnings were allegedly supplemented by payments, in the form of concessions granted to extract natural resources, from the host state.[44]

In Sierra Leone, the presence of valuable natural resources apparently influenced the shape of EO's intervention. It is clear that the company's primary strategic goal was the removal of rebels from diamond mining areas. EO's strategy was to push the RUF away from Freetown, opening supply lines to the government,[45] but thereafter, their first objective was to capture diamond areas.[46] Shearer argues that EO's strategy was purely financial—they needed the mining areas to be open to ensure that Branch-Heritage's diamond mining

---

[41] Singer (2003a: 192).   [42] Ibid. 193.   [43] Ibid. 194. See also Dorney (1998: 27).
[44] O'Brien (1998: 85, 86) and Arnold (1999: 118).
[45] Shearer (1997a: 204) and Douglas (1999: 314).
[46] Shearer (1997a: 204) and Arnold (1999: 134).

concessions would be lucrative and that they would get paid.[47] After the main rebel threat was driven back at Freetown, EO struck first at the diamond mining area of Koidu in June of 1995. In July, EO moved to the diamond fields at Kono, the same area in which Branch had just been granted the concession. EO quickly had the Kono diamond operation up and running.[48]

EO attacked the RUF in diamond areas long before launching attacks on the rebels' military installations.[49] In some ways, this may have simply been a good strategy, as the cutting off of funds to the rebels would weaken their efforts. However, peace only seemed to come to the parts of the country rich in natural resources. As Harding puts it, 'wherever they [EO] went, civilians stopped dying. The trouble was that they only went where the payoff was high'.[50] RUF bases were concentrated in Bo and Kenema, away from the diamonds[51] and the first attack on their bases came in December 1995;[52] it took EO seven months to launch its first attack on an RUF base.

In PNG, the presence of natural resources may have inspired Sandline's interest in the conflict. The contract between Sandline and PNG called for a US $36 million payment (after a 'discount' of $1.3 million), amounting to 150 per cent of the PNG armed forces' annual budget; the huge sum was to come from 'unauthorized budget cuts and the nationalization and sale of the Panguna mine'.[53]

International Pressure may have Led to the End of the Missions

The third similarity shared by all three cases of PMC intervention is that international attention appears to have played a role in ending the missions. EO's departure from Angola was obscured by a complicated cloud of international interference. There seems to be no doubt that the American government heavily pressured their Angolan counterparts to fire EO. There is, however, disagreement about the reason behind this pressure. Singer, Reno, and Spicer argue that President Clinton pressured the Angolans to remove EO and replace them with the American private security firm, MPRI.[54] As Singer puts it, people within the industry felt that Clinton was 'shilling' for MPRI.[55] Howe argues, conversely, that Clinton's concern was that EO's continued presence was causing UNITA to drag its heels in following the timetable set out in the peace agreement, and that Clinton had applied pressure on the Angolan

---

[47] Shearer (1997b: 853).   [48] Reno (1998: 131).   [49] Francis (1999: 322).
[50] Harding (1997: 93).   [51] Douglas (1999: 183).   [52] Ibid. 182.
[53] Singer (2003a: 193).
[54] Spicer (1999a: 50–1), Reno (2000: 65), and Singer (2003a: 109).
[55] Singer (2003a: 276, n. 32).

President dos Santos to end his involvement with EO during a state visit to Washington in December 1995.[56]

EO's departure from Sierra Leone occurred under similar international pressure, and their January 1997 withdrawal has been attributed to several factors. There is evidence suggesting that the IMF pressured the Kabbah government to avoid renewing their contract with EO,[57] or to reduce the nation's budget, which would have the inevitable (and foreseeable) effect of forcing a reduction in payment to EO.[58] Another interpretation has it that budgetary pressures were responsible for Kabbah's decision, but so too was the discomfiture of the Kabbah regime in the face of international criticism. It seemed that Kabbah 'did not only want to save the costs of the EO presence, but was also embarrassed by it'.[59] James Jonah, the Sierra Leonean finance minister in 1996–7, suggests that while the IMF's pressure was purely financial, the Kabbah government was not too enthusiastic about EO and therefore predisposed to not renewing the contract.[60] International pressure and domestic lack of enthusiasm were responsible for EO's departure.

In the case of PNG, international pressure to remove the PMC was direct and intense. Australia, PNG's primary donor and the regional security power, came out strongly against the Sandline intervention, and expressed its concerns in no uncertain terms to its allies and the international media.[61]

How Allegations about PMCs Demonstrate the Continued Influence of the Anti-Mercenary Norm

The allegations made against PMCs reflect the influence of the anti-mercenary norm. The charges that PMCs were being paid by mining concessions to related companies, regardless of whether or not they were conclusively proved, stuck. These charges undermined PMC attempts to portray themselves as non-mercenary. The existence of concessions and the apparent predilection of PMCs to intervene in countries with lucrative and easily extracted natural resources seemed to suggest that the new dogs of war were just as keen on working for their own interests as the old. The fact that these companies were private entities designed to be financially successful did little to diminish the comparison.

There are, of course, perfectly plausible reasons for the incidence of PMC missions in natural-resource rich areas. These companies have to be paid, and the only way for many states to pay is by exploiting their natural resources.

[56] Howe (1998: 313, n. 18). [57] O'Brien (1998: 86). [58] Howe (1998: 321).
[59] Shearer (1997b: 855). [60] Interview with James Jonah.
[61] Dorney (1998: 227), Arnold (1999: 79), and Dinnen (1999: 287).

In Angola and Sierra Leone, illicit extraction of natural resources was also funding the rebels the PMC was hired to defeat and needed to be stopped. However, the presence of a clear financial incentive, and alleged links to companies in a position to take advantage of natural resource opportunities, has not helped PMCs to avoid the mercenary label. The allegations seem to demonstrate that PMCs, despite protestations that they work in the interests (and so for the cause of) the state which hires them, are still mercenaries in the sense that they do not really share the same cause as their employers.

Similarly, the allegation that other states and international organizations have pressured those states who have hired PMCs to end that assistance contributes to the perception that these companies might be unethical.

The similarities between these three operations provide a window into how the proscriptive norm against mercenary use retains its influence. Examining the status of the UN Convention in the 1990s and the major operations of PMCs sets the stage for further discussion. Even though PMCs with the ability to transform a conflict had emerged, and international enthusiasm for formal legal regulation of mercenaries appeared to be waning, the norm against mercenary use nonetheless retained significant influence over PMCs themselves.

Only the Lonely: PMC Use Occurs Only in Peripheral Areas with No Other Options

Moreover, the appearance and use of PMCs in three cases does not present a robust challenge to the norm against mercenary use. Not only are there only three significant cases of combat assistance by PMCs, but all these cases occurred in peripheral and extremely weak states. Most states simply do not contemplate the use of PMCs to provide combat assistance. States that do consider using this type of private force have to avoid two different types of knee-jerk reactions. First, there is the implicit belief that strong states simply do not need to use mercenaries; therefore, a state which requires the assistance of private force is weak, and not even a proper state. 'Today', Thomson writes, 'real states do not buy mercenaries'.[62] Second, there is the taint that comes from associating with mercenaries. The difficulties caused by these two reactions have meant that only states in truly dire straits have chosen to employ PMCs, and these states have been forced to justify the decision to the international community, and perhaps more significantly, to themselves.

[62] Thomson (1994: 96).

218   *Mercenaries*

In two of the cases discussed above, the world had effectively abandoned the state to the horrors of its own civil war. Despite repeated attempts, Sierra Leone could not get the UN involved[63] until after two PMCs had come and gone; PNG was given aid by Australia, but this aid was heavily restricted by conditions which prevented its use in the war against the BRA.[64] Three UN missions in Angola[65] had not had a great impact on the crisis. In Sierra Leone and Angola, the situation was truly desperate, with rebels closing in on the capital city and in control of a vast swathe of countryside. PNG's military had 'demonstrated [its] lack of capability to defeat BRA'.[66] Without formal and legitimate international intervention, these states had no choice but to employ private military force to ensure rebels did not take over.

The choice to hire mercenaries indicates state desperation in another way. Hiring private force was a final indication that the state had failed and could no longer provide security for its own citizens. The 'decision by a government to employ outside military assistance is an admission of its own forces' failure. It is likely to cause severe loss of face for its military personnel'.[67] The decision to use private force in this sort of scenario should not be taken as an endorsement of mercenaries, but as an act of desperation. Had other options been available, the states in question would have pursued them.

Continued International Hostility to Private Force: Puritanical Norms

PMCs were only used in three cases, by peripheral and desperate states, and were dogged by accusations that reinforced the norm against mercenary use. Moreover, we would expect that, if PMCs seriously eroded the anti-mercenary norm, there would be little or no international reaction to the use of force. In fact, PMCs were widely perceived to be morally problematic, even in cases where they were supporting a state facing a far worse fate.

The norm against mercenary use in the late 1990s was so powerful it had become puritanical. A puritanical norm makes an unreflective condemnation without attention to the facts. Actors may follow the dictates of this kind of norm without thinking about it, leading to knee-jerk negative reactions. In some cases, adhering to a puritanical norm may lead states to behave in a way that does not seem rational, in terms of cost-benefit analysis. The norm against mercenary use is an example of this type of norm. By the time PMCs

---
[63] Shearer (1997*b*: 855).   [64] Singer (2003*a*: 177).
[65] There has since been a fourth, MONUA, which arrived after EO's departure.
[66] Singer (2003*a*: 195).   [67] Shearer (1997*a*: 205).

appeared on the scene in the 1990s, there was a strong tradition of thought which asserted that mercenaries were immoral, going, as we have seen, as far back as the twelfth and thirteenth centuries. A norm against mercenary use had been institutionalized and was supported by the norms associated with national self-determination and decolonization. There is also a clear thread of continuity between the pre-nineteenth century variants of the anti-mercenary norm and those of the twentieth and twenty-first centuries: the same belief that mercenaries are negative actors because they do not fight for the proper cause and as a result undermine the group which hires them has existed for centuries. So, too, has a belief that mercenaries are less threatening when they are uncontrolled. The long history of the norm against mercenary use, its recent institutionalization, and the support it receives from similar norms have resulted in almost automatically negative responses to the use of private force no matter the facts of the case.

The knee-jerk anti-mercenary reaction and fears about mercenary use have resulted in a situation where states left with no other option are condemned for ending bloody civil wars with private fighters. In theory, a state ought to be able to use any legal means to defend itself, as enshrined in Article 51 of the UN Charter.[68] So, why is a state unable to hire a private force to assist in what would seem to be the legitimate goal of self-defence? Brauer argues that 'it is not all clear why countries...should be prevented from hiring foreigners in the training of regular troops and supplementing of national armed forces in battle'.[69] Hiring mercenaries might actually *reinforce* state sovereignty because one of the attributes of a sovereign state is the ability to employ whom it chooses in order to augment security.[70] As we have seen, wars in Sierra Leone, Angola, and PNG were prolonged and bloody. The country's economic situation in each case had been greatly damaged by continuing hostilities. Assistance from the international community was not forthcoming. Sylvester Rowe, the Sierra Leonean ambassador to the UN and a former Kabbah government official, points out that after Kabbah was deposed by a poorly organized and dangerous military junta, it appeared as if the Nigerian-led peacekeeping force might be withdrawn. 'What do we do', he asked, '...the legitimate government of Dr Kabbah did what it had to do'.[71] Under these circumstances, the right of a state to survival must surely be weighed against the potential dangers of a PMC.

A moral position against mercenary use is, in some cases, perverse. Condemning the use of private force, even in situations where states have no

---

[68] Zarate (1998: 80).   [69] Brauer (1999: 131).   [70] Herbst (1999: 115).
[71] Interview with Ambassador Sylvester Rowe.

other choice, seems to be deeply unfair. If 'other nations, individually or collectively, are not going to contribute to multilateral peacekeeping or peacemaking forces, shouldn't a state have a right to hire a force able to keep order? It seems distinctly odd, both legally and morally, to argue that a state is somehow required to depend on whatever conscripts it can muster and train them as best it can, rather than obtain expert assistance from outside'.[72]

It is even more odd to condemn a state for receiving expert *private* assistance to solve its dire security problems when expert *public* assistance receives plaudits from the world community. American and French interventions to end hostilities in Liberia and Côte d'Ivoire, for example, were praised for working to end severe crises. If the object is to create peace, surely it does not matter whether or not the peacemaker is publicly or privately motivated. As Sam Kiley, the *London Times* Africa correspondent, noted in relation to Sierra Leone, 'the redeployment of mercenaries in this blighted nation would be an act of genuinely ethical foreign policy'.[73]

The question is, then, why deep concern over the use of private force somehow outweighs the use of such force in self-defence by sovereign states in desperate situations. The answer is that the norm against mercenary use now lies so deep and a negative view has become so automatic that considerations of necessity are no longer taken in to account. The puritanical norm against mercenary use prevents clear thinking on whether and in what circumstances mercenaries might be useful, leading to condemnation of the use of private force whether that force is directed towards stopping a war or towards promoting it.

The puritanical turn in the norm against mercenary use is particularly visible within the UN. The disjunction between the facts of PMC action and the nature of the UN response represents a situation where states reacted automatically in terms of the norm without analysing the facts, and can be seen in two different areas. First, the debate about PMCs in the UN led by the Special Rapporteur in the 1990s was cast in terms of self-determination, which was no longer clearly associated with the problems caused by mercenaries. Second, officials in the UN left no doubt that a more active role for PMCs in terms of peacekeeping would be impossible. A closer look at the UN position illustrates that the norm against mercenary use was so puritanical in the 1990s that it actually obscured the facts of private military action.

---

[72] Adams (1999: 7).   [73] Shearer (1999: 90).

Self-Determination and the Special Rapporteur

One of the primary sources of international commentary on the mercenaries question comes from the UN's former Special Rapporteur on the question, Enrique Bernales Ballesteros. Ballesteros was appointed in the early 1980s and was the UN's longest continuously serving Special Rapporteur until he was replaced in July 2004 by Shaista Shameem. Ballesteros' work goes through the UN High Commission for Human Rights, and ran parallel to the work of the Ad Hoc Committee in the 1980s. Indeed, the two groups came to blows on the subject of which was best equipped to deal with the mercenaries question.[74] Ballesteros' mandate stems from the argument that mercenaries violate the right of states to national self-determination. His investigations proceed from a series of UN General Assembly resolutions making this point throughout the 1980s.[75]

The difficulty of this approach is that it continued throughout the 1990s, with the advent of PMCs. Ballesteros' reports during the 1990s refer to the challenges mercenaries pose for self-determination. PMCs represent 'a danger to the economies, democracy and self-determination of peoples',[76] by 'the very nature and scope of their activities and [their] methods'.[77] Ballesteros noted in 2000 that his reports have always referred to 'mercenary activities as a criminal act that prevents or impedes the exercise by peoples of the right to self-determination and that such activity is also a violation of human rights'.[78] During the 1960s and 1970s, the use of mercenaries by secessionist subnational groups, as in Katanga and Biafra, clearly acted against the self-determination of the former colonial state. But it is hard to see how PMC action in the 1990s was undermining national self-determination, because they were working *for* sovereign states.

It is curious that the same language of self-determination persists in the Ballesteros reports of the 1990s. In Sierra Leone and Angola, EO was *supporting* the state as a whole against the incursions of rebel groups. The RUF was a particularly illegitimate rebel group, and well-known for its use of atrocities as a terror tactic.[79] EO was hired specifically by the sovereign state to prevent the rebel group from destroying the post-colonial state, a task which would seem to be the polar opposite of the use of mercenaries in the cases

---

[74] Statements of Sweden and Japan UN Doc A/C.6/43/SR.51 at paras. 10, 12 respectively.

[75] There has been a resolution entitled 'Use of mercenaries as a means of violating human rights and impeding the exercise of the right of peoples to self-determination' every year from 1986 to 2004, beginning with UN Doc A/Res/41/102 and ending with UN Doc A/Res/59/78.

[76] UN Doc E/CN/.4/1998/31 at p. 11. Also addressed in UN Doc E/CN/.4/1997/24 at pp. 23 and 24.

[77] UN Doc E/CN/.4/1998/31 at p. 33.   [78] UN Doc A/55/334 at p. 7.

[79] See Macgregor (1999: 16) and Amnesty International (1996) for details.

outlined in Chapter 6. Ballesteros uses the language of self-determination to condemn mercenaries who were upholding the wishes of the sovereign state and preventing secession, which seems out of step with reality.

Of course, as we saw in Chapter 6, the norm of national self-determination and the appropriate cause aspect of the anti-mercenary norm are closely related. Ballesteros' outmoded form of condemnation indicates the strength of the association between these two norms. Both condemnation of mercenaries and condemnation of forces seeking to subvert national self-determination remained powerful tools, and so became particularly effective together. Ballesteros' censure of PMCs uses the language of appropriate motivation, and shares the concerns about the dangers of using outsiders in an internal conflict. Criticism of mercenaries in terms of self-determination lingered on long after mercenaries were actually threatening self-determination.

The UN: Doors Closed to PMCs

The final way in which the norm's puritanical effect has influenced state behaviour is in the lack of serious debate about where PMCs could be used efficiently, particularly by the UN. Zarate suggests that PMCs could 'fill a void' left by problems with UN peacekeeping.[80] Among senior officials at the UN, even when there is a recognition that PMCs might have a useful role to play, fear of the puritanical anti-mercenary response of states means the option is not seriously considered.[81] The proscriptive norm against mercenary use has resulted in UN condemnation of the private military option even in situations where it could be useful, and has resulted in the bizarre response that an intractable civil war is preferable to the use of PMCs.

Within the UN, the possibilities of using private force have been mooted on several occasions. Reno quotes a UN official as saying that 'the idea of private armies helping to settle some of Africa's problems does have an appeal. No particular country will have to pay for the services, which forces some kind of hard thinking on regimes not noted for their clarity of mission'.[82] Indeed, it has been widely recognized that the private force option might be cheaper than peacekeeping[83] and that in some circumstances, particularly where conventional aid no longer works, it might provide better or more feasible assistance than a UN mission.[84] In particular, a PMC like EO operated in situations where a mission was considered desirable by Western states, although political and economic costs made intervention impossible, and in circumstances where the UN was unlikely to agree to the type of mission

[80] Zarate (1998: 161).   [81] See below.   [82] Reno (1998: 70).
[83] Shearer (1998b: 90) and Coker (1999: 108).   [84] Reno (2000: 68).

required, particularly in situations where aggressive peace enforcement was necessary to resolve the situation.[85]

Some UN humanitarian missions used private military force to secure the delivery of humanitarian supplies, or to arrange transport into dangerous areas.[86] A PMC associated with Sandline flew Office of the Commission of Humanitarian Affairs (OCHA) aid workers on missions in Sierra Leone after Sandline's company's withdrawal.[87] OCHA were always uncomfortable about the arrangement, in part because of the humanitarian principle of avoiding association with armed groups of any kind, but were willing to make exceptions in order to deliver desperately needed aid.[88]

Officials inside the UN and commentators outside it have recognized that private military force might play a useful role, either replacing or complementing existing UN peacekeeping missions or protecting the delivery of humanitarian aid. When asked about the use of mercenaries in peacekeeping during a press conference, Kofi Annan 'bristled'[89] at the suggestion that the UN would ever consider working with mercenaries, arguing that 'first of all, I don't know how one makes a distinction between respectable and non-respectable mercenaries'. Annan went on to remark that he was not aware he had made any statements implying that he would accept the use of mercenaries in tasks associated with peacekeeping, but had looked at 'the possibility of bringing in other elements—not necessarily troops from Governments—who might be able to provide security, assist the aid workers in the United Nations High Commissioner for Refugees (UNHCR) and protect them' when no aid from governments was forthcoming to separate armed fighters from refugees on the Rwanda–Zaire border.[90] The Secretary General reiterated these remarks in the Ditchley Foundation lecture, which he delivered in 1998, pointing out that:

Some have even suggested that private security firms, like the one which recently helped restore the elected President to power in Sierra Leone, might play a role in providing the United Nations with the rapid reaction capacity it needs. When we had need of skilled soldiers to separate fighters from refugees in the Rwandan refugee camps in Goma, I even considered the possibility of engaging a private firm. But the world may not be ready to privatize peace.[91]

---

[85] Howe (1998: 309). The UN missions in Angola were observer missions and could not take the kind of aggressive action EO was able to take.
[86] Ibid. 312.   [87] Interview with James Jonah; Interview with Amjad Abbashar.
[88] Interview with Amjad Abbashar.   [89] Shearer (1998b: 68).
[90] Transcript of a press conference with Secretary General Kofi Annan, 12 July 1997, available at <http://www.un.org/News/Press/docs/1997/19970612.sgsm6255.html>.
[91] Text of thirty-fifth annual Ditchley Foundation Lecture, given by Secretary General Kofi Annan, 26 June 1998. United Nations Press Release SG/SM/6613, available at <http://www.un.org/News/Press/docs/1998/19980626.sgsm6613.html>.

Interviews with UN officials indicate that the depth of international dislike for mercenaries would prevent the UN from ever using private force in a peacekeeping capacity, no matter how useful they might be. David Harland, then the chief of the Best Practices Unit in the Department of Peacekeeping Operations (DPKO) believes that the potential use of PMCs faces a very serious obstacle in the form of political liabilities created by the negative images of mercenaries.[92] Michael Møller, formerly the Director for Political Peacekeeping and Humanitarian Affairs in the Executive Office of the Secretary-General, believes that the stigma of mercenaries because of their image as 'roughnecks' interested only in 'greed and profit' would make it impossible for PMCs to be used in a peacekeeping context, even though their staff might be superior to some of the peacekeeping contingents currently provided to the UN.[93] Abiodun Williams, the former Director of the Strategic Planning Unit in the Executive Office of the Secretary-General, points out that there would be implications for the host state of using private force which would make it an undesirable option.[94] While UN officials can see the merits of private force privately, they believe that member states' dislike of mercenaries would prevent the option from ever being seriously mooted.[95]

Member states undoubtedly disapprove of the idea that PMCs might be used in UN peace operations. Many 'member states and staff at the UN take the view that PMCs are immoral organisations, who have traditionally served autocratic and unpopular governments and whose operations are littered with human rights abuses. There is also a perception amongst staff and Member States from the Third World that they are also inherently racist'.[96]

The appearance of PMCs in the 1990s does not deal the anti-mercenary norm a significant blow. These companies were only used in three cases, all three of which were peripheral states with no real options. Strong states still do not consider the use of private combat assistance. If PMCs genuinely posed a challenge to the norm against mercenary use, we would expect to see them to be openly embraced by the international community and for their appearance to go unaccompanied by criticism. In fact, PMCs were dogged by controversy after their appearance on the international stage. PMCs were never widely enough used nor accepted to pose a serious challenge to the norm against mercenary use. However, the most compelling evidence for the continued

---

[92] Interview with David Harland.   [93] Interview with Michael Møller.
[94] Interview with Abiodun Williams.
[95] The reaction to the PSC Blackwater's suggestion that it could provide peacekeeping troops further reinforces this point and will be discussed below.
[96] Cranfield University Study, submitted as a memorandum to the House of Commons Foreign Affairs Committee. Quoted in: House of Commons Foreign Affairs Committee (2001–2: 26).

strength of the anti-mercenary norm comes from the fact that the sorts of combat services PMCs provided were too controversial to become openly accepted. The anti-mercenary norm explains why PMCs disappeared from the international stage almost as abruptly as they had arrived upon it.

7.2. PRIVATE FORCE AND THE SHIFT AWAY FROM COMBAT OPERATIONS

In order to explain the shift from combat-oriented PMCs to PSCs that eschew combat, this section first outlines the nature of the private security industry before turning to a discussion of how the norm against mercenary use can explain the transition from combat to non-combat companies.

The market for PSCs has exploded, at the same time the market for PMCs has diminished. There are at least 20,000 individual employees of PSCs operating in Iraq, and the latest estimates suggest that that number could be as high as 100,000.[97] During the initial phase of the invasion in 2003, one in ten of the personnel attached to the US forces were PSC employees. Tim Spicer started a new, non-combat company in 2003. The company, Aegis Risk Management, was awarded a multimillion dollar contract in Iraq,[98] demonstrating the success of his new approach. These companies are more notable for the services they do not provide than for the services they do: the companies today working in Iraq explicitly avoid the use of combat, and some even seek to minimize the prospect of using force by ensuring that as few of their employees as possible use arms.

PSCs provide four main types of services: logistical support, operational or tactical support, military advice and training, and policing or security. Logistical support entails tasks such as the preparation and delivery of food, laundry, and maintenance at military bases. The American company KBR is a good example of a logistical support company.[99] Private logistical support, given its distance away from active combat, lies extremely far away from the sorts of behaviour proscribed by the anti-mercenary norm.

PSCs also provide operational or tactical support;[100] this type of support can best be explained as the provision of services normally considered the sole purview of national armed forces. These services may include military interrogation, and even the operation and support of weapons systems. During *Operation Enduring Freedom* in Iraq in 2003, Alt-64 *Apache* helicopters and

---

[97] Merle (2006) [98] Norton-Taylor (2004).
[99] Avant (2005a: 20). [100] Singer (2004b) and Avant (2005a: 16).

226   *Mercenaries*

B-2 bombers were supported by contractors,[101] and contractors were used to operate missile guidance systems on US ships, as well as the computer systems for unmanned aerial vehicles (UAVs).[102]

PSCs also provide security and policing. These services are particularly widespread in Iraq and Afghanistan, where PSCs have provided security for military and political assets, including installations, individuals, and convoys.[103] Paul Bremer, head of the Coalition Provisional Authority in Iraq, and Hamid Karzai, president of Afghanistan, have been protected by the American companies Blackwater and DynCorp respectively. In some cases PSCs act as police themselves: DynCorp routinely provides the military police that make up American contributions to international missions,[104] including in East Timor and Kosovo. PSCs have also been used to develop and run police and security services. The South Africa-based company Erinys trained, managed, and equipped the 16,000-strong Iraq Oil Protection Force.[105] Security services can also be sold to the private sector and to NGOs. In war-zones such as Iraq and Afghanistan, virtually all private companies, from the media to telecommunications to extractive industries, require security to do their jobs, and this is usually provided by PSCs.[106] Cockayne identifies three main roles for private security in the NGO and humanitarian sector: guarding installations; providing mobile security escorts; guarding third parties (such as refugee populations); and, less commonly, security analysis and intelligence provision.[107] Avant has provided extensive analysis of the use of private security by the World Wildlife Fund.[108]

Providing military advice and training constitutes a significant portion of PSC business. PSCs train armed forces, police forces, and auxiliary forces. The American company MPRI provided training for Croatian forces that was so effective that its protégés had striking success during *Operation Storm*, the offensive to take back Serb-held territory in the Krajina during the summer of 1995. The Croatian victory showed such remarkable improvement that MPRI has been dogged by accusations that its personnel must have accompanied their trainees during the mission itself,[109] an accusation that persists despite the absence of evidence. PSCs also provide training as part of post-war reconstruction efforts: DynCorp has trained both the Iraqi and Afghan police forces.[110]

[101] Avant (2004).   [102] Isenberg (2004: 21).   [103] Singer (2004b: 6).
[104] Avant, *Market for Force*, p. 21. Avant (2005a: 21).
[105] Erinys, 'The Erinys Iraq Oil Protection Force: Infrastructure Security in a Post-Conflict Environment.'
[106] Occasionally larger companies have in-house security expertise.
[107] Cockayne (2006).   [108] Avant (2005a).
[109] Adams (1999) and Brayton (2002: 310).
[110] For a more extensive discussion of the private security industry see Percy (2006).

The Disappearance of Combat and Today's Private Security Industry

The notoriety achieved by PMCs, and the apparent ubiquity of PSCs in contemporary conflicts, might at first seem to suggest that the anti-mercenary norm is losing its influence. However, the evolution of private force, from combat-oriented PMCs to combat-avoiding PSCs, demonstrates the continued salience of the norm against mercenary use. This section argues that the anti-mercenary norm provides a compelling explanation for the decline of PMCs providing combat services, and demonstrate how it shapes the private security industry's structure and prospects.

In the late 1990s, the prospects for PMCs appeared rosy as continued conflicts in Africa and elsewhere suggested a large quantity of available clients.[111] Commentators emphasized that the demand for PMCs would continue to rise, especially in countries rich in natural resources and prone to conflict. In 1999, Tim Spicer said in relation to whether or not Sandline would engage in combat and accompany clients on operations, 'of course we will. I use the analogy of a boat builder. If I built you a boat and you paid for it and said to me, "OK, let's go for a test run," and I refused, you would be very dubious about that vessel'.[112] But after the debacles in PNG and Sierra Leone, the provision of combat services began to sputter out. EO and Sandline no longer exist. They were pushed out of business in part by normative dislike and in part by formal regulation reflecting that dislike. EO went out of business in January 1999 because of a shrinking client base and its unsavoury mercenary image.[113] British[114] and South African[115] pressure may have contributed to the company's demise. Sandline, allegedly EO's sister company, was arguably created to avoid the problems EO had with public perception.[116] Having developed its own image problems after the Sierra Leone and Bougainville dramas, Sandline closed its doors in 2004. The demise of Sandline means that there are no longer any PMCs which will openly admit to engaging in combat. PMCs were too controversial to have the sort of legitimate reputation they desired, and the market for such activities was restricted to the desperate. Even those states in obvious need were criticized for their decision to use private force, and the prospect of future regulation meant that the available market would have been even smaller. As we see, however, while the door for private combat companies has been closed, many of these companies have been pushed into the private security industry.

---

[111] Adams (1999: 1) and O'Brien (2000: 71). [112] Spicer (1999b).
[113] Shearer (1999: 82). [114] Brauer Ibid. 130. [115] Howe (1998: 327).
[116] Pech (1999: 93).

In the summer of 2003, the British-based firm Northbridge Security Services offered combat-based assisted to the government of Côte d'Ivoire, but pressure from the international community and from the Foreign and Commonwealth Office scuppered the mission. Jack Straw, the UK Foreign Secretary, decried the potential use of mercenaries and said it would threaten the peace process.[117] The UN Security Council urged 'all Ivorian parties to refrain from any recruitment or use of mercenaries or foreign military units and [expressed] its intention to consider possible actions to address this issue'.[118] Instead, the French provided peacekeeping to the beleaguered nation. It began to appear that private military assistance to unstable countries was not an automatic option.

Indeed, by 2003, the industry had already taken significant steps away from the provision of active combat. Tim Spicer started the new company Aegis Risk Management in 2003, with the explicit intention of excluding combat from the company's range of services.[119] None of the members of the British Association of PSCs, launched in February 2006, provide any sort of offensive combat services.[120] The American-based International Peace Operations Association (IPOA) and its members also eschew the use of force.[121] In other words, in less than ten years, the market for private force has transformed from one where Tim Spicer was able to argue it would be illogical for his company *not* to engage in active combat, to a market where the provision of active combat is so unlikely that even the mention of the idea is met with a chorus of negative responses, and where no company believes that it is in its interests to provide offensive force. This transformation is so remarkable that it prompts the question of how the market changed so swiftly.

The transformation of the market for private force can be explained in terms of the norm against mercenary use. There is no longer a market for the provision of active combat services, and PSC officials are quick to point out that this is because combat services are publicly unacceptable, which makes them so controversial that they are not viable. Christopher Beese, the chief administrative officer of ArmorGroup, argues that the 'public relations exercise' involved in providing offensive combat services would be next to impossible, and that these sorts of services should not be provided by the private sector.[122] In an interview, John Holmes, director of Erinys, echoes these concerns, pointing out that combat services are viewed by the public to be

---

[117] Allison (2003).
[118] S/Res/1479 (2003). This resolution, dating from 13 May, clearly refers to the Northbridge offer as well as the mercenaries already active in Côte d'Ivoire.
[119] Interview with Tim Spicer, September 2003.
[120] Interview with Andrew Bearpark, September 2006.
[121] Interview with Doug Brooks, September 2006.
[122] Interview with Christopher Beese, September 2006.

unacceptable, and that moreover, most companies would not be comfortable providing these services anyway.[123]

It is also striking that among the panoply of military services now contracted out by governments, particularly in the UK and in the United States, combat services are excluded. There has been no attempt to privatize command and control of military missions, as there was in Sierra Leone and Angola. This is partly because strong states like the United States and the UK do not require external assistance in military command, but they do require other types of military assistance. The fact that strong states simply do not need to hire PMCs providing combat services underlines the point that real states do not use mercenaries. More remarkable still is the fact that even weak states today are strongly discouraged from hiring a PMC to provide combat assistance, as was the case in Côte d'Ivoire.

It is true that many of the services PSCs do provide may fall in to a grey area between offensive and defensive uses of force. For example, in securing an oil pipeline, it may be difficult to assess whether or not PSCs are using force offensively or defensively. However, it is important to note that the PSC services that are most controversial are those that fall most completely into this grey area. For example, the US military establishment has expressed concerns over the use of private contractors to operate UAVs given that they might be considered unlawful combatants,[124] and there is a generally high level of concern about the use of private contractors to conduct military interrogations. PSCs themselves work hard to ensure that they are not perceived to be providing offensive combat services. Christopher Beese points out that ArmorGroup avoids anything to do with guns: carrying them, supplying them, and training people in their use.[125]

The use of PSCs by non-governmental organizations and the UN also highlights the degree to which the industry has transformed itself. The UN and many NGOs commonly use PSCs to provide security, for personnel, for humanitarian aid, and in refugee camps. In these roles, PSCs work defensively and oriented away from combat. However, the UN and many NGOs view even this type of security as controversial, and are reluctant to speak on the record about their use of PSCs. Many NGOs express 'feelings of horror and outrage' over having to work with PSCs, and are sensitive about 'the bad publicity that might result from them openly discussing their use of commercial security providers'.[126] Even within governments, departments focused on development or on aid, like DFID in the UK, are reluctant to associate themselves too openly with PSCs. One senior industry official reports that a DFID

---

[123] Interview with John Holmes, London, 14 September 2006.
[124] Schreier and Caparini (2005: 57).
[125] Interview with Christopher Beese, 13 September 2006. [126] Cockayne (2006: 3).

contract was not awarded to ArmorGroup because its name sounded too 'military'.[127]

Within the UN, institutionalized hostility to PSCs as the latest manifestation of mercenary behaviour on the world stage persists.[128] The continued association between mercenaries, PMCs, and PSCs is reflected in the fact that the UN Working Group on Mercenaries, the replacement for the Special Rapporteur, is the actor tasked with dealing with the private security industry. A statement from PSCs[129] is appended to the final (2005) Special Rapporteur's report. In the statement, the companies argue that considering they are:

frequently employed by UN member states and the UN own [sic] entities, we strongly recommend that the UN re-examine the relevance of the term 'mercenary'. This derogatory term is completely unacceptable and is too often used to describe fully legal and legitimate companies engaged in vital support operations for humanitarian peace and stability operations.[130]

The Working Group demonstrates the influence of the anti-mercenary norm in another way. The Group has stated that one of its main priorities is examining 'the role of the State as the primary holder of the monopoly of the use of force, and related issues such as sovereignty and State responsibility to protect and ensure respect for human rights by all actors'.[131] In other words, one of the questions that preoccupies the UN Working Group is related to the control aspect of the norm.

The disappearance of PMCs providing combat and of combat services from the industry has been even more pronounced than a simple shift away from a particular service would suggest. Rather, the evolution away from a combat-oriented industry is profound, and it is hard to imagine a return towards the legitimate provision of combat services in the near future. There are two pieces of evidence that suggest that the shift away from combat is more profound than a fluctuation in the market.

---

[127] Confidential interview.   [128] Percy (forthcoming 2007b).
[129] American Equipment Company (AMECO); Blackwater USA; Demining Enterprises International; EarthWind Holding Corporation (Groupe EHC); Hart; International Charters Incorporated (ICI) of Oregon; IPOA; J-3 Global Solutions; Medical Support Solutions (MSS); MPRI; Pacific Architects and Engineers (PAE); Security Support Solutions (3S); Special Operations Consulting-Security Management Group (SOC-SMG); Triple Canopy; and AEGIS signed the statement. See UN Doc A/60/263, 17 August 2005. These companies, despite being referred to as PMCs, are clearly PSCs in that they do not provide combat services.
[130] UN Doc A/60/263, p. 21.
[131] UN Doc E/CN.4/2006/11 at p. 5, 11. At the time of writing the Group planned to convene a round table on the subject.

First, even the suggestion that a company might be involved in a more active military role has been met both with derision and disapproval. In the spring of 2006, the American company Blackwater suggested that it could provide a brigade-sized peacekeeping force to deal with the situation in Darfur. Peacekeeping forces are not even active combat forces. Blackwater itself asserted that it would not undertake offensive operations,[132] and yet this suggestion has been greeted with significant disapproval from other PSCs[133] and derision from commentators who know the industry well. Peter Singer remarked that 'it would be a great idea if Martians came and acted in Darfur, too...it's not on the table except in the minds of the companies'.[134]

Second, the industry itself sees its future lying noticeably far away from combat-oriented activities. The PSC Erinys is pursuing the idea that it might provide human rights training for companies wanting to bring themselves in line with the Voluntary Principles on Human Rights.[135] Aegis has suggested that PSCs might be able to act as 'direct providers of humanitarian aid and development assistance' and to coordinate the delivery of humanitarian aid.[136] Even industry organizations emphasize that the future of the industry excludes combat, and might even exclude the sort of security services considered acceptable today. Andrew Bearpark of the BAPSC argues that there are four main areas for the private security industry: military support, corporate support, support for reconstruction efforts, and security sector reform.[137] The industry will then be far broader in the future than it is today. The American-based IPOA goes further still and does not even use the term PSC in its title, focusing instead on the provision of peacekeeping and post-conflict reconstruction.

The shift from PMCs, with their focus on combat services, to PSCs, with their active avoidance of combat, can be explained by the norm against mercenary use. PSCs are less controversial than PMCs because they avoid offensive combat, and therefore can minimize the effect of the charge that they are fighting (and therefore killing) in exchange for financial gain. It can be argued that the difference between offensive and defensive combat is minimal, and that PSCs might actually be quite likely to use force. However, the industry in the UK and in the United States are clearly attempting to move away even from this potential grey area, either by avoiding carrying arms, or by embarking on unarmed or lightly armed humanitarian rather than traditional security services.

---

[132] Willis Witter. 'Private Firms Eye Darfur.' *The Washington Times*, 2 October 2006.
[133] Interviews with PSC officials, 2006.
[134] Willis Witter. 'Private Firms Eye Darfur.' *The Washington Times*, 2 October 2006.
[135] Interview with John Holmes, September 2006.   [136] Donald (2006: 65).
[137] Interview with Andrew Bearpark, September 2006.

The presence of a sizeable private security industry thus does not pose a major challenge to the continued influence of the norm against mercenary use. Rather, the initial growth of PSCs and the way they see themselves growing in the future demonstrates that the anti-mercenary norm is still influential, and still shapes both the opportunities available to PSCs and the ways states and other actors use them. Moreover, the parameters within which the private security industry currently operates are also influenced by the anti-mercenary norm.

7.3. THE ANTI-MERCENARY NORM AND ITS INFLUENCE ON THE PROVISION OF PRIVATE FORCE TODAY

The anti-mercenary norm has had an effect on the provision of private force more widely. Its influence on the evolution of the industry away from combat is visible, but the norm against mercenaries has also shaped the relationship between states and PSCs. Understanding the anti-mercenary norm can also help reveal why PSCs will find it difficult to escape the mercenary label. This section examines these two points in turn.

State Control, Regulation, and Private Force

One of the more noticeable differences between PSCs and PMCs is their relationship with their home state, or the state they operate from. In a sense, the move towards industry regulation is the latest iteration of the 'control' aspect of the norm, solidified first in the fifteenth and sixteenth centuries, and then again in the nineteenth century. States are less troubled by private force when they believe it less likely to run amok. As Jack Straw argues in the introduction to the British Government's Green Paper on the question, 'one of the reasons for considering the option of a licensing regime is that it may be desirable to distinguish between reputable and disreputable private sector operators, to encourage and support the former while, as far as possible, eliminating the latter'.[138] Regulation reduces the possibility that the state might become embroiled in disputes because of the unauthorized mercenary actions of its citizens. States have used regulation to bring PMCs under control and to ensure PSCs act in the state's interest.

[138] Jack Straw, in House of Commons Foreign Affairs Committee (2002a: 5).

PMCs maintained an uneasy relationship with their home states, and their home states responded by tightening control over the companies in question. South Africa created legislation in response to concerns expressed about EO, in order to 'leash the dogs of war'.[139] The Regulation of Foreign Military Assistance Act (1998) differentiates between mercenary activity, which it defines as 'direct participation as a combatant in armed conflict for private gain' and 'foreign military assistance' which is defined as military advice or training short of combat, security services, or any activity which may have the effect of assisting a party to armed conflict or overthrowing the government. The Act bans mercenary activity outright, and requires any type of foreign military assistance to be examined by the National Conventional Arms Control Committee, which looks at the relationship of the intended recipient to the armed conflict, and provides a licence which it retains the power to revoke.[140] The effect of this legislation is to ban the practice of selling military services abroad, except in circumstances where it is authorized by the government.

Since 2005, the South African government has been debating the creation of new legislation to deal with the issues caused by private force. The Prohibition of Mercenary Activities and Prohibition and Regulation of Certain Activities in Areas of Armed Conflict Bill passed through the committee stage in late August 2006. It will now have to be passed by both houses and signed into law by the President. The Bill tightens the relationship between the South African state and all types of South African actors working in war zones abroad, including PMCs and PSCs.

The British government also considered the control of PMCs. In 1998, the Report of the Sierra Leone Arms Investigation (the 'Legg Report') analysed the Sandline ('arms to Africa') scandal and called for a British government Green Paper into the regulation of PMCs.[141] The Green Paper was released in February 2002, and argues that regulation is necessary because of the practical problems that might be caused by the actions of a British-based military company, such as undermining British policy. In other words, the Green Paper was prompted by the need to assert control over PMCs based in Britain. The Green Paper suggests six options for regulation: a ban on military activity abroad; a ban on recruitment for military activity abroad; a licensing regime for military services; a system of regulation and notification; a general licence for companies; and self-regulation, or the creation of a voluntary code of conduct.[142] In

---

[139] Avant (2005a: 161).
[140] Articles South Africa, Regulation of Foreign Military Assistance Act, available at <http://www.up.ac.za/publications/gov-acts/1998/act15.pdf>.
[141] Legg and Ibbs (1998).
[142] House of Commons Foreign Affairs Committee, 'Options for Regulation,' pp. 20–1, 22–7 House of Commons Foreign Affairs Committee (2002a: 20–1, 22–7).

August 2002, the House of Commons Foreign Affairs Committee responded with the publication of a report, 'Private Military Companies', which recommends that the US model be carefully examined,[143] that a licensing regime be created requiring disclosure of the company's structures and policies,[144] and that a monitoring and evaluation regime be created.[145] Responding, the Secretary of State for Foreign and Commonwealth Affairs agreed to look into these recommendations.[146] However, no further action has been taken on the Green Paper, in part because the transformation in the industry from PMCs to PSCs, and the demise of Sandline have meant that many of its recommendations are out of date.[147]

In contrast, the relationship between home states and PSCs is both tighter and less controversial. In the United States, the Arms Export Control Act of 1968 requires American companies offering military services to foreign nationals to be registered with and licensed by the State Department. Congressional notification is required before contracts in excess of $50 million are approved.[148] The result is that American PSCs embark only on projects approved by the US government, and the relationship between the two is extremely tight. It is hard to see how US-based PSCs threaten the control aspect of the norm.

In the UK, the relationship between PSCs and the government is informal. It is common practice for British-based PSCs to alert the government before embarking on any contracts,[149] and the British government has been known to prevent the actions of companies if it disapproves, as it did with Northbridge Security Services in Côte d'Ivoire. The UK government manages to exert a fair degree of informal control over PSCs, and one of the stated goals of the Green Paper is to ensure that any regulatory regime would make sure that the actions of a private military or security company are congruent with British foreign policy. The Foreign Affairs Committee's response to the Green Paper makes it very clear that a strong distinction between combat and non-combat troops should be maintained,[150] a suggestion with which the Secretary of State concurs.[151] In fact, the British recommendations go so far as to suggest that the *government itself* might wish to consider 'the option of developing a publicly funded armed service cadre to provide on a commercial basis the

---

[143] Ibid. 11.   [144] Ibid. 35.   [145] Foreign Affairs Committee (2001–2: 39).
[146] Ibid. 5–6.   [147] Percy (2006, ch.3).
[148] House of Commons Foreign Affairs Committee (2002a: 38). For a more detailed discussion of the American system, see Percy (2006).
[149] Interviews with Beese and Holmes.
[150] House of Commons Foreign Affairs Committee (2001–2: 29).
[151] Foreign Affairs Committee (2001–2: 4).

New Model Mercenaries 235

tasks currently being undertaken by PMCs'.[152] The Secretary of State agreed to consider the possibility while recognizing that there 'would be risks inherent in setting up an operation which might be seen as amounting to a publicly owned PMC'.[153] In other words, there might be problems with negative public perception if the government went into the private military business. While the degree of control over British-based PSCs is not as high as it is in the United States, government efforts to control private force and bring it in line with official state policy are still clearly in line with the control aspect of the anti-mercenary norm.

It is worth pointing out that the often-discussed deficiencies in these regulatory regimes[154] and proposals do not necessarily undermine the control aspect of the anti-mercenary norm. Even weak regulatory regimes enhance state control over the use of force. In the United States, the regulatory system is often criticized for putting *too much* control in the hands of the executive branch of government, at the expense of other branches.[155] We may disapprove of the way in which the Western state uses private force, but its control over the political decision to use private force seems undisputed.[156]

Indeed, today's legitimate market for private force is characterized by a significant and growing degree of state control over the use of force.[157] The twenty-first century market for force is a state-to-state-based exchange of private violence, whereby private assistance for training and reconstruction is sent from strong states to weak, and where strong states use private force to supplement their own forces and free up regular personnel for frontline duties. The shift from PMCs to PSCs is not just a shift from combat to non-combat operations, but also a shift from individual, entrepreneurial companies operating at arm's length from their home state to companies that work exclusively or primarily for their home state or on projects approved by their home state. This shift resembles the transition from entrepreneurial bands of mercenaries to the state-to-state-based exchange of mercenaries prior to the nineteenth century.

---

[152] House of Commons Foreign Affairs Committee (2002*a*: 43).
[153] Foreign Affairs Committee (2001–2: 6).
[154] Singer (2004*a*), Holmqvist (2005), Schreier and Caparini (2005), and Percy (2006).
[155] Avant (2005*a*).
[156] The relationship between PSCs and the states in which they operate is different, and the PSC might well threaten state control over force in the host state. Ibid, Holmqvist (2005). However, they are sent as the agent of a strong state to pursue its goals, and so the dangers PSCs pose to weak or post-conflict states do not undermine the pure control aspect of the norm.
[157] This enhanced control is frequently not enhanced popular control, a point that will be addressed below.

Appropriate Cause, Control, and Private Force: Lines of Continuity

For all that PSCs differ from PMCs and mercenaries, and given the ways in which the structure and operations of PSCs avoid aspects of the anti-mercenary norm, it is important to note that PSCs do not avoid the anti-mercenary norm entirely. There is a clear line of continuity that runs between mercenaries, PMCs, and PSCs, and it stems from the threat that private force poses to the appropriate cause aspect of the norm. A second type of objection to the private security industry is that, just as mercenaries made it easier for the state to go to war and to repress its people in the past, private military and private security companies might make it easier for modern states to fight war and also reduce democratic control over war.[158] This argument finds echoes in theories of the democratic peace, which argue that public opinion can exert a strong effect on making a state more reluctant to go to war, particularly if too many soldiers are killed or if soldiers' lives are placed in harm's way. As Kant argues, 'if the consent of the citizens is required in order to decide that war should be declared...nothing is more natural than that they would be very cautious in commencing such a poor game, decreeing for themselves all the calamities of war'.[159] One objection to the private security industry is that it removes or lessens the restraints of public opinion, because the public will not notice or will be less worried about the deaths of private fighters than they would be about the killings of soldiers.[160] The use of PMCs might lead to a reduction of democracy in states which hire these companies by diminishing democratic oversight of decisions to go to war.

Many commentators have noted that PMCs and PSCs are problematic because they might encourage covert wars,[161] or act as proxies in conflicts in which the state finds it politically inexpedient to get involved.[162] Both covert wars and the use of proxies allow states to enter into conflict without the usual range of democratic oversight. Even in open conflicts, the use of private military personnel instead of regular soldiers not only loosens the aforementioned constraint of public opinion but significantly reduces the number of obstacles to continuing a prolonged conflict. The current war in Iraq demonstrates the significant political obstacles to mobilizing larger numbers of troops. Because PSCs can perform a variety of military tasks, they can free up regular soldiers.

---

[158] A similar argument can be found in Avant (2005b: 155–6).
[159] Kant ([1795] 1983: 113).
[160] This restraint is of course merely a restraint and cannot end war. Doyle (1983: 230).
[161] Zarate (1998: 148), Francis (1999: 323), and Singer (2003b: 48).
[162] O'Brien (1998), Francis (1999: 333–4), Shearer (1999: 82), and Reno (2000: 65).

The obstacles to increasing the number of PSC personnel on the ground are also far less significant than those in the way of mobilizing larger numbers of regular troops. The state might also find it easier to sustain wars that might go against public opinion because of the presence of PSCs. While pre-nineteenth century commentators worried that the use of mercenaries would lead to domestic tyranny, today the concern is that private force could lead to tyrannical foreign policy detached from popular control.

Another way of looking at the same problem is to argue that PMCs and PSCs simply erode the citizen's duty to the state, which is important for a democracy. The fact that PMCs might not display loyalty to the community left the writers of the UK Green Paper,

> uneasy. To encourage such activity seems contrary both to our values and to the way in which we order society. In a democracy it seems natural that the state should be defended by its own citizens since it is their state. And it is not an accident that the business of fighting for money often brings in unattractive characters.[163]

Mercenaries, PMCs, and PSCs all have the potential to upset the relationship between the state and the citizen, and could make it easier for the state to use force, become tyrannical, or sustain an unpopular war. It is important to note here that this criticism relates to the state as much as it does to the private fighter. The state that decides to privatize aspects of the use of force is more morally responsible for the disruption of democratic control over the use of force than the private actor it hires. PSCs would not exist unless there were a demand for their services, and responsibility thus lies with the state. That said, the persistence of this objection to private force and its applicability to all types of private force helps explain why the mercenary label has been hard for the industry to shake. Private fighters of all kinds are linked because they are subject to the same criticism: that they disrupt the military relationship between the citizen and the state.

In a sense, the state has enhanced its control over the use of private force, by insisting upon regulatory controls and a tight relationship with PSCs based on its territory. However, popular control over the use of force has been simultaneously diminished. The use of private force by strong states detaches their citizens from the decision to go to war, and the use of PSCs in post-conflict states without effective regulation prevents the citizens of post-conflict states from controlling the armed agents working on their territory. PSC employees working in Iraq were immunized from local prosecution and there was no effective mechanism to prosecute them under American law.[164]

---

[163] House of Commons Foreign Affairs Committee (2002b: 18).
[164] Isenberg (2004), Holmqvist (2005), and Percy (2006).

The market for private force from the fourteenth to the seventeenth centuries experienced similar tensions. As states tightened their control on the use of private force, fears that mercenaries might be used to enhance state power, promote tyranny, and undermine popular control over the use of force also arose. One of the consequences of a state-to-state-based exchange of private force may be that state control is enhance at the expense of popular control.

7.4. THE FUTURE OF THE ANTI-MERCENARY NORM

The development of PMCs and later PSCs has occurred in ways that are consistent with, rather than a challenge to, the anti-mercenary norm. Rather, these two types of private force have developed in ways consistent with the norm. But as the world again becomes used to the idea of exchanging military might for financial gain, is it possible that the norm against mercenary use may disappear? Or, perhaps, *should* the anti-mercenary norm wither away, now that it has become puritanical and is applied unreflectively regardless of the facts of the situation?

One of the reasons for the anti-mercenary norm's continued strength has been its effective institutionalization. Price argues in relation to the chemical weapons taboo that early institutionalization will mean that a norm is stronger than it otherwise would be.[165] It could also be argued that even when institutionalization is not particularly effective, a norm's early arrival on the international stage guarantees it attention, press, and discussion, all of which strengthen and prolong its influence. The international law created to regulate mercenaries was flawed and unworkable; there was disagreement about the shape it ought to take and the techniques it ought to use to control private force. Even so, the fact that almost as soon as twentieth century mercenaries appeared, they were condemned by the UN and states began to speak out against them resulted in constant bad press for private fighters. The early adoption of laws[166] to control mercenaries left many with a sense that mercenaries and PMCs are banned by international law, even though in reality no such explicit ban exists.[167]

The anti-mercenary norm was also institutionalized as part of the bundle of what might be termed the national self-determination regime. It has been said that the UN since 1945 has been as a decolonization machine,[168] and anti-mercenary sentiment and legislation was a part of that machine. The inclusion

---

[165] Price (1997*a*: 35). See the discussion in Chapter 1 for more detail.
[166] See Chapter 5.   [167] Singer (2004*a*: 531).   [168] Clarke and Herbst (1996: 80).

of anti-mercenary provisions in General Assembly resolutions promoting or protecting self-determination extended the life of the former by attaching to the latter. As long as the debate about national self-determination gained speed, it did not matter if concerns about mercenaries lost steam, because the two were associated both in the public eye and in the letter of UN documents. An excellent example of this is the repeated resolutions through the 1980s and 1990s which reiterate the dangers of practices which undermine self-determination, including mercenarism. A resolution declaring the practice of mercenarism to be a criminal act, alongside other acts which threatened national self-determination, was reiterated every year from 1979 to 1998.[169] In addition, the mention of mercenaries in other international legal instruments, including the General Assembly's Definition of Aggression[170] and the Draft Code of Crimes against the Peace and Security of Mankind[171] meant that the idea of mercenarism as a criminal act was kept alive in other instruments. Indeed, the mere fact that mercenarism is *included* in the Draft Code alongside crimes like genocide and slavery demonstrates the degree to which international lawmakers disliked the idea of private force. Even if the UN Convention and Article 47 were flawed, anti-mercenary feeling was embedded in other documents and associated with other ideas, allowing it to flourish.

The repeated mention of anti-mercenarism in UN documents and in documents of international law, including the Draft Code, had a further institutionalizing effect. Those working *within* international institutions, in particular the ILC and various organs of the UN, were left with a constant impression that mercenaries were illegal actors needing control. Those 'in the know' knew that mercenaries were dangerous, and these individuals were responsible for making policy in the event that any mercenary action causes problems. Thus, it is not surprising that when PMCs emerged in the 1990s that they were dealt with within the parameters of existing international law and the UN's traditional approach, even though, as will be argued below, these approaches did not apply to the situation.

The institutionalization of the anti-mercenary norm also ensured a barrage of criticism whenever mercenary action came to the fore. UN disapproval kept the mercenary issue in the public eye, and constant criticism reminded the international community that private fighters were dangerous and troublesome actors. Hollywood stars often hire publicists, whose role it is to keep

---

[169] Res 36/9, 28 Oct 1981. UN Doc A/36/622. '*Reaffirms* that the practice of using mercenaries against national liberation movements and sovereign States constitutes a criminal act and that the mercenaries themselves are criminals' and calls upon legislation to be enacted by states.
[170] GA Resolution 3314 (XXIX) 1974. Article 3(g) of the definition states that the sending of armed bands, groups, irregulars, or mercenaries to commit acts of aggression.
[171] See McCormack and Simpson (1994) for a draft of the code.

the star's name on the public's lips, and to make sure the star's good image, or 'brand', maintains its visibility and allure. To a large extent, the UN has acted as a sort of world-class publicist in reverse for mercenaries. Constant attention in the General Assembly and by the High Commission for Human Rights has meant that mercenaries have been branded malevolent in the public eye. Institutionalization of a norm, even when incomplete or ineffective, can influence state behaviour.

However, despite the early institutionalization of the anti-mercenary norm, it is not clear it will persist. First, relying on norms of decolonization and national self-determination for continued strength may not in the future be as effective as it has been in the past. Self-determination and decolonization were powerful norms in the early 1970s, 1980s, and early 1990s, but it remains to be seen whether or not they will have continued salience in the future.

Second, the institutionalization of the anti-mercenary norm in ineffective law may ultimately lead to problems. Anti-mercenary law has never been used, and the failure to use a legal instrument can be just as damning as repeated violations of that instrument. If a law exists to control mercenaries but loopholes prevent its application, the repeated non-enforcement of law will begin to look like a series of violations of the law's intent, even though the use of mercenaries in some circumstances might not threaten the letter of the law. In other words, it might begin to look as though because anti-mercenary law is so ineffective, states were never committed to it, and so the fact it does not apply to private security companies indicates a lack of will rather than poorly designed law. The international community's *inability* to respond legally to the presence of private military and private security companies appears like a lack of will, and these failures have overshadowed the initial normative commitment to controlling mercenaries. The 'general absence of law within this critical realm stands as a clear challenge to the belief that legal norms underscore good behaviour in the international arena...if laws are absent, unclear, or seen as inappropriate, the respect for them and their resultant effectiveness certainly will be diminished'.[172] Institutionalizing the anti-mercenary norm in such problematic law will mean that the anti-mercenary norm has had to hold fast against the erosion of constant failure in the control and regulation of mercenaries and other private actors who use force.[173]

Despite weak law dealing with mercenaries and the association with norms that may decline in importance, the basic point holds true: early institutionalization has left a lingering sense that private force is morally problematic. Examining the anti-mercenary norm from a different perspective provides a less bleak view of its future prospects. Because the anti-mercenary norm

---

[172] Singer (2004a: 524). [173] For further discussion, see Percy (forthcoming, 2007a).

contains two components, both would have to erode for the norm itself to lose strength. Even if one becomes less important, the other may still persist. At different periods, the components of the anti-mercenary norm have ebbed and flowed in strength. Sometimes one aspect of the norm is most relevant, and sometimes the other. It might well be that the shifting relationship between the elements that compose the anti-mercenary norm gives it the flexibility necessary to survive.

The fact that the anti-mercenary norm seems to have become puritanical may also result in its future longevity. The almost automatically negative response to all types of private force, even brand new ones, ensures the continued life of the norm. PMCs and PSCs have struggled to differentiate themselves from mercenaries. PSCs have insisted they are different from PMCs, who engage in combat and are more 'mercenary'. 'Whilst I do not object to the *Oxford English Dictionary* definition of the word', explained Tim Spicer in his Sandline days, 'I do object to the images it conjures up in people's minds... we don't like the "Rambos", the psychopaths, the killers. In the conflicts in which we become involved they actually work for the other side'.[174] Of course, Spicer might be wise to object to the OED definition as well, because 'mercenary' is used as adjective meaning 'a person whose actions are motivated primarily by personal gain, often at the expense of ethics'.[175] As we have seen, PSCs are particularly exercised by the fact the UN body dealing with them has the word 'mercenary' in the title. Numerous PSC officials have pointed out that this approach is problematic and that they are less enthusiastic about the Working Group as a result.[176]

Because the word mercenary has itself become pejorative, it reinforces the idea that all manifestations of private force are inherently problematic. Another demonstration of the strength of the mercenary label is that it is now being used by a variety of parties as a way to condemn international interference of any kind, even if that interference is not mercenary. During the recent war in Iraq, both sides referred to the fighters of the other as mercenary. The Iraqi Minister of Information referred to 'hordes of British and American mercenaries',[177] and General Tommy Franks accused Syria of allowing foreign 'mercenaries' to enter to assist Iraq.[178] The use of mercenary as a pejorative term in a variety of contexts indicates that states recognize that other states will make an immediate association with negative images should a fighter be branded a mercenary. As a rhetorical device, calling a fighter of whom one

---

[174] Spicer (1999b: 165).   [175] Oxford English Dictionary.
[176] Interviews with Brooks, Beese, Bearpark, and Holmes.
[177] Grove (2003). The Iraqi foreign minister also referred to American troops as mercenaries and 'louts'. Lamb (2003).
[178] Cornwell (2003).

disapproves a mercenary can only be useful if others also consider mercenaries to be beyond the pale. Companies providing private force would only work to avoid the mercenary label if they believed it to be problematic. As long as the word mercenary carries so much power, it will be hard for the anti-mercenary norm to erode. Every new variation of private force will start out having to work against a pejorative label.

It is also possible that a growing disjunction between the reality of private force and the anti-mercenary norm may eventually force the latter to change. Clinging on to the idea that all private fighters are inherently problematic in the light of evidence to the contrary may prove to be unsustainable. However, the continued normative concerns prompted by PSCs, and the use of mercenaries in unsavoury plots around the world, are likely to mean that the anti-mercenary norm does not fall completely out of step with reality.

Finally, the future of the conflict in Iraq is crucial in determining the future of the anti-mercenary norm. If the war in Iraq continues to be perceived as a failure that the public never truly supported, it may very well be that the anti-mercenary norm gets reinforced. There are notable parallels between the American Revolution and the war in Iraq. In both cases, a major power fought a controversial war that lacked public support. During the American Revolution, the use of mercenaries began to be associated with wars so unpopular that Britain was unable to persuade British men to fight. The fact that Britain had to pay 'hirelings' in a war about freedom was considered especially problematic, and the unpopularity of the war began to infect the already unpopular means used to fight it. It became harder to use mercenaries in subsequent conflicts, like the Crimea, because they were seen as part and parcel of an unsuccessful and unpopular war. In Iraq, the United States and the UK have failed to convince enough of their own people to fight for the liberation of Iraqis; private companies fill the gap left by recruitment failures. Moreover, an increasingly unpopular war may force questions as to why the United States and its allies had to rely so heavily on private force. Fortuitous circumstances assist the evolution of all norms, and in this case, an unhappy experience in Iraq may enhance the anti-mercenary norm.

7.5. CONCLUSION

While the events of the 1990s and afterwards may at first suggest that the anti-mercenary norm has lost its influence, a closer examination reveals that it is impossible to understand the 1990s without understanding the anti-mercenary norm. Far from being eroded by events, the anti-mercenary norm pushed PMCs into oblivion and shaped the burgeoning PSC industry. The growth of a non-combat industry tightly aligned with the state directly conforms to the anti-mercenary norm, but is not entirely uncontroversial. PSCs, like other types of private force, upset the traditional relationship between the citizen and the state. Private force allows the state to embark on war more easily, and to sustain unpopular wars. PSCs do not entirely escape the anti-mercenary norm. Despite the growth of an active private security industry, the norm against mercenary use may not decline. The anti-mercenary norm's two components make it flexible enough to withstand historical changes.

Conclusion

Mercenaries and their employers must constitute one of the quintessential love-hate relationships of international politics. Private fighters have always been useful, but those in a position to make decisions about which type of force to use have never accepted them with wholehearted enthusiasm. Mercenaries have often been hired only out of desperation or despair. Moral reservations about the advisability of using a soldier motivated only by financial gain have been coupled with a belief that only certain actors within a polity and among polities are entitled to use force at all. In the medieval period, the church-sanctioned use of violence was restricted to the nobility, and by the end of the seventeenth century the sovereign state took for itself the aristocratic right to wage war. Even though rulers have loved the idea of hiring soldiers only when necessary, they (and their people) simultaneously hated the resort to private actors who were connected to the cause for which they were hired to fight by money only, and who, by retaining the right to wage war for themselves, challenged the institution of war itself.

On the employer side, states, kings, popes, princes, and other rulers who have been in a position to hire mercenary force have never been able to do so without constraint. Sometimes, the constraints on employers have been externally imposed, by the 'popular control' aspect of the norm. Public opinion turned against mercenary use in nineteenth century Europe and remained strongly opposed to the use of private force across the world during the twentieth century, and remains opposed today. Public moral disapproval has been shared privately by employers themselves. The external constraints on employers have mainly been moral, based on a belief that to fight for money, without sharing the goals of the hiring group, is problematic. In medieval Europe, mercenaries upset the social order because they did not fight for a just cause. In renaissance Italy, Machiavelli feared the *condottieri* on republican grounds, believing that mercenaries undermined the fabric of the republic because they prevented the citizens of the republic from doing their civic duty and fighting for the state, and because their selfish motivation meant that they could never be as effective as citizens. Machiavelli's republican opposition to mercenaries can be traced directly through history to today's objections about

PSCs. The American revolutionaries, the French revolutionaries, Prussian reformers, and Victorian Britons all argued that fighting for a financial, selfish motive rather than out of patriotism or devotion to the national cause would not only make mercenaries poorer soldiers, but would make society itself poorer by ignoring the duty the citizen has to serve the state.

Employers also faced self-imposed constraints on the use of private force. These constraints stem from the 'authoritative control' aspect of the norm against mercenary use. Even in its earliest days, the use of mercenaries had to be controlled to be remotely tenable. A free-ranging, freewheeling system of freelance soldiers could (and did) lead to mayhem and social disorder. Employers chose to use mercenaries under increasingly constrained circumstances to avoid these problems. In medieval Europe, states developed prototype standing armies and began to hire foreigners only as part of long-standing alliance arrangements with other states. By the end of the seventeenth century, as states across Europe had grown stronger, the independent mercenary contractor no longer existed and the mercenary industry was a state-to-state-based exchange of troops based on bilateral agreements. Employers wanted control over private force for practical reasons, as uncontrolled mercenaries were dangerous to both states and individuals, but also for moral reasons.

The idea that only certain groups in society have the right to wage war is an old one, although it has taken many forms. The argument that only nobles, or the rulers of sovereign states, or the governments of sovereign states, have the right to use force is a highly normative argument. The right to use force is located in the hands of the few, and that right is buttressed and justified by normative ideas, like the medieval social order or *raison d'état* or the divine right of kings or the theory of the sovereign state. As long as independent mercenaries existed, they challenged these norms as well as posing genuine practical problems for rulers.

Mercenaries, as employees, have also been constrained by the norm against the use of private force. These constraints have often come in the form of contracts, whether between a mercenary captain and a city-state, between a state and another state, between a mercenary and a colonial power, or a PMC and a troubled state. But these constraints have often been more explicitly moral and deeply condemnatory. Medieval mercenaries were excommunicated and penalized by the Church. Italian *condottieri* were castigated by renaissance humanists and often became citizens of the states that hired them. The Swiss turned their backs on their mercenary past in 1848 by outlawing the long Swiss tradition of exporting mercenaries, succumbing to the arguments of nationalists and humanists like Zwingli. The mercenary of 1960s and 1970s Africa was forced to act at the margins of respectability, often for causes lacking international support or completely illegal, like the raising of troops for *coups d'état*. PMCs and PSCs have had to struggle to overcome the mercenary label to develop effective business, and their prospects are greatly constrained by the ongoing belief that to use mercenaries is simply immoral.

We have seen how the norm against mercenary use has constrained states in deciding whether or not to use private force, and how to compose their armies. The norm against mercenary use has also made life more difficult for mercenaries themselves, shaping the kinds of opportunities available and so the kind of mercenary best able to meet those opportunities. The *condottieri*, the Hessians, and today's PMCs and PSCs had and have a particular construction so as not to upset, or to challenge only minimally, prevailing beliefs about who has the right to wage war.

The norm against mercenary use has explained four different puzzles in international history. First, anti-mercenary feeling can help illustrate why states got control over the independent mercenary and established a controlled international trade in mercenaries. Second, the norm against mercenary use can help explain why, even though the controlled trade in private fighters was effective, it was abandoned in favour of citizen armies across Europe in the nineteenth century. Third, it is impossible to understand why international law on mercenaries is so flawed without understanding that states were attempting to adhere to a very strong norm against mercenary use which was difficult to translate into law, and was simultaneously supported by the norms of national self-determination and undermined by the norms of state responsibility and freedom of movement. Fourth, the growth of PMCs, their disappearance, and the rise of PSCs cannot be understood without understanding the normative obstacles modern-day mercenaries face, and the international community's response to the emergence of PMCs is likewise impossible to understand without attention to widespread normative discomfort with the use of private force.

The norm against mercenary use not only helps explain these four puzzles, but also reveals three further points about the role of norms in international politics. First, the norm against mercenary use is a good example of a soft, uncodified norm. The norm against mercenary use has only been formally codified recently, and the resulting law is unwieldy and unworkable. The persistence of the norm against mercenary use suggests that norms do not need to be formally or effectively codified in order to retain an influence over state behaviour. Moreover, the relationship between law and norms is not straightforward. A strong underlying norm can still result in weak and ineffective law.

Second, the norm against mercenary use flies in the face of certain expectations of state behaviour. The rationalist view of norms, outlined in Chapter 1, would be perfectly consistent with the control aspect of the norm. States have created a norm about the control of private force because it serves their needs by diminishing the negative effects of private fighters and enhancing their potential benefits. But what we have seen is that the appropriate cause and popular control components of the norm are far more important. The belief that mercenaries ought to be controlled or outlawed because there is something morally problematic about killing for money rather than ideals has played a large part in all four of the puzzles addressed in this book. States have had a long history of making decisions about which type of force to use on the basis of an ethical objection to mercenaries and their financial motivation. Their citizens have had a long history of worrying about whether using private force upsets popular control over the decision to wage war. We have seen states and regimes of all kinds and from all eras thinking ethically about which type of force to use and seeking to control mercenaries tightly or outlaw them outright on moral grounds. The long history of ethical objections to mercenaries suggests that states are indeed profoundly influenced by moral beliefs about war.

The norm against mercenary use is also an excellent example of a norm with a 'dark side'.[1] Norms are not always useful, good, or functional. They can lead states down negative or inefficient paths just as they can lead states to agreement and positive outcomes. The norm against mercenary use is in many ways a puritanical norm, which no longer applies to the actual behaviour that it initially regulated. Our moral dislike of mercenaries may no longer be grounded in the realities of mercenary behaviour, and the potential benefits of private force may be obscured by the great strength of the anti-mercenary norm.

[1] Tannenwald (forthcoming).

APPENDIX 1

Definition of a Mercenary from the International Convention against the Recruitment, Use, Financing and Training of Mercenaries

1. A mercenary is any person who:
   (a) Is specially recruited locally or abroad in order to fight in an armed conflict;
   (b) Is motivated to take part in the hostilities essentially by the desire for private gain and, in fact, is promised, by or on behalf of a party to the conflict, material compensation substantially in excess of that promised or paid to combatants of similar rank and functions in the armed forces of that party;
   (c) Is neither a national of a party to the conflict nor a resident of territory controlled by a party to the conflict;
   (d) Is not a member of the armed forces of a party to the conflict; and
   (e) Has not been sent by a State which is not a party to the conflict on official duty as a member of its armed forces.
2. A mercenary is also any person who, in any other situation:
   (a) Is specially recruited locally or abroad for the purpose of participating in a concerted act of violence aimed at:
      (i) Overthrowing a Government or otherwise undermining the constitutional order of a State; or
      (ii) Undermining the territorial integrity of a State;
   (b) Is motivated to take part therein essentially by the desire for significant private gain and is prompted by the promise or payment of material compensation;
   (c) Is neither a national nor a resident of the State against which such an act is directed;
   (d) Has not been sent by a State on official duty; and
   (e) Is not a member of the armed forces of the State on whose territory the act is undertaken.

References

Adams, T. K. (1999). 'The New Mercenaries and the Privatization of Conflict'. *Parameters, US Army War College Quarterly*, XXIX(2): 1–12.
Addington, L. H. (1994). *The Patterns of War since the Eighteenth Century*. Bloomington, IN: Indiana University Press.
Allison, R. (2003). 'Mercenary Warning for UK Firm'. *The Guardian*, 2 April 2003.
Allmand, C. (1971). 'The War and Non-Combatant', in K. A. Fowler (ed.), *The Hundred Years War*. London and Basingstoke, UK: Macmillan.
Allott, P. (2000). 'The Concept of International Law', in M. Byers (ed.), *The Role of Law in International Politics*. Oxford: Oxford University Press, pp. 69–90.
Amnesty International (1996). 'Sierra Leone: Towards a Future Founded on Human Rights', AFR:51/05/96, Online Pagination: Accessed 18 December 2004. Available at http://web.amnesty.org/library/Index/ENGAFR510051996?open&of=ENG-2AF
Anderson, E. N. (1939). *Nationalism and the Cultural Crisis in Prussia, 1806–1815*. New York: Farrar and Rhinehart.
Armstrong, L. (2000). 'Enemies of God, Pity and Mercy', *Canadian Journal of History*, 35(2): 293–96.
Arnold, G. (1999). *Mercenaries: The Scourge of the Third World*. London: Macmillan.
Asch, R. (1997). *The Thirty Years' War: The Holy Roman Empire and Europe, 1618–1648*. New York: St. Martin's Press.
Atwood, R. (1980). *The Hessians: Mercenaries from Hessen-Kassel in the American Revolution*. Cambridge: Cambridge University Press.
Avant, D. (2000). 'From Mercenary to Citizen Armies', *International Organization*, 54(1): 41–72.
_____ (2004). 'Think Again: Mercenaries', *Foreign Policy*: 20–8.
_____ (2005a). *The Market for Force: The Consequences of Privatizing Security*. Cambridge: Cambridge University Press.
Bailyn, B. (1967). *The Ideological Origins of the American Revolution*. Cambridge and London: Belknap Press.
Barnett, C. (1970). *Britain and Her Army 1509–1970: A Military, Political and Social Survey*. Harmondsworth, UK: Penguin Books.
Barnie, J. (1974). *War in Medieval Society*. London: Weidenfeld and Nicolson.
Bartelson, J. (1995). *A Genealogy of Sovereignty*. Cambridge: Cambridge University Press.
Bayley, C. C. (1961). *War and Society in Renaissance Florence*. Toronto, Canada: University of Toronto.
_____ (1977). *Mercenaries for the Crimea: The German, Swiss and Italian Legions in British Service, 1854–1856*. London: McGill-Queen's University Press.

Beck, R. J., Arend, A. C., and vander Lugt, R. D. (1996). *International Rules: Approaches from International Law and International Relations*. Oxford: Oxford University Press.

Bertaud, J.-P. (1988). *The Army of the French Revolution*. Translated by R. R. Palmer. Princeton, NJ: Princeton University Press.

Beshir, M. O. (1972). *Mercenaries in Africa*. Khartoum: Khartoum University Press.

Best, G. (1980). *Humanity in Warfare: The Modern History of the International Law of Armed Conflicts*. London: Weidenfeld and Nicolson.

—— (1982). *War and Society in Revolutionary Europe*. Leicester, UK: Leicester University Press.

Besterman, T. ([1776] 1964). *Voltaire's Correspondence*. Geneva, Switzerland: Institut et Musée Voltaire.

Black, J. (1994). *European Warfare 1660–1815*. London: UCL Press.

—— (2002). 'European Warfare 1864–1913', *European Warfare 1815–2000*. Houndmills, Basingstoke, UK and New York: Palgrave: 51–78.

Blackstone, W. ([1765] 1979). *Commentaries on the Laws of England*. 1. Chicago, IL and London: University of Chicago Press.

Blanning, T. C. W. (1996). *The French Revolutionary Wars 1787–1802*. London: Arnold.

Bonjour, E., Offler, H. S., and Potter, G. R. (1952). *A Short History of Switzerland*. Oxford: Clarendon Press.

Bonwick, C. (1991). *The American Revolution*. Houndmills, Basingstoke, UK and London: Palgrave.

Bowen, H. V. (1998). *War and British Society, 1688–1815*. Cambridge: Cambridge University Press.

Brauer, J. (1999). 'An Economic Perspective on Mercenaries, Military Companies and the Privatization of Force'. *Cambridge Review of International Affairs*, XIII(1): 130–45.

Brayton, S. (2002). 'Outsourcing War: Mercenaries and the Privatization of Peacekeeping', *Journal of International Affairs*, 55 (303–29).

Brown, Michael, Lynn-Jones, S., and Miller, S. (eds) (1996). *Debating the Democratic Peace*. Cambridge, MA: MIT Press.

Brown, S. D. B. (1989). 'Military Service and Monetary Reward in the Eleventh and Twelfth Centuries'. *History*, 74(240): 20–38.

Buel Jr., R. (1984). Samson Shorn: 'The Impact of the Revolutionary War on the Estimates of the Republic's Strength', in R. Hoffman and P. J. Albert (eds), *Arms and Independence: The Military Character of the American Revolution*. Charlottesville, VA: University Press of Virginia, pp. 141–65.

Bull, H. (1977). *The Anarchical Society: A Study of Order in World Politics*. Houndmills, Basingstoke, UK and London: Macmillan.

Burchett, W. and Roebuck, D. (1977). *The Whores of War: Mercenaries Today*. Harmondsworth, UK: Penguin Books.

Burmester, S. (1978). 'The Recruitment and Use of Mercenaries in Armed Conflict', *American Journal of International Law*, 72(1): 37–56.

Caferro, W. (1994). 'Mercenaries and Military Expenditure: The Cost of Undeclared Warfare in XIVth Century Siena', *Journal of European Economic History*, 23(2): 219–47.

Carp, E. W. (1987). 'The Problem of National Defense in the Early American Republic', in J. P. Greene (ed.), *The American Revolution: Its Character and Limits*. New York and London: New York University Press.

Cassese, A. (1980). 'Mercenaries: Lawful Combatants or War Criminals?' *Zeitschrift für ausländisches öffentliches Recht und Völkerrecht*, 40: 1–30.

Cesner, R. E. and Brant, J. W. (1977). 'Law of the Mercenary: An International Dilemma', *Capital University Law Review*, 6: 339–70.

Challener, D. (1965). *The French Theory of the Nation in Arms: 1866–1939*. New York: Russell & Russell.

Checkel, J. T. (1998). 'The Constructivist Turn in International Relations Theory', *World Politics*, 50(2): 324–48.

Chibnall, M. (2000). 'Mercenaries and the *Familia Regis* under Henry I', *Piety, Power and History in Medieval England and Normandy*. Aldershot, UK: Ashgate: XVIII: 16–23.

Childs, J. (1982). *Armies and Warfare in Europe 1648–1789*. New York: Holmes and Meier Publishers.

Clapham, C. (1996). *Africa and the International System*. Cambridge: Cambridge University Press.

——— (1999). 'African Security Systems: Privatization and the Scope for Mercenary Activity', in G. Mills and J. Stremlau (eds), *The Privatization of Security in Africa*. Johannesburg, South Africa: South African Institute of International Affairs.

Clark, I. (1988). *Waging War: A Philosophical Introduction*. Oxford: Clarendon Press.

Clarke, W. and Herbst, J. (1996). 'Somalia and the Future of Humanitarian Intervention', *Foreign Affairs*, 75(2): 70–85.

Cleary, S. (1999). 'Angola: A Case Study of Private Military Involvement', in J. Cilliers and P. Mason (eds), *Peace, Profit or Plunder?: The Privatization of Security in War-Torn African Societies*. Johannesburg, South Africa: Institute for Security Studies.

Cobban, A. (1969). *The Nation State and National Self-Determination*. London: Collins Fontana Library.

Cobbett (1776). *Cobbett's Parliamentary History of England: From the Norman Conquest in 1066 to the Year 1803*. 18. London: R. Bagshaw.

Cockayne, J. (2006). *Commercial Security in Humanitarian and Post-Conflict Settings: An Exploratory Study*. New York: International Peace Academy.

Cogliano, F. D. (2000). *Revolutionary America: 1763–1815*. London and New York: Routledge.

Cohen, E. A. (1985). *Citizens and Soldiers: The Dilemmas of Military Service*. Ithaca, NY and London: Cornell University Press.

Coker, C. (1999). 'Outsourcing War', *Cambridge Review of International Affairs*, XIII(1): 94–113.

Conacher, J. B. (1987). *Britain and the Crimea, 1855–56: Problems of War and Peace*. New York: St. Martin's Press.

Contamine, P. (1984). *War in the Middle Ages*. Translated by M. Jones. Oxford: Blackwell.

Conway, S. (2000). *The British Isles and the War of American Independence*. Oxford: Oxford University Press.

Corfu Channel Case (UK v. Albania), ICJ Reports (1949).
Cornwell, T. (2003). 'US Warns Syria against Support for Iraq', *The Scotsman*, 14 April 2003.
Corvisier, A. (1979). *Armies and Societies in Europe, 1494–1789*. Translated by A. T. Siddall. Bloomington, IN and London: Indiana University Press.
Craig, G. A. (1964). *The Politics of the Prussian Army 1690–1945*. Oxford: Clarendon Press.
Davis, G. R. C. (1963). *Magna Carta*. London: Trustees of the British Museum.
De Bustamente, A. S. (1908). 'The Hague Convention Concerning the Rights and Duties of Neutral Powers and Persons in Land Warfare', *American Journal of International Law*, 2(1): 95–120.
De St. Jorre, J. (1972). *The Nigerian Civil War*. London: Hodder and Stoughton.
De Venette, J. (1953). *The Chronicle of Jean De Venette*. Translated by J. Birdsall. R. A. Newhall. Oxford: Oxford University Press.
Desch, M. C. (1998). 'Culture Clash: Assessing the Importance of Ideas in Security Studies', *International Security*, 23(1): 141–70.
Dessler, D. (1989). 'What's at Stake in the Agent-Structure Debate?', *International Organization*, 43(3): 441–73.
Dinnen, S. (1999). 'Militaristic Solutions in a Weak State: Internal Security, Private Contractors and Political Leadership in Papua New Guinea', *Contemporary Pacific*, 11(2): 279–303.
Diplock, Lord, Walker-Smith, D., and de Freitas, G. (1976). Report of the Committee of Privy Counsellors Appointed to Inquire into the Recruitment of Mercenaries. London: Stationery Office.
Donald, D. (2006). After the Bubble: British Private Security Companies after Iraq. London: Royal United Services Institute, Whitehall Papers.
Dorney, S. (1998). *The Sandline Affair: Politics and Mercenaries in the Bougainville Crisis*. Sydney, Australia: ABC Books.
Douglas, I. (1999). 'Fighting for Diamonds—Private Military Companies in Sierra Leone', in J. Cilliers and P. Mason (eds), *Peace, Profit or Plunder?: The Privatization of Security in War-Torn African Societies*. Johannesburg, South Africa: Institute for Security Studies.
Doyle, M. (1983). 'Kant, Liberal Legacies and Foreign Affairs', *Philosophy and Public Affairs*, 2, 3, and 4.
Dumbauld, E. (1937). 'Neutrality Laws of the United States', *The American Journal of International Law*, 31(2): 258–70.
Dupuy, T. N. (1977). *A Genius for War*. London: Macdonald and Jane's.
Ellis, J. (1973). *Armies in Revolution*. London: Croom Helm.
Enloe, C. H. (1978). 'Mercenerizaton', *US Military Involvement in Southern Africa*.
Erinys. The Erinys Iraq Oil Protection Force: Infrastructure Security in a Post-Conflict Environment. London and Johannesburg: Erinys.
Esdaile, C. J. (1995). *The Wars of Napoleon*. London and New York: Longman.
Falk, R. (2002). 'Self-Determination under International Law: The Coherence of Doctrine Versus the Incoherence of Experience', in W. Danspeckgruber (ed.), *The*

Self-Determination of Peoples: Community, Nation and State in an Interdependent World. Boulder, CO: Lynne Rienner, pp. 31–66.
Fantosme, J. (1981). *Jordan Fantosme's Chronicle*. Translated by R. C. Johnston. Oxford: Clarendon Press.
Finer, S. E. (1976). 'The Second Oldest Trade', *The New Society*, 15 July 1976, 129–31.
Finnemore, M. (1993). 'International Organizations as Teachers of Norms: The United Nations Educational, Scientific, and Cultural Organization and Science Policy', *International Organization*, 47(4): 565–97.
—— (1996a). 'Constructing Norms of Humanitarian Intervention', in P. J. Katzenstein (ed.), *The Culture of National Security: Norms and Identities in World Politics*. New York: Columbia University Press.
—— (1996b). 'Norms, Culture and World Politics: Insights from Sociology's Institutionalism', *International Organization*, 50(2): 325–47.
Finnemore, M. and Sikkink, K. (1998). 'International Norm Dynamics and Political Change', *International Organization*, 52(4): 887–917.
Florini, A. (1996). 'The Evolution of International Norms', *International Studies Quarterly*, 40(3): 363–89.
Ford, G. S. (1965). *Stein and the Era of Reform in Prussia, 1807–1815*. Gloucester, MA: Peter Smith.
Foreign Affairs Committee (2001–2). *Ninth Report of the Foreign Affairs Committee: Private Military Companies. Response of the Secretary of State for Foreign and Commonwealth Affairs*. London: The Stationery Office Ltd.
Forrest, A. (1989). *Conscripts and Deserters: The Army and French Society During the Revolution and Empire*. Oxford: Oxford University Press.
—— (1990). *The Soldiers of the French Revolution*. Durham, NC: Duke University Press.
—— (2003). '*La Patrie En Danger*: The French Revolution and the First *Levée En Masse*', in D. Moran and A. Waldron (eds), *The People in Arms: Military Myth and National Mobilization since the French Revolution*. Cambridge: Cambridge University Press, pp. 8–32.
Fowler, K. A. (1971). 'Introduction: War and Change in Late Medieval France and England', in K. A. Fowler (ed.), *The Hundred Years War*. London and Basingstoke, UK: Macmillan.
—— (2001). *Medieval Mercenaries. 1: The Great Companies*. Oxford: Blackwell.
France, J. (1999). *Western Warfare in the Age of the Crusades, 1000–1300*. Ithaca, NY: Cornell University Press.
Francis, D. J. (1999). 'Mercenary Intervention in Sierra Leone: Providing National Security or International Exploitation?', *Third World Quarterly*, 20(2): 319–38.
Fredland, E. and Kennedy, A. (1999). 'The Privatization of Military Force: Economic Virtues, Vices and Government Responsibility', *Cambridge Review of International Affairs*, XIII(1): 147–63.
French, D. (1990). *The British Way in Warfare 1688–2000*. London: Unwin Hyman.
Gasser, H.-P. (1987). 'An Appeal for Ratification by the United States', *American Journal of International Law*, 81(4): 912–25.

Gesta Stephani, Regis Anglorum (1976). Translated by K. R. Potter. Oxford: Clarendon Press.

Gilliard, C. (1955). *A History of Switzerland*. Translated by D. L. B. Hartley. London: George Allen and Unwin.

Goertz, G. and Diehl, P. (1992). 'Towards a Theory of International Norms', *Journal of Conflict Resolution*, 36(4): 634–64.

Goldstein, J. and Keohane, R. O. (eds) (1993). *Ideas and Foreign Policy: Beliefs, Institutions and Political Change*. Ithaca, NY and London: Cornell University Press.

Gong, G. (1984). *The Standard of 'Civilization' in International Society*. Oxford: Clarendon Press.

Gooch, J. (1980). *Armies in Europe*. London: Routledge and Kegan Paul.

Green, L. C. (1979). 'The Status of Mercenaries in International Law', *Manitoba Law Journal*, 9(3): 201–46.

Griffith, P. (1989). *Military Thought in the French Army, 1815–51*. Manchester, UK: Manchester University Press.

Grove, L. (2003). 'The Reliable Source', *Washington Post*, 10 April 2003.

Guerlac, H. (1986). 'Vauban: The Impact of Science on War', in P. Paret, G. A. Craig, and F. Gilbert (eds), *Makers of Modern Strategy: From Machiavelli to the Nuclear Age*. Princeton, NJ: Princeton University Press, pp. 64–90.

Hale, J. R. (1985). *War and Society in Renaissance Europe*. Leicester, UK: Leicester University Press.

Hampson, F. (1991). 'Mercenaries: Diagnosis before Prescription', *Netherlands Yearbook of International Law*, 3: 4–37.

Hansard (1854–7). *Parliamentary Debates*. CXXXVI. London and Basingstoke, UK: Cornelius Buck.

Harding, J. (1997). 'The Mercenary Business: "Executive Outcomes"', *Review of African Political Economy*, 71: 87–97.

Hempstone, S. (1962). *Rebels, Dividends and Mercenaries: The Katanga Story*. New York: Frederick A. Praeger.

Henley, J. (2000). 'Dogs of War in Nudist Camp', *The Guardian*, 19 August 2000.

Herbst, J. (1999). 'The Regulation of Private Security Firms' in G. Mills and J. Stremlau (eds), *The Privatization of Security in Africa*. Johannesburg, South Africa: South African Institute of International Affairs, pp. 107–27.

Higgins, R. (1994). *Problems and Process: International Law and How We Use It*. Oxford: Clarendon Press.

Hindley, G. (1971). *Medieval Warfare*. London: Wayland Publishers.

Hobsbawm, E. J. (1965). 'The Crisis of the Seventeenth Century', in T. Aston (ed.), *Crisis in Europe: 1560–1660*. London: Routledge and Kegan Paul.

Hollister, C. W. (1965). *The Military Organization of Norman England*. Oxford: Clarendon Press.

Holmqvist, C. (2005). *Private Security Companies: The Case for Regulation*. Stockholm: Stockholm Institute for Peace Research.

Holt, E. (1969). *The Carlist Wars in Spain*. London: Putnam.

Holt, J. C. (1992). *Magna Carta*. Cambridge: Cambridge University Press.
Hoover, M. J. (1977). 'The Laws of War and the Angolan Trial of Mercenaries: Death to the Dogs of War', *Case Western Reserve Journal of International Law*, 9: 323–406.
Hoppit, J. (2000). *A Land of Liberty? England 1689–1727*. Oxford: Oxford University Press.
House of Commons Foreign Affairs Committee (2001–2). *Private Military Companies*. London: The Stationery Office Ltd.
____ (2002*a*). *Private Military Companies: Options for Regulation*. London: The Stationery Office Ltd.
Housley, N. (1999). 'European Warfare: C.1200–1320', in M. Keen (ed.), *Medieval Warfare: A History*. Oxford: Oxford University Press.
Howe, H. M. (1996). 'South Africa's 9-1-1 Force', *Armed Forces International Journal*: 38–9.
____ (1998). 'Private Security Forces and African Stability: The Case of Executive Outcomes', *Journal of Modern African Studies*, 36(2): 307–31.
____ (2001). *Ambiguous Order: Military Forces in African States*. Boulder, CO: Lynne Rienner.
International Committee of the Red Cross (1987). *Commentary on the Additional Protocols of 8 June 1977 to the Geneva Conventions of 12 August 1949*. Geneva, Switzerland: Martinus Nijhoff.
Isenberg, D. (2004). A Fistful of Contractors: The Case for a Pragmatic Assessment of Private Military Companies in Iraq. London: British American Security Information Council.
Jackson, R. H. (1993). 'The Weight of Ideas in Decolonization: Normative Change in International Relations', in J. Goldstein and R. O. Keohane (eds), *Ideas and Foreign Policy*. Ithaca, NY and London: Cornell University Press.
____ (2000). *The Global Covenant*. Oxford: Oxford University Press.
Jepperson, R. L., Wendt, A., and Katzenstein, P. J. (1996). 'Norms, Identity and Culture in National Security', in P. J. Katzenstein (ed.), *The Culture of National Security: Norms and Identity in World Politics*. New York: Columbia University Press, pp. 33–75.
Joenniemi, P. (1977). 'Two Models of Mercenarism: Historical and Contemporary', *Instant Research on Peace and Violence*, VII(3–4): 184–96.
Kaeuper, R. W. (1988). *War, Justice and Public Order: England and France in the Later Middle Ages*. Oxford: Clarendon Press.
Kandeh, J. D. (1998). 'Ransoming the State: Elite Origins of Subaltern Terror in Sierra Leone', *Journal of African Political Economy*, 81: 349–66.
Kant, I. ([1795] 1917). *The Perpetual Peace*. Translated by M. Campbell-Smith. London: George Allen and Unwin.
____ ([1795] 1983). 'Perpetual Peace and Other Essays'. Indianapolis: Hackelt Publishing Company.
Katzenstein, P. J. (ed.) (1996*a*). *The Culture of National Security: Norms and Identity in World Politics*. New York: Columbia University Press.

Katzenstein, P. J. (ed.) (1996b). 'Introduction', in P. J. Katzenstein (ed.), *The Culture of National Security: Norms and Identity in World Politics*. New York: Columbia University Press.

Keen, M. (1966). *The Laws of War in the Late Middle Ages*. London: Routledge and Kegan Paul.

———(1999a). 'Introduction', in M. Keen (ed.), *Medieval Warfare: A History*. Oxford: Oxford University Press: 1–9.

———(1999b). 'The Changing Scene: Guns, Gunpowder and Permanent Armies', in M. Keen (ed.), *Medieval Warfare: A History*. Oxford: Oxford University Press: 273–91.

Keohane, R. O. (1984). *After Hegemony: Cooperation and Discord in the World Political Economy*. Princeton, NJ: Princeton University Press.

———(1988). 'International Institutions: Two Approaches', *International Studies Quarterly*, 32(4): 379–96.

———(1995). 'Hobbes' Dilemma and Institutional Change in World Politics: Sovereignty in International Society', in H.-H. Holm and G. Sørensen (eds), *Whose World Order?: Uneven Globalization and the End of the Cold War*. Boulder, CO: Westview Press: 165–87.

Kinsey, C. (2005). 'Challenging International Law: A Dilemma of Private Security Companies', *Conflict, Security and Development*, 5(3): 269–93.

———(2006). *Corporate Soldiers and International Security: The Rise of Private Security Companies*. London: Routledge.

Kitchen, M. (1975). *A Military History of Germany from the Eighteenth Century to the Present Day*. London: Weidenfeld and Nicolson.

Klotz, A. (1995). *Norms in International Relations: The Struggle against Apartheid*. Ithaca, NY: Cornell University Press.

Krasner, S. D. (1989). 'Sovereignty: An Institutional Perspective', in J. A. Caporaso (ed.), *The Elusive State: International and Comparative Perspectives*. Newbury Park: Sage.

Kratochwil, F. (1989). *Rules, Norms and Decisions*. Cambridge: Cambridge University Press.

———(2001). 'How Do Norms Matter?', in M. Byers (ed.), *The Role of Law in International Politics: Essays in International Relations and International Law*. Oxford: Oxford University Press.

Kratochwil, F. and Ruggie, J. (1986). 'International Organization: A State of the Art on the Art of the State', *International Organization*, 40(4): 753–75.

Kwakwa, E. (1990). 'The Current Status of Mercenaries in Armed Conflict', *Hastings International and Comparative Law Review*, 14: 68–91.

Lamb, D. (2003). 'Defiance Personified: Minister Still Hurls Insults', *Los Angeles Times*, 9 April 2003.

Layeb, A. (1989). 'The Need for an International Convention against Mercenaries and Mercenarism', *African Journal of International and Comparative Law*, 1: 466–81.

Lee, J. M. (1969). *African Armies and Civil Order*. London: Chatto and Windus.

Legg, Sir T. and Ibbs, Sir R. (1998). *Report of the Sierra Leone Arms Investigation*. London: The Stationery Office Ltd.

Legro, J. (1995). *Cooperation under Fire: Anglo-German Restraint During World War II*. Ithaca, NY: Cornell University Press.

Lockwood, G. H. (1976). 'Report on the Trial of Mercenaries: Luanda, Angola, June 1976', *Manitoba Law Journal*, 7: 183–202.

Lowe, V. (2001). 'The Politics of Law-Making: Are the Method and Character of Norm Creation Changing?', in M. Byers (ed.), *The Role of Law in International Politics: Essays in International Relations and International Law*. Oxford: Oxford University Press.

Lynch, T. and Walsh, A. J. (2000). 'The Good Mercenary?', *The Journal of Political Philosophy*, 8(2): 133–53.

Lynn, J. A. (1984). *The Bayonets of the Republic: Motivation and Tactics in the Army of Revolutionary France, 1791–94*. Urbana and Chicago, IL: University of Illinois Press.

—— (1989). 'Toward an Army of Honour: The Moral Evolution of the French Army, 1789–1815', *French Historical Studies*, 16(1): 152–73.

—— (2001). 'The Treatment of Military Subjects in Diderot's *Encyclopédie*', *The Journal of Military History*, 65(1): 131–65.

MacFarlane, S. N. (1985). *Superpower Rivalry and Third World Radicalism*. London and Sydney, Australia: Croom Helm.

Macgregor, A. (1999). Quagmire in West Africa: International Journal. 2000.

Machiavelli, N. ([1513] 1992). *The Prince*. New York and London: Norton.

Mackesy, P. (1964). *The War for America: 1775–1783*. London: Longmans.

—— (1984). 'What the British Army Learned', in R. Hoffman and P. J. Albert (eds), *Arms and Independence: The Military Character of the American Revolution*. Charlottesville, VA: University Press of Virginia, pp. 191–215.

Major, M.-F. (1992). 'Mercenaries and International Law', *Georgia Journal of International and Comparative Law* 22. Online Pagination: 1–35 Accessed 22 March 2003. Available at www.westlaw.com

Mallett, M. E. (1974). *Mercenaries and Their Masters: Warfare in Renaissance Italy*. London: The Bodley Head.

—— (1999). 'Mercenaries', in M. Keen (ed.), *Medieval Warfare*. Oxford: Oxford University Press.

Malone, D. (1998). *Decision-Making in the UN Security Council: The Case of Haiti, 1990–1997*. Oxford: Clarendon Press.

Map, W. (1983). *De Nugis Curialium*. Translated by M. R. James, C. N. J. Brooke, and R. A. B. Mynors. Oxford: Clarendon Press.

March, J. G. and Olsen, J. P. (1998). 'The Institutional Dynamics of International Political Orders', *International Organization*, 52(4): 943–69.

Marston, G. (1982). 'United Kingdom Materials on International Law', *British Yearbook of International Law*, LIII: 337–569.

Martin, R. (1977). 'Mercenaries and the Rule of Law', *Review of International Comm. Jurists*: 51–7.

Mayall, J. (1990). *Nationalism and International Society*. Cambridge: Cambridge University Press.

Mayer, H. A. (2000). 'The Continental Army', in J. P. Greene and J. R. Pole (eds), *A Companion to the American Revolution*. Oxford: Blackwell.

McCormack, J. (1993). *One Million Mercenaries: Swiss Soldiers in the Armies of the World*. London: Leo Cooper.

McCormack, T. L. H. and Simpson, G. J. (1994). 'The International Law Commission's Draft Code of Crimes against the Peace and Security of Mankind: An Appraisal of the Substantive Provisions', *Criminal Law Forum*, 5(1): 1–55.

McDougal, M. S. and Lasswell, H. D. ([1959] 1996). 'The Identification and Appraisal of Diverse Systems of Public Order', in R. J. Beck, A. C. Arend, and R. D. Vander Lugt (eds), *International Rules: Approaches from International Law and International Relations*. Oxford: Oxford University Press, pp. 113–41.

McElroy, R. W. (1992). *Morality and American Foreign Policy*. Princeton, NJ: Princeton University Press.

McNeill, W. H. (1982). *The Pursuit of Power: Technology, Armed Force, and Society since A.D. 1000*. Oxford: Blackwell.

—— (1983). *The Pursuit of Power: Technology, Armed Force, and Society since A.D. 1000*. Oxford: Blackwell.

Mead Earle, E. (1986). 'Smith, Hamilton, List', in P. Paret, G. A. Craig, and F. Gilbert (eds), *Makers of Modern Strategy: From Machiavelli to the Nuclear Age*. Princeton, NJ: Princeton University Press, pp. 217–61.

Mearsheimer, J. J. (1994–5). 'The False Promise of International Institutions', *International Security*, 19(3): 5–49.

Merpe, R. (2006). 'Census Counts 100,000 Contracts in Iraq', *Washington Post*, 5 December 2006.

Middlekauf, R. (1982). *The Glorious Cause: The American Revolution 1763–1789*. New York and Oxford: Oxford University Press.

Mills, G. and Stremlau, J. (eds) (1999*a*). *The Privatization of Security in Africa*. Johannesburg, South Africa: South African Institute of International Affairs.

—— —— (1999*b*). 'Introduction', in G. Mills and J. Stremlau (eds), *The Privatization of Security in Africa*. Johannesburg, South Africa: South African Institute of International Affairs.

Mockler, A. (1969). *The Mercenaries*. London: Macdonald.

—— (1985). *The New Mercenaries*. London: Sidgwick and Jackson.

Montesquieu ([1748] 1989). *The Spirit of the Laws*. Translated by A. M. Cohler, B. C. Miller, and H. S. Stone. Cambridge: Cambridge University Press.

Moore, F. (1859). *Diary of the American Revolution from Newspapers and Original Documents*. 1. New York: Charles Scribner.

Moore, J. B. (1906). 'Hostile Expeditions', A Digest of International Law as embodied in diplomatic discussions, treaties and other international agreements, international awards, the decisions of municipal courts, and the writings of jurists, and especially in documents, published and unpublished, issued by presidents and secretaries of states of the United States, the opinions of the Attorneys-General and the decisions of courts, federal and state. VII: 917–35.

Moran, D. (2003a). 'Introduction: The Legend of the *Levée En Masse*', in D. Moran and A. Waldron (eds), *The People in Arms: Military, Myth and National Mobilization since the French Revolution*. Cambridge: Cambridge University Press: 1–7.

——— (2003b). 'Arms and the Concert: The Nation in Arms and the Dilemmas of German Liberalism', in D. Moran and A. Waldron (eds), *The People in Arms: Military Myth and National Mobilization since the French Revolution*. Cambridge: Cambridge University Press.

Mortimer, G. (2002). *Eyewitness Accounts of the Thirty Years War 1618–1648*. Houndmills, Basingstoke, UK and London: Routledge.

Mourning, P. W. (1982). 'Leashing the Dogs of War: Outlawing the Recruitment and Use of Mercenaries', *Virginia Journal of International Law*, 22: 589–612.

Müller, H. (1993). 'The Internalization of Principles, Norms, and Rules by Governments: The Case of Security Regimes', in V. Rittberger (ed.), *Regime Theory and International Relations*. Oxford: Clarendon Press.

Musah, A. F. and Fayemi, J. K. (eds) (2000a). *Mercenaries: An African Security Dilemma*. London and Stirling, VA: Pluto Press.

——— (2000b). 'Africa in Search of Security: Mercenaries and Conflicts—an Overview', in A. F. Musah and J. K. Fayemi (eds), *Mercenaries: An African Security Dilemma*. London and Stirling, VA: Pluto Press.

Nadelmann, E. A. (1990). 'Global Prohibition Regimes: The Evolution of Norms in International Society', *International Organization*, 44(4): 479–526.

Norton-Taylor, R. (2004). 'Big Role Predicted for Security Firms', *The Guardian*, 6 December 2004.

Nossal, K. R. (1998). 'Roland Goes Corporate: Mercenaries and Transnational Security Corporations in the Post-Cold War Era', *Civil Wars*, 1(1): 16–35.

O'Brien, K. A. (1998). 'Military Advisory Groups and African Security: Privatized Peacekeeping?', *International Peacekeeping*, 5(3): 78–105.

——— (2000). 'Private Military Companies and African Security 1990–1998', in A. F. Musah and J. K. Fayemi (eds), *Mercenaries: An African Security Dilemma*. London and Stirling, VA: Pluto Press.

Owen, J. M. (1994). 'How Liberalism Produces Democratic Peace', *International Security*, 19(2): 87–125.

Palmer, R. R. (1986). 'Frederick, Guibert, Bülow', in P. Paret, G. A. Craig, and F. Gilbert (eds), *Makers of Modern Strategy: From Machiavelli to the Nuclear Age*. Princeton, NJ: Princeton University Press, pp. 91–119.

Paret, P. (1966). *Yorck and the Era of Prussian Reform 1807–1815*. Princeton, NJ: Princeton University Press.

——— (1986). 'Napoleon and the Revolution in War', in P. Paret, G. A. Craig, and F. Gilbert (eds), *Makers of Modern Strategy: From Machiavelli to the Nuclear Age*. Princeton, NJ: Princeton University Press, pp. 123–42.

——— (1992). *Understanding War: Essays on Clausewitz and the History of Military Power*. Princeton, NJ: Princeton University Press.

Parker, G. (ed.) (1997). *The Thirty Years' War*. London: Routledge.

Parkinson, R. (1970). *Clausewitz: A Biography*. London: Wayland Publishers.

Pech, K. (1999). 'Executive Outcomes: A Corporate Conquest', in J. Cilliers and P. Mason (eds), *Peace, Profit or Plunder?: The Privatization of Security in War-Torn African Societies*. Johannesburg, South Africa: Institute for Security Studies.

Percy, S. (2006). *Regulating the Private Security Industry*. Adelphi Paper 384. London: Routledge and the International Institute of Strategic Studies.

——— (forthcoming, 2007a). 'Mercenaries: Strong Norm, Weak Law', *International Organization*, 61(2): 367–97.

——— (forthcoming, 2007b). 'Morality and Regulation', in S. Chesterman and C. Lehnhardt (eds), *From Mercenaries to Market: The Rise and Regulation of the Private Military Industry*. Oxford: Oxford University Press.

Philpott, D. (2001). *Revolutions in Sovereignty: How Ideas Shaped Modern International Relations*. Princeton, NJ: Princeton University Press.

Pocock, J. G. A. (1965). 'Machiavelli, Harrington and English Political Ideologies in the Eighteenth Century', *The William and Mary Quarterly*, 22(4): 549–83.

——— (1975). *The Machiavellian Moment: Florentine Thought and the Atlantic Republican Tradition*. Princeton, NJ: Princeton University Press.

Porch, D. (1974). *Army and Revolution in France 1815–1848*. London and Boston, MA: Routledge and Kegan Paul.

Posen, B. R. (1993). 'Nationalism, the Mass Army, and Military Power', *International Security*, 18(2): 80–124.

Potter, G. R. (1976). *Zwingli*. Cambridge: Cambridge University Press.

Preston, R. A. and Wise, S. F. (1979). *Men in Arms: A History of Warfare and Its Interrelationships with Western Society*. New York: Holt, Rinehart and Wilson.

Prestwich, M. (1996). *Armies and Warfare in the Middle Ages: The English Experience*. New Haven, CT and London: Yale University Press.

Price, R. (1995). 'A Genealogy of the Chemical Weapons Taboo'. *International Organization*, 49(1): 73–103.

——— (1997a). *The Chemical Weapons Taboo*. Ithaca and London: Cornell University Press.

——— (1997b). 'Moral Norms in World Politics'. *Pacifica Review*, 9(1): 45–72.

——— (2004). 'Emerging Customary Norms and Anti-Personnel Landmines', in C. Reus-Smit (ed.), *The Politics of International Law*. Cambridge: Cambridge University Press.

Price, R. and Tannenwald, N. (1996). 'Norms and Deterrence: The Nuclear and Chemical Weapons Taboo', in P. J. Katzenstein (ed.), *The Culture of National Security*. Ithaca, NY and London: Cornell University Press: 114–52.

Ray, J. L. (1989). 'The Abolition of Slavery and the End of International War', *International Organization*, 43(3): 405–39.

Redlich, F. (1964a). *The German Military Enterpriser and His Work Force: A Study in European Economic and Social History*. 1. Wiesbaden, Germany: Franz Steiner Verlag GMBH.

——— (1964b). *The German Military Enterpriser and His Work Force: A Study in European Economic and Social History*. 2. Wiesbaden, Germany: Franz Steiner Verlag GMBH.

Reno, W. (1997). 'War, Markets and the Reconfiguration of West Africa's Weak States', *Comparative Politics*, 29(4): 493–510.
—— (1998). *Warlord Politics and African States*. Boulder, CO: Lynne Rienner.
—— (2000). 'Internal Wars, Private Enterprise and the Shift in Strong State-Weak State Relations', *International Politics*, 37: 57–74.
'Resources, Primary Industry and Conflict in Sierra Leone'. (1997). *Conciliation Resources Paper*. Online Pagination: Accessed 17 December 2004. Available at http://www.c-r.org/pubs/occ_papers/briefing3.shtml
Risse, T. and Sikkink, K. (1999). 'The Socialization of International Human Rights Norms into Domestic Practices: Introduction', in T. Risse, S. C. Ropp, and K. Sikkink (eds), *The Power of Human Rights: International Norms and Domestic Change*. Cambridge: Cambridge University Press.
—— Ropp, S. C., and Sikkink, K. (eds) (1999). *The Power of Human Rights: International Norms and Domestic Change*. Cambridge: Cambridge University Press.
Roberts, A. (1999). 'Beyond the Flawed Principle of National Self-Determination', in E. Mortimer (ed.), *People, Nation and State: The Meaning of Ethnicity and Nationalism*. London: I.B. Tauris.
Rogers, A. (2000). *Someone Else's War*. London: Collins.
Rogers, C. (1999). 'The Age of the Hundred Years War', in M. Keen (ed.), *Medieval Warfare: A History*. Oxford: Oxford University Press, pp. 136–60.
Ropp, T. (1959). *War in the Modern World*. Durham, NC: Duke University Press.
Rosenne, S. (ed.) (1997). *The International Law Commission's Draft Articles on State Responsibility*. Dordrecht, The Netherland: Martinus Nijhoff.
Rosinski, H. (1966). *The German Army*. London: Pall Mall Press.
Rothenberg, G. E. (1977). *The Art of Warfare in the Age of Napoleon*. London: B.T. Batsford.
Rousseau, J.-J. ([1755] 1987). 'A Discourse on Political Economy', in D. Diderot (ed.), *Jean-Jacques Rousseau: The Basic Political Writings*. Indianapolis and Cambridge: Hackett Publishing Company, pp. 111–38.
Royster, C. (1979). *A Revolutionary People at War*. Chapel Hill, NC: University of North Carolina Press.
Russell, F. H. (1975). *The Just War in the Middle Ages*. Cambridge: Cambridge University Press.
Russett, B. M. (1993). *Grasping the Democratic Peace: Principles for a Post-Cold War World*. Princeton, NJ: Princeton University Press.
Sandoz, Y. (1999). 'Private Security and International Law', in J. Cilliers and P. Mason (eds), *Peace, Profit or Plunder?: The Privatization of Security in War-Torn African Societies*. Johannesburg, South Africa: Institute for Security Studies, pp. 208–26.
Saunders, F. S. (2004). *Hawkwood: Diabolical Englishman*. London: Faber and Faber.
Schama, S. (1989). *Citizens: A Chronicle of the French Revolution*. London: Viking.
Schreier, F. and Caparini, M. (2005). Privatising Security: Law, Practice and Governance of Private Military and Security Companies. Geneva, Switzerland: Geneva Centre for the Democratic Control of Armed Forces.

Schwarzenberger (1971). 'Terrorists, Guerrilleros and Mercenaries', *Current Legal Problems*, 24: 257–82.

Shanahan, W. O. (1966). *Prussian Military Reforms 1786–1813*. New York: AMS Press.

Shearer, D. (1997a). 'Dial an Army', *The World Today*: 203–5.

Shearer, D. (1997b). 'Exploring the Limits of Consent: Conflict Resolution in Sierra Leone', *Millennium*, 26(3): 845–60.

____ (1998a). *Private Armies and Military Intervention*. Adelphi Paper 318. Oxford: International Institute of Strategic Studies.

____ (1998b). 'Outsourcing War', *Foreign Policy*: 68–80.

____ (1999). 'Private Military Forces and the Challenges for the Future', *Cambridge Review of International Affairs*, XIII(1): 80–92.

Showalter, D. E. (1980). 'The Retaming of Bellona: Prussia and the Institutionalization of the Napoleonic Legacy, 1815–1876', *Military Affairs*, 44(2): 67–3.

____ (2002). 'Europe's Way of War 1815–64', in J. Black (ed.), *European Warfare 1815–2000*. Houndmills, Basingstoke, UK and New York: Palgrave.

Sikkink, K. (1993). 'The Power of Principled Ideas: Human Rights Policies in the United States and Western Europe', in J. Goldstein and R. O. Keohane (eds), *Ideas and Foreign Policy*. Ithaca, NY and London: Cornell University Press.

Simon, W. M. (1954). 'Variations in Nationalism During the Great Reform Period in Prussia', *The American Historical Review*, 59(2): 305–21.

____ (1971). *The Failure of the Prussian Reform Movement, 1807–1819*. New York: Howard Fertig.

Simpson, M. C. M. ([1855] 1872). *Correspondence and Conversations of Alexis De Tocqueville with Nassau William Senior from 1834 to 1859*. 2. London: Henry S. King & Co.

Singer, P. W. (2003a). *Corporate Warriors: The Rise and Fall of the Privatized Military Industry*. Ithaca, NY and London: Cornell University Press.

____ (2003b). 'Corporate Warriors: The Rise and Fall of the Privatized Military Industry'.

____ (2004a). 'War, Profits and the Vacuum of Law: Privatized Military Firms and International Law', *Colombia Journal of Transnational Law*, 42(2): 521–49.

____ (2004b). The Private Military Industry and Iraq: What Have We Learned and Where to Next? Geneva, Switzerland: Geneva Centre for the Democratic Control of Armed Forces.

Skinner, Q. (1981). *Machiavelli*. Oxford: Oxford University Press.

____ (1988). 'Meaning and Understanding in the History of Ideas', in J. Tully (ed.), *Meaning and Context: Quentin Skinner and His Critics*. Oxford: Polity Press, pp. 29–68.

Smith, A. ([1766] 1978). *Lectures on Jurisprudence*. Oxford: Oxford University Press.

____ ([1776] 1976). *An Inquiry into the Nature and Causes of the Wealth of Nations*. 2. Chicago, IL and London: University of Chicago Press.

Smith, E. B. (2002–3). 'The New Condottieri and US Policy: The Privatization of Conflict and Its Implications', *Parameters, US Army War College Quarterly* (Winter): 104–19.

Special Subcommittee on Investigations of the Committee on International Relations (1976). *Mercenaries in Africa: Special Subcommittee on Investigations of the Committee on International Relations.* 94th Congress: 2nd Session.

Spicer, T. (1999a). *Unorthodox Soldier: Peace and War and the Sandline Affair.* Edinburgh, UK and London: Mainstream Publishing.

―――― (1999b). 'Interview with Lt. Col. Tim Spicer', *Cambridge Review of International Affairs*, XIII(1): 165–71.

Starkey, A. (2003). *War in the Age of Enlightenment, 1700–1789.* Westport, CT and London: Praeger.

Stephens, W. P. (1986). *The Theology of Huldrych Zwingli.* Oxford: Clarendon Press.

Stewart, J. H. (1951). *A Documentary Survey of the French Revolution.* New York: Macmillan.

Tannenwald, N. (1999). 'The Nuclear Taboo: The United States and the Normative Basis of Nuclear Non-Use', *International Organization*, 53(3): 433–68.

―――― (forthcoming). *The Nuclear Taboo: The United States and the Non-use of Nuclear Weapons Since 1945.* Cambridge: Cambridge University Press.

Taulbee, J. L. (1985). 'Myths, Mercenaries and Contemporary International Law', *California Western International Law Journal*, 15: 339–63.

Thomas, G. (1984). *Mercenary Troops in Modern Africa.* Boulder, CO: Westview Press.

Thomas, W. (2001). *The Ethics of Destruction.* Ithaca, NY and London: Cornell University Press.

Thomson, J. E. (1990). 'State Practices, International Norms and the Decline of Mercenarism', *International Studies Quarterly*, 34: 23–47.

―――― (1994). *Mercenaries, Pirates, and Sovereigns: State-Building and Extraterritorial Violence in Early Modern Europe.* Princeton, NJ: Princeton University Press.

Tickler, Peter (1987a). *The Modern Mercenary: Dog of War or Soldier of Honour.* Wellingborough, Northamptonshire, UK: Patrick Stephens.

―――― (1987b). 'The Modern Mercenary: Dog of War or Soldier of Honour'.

Tilly, C. (1990). *Coercion, Capital and European States, AD 990–1990.* Oxford: Blackwell.

Trease, G. (1970). *The Condottieri: Soldiers of Fortune.* London: Thames and Hudson.

Van Creveld, M. (1991). *The Transformation of War.* New York and London: The Free Press.

Van Deventer, H. (1976). 'Mercenaries at Geneva', *American Journal of International Law*, 70(4): 811–16.

Ventner, A. J. (1995). 'Mercenaries at Work', *West Africa*, 23–9 October 1995, 1633–5.

Vines, A. (1999). 'Mercenaries and the Privatisation of Force in Africa', in G. Mills and J. Stremlau (eds), *The Privatization of Security in Africa.* Johannesburg, South Africa: South African Institute of International Affairs.

Voltaire ([1764] 1962). *Philosophical Dictionary.* Translated by P. Gay. 1. New York: Basic Books.

Waltz, K. N. (1979). *Theory of International Politics.* Reading: Addison-Wesley.

Wendt, A. (1987). 'The Agent-Structure Problem in International Relations Theory', *International Organization*, 41(3): 335–70.

Wendt, A. (1992). 'Anarchy Is What States Make of It: The Social Construction of Power Politics', *International Organization*, 88(2): 384–96.
―――― (1999). *Social Theory of International Politics*. Cambridge: Cambridge University Press.
White, C. E. (1989). *The Enlightened Soldier: Scharnhorst and the Militärische Gesellschaft in Berlin, 1801–1805*. New York, Westport, CT and London: Praeger.
Whiteclay Chambers II, J. (2003). 'American Views of Conscription and the German Nation in Arms in the Franco-Prussian War', in D. Moran and A. Waldron (eds), *The People in Arms: Military Myth and National Mobilization since the French Revolution*. Cambridge: Cambridge University Press.
Yearbook of the United Nations (1979). 33. New York: United Nations.
Yee, A. S. (1996). 'The Causal Effects of Ideas on Policies', *International Organization*, 50(1): 69–108.
Yusuf, A. A. (1979). 'Mercenaries in the Law of Armed Conflict', in A. Cassese (ed.), *The New Humanitarian Law of Armed Conflict*. Napoli: Editoriale scientifica.
Zarate, J. C. (1998). 'The Emergence of a New Dog of War: Private International Security Companies, International Law, and the New World Disorder', *Stanford Journal of International Law*, 34(Winter): 75–162.

Index

Aegis 225, 228, 231
American Revolution 60, 100–1, 114, 123, 125–6, 128, 138–9, 147–9, 152, 154, 166, 242, 245
Angola 207–8, 218, 229
   Mercenary involvement 1976 182, 186
   Trial of mercenaries 1976 177, 181, 186, 187, 188
   Executive Outcomes involvement in 209–11, 213–15, 221
Annan, Kofi 223
Anti-mercenary norm 3–4, 7, 10–12, 66–7
   Cause aspect of the norm 65, 68–9
   Control aspect of the norm 57, 66, 78–85, 173, 175–6, 203, 230, 232–5
AmorGroup 228–30
Article 47, Protocol I additional to the Geneva Conventions 168–78, 181–2, 190, 193, 208, 239
Auerstädt, battle of (1806) 100, 108, 137, 139, 142, 145
Avant, Deborah 5, 95–6, 105–11, 120, 122, 135, 164, 226

Ballesteros, Enrique Bernales de *see* Special Rapporteur on Mercenaries 221–2
Barlow, Eeben 209–10
Bearpark, Andy 231
Beese, Christopher 228–9
Benin 187, 190
Berenhorst, Georg Heinrich von 138, 140
Bernadotte, Jean-Baptiste 110
Biafra 184 n, 187, 189, 221
Bill of Rights (Great Britain) (1689) 150
Blackstone, William 150
Branch Heritage Group 213
British Association of Private Security Companies (BAPSC) 228
British Legion 104, 158
Bunche, Ralph 185

Cardwell, Reforms 163–4
Cassese, Antonio 168–9
Chan, Sir Julius 211
Charles VII (king of France) 82–3
Cobden, Richard 159
Comoro Islands 187

Commission of Enquiry (Angola) 186–8
compagnies d'ordonnance 8, 83
condottieri 157
   types of contract 75, 85–6
   Siena and 86, 75
Congo 161, 167, 182–3, 185–8, 196, 208 n
Congress of Vienna (1815) 160
Congress of Verona (1822) 160
Convention of 23 August 1793 132
Côte d'Ivoire 220, 228–9, 234
citizen army 121–3, 126, 128–9, 136, 142–3, 145, 147–9, 163–5
Clausewitz, Carl Philipp Gottfried von 141
Clinton, William Jefferson 215
Constructivism 14, 17–18, 21, 25, 33–4, 46
Crimean War 149, 155–7, 161, 166

Decken, Friedrich van der 142
Declaration against Aggression 239
Declaration of Independence (1776) 125
Denard, Bob 187
Diderot, Denis 129 n
Diplock, Kenneth (Lord Diplock) 177, 197
   Diplock Report 117, 193 n, 196–7
Disraeli, Benjamin 157–8
DynCorp 226–7

Encyclopédie 129 n, 130
Enlightenment 105–7, 109, 128–9, 131, 147
Equatorial Guinea 1
Erinys 226, 228, 231
Executive Outcomes (EO) 206–16, 221–2, 227, 233

Filibusters 116–17
FNLA (National Liberation Front of Angola) 186
Foreign enlistment legislation 156, 196
   Great Britain 113, 116–17, 157, 162
   Prussia 117–18
   United States 115–16, 156, 196
Frederick the Great (king of Prussia) 100, 131, 136, 138–40
Frederick William II (king of Prussia) 143
Frederick William III (king of Prussia) 143
Free Companies 2, 8, 59, 81–3, 85
freedom of movement 193, 195–8, 202–3

French Foreign Legion 58–9, 61, 64, 135, 172, 205
French Revolution 94, 96, 100, 102–3, 109–10, 112, 116, 128–30, 132, 140

Georgiou, Costas 'Callan' 186
Gneisenau, August von 110, 143
Gong, Gerritt 24, 108
Green, Leslie 182
Green Paper (UK) 232–4, 237
Guibert, Comte de (Jacques Antoine Hippolyte) 98, 100
Gurkhas 58–9, 61, 64, 164, 172, 205
Gurkha Security Guards (GSG) 210

Hague Conventions 197
Harland, David 224
Harrington, Samuel 124, 127, 149, 151
Hawkwood, Sir John 75
Hessians 60, 123, 126, 128, 138–9, 147–8, 154, 158, 246
Hessen-Kassel 114, 123, 138–9, 152
Hoare, Mike 187–8
Hundred Years War 59, 75, 78, 81, 83, 88

international law 53, 95, 111, 114, 162, 167–9, 178, 191–3, 198–205, 238–9
customary international law 18–19
International Covenant on Civil and Political Rights 197
International Peace Operations Association (IPOA) 228

Jaucourt, Louis de 130
Jefferson, Thomas 115
Jena, battle of (1806) 100, 108, 137–40, 142, 144–5
Jonah, James 216
just cause 54, 63, 65, 69, 71–3, 79–80, 82–3, 141
just war 54–5, 72
just title 72, 78, 80

Kabbah, Ahmed Tejan 210–11, 216, 219
Kant, Immanuel 138, 236
Kinsey, Christopher 3–4 n, 206

Lateran Council (1179) 38, 59, 80
Legg Report 233
levée en masse 98, 102, 104–5, 107, 132, 134, 147

Machiavelli, Niccolò 76–7, 82, 91, 107, 124

Magna Carta (1245) 71
Map, Walter 80
mercenaries
  cotereaux 59, 73, 80
  definition of 49–66
  écorcheurs 68, 82–3
  landsknechts 87
  routiers 59, 68, 73, 80
  vagabond mercenaries 59–60, 63
Military Professional Resources Incorporated (MPRI) 61, 215, 226
Military Reorganization Commission (Prussia) 143
Møller, Michael 224
Montesquieu (Charles de Secondat, Baron de) 98
Montlovier, Jean-Denis de 130
MPLA (Popular Movement for the Liberation of Angola) 186

Napoleon 102, 134–5, 137, 143, 145–6, 161, 165
Napoleonic Wars 98, 103–5, 110, 120, 122, 134, 155–6
National Conventional Arms Control Committee (South Africa) 233
National Provisional Ruling Council (NPRC) (Sierra Leone) 210, 213
Neutrality laws 111–15, 117 167
  United States 115–19
Norms
  causation and 42–3
  definition of 14–15, 17–18
  distinction between norms and interests 20–3
  evolution of 32–5, 37–9
  institutionalization of 25–7, 30–1, 38
  methodological problems associated with study of 40–3
  norm entrepreneurs 38, 41
  proscriptive norms 15, 18, 30–1, 34, 39, 45, 48, 65–7
  puritanical norm 32, 218, 220, 222,
  relationship with law 18–19, 25–6

Papua New Guinea (PNG) 207, 211–12, 214–16, 218–19, 227
Peace of Paris (1814–15) 160
Petrarch (Francesco Petrarca) 75
Posen, Barry 97, 99, 105
Price, Richard 50, 238
Privateering 115–17

private military companies (PMCs) 59–60, 62–3, 65, 176, 206–9, 211–43
private security companies (PSCs) 59–62, 64–5, 206–7, 225–43
Prohibition of Mercenary Activities and Prohibition and Regulation of Certain Activities in Areas of Armed Conflict Bill (South Africa) 233

Realism *see* structural realism
Rebel United Front (RUF) 210, 214–15, 221
Redlich, Fritz 87–9, 117
Regulation of Foreign Military Assistance Act (South Africa) 233
Republicanism 124, 129, 133
Rosen, Count Carl Gustav von 189 n, 199 n
Rousseau, Jean-Jacques 129–30, 162
Rowe, Sylvester 219

Saint Lambert, Jean François de 130
Sandline 206–8, 210–16, 223, 227, 233–4, 241
Sankoh, Foday 210
Scharnhorst, Gerhard von 110, 140–1, 143–4
Scutage 70
self-determination 26, 29–30, 35, 37, 54, 179, 180–1, 183–5, 189–94, 205, 219–22, 238–40
Seychelles 187, 208 n
Shameem, Shaista *see* Special Rapporteur on Mercenaries
Sierra Leone 53, 196 n, 210–23, 227–9, 233
Singer, Peter W. 62 n, 215, 231
Singirok, Jerry 212
Smith, Adam 101, 149
Special Rapporteur on Mercenaries 220–1, 231
  Ballesteros, Enrique Bernales de 221–2
  Shameem, Shaista 221
Spicer, Tim 53, 55, 215, 241
  Aegis and 225, 228
  Sandline and 211–12, 214
Standing army 83, 86, 119, 163, 166
State responsibility 30, 169, 193, 198–203, 230
Stein, Heinrich Friedrich Karl Reichsfreiherr vom und zum 140

Strasser, Valentine 210, 213
structural realism 15, 17, 20–2, 44–5, 47–8, 96–7, 99–100, 119
Swiss Guards 173
Switzerland 74, 91
  Mercenaries operating from 74
  Alliance with French 73, 84–5
  Abolition of mercenary use 73, 77, 84

Tannenwald, Nina 46–7
Taylor, Charles 210
Thomson, Janice 111–20, 217
Perpetual Peace Treaty of 1516 84

United Nations 40, 182–3
  Declaration on Human Rights (UNDHR) 197–8
  General Assembly 181–3, 190–1, 239–40
  High Commission for Human Rights (Human Rights Council) 27, 40, 221, 240
  International Convention against the Recruitment, Use, Financing and Training of Mercenaries (see also UN Convention) 169
  Security Council 27, 181–3, 190–1, 194, 228,
UNITA (National Union for the Total Independence of Angola) 186, 209, 215
UN Convention 176–7, 191, 193, 195, 198–204, 207–8, 217
Urban V, Pope 81
  Cogit nosi 81
Urquhart, Brian 183, 185

Voltaire (François-Marie Arouet) 130–1

Wallenstein, Albrecht von 87–9
Washington, George 101, 127
Wellington, Duke of (Arthur Wellesley) 99, 104, 110, 155–8, 163
Williams, Abiodun 224
Württemberg 117, 119

Zwingli, Huldrych 73–5, 91